Quality and Communicability for Interactive Hypermedia Systems:
Concepts and Practices for Design

Francisco V. Cipolla–Ficarra
Alaipo, Italy

T0320546

Information Science REFERENCE

INFORMATION SCIENCE REFERENCE

Hershey · New York

Director of Editorial Content:	Kristin Klinger
Director of Book Publications:	Julia Mosemann
Acquisitions Editor:	Joel Gamon
Development Editor:	Joel Gamon
Publishing Assistant:	Kurt Smith, Jamie Snavely
Typesetter:	Deanna Zombro
Quality control:	Jamie Snavely
Cover Design:	Lisa Tosheff
Printed at:	Yurchak Printing Inc.

Published in the United States of America by
Information Science Reference (an imprint of IGI Global)
701 E. Chocolate Avenue
Hershey PA 17033
Tel: 717-533-8845
Fax: 717-533-8661
E-mail: cust@igi-global.com
Web site: http://www.igi-global.com/reference

Library of Congress Cataloging-in-Publication Data

Quality and communicability for interactive hypermedia systems : concepts and practices for design / Francisco V. Cipolla-Ficarra, editor.
     p. cm.
  Includes bibliographical references.
  Summary: "This book introduces a new professional in the context of the information science, technology, and management called an 'heuristic assessor of qualitative communicability in interactive systems'"--Provided by publisher.
  ISBN 978-1-61520-763-3 (hardcover) -- ISBN 978-1-61520-764-0 (ebook) 1. Interactive multimedia. 2. Web sites--Design. 3. User interfaces (Computer systems) 4. Human-computer interaction. I. Cipolla-Ficarra, Francisco V. (Francisco Vicente), 1963-
  QA76.76.I59Q35 2010
  006.7--dc22
                                             2009036021

British Cataloguing in Publication Data
A Cataloguing in Publication record for this book is available from the British Library.

All work contributed to this book is new, previously-unpublished material. The views expressed in this book are those of the authors, but not necessarily of the publisher.

Table of Contents

Detailed Table of Contents

Chapter 1

Emma Nicol, University of Strathclyde, UK

Simulation and game-based learning are powerful modes of learning that are used in many fields including subjects as diverse as medicine and aviation. While institutes of further and higher education are making increasing use of VLEs to deliver teaching and learning, there are currently few examples of simulated environments for learning. The SIMPLE (Simulated Professional Learning Environment) and Cyberdam environments are two of the few dedicated simulation environments. This chapter will look at both of these environments and the results of user evaluations to determine what makes a simulation environment successful and what aspects of a simulation environment would have to be evaluated in order to establish its communicability.

Chapter 2

Andreas Kratky, USC School of Cinematic Arts, USA
Juri Hwang, USC School of Cinematic Arts, USA

The question of how to design and implement efficient remote learning environments gains a new quality in the light of extensive digital education projects such as the One Laptop Per Child (OLPC) initiative. At the core of this consideration is not only the task of developing content for very different cultural settings but also the necessity to reflect the effects of learning processes that operate exclusively with digitally mediated content. This chapter outlines the design strategies of the project Venture to the Interior, an interactive experience that presents selected objects from the collections of the Museum of Natural History in Berlin, Germany, and displays them in a context reflecting the museum as an institution and the practices of collecting as knowledge constitution. The project investigates the role of objects as knowledge devices and the possibilities for a translation of the didactic effects of experiential learning into virtual environments.

Chapter 3

A. Bellucci, Universidad Carlos III, Spain
A. Malizia, Universidad Carlos III, Spain
P. Diaz, Universidad Carlos III, Spain
I. Aedo, Universidad Carlos III, Spain

In the last 20 years we have assisted to the birth and growth of the World Wide Web. It rapidly changed from a tool conceived for scientists at CERN, into a global information network, populated by billions of users. Currently, we are experiencing another change within the Web paradigm, where the Web is viewed as a read/write tool enhancing users' collaboration and participation in information creation, consuming and sharing. Web 2.0, intended as a second step in the Web's evolution, is a complex topic and therefore it is difficult to clearly define it. It concerns viewing the Web as a platform for the development of Rich Internet Applications that go beyond the page metaphor of Web 1.0. It lies on the ideas of 1) users' participation; 2) users production of content and; 3) data remixability, so that Web applications and services can be employed as social tools allowing mass users collaboration and information sharing. The authors describe in this chapter, the main concepts behind the Web 2.0 paradigm, together with the technological aspects and design patterns that demonstrate this new way to use and perceive the Web. In second stance, they highlight future directions and research trends which are leading to the next Web's evolution phase: the Social Semantic Web.

Chapter 4

Maria Claudia Buzzi, IIT-National Research Council, Italy
Marina Buzzi, IIT-National Research Council, Italy
Barbara Leporini, ISTI-National Research Council, Italy

Accessibility is essential for every system or product in order to guarantee equal opportunity for access and use to all, including the differently-abled. Thus it is crucial to remove any technological barriers for special needs users, who explore the Internet by assistive technologies. However, ensuring efficient and satisfactory (in other words, usable) interaction with user interfaces (UIs) of products or services must occur in the design phase, in order to produce UIs that are universally simple to understand, rapid and easy to use. Applying accessibility and usability criteria from the very beginning of the design phase is much less costly than introducing it later, so specific guidelines should be followed from the earliest stages of the design process. In the long run, creating accessible and usable Web UIs will improve overall efficiency and effectiveness of interaction for any individual and organization.

Chapter 5

Francisco V. Cipolla-Ficarra, ALAIPO, & AInCI, Spain
Maria Valeria Ficarra, AInCI, & ALAIPO, Spain

In the current chapter the authors present a heuristic and diacritical analysis of the communicability in Web 1.0 and Web 2.0 carried out in the contents of the websites of Southern Europe, especially between Italy and Spain. The real examples that will be presented are related to the loss of the veracity of on-line information and the decay of credibility of the traditional information sources, such as digital newspapers, university context and the industrial or commercial sector. These results are directly related to the statistical aspect and the new phenomenon of the star enunciator and the use of statistics in the Internet, especially in websites such as university websites, social networks, digital newpapers and magazines, portals, etc., whose consequence in the short and middle term may be the total destruction of transparency in the communication process among the users of the interactive systems and the freedom of access to true online information.

Chapter 6

Jorge Roa, CIDISI-UTN-FRSF-CONICET, Argentina
Milton Pividori, CIDISI-UTN-FRSF-CONICET, Argentina
Ma. De los Milagros Gutiérrez, CIDISI-UTN-FRSF-CONICET, Argentina
Georgina Stegmayer, CIDISI-UTN-FRSF-CONICET, Argentina

In Artificial Intelligence courses, the development of intelligent agents is a common practical work. However, it is a programming extensive and consumed time practice that much of the time the student can not solve in full and in time. In this work the authors present FAIA, a framework to develop intelligent agents giving a partially design solution. With FAIA the teacher and student will have benefits, for the first, it helps in the teaching and evaluation process, while for the second, it helps to guide in the correct design and learning process.

Chapter 7

Rocío Andrea Rodríguez, National University of La Matanza, Argentina
Daniel Alberto Giulianelli, National University of La Matanza, Argentina
Pablo Martín Vera, National University of La Matanza, Argentina
Artemisa Trigueros, National University of La Matanza, Argentina
Isabel Beatriz Marko, National University of La Matanza, Argentina

E-Governance aims to provide high quality of government for citizens with. It covers services, information delivery and interactive community / government communication. This goal can be achieved by adopting the ICT (Information and Communication Technologies) tools in the government web site´s design and contents. This communication channel allows a redefinition of the traditional role played by each one of the actors of the relation. The government as provider of: services, information, transparency and interactive communication. The citizens acting as active subjects with their government, using services, receiving information, controlling the government´s decisions and returning feedback to them. This feedback includes opinions, complaints and suggestions delivered by the web sites' interactive tools. This research surveyed if the implementation of ICT tools regarding national and international norms and regulations for web sites development and content, increases the fulfillment of the key concepts of e-governance: e-democracy, e-services, e-transparency and active and passive communication. 30 local

government web sites of Argentine were analyzed by checking if they implemented the ICT tools expressed by the seven basic concepts of design and contents: Navigability, Veracity, Friendliness, Functionality, Accessibility, Usability and Information through 152 weighed aspects that fulfill these seven concepts. The analysis of the score obtained by the web sites showed their e-governance development level and what aspects they have to implement to improve e-governance quality.

Chapter 8

The construction of educational games requires knowledge from very diverse fields, like pedagogy, cognitive psychology, computer graphics, simulation and software engineering. Teachers, mathematicians and engineers have different views from the issues involved; bringing together these professionals in a coherent manner can be a challenging task. This work describes tools to help organize the design and decisions during the implementation of an educational game. The tools facilitate the communication between project members and serve to document design options in different stages.

Chapter 9

Aspect-Oriented Software Development (AOSD) aims at solving the problem of encapsulating crosscutting concerns, which orthogonally crosscut the components of a system, in units called aspects. This encapsulation improves the modularization of a system and in consequence its maintenance and evolution. In this work, the authors propose a systematic process for the migration of object-oriented systems to aspect-oriented ones. This migration is achieved in two main phases: crosscutting concern identification (aspect mining) and code transformation (aspect refactoring). The aspect mining phase is based on dynamic analysis and association rules to identify potential crosscutting concerns. The aspect refactoring phase, on the other hand, uses inference rules to identify the refactoring that can be applied. The whole process is described and its application on a real system is assessed.

Chapter 10

To understand historic developments of the past the authors normally turn to facts: Archival records, testimonies or remains from the past – they are looking for tangible evidence to reconstruct the past. In particular in respect to the technological development that originated at the turn from the 19th to the 20th

century the role of deterministic interpretations has been very strong. The focus is on technologies and how they improved along an inevitable time line towards technical perfection (Marvin, 1988). Another historic perspective that takes the social aspects into account mainly traces how people negotiated the old and the new and how technologies changed the social fabric. What stays out of the focus of most research is what people in the past felt and thought and how their imagination of what is possible and desirable influenced the development of technologies and the society. The following will use the example of the interactive media art piece The Imaginary 20th Century to discuss an approach to turn the attention to the re-construction of historical imagination with a particular focus on the imaginative processes and their communication to a current audience.

Chapter 11

In the current chapter are analyzed the main reasons for which it is necessary to count with a new profile in design, realization and assessment of the interactive systems. The whole of the observations and proposals is the result of theoretical research, experiences in projects of interactive multimedia systems in the public and private Spanish and Italian university context in the last two decades. Through all this time it has been seen how the lack of training among the professionals in the interactive systems, especially in some university environments, not only has increased the production costs but the detection of a low quality of design and communicability has discouraged the interaction of the novel users with these systems. One of the goals that the authors set ourselves is to determine the set of necessary knowledge and/or experiences that these professionals must possess to carry out satisfactorily the interactive systems of the present and the future, in the least possible production time, with reduced costs and a high final quality. Obviously, the key factor of these shortcomings lies in the university educational systems and in the organization of the contents in the study plans, leaving behind the business factor of university teaching. Therefore, they have structured the current work in the following way: study of the evolution of the multimedia systems, anchoring of the notions related to communication, determination of the main areas of knowledge of the future professional, analysis of the software quality, signalling of the business-oriented factors in the structuring of the university study plans, especially related to degrees, engineering titles and masters.

Preface

If you have built castles in the air, your work need not be lost; that is where they should be. Now put the foundations under them.

Henry David Thoreau (1817-1862)

In the word communicability we find implicitly the notion of quality. However, in the current book we use the word quality to boost the idea of seeking it in the implicit and explicit process of communication in the interactive multimedia/hypermedia systems. Here we understand as communicative process the continuous feedback between the user and the contents in the dynamic and static means of the hypermedia system. In this qualitative feedback the user comes into direct contact with the design aspects of the interactive system, such as the cognitive model used by the designer or his team.

In our case, we consider the design of these hypermedial on-line and off-line systems made up by several categories bi-directionally interrelated among them, such as presentation, navigation, structure, connectability and panchronism and content. In the presentation, all the variables related to metaphor, the graphical aspects of the interface (colors, typography, photographies, maps, etc.), the topographical disposition of each one of the static and dynamic means, etc come into play. Navigation represents the set of possibilities that the user has in each moment in the interaction of knowing where he is, where he comes from and where she/he can go, the different ways of activating and disactivating the dynamic means, etc. The structure is the architecture that makes up the nodes and links in the system, the modalities of access to the hyperbase data, that is to say, index or menu, direct search, etc. It is understood as panchronism the synchronization among the different dynamic means of an interactive system, for instance, the audio with animations, the audio with video subtitles, the face movements of the virtual characters or synthesis with the voice, etc. The content is mainly aimed at the study of the text organization and exceptionally the static images, as in the first hypertextual systems, for instance. All these categories and their different components make up our notion of design of an interactive system.

As it can be seen, it is an area which belongs to software and computer science engineering, human computer interaction and usability engineering. However, in contrast to what was partially established during the last two decades, in the design of interactive systems by the three enunciated engineerings, here we consider essential the communication variable from the perspective of social sciences. That is to say, communicability exists in the interaction between formal sciences and factual sciences enunciated by Mario Bunge[1]. This communicative perspective is essential even to avoid the butterfly system of redundance, vagueness, ambiguity and lack of originality in numerous research works as can be seen in the following graphics:

Figure 1. Originality equal to zero in 'butterfly' research

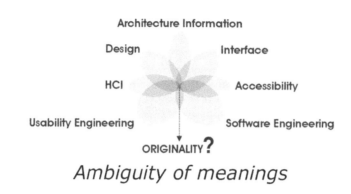

Ambiguity of meanings

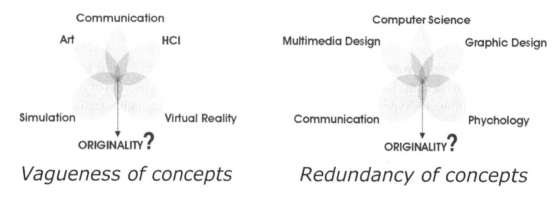

Vagueness of concepts   Redundancy of concepts

The problem in this mistake that is currently being caused in the lack of an analysis methodology of the real requirements of the users through the usability heuristic techniques is due to the difference of university study programs among the different continents. For instance, in software engineering, with the purpose of improving the quality of the products and services, the incorporation of psychologists, anthropologists, sociologists in the analysis team was promoted. This happened at the dawn of the nineties, that is to say, it coincided in time with the principles of usability engineering as stated by Jakob Nielsen[2]. Those were years in which the personal computers compatible with IBM and with Windows operating systems had erupted in daily life. The momentum of the phenomena put to rest in many cases the traditional typewriter, thanks to the first word processors, such as the Wordstart or WordPerfect.

This phenomenon, joined to the first bases of commercial data of easy programming such as dBase, the calculation sheets with graphics, was due to generate a fast change in the attitude of users towards computers because they would not only have them in their daily working activity, but also in the home. Besides, it was a period in which the first video games through the computer made their appearance in the family context. That is to say, a time where usability had its great protagonism, especially because of the yearning to learn to use the operating systems, educative applications, pastimes, etc., by millions of users in the whole world. Simultaneously, the aegis of the personal computer (hardware and software more efficient and at a lower cost), the evolution of the interactive systems took place, going from hypertext to interactive multimedia until reaching the off-line hypermedia systems, with its star being in the mid-nineties in Europe the CD-ROM support, to then be replaced by the current DVD, before the end of the millenium. Also in the mid-nineties the use of the Internet was democratized and the first

hypermedia systems started to be on-line. In all this evolution those software, hardware, telecommunications professionals, etc. played an active role, whereas the professionals required for the quality of the software coming from the social sciences were left behind in second place.

Now in the history of sciences, the social sciences have always had fewer financial resources for research in those university studies centers where they coexist with formal and with factual sciences. This is one of the reasons why communicability has not been considered in the design of interactive systems and even in the recent maps that have been made of the different areas that make up the User-Centered Design[3]. The problem lies in many cases in the management of those funds, that is, a technician or an engineer is preferred to a holder of a bachelor degree in social sciences. This reality is the common denominator in many Latin cultures. In contrast, in the English speaking environment, the motives respond to the structuring of university careers. For instance, the studies about informatics, telecommunications, systems, etc., lacked subjects related to the social training of the future professional, that is to say, sociology, social psychology, cultural systems, etc. A great exception to this rule in the American continent is to be found in the old syllabuses of several public universities in the South and Central America. A way to make up for this shortcoming in the training of the future computer professional in Europe, has been to take short-duration masters courses. Here it is necessary to make a distinction between official masters in the public institutions of the state from those that pursue a purely market-oriented purpose taken in private universities and subsidized by regional governments. The latter usually even have an external appearance and a plan of study (the names of the subjects, for instance) similar to those of the public or state university institutions, but the degree of the requirements to the student body is practically null. Consequently, both the European computer experts and their American counterparts lack theoretical knowledge or experiences in social sciences. This lack has seriously damaged the speed of the evolution of high quality interactive systems.

The methods and techniques presented for the assessment of the quality of the software in general and belonging to the field of heuristics, stem from the social sciences and the statistics that were applied to the studies made in the social or mass communication media. With regard to the terms *social* or *massive*, the former have a lesser power of persuasion and manipulation of communication as compared to the latter, although the receptor of the message is the general public or what we would nowadays call on the Internet, a virtual community or social network. Another difference between both notions lies in the final purpose such as for example the common welfare of all, in the social media, in contrast to the business-like nature of the mass media. That is to say, the receptors of the multimedia contents may have a bigger or lesser critical ability or reflexive, at the moment of making decisions. In both cases, the techniques used by statistics to gather information from the public at large, such as interviews, direct and indirect observations, lab trials, etc., have always taken this great differentiation into account. With the first commercial hypertextual systems and in off-line support usability engineering was born in the 1990s. From mathematics and computer science began a convergence towards social sciences with the purpose of finding the final quality of the commercial products and aimed at the users of the whole world.

However, this convergence was aimed at the acceptability of the systems. In regard to this, Jakob Nielsen established the difference between social acceptability and practical acceptability. In the latter, he cited several components such as compatibility of the system, reliability, cost, usefulness, etc. In Nielsen's concept of usefulness is the origin of the usability notion with its five principles: easy to learn, efficient to use, few errors, easy to remember and subjectively pleasing[4]. However, the communicative factor that lies implicit in any interaction process in the old and new means of social communication is not taken into account. The current compendium is somehow intended to fill this gap. The main goal is

to increase the quality of communicability in interactive systems and to introduce a new professional in the context of the information science, technology and management called an "heuristic assessor of qualitative communicability in interactive systems". The secondary targets are to present a series of works in which it is possible to analyze the current state of the new technologies in several American and European universities and to create an area of excellence among the formal and factual sciences aimed at constantly increasing the quality of interactive systems, especially those related to multimedia/ hypermedia on-line and off-line. We briefly present each one of the works developed by their authors.

In the first chapter, "*Communicability in Educational Simulation*", its author Emma Nicol presents two examples of the first generation of dedicated educational simulation engines, that is, software dedicated to the building and running of educational simulations. The work begins with a discussion of the history of simulation in learning with a focus on professional learning, and goes on to discuss the virtual environments of SIMPLE and Cyberdam and their genesis in the virtual town of Ardcalloch. A discussion is made of evaluation outcomes from both of these projects, the implications for professional learning in higher education and a discussion is made of possible future directions for simulation environments of this type. Definitions of the various types of simulation are offered and simulation's place within the wider context of e-learning and gaming is outlined. Taking her lead from earlier work by Cipolla-Ficarra, the author proposes some additional communicability measures for simulation environments.

In "*Venture to the Interior: Virtual Object Lessons*" the authors, Andreas Kratky and Juri Hwang, present an extension of the project One Laptop Per Child (OLPC), which to puts computers for the learning process within the reach of all students. In it are described a series of strategies followed in the work 'Venture to the Interior' using digital content belonging to the Museum of Natural History in Berlin, Germany. The project has demonstrated the interesting possibility of educating using tangible and historical objects of the mixed reality environment. This end has been achieved using a combination of bidirectional and three-dimensional graphic informatics techniques. Aside from the use of the key features of digital photography. the objects are presented in their context with a high visual quality which facilitates human-computer interaction.

In the research presented by A. Bellucci, A. Malizia, P. Díaz, I. Aedo, with the title "*The Anatomy of Web 2.0: The Web as a Platform to Promote Users' Participation and Collaboration*" its authors carry out a diachronic analysis of the different versions of the Internet, that is to say, past, present and future of the net. A meticulous historic description stresses each one of the main characteristics and components that the current net offers to the user. In its pages there are each of the services of the new generation aimed at the Web 2.0 and Web 3.0 virtual community. This text is a detailed summing-up of the technological evolution of the Internet, in very multifarious sectors which range from entertainment to on-line training.

Maria Claudia Buzzi, Marina Buzzi and Barbara Leporini are authors of the work titled "*Accessibility and Usability of Web Content and Applications*" where are presented the main aspects related to the access to the contents and the use of interactive systems for users without physical hindrances or those who have some kind of disability. Besides, they make a complete description accompanied by several examples of the advantages of usability and accessibility of on-line information. A case study –web interaction of totally blind persons serves to show us the main aspects of their research work, especially from the point of view of the simplification of the user computer interaction, such as their general guidelines for simplifying interaction via use of a screen reader and the increase of quality in the interaction of all the kinds of potential users, with the on-line multimedia systems mainly.

In the chapter named "*A Diacritical Study in Web Design: Communicability Versus Statistical Manipulation,*" the authors present a heuristic study of credibility destruction on-line through the statistics and the persuaders and manipulators of the information in the virtual communities, named as "star enunciators". The analysis of the communicability for education, industrial information and general news, carried out in the contents of the websites of Southern Europe, particularly between Italy and Spain. A series of examples in the evolution of the web make it plain how the transparency of information disappears in those environments where the parochialism defined by Saussure prevails. Besides, basic and frequent statistics notions are presented to be used by the communicability evaluators.

In the work titled "*How to Develop Intelligent Agents in an Easy Way with FAIA,*" the authors, Jorge Roa, Milton Pividori, Ma. De los Milagros Gutiérrez and Georgina Stegmayer present the importance of the relationship between artificial intelligence and games in the university educational environment, in the context of engineering. In it is made a comparison of FAIA (Framework for Intelligent AI Agents) with existing approaches. After that, the framework architecture is shown in detail, its components and the concepts involved in its design. We also find some examples of FAIA instantiation with an agent that solves a search problem and an agent that uses situation calculus to decide its movements are explained and exemplified with real problems in detail. Finally, the main advantages of the FAIA framework are cited.

In the chapter "*E-Governance Survey on Municipalities Web Sites*" the authors, Rocío Andrea Rodríguez, Daniel Alberto Giulianelli, Pablo Martín Vera, Artemisa Trigueros and Isabel Beatriz Marko, analyze the main advantages of distance government through the use of the new technologies to speed up the citizen's negotiations in front of the public institutions, for instance. Their work is aimed basically at usability, tending to improve the quality of the design of the on-line information in regard to government management in city councils. In this regard a series has been made of detailed heuristic assessments of 30 Argentinian websites, whose results and conclusions are presented in a detailed way in an Annex 2 (see annex section).

André Koscianski, author of "*Changing the Rules: Injecting Content into Computer Games,*" starts with a brief state of the art and the historic evolution where the importance of the video games in education is made clear. Under an interdisciplinary perspective it presents in detail the different stages of design, the importance of the communicative process among programmers, professors and artists for the generation of the video games with educational purposes. A set of examples are presented along its pages. Also are made clear the main advantages of introducing the video games in the classroom.

In "*An Integrated Process for Aspect Mining and Refactoring,*" its authors Esteban S. Abait, Santiago A. Vidal, Claudia A. Marcos, Sandra I. Casas and Albert A. Osiris Sofia present essential aspects inside object-oriented programming by using implicit criteria of the communicability inside software engineering. They propose a systematic process for the migration of object-oriented systems to aspect-oriented ones. The migration is achieved in two main steps; crosscutting concern identification (aspect mining) and code transformation (aspect refactoring) A detailed description of the process allows having an overall view of the problems to be faced and the developed solution. Besides, the results of JHotDraw, to Java object-oriented framework. (JHotdraw is a framework for drawing structured 2D graphics).

With a detailed explanation of the concepts behind the interactive media art piece *The Imaginary 20th Century,* Andreas Kratky, author of the chapter "*The Imaginary 20th Century: Reconstructing Imagination*", examines the possibilities of interactive media to convey the an understanding for the mental climate of the historic period of the turn of the 19th to the 20th century. He explains how the piece uses a large database of period documents the piece reconstructs the imaginative processes how people

imagined their future extrapolating from the information available. After a methodological discussion of imagination and the processes involved the chapter outlines the concepts of the art piece, the selection of materials and the aesthetic decisions that were made for the piece.

In the chapter *"Communicability Era: New Professionals for Interactive Systems"* its authors, present the profile of a new professional in the context of design and communicability. This professional possesses a set of skills and/or experiences deriving from several sectors of the formal and factual sciences. The work begins with a brief description of the state of the art in education and the new technologies, stressing the intersection between both. Then are presented each one of the areas of knowledge of the new professional and the main reasons why the epistemological principles of the sciences should be followed, ruling out the mercantilistic factor in the public or state educative institutions. Simultaneously, a constant study of the terminology used in the design is made, the communicability, software and system engineering, usability engineering and human-computer interaction.

In the Annex 1 are the main notions of descriptive statistics. Besides, there is a series of examples in regard to the loss of credibility of the information in the interactive systems on-line, deriving mainly from the education and the entrepreneurial sector and the mass media (the surnames have been eliminated or modified to keep the anonymity of the 'star enunciators' and their collaborators). In the second annex are the detailed results of the research work made in Chapter 7 *"E-Governance Survey on Municipalities Web Sites"*.

Finally, in the section of additional bibliography, the reader who is interested may find books, magazines links to websites, etc. to go deeper into each one of the subjects that the several authors have presented along these pages.

ENDNOTES

[1]   Bunge, M. (2001). *Philosophy of the Social Sciences, 31*(3), 404-423.
[2]   http://www.useit.com/
[3]   Sanders, L. (2008). An Evolving Map of Design Practice and Design Research. *Interactions.* Vol. 15 (6), p. 13-17.
[4]   Nielsen, J. (1993). *Usability Engineering.* London: Academic Press.

Acknowledgment

I would like to thank the following people for their helpful comments and assistance on the present book: Maria Ficarra, Emma Nicol, Joel Gamon, Carlos Albert and Miguel C. Ficarra.

Francisco V. Cipolla-Ficarra
Cerro Colorado –Archaeological, Cultural and Natural Park, August 2009

Chapter 1
Communicability in Educational Simulations

Emma Nicol
University of Strathclyde, UK

ABSTRACT

Simulation and game-based learning are powerful modes of learning that are used in many fields including subjects as diverse as medicine and aviation. While institutes of further and higher education are making increasing use of VLEs to deliver teaching and learning, there are currently few examples of simulated environments for learning. The SIMPLE (Simulated Professional Learning Environment) and Cyberdam environments are two of the few dedicated simulation environments. This chapter will look at both of these environments and the results of user evaluations to determine what makes a simulation environment successful and what aspects of a simulation environment would have to be evaluated in order to establish its communicability.

INTRODUCTION

Higher education has been undergoing radical change in recent times with regard to ever increasing student numbers, decreasing funding, and staffing and other resource issues. In response to these increasing pressures, higher education institutions are turning increasingly to the use of digital technology to facilitate the teaching and administration of undergraduate and postgraduate courses. Rather than relying solely on VLEs, which are in many cases

DOI: 10.4018/978-1-61520-763-3.ch001

acting as little more than repositories for course information and other resources, currently there is a small but growing number of institutions throughout the UK, and increasingly, beyond, that are having great success in employing dedicated simulation technology to facilitate teaching and learning on their courses, and it is with these dedicated simulation engines with which this chapter concerns itself. The chapter will begin by looking at the historical use of simulation in learning and will review the research that has accompanied this. What then follows is a discussion of the current use of dedicated simulation environments in higher education with reference to

a few successful examples of their deployment in a number of institutions and countries, in a variety of subject disciplines and at various different levels of education. There will be a discussion of the factors that have combined to produce successful simulations in these environments, in particular the design of the simulation itself and the usability and communicability aspects of the software on which the simulations run. The chapter continues by making recommendations for the successful design, development and use of digital simulations in higher education with reference to communicability, and with regard also to the human interaction requirements of the user groups involved. It concludes by considering possible future directions for simulation in higher education.

WHAT WE MEAN BY SIMULATION

In recent years the term simulation has become associated with a wide range of different types of instructional exercises and experiences. It is important to distinguish between *symbolic* simulations and *experiental* simulations (Jonassen, 2003). Symbolic simulations are those simulations that 'depict the characteristics of a particular population, system or process through symbols; and the user performs experiments with variables that are a part of the program's population' (Encyclopedia of Educational Technology, 2009). Symbolic simulations are often employed in fields such as economics, management, and the sciences (Windschitl & Andre, 1998). The use of flight and other simulations in the teaching of engineering sciences for example has been commonplace for many decades, and Monte Carlo type simulations are often to be found on the curriculum of management degree courses. *Experiential* simulations by contrast are generally based on case studies or scenarios and include role-play and activity in an environment that reconstructs aspects of real life (Maharg, 2006a). The use of experiential simula-

tions is most common in social science subjects and in professional learning. Increasingly, the distinctions between the two types of simulation are lessening in part because of the recent advances in the technology that can be used to support them (Barton & Maharg, 2006).

SIMULATION IN EDUCATION

There is a long history of the use of simulation in education in a variety of disciplines, with the tools required often being little more than the humble paper and pen. There are many recorded instances from throughout the 20th century, for example, of mock courts being used to teach legal procedures to law students, a practice that continues in countless higher education institutions to this day. In recent times, much of the pioneering work on educational simulations has been carried out in the field of medical education. Patients are now routinely simulated to allow trainee doctors and nurses to gain experience in how to interact with potential future patients by responding appropriately to the needs and requirements of the simulated patient. The nature of the knowledge and skills gained from taking part in such simulation activities is often more complex than might be imagined. In a study by Stedeford (2003), a simulation approach was used to assess not only the patienthandling skills of the students, but also their medical knowledge. The study showed that the use of this educational approach meant that students improved in both areas, allowing them to learn the synthesis of skills and knowledge that they would use in the workplace.

Simulations allow the learner to get as close to genuine practice of their chosen field without any of the risks or consequences that having them act in the real world might incur. Taking part in a simulation exercise allows students to interact in a close to realistic setting, free from the dangers of harming clients or patients, free from the risk of losing the company millions or at worst causing

death or severe injury. They allow students the chance to make mistakes and to learn from them long before they are in the situation where their actions could have far reaching consequences. Taking part in a simulation exercise might allow students to perform tasks that they might not be permitted to do during internships or traineeships for example.

During the eighties and nineties, a number of studies that sought to evaluate the effectiveness of simulations as a learning tool pointed to only limited gains from the use of simulation in learning (Bangert-Drowns et al, 1985; Rieber & Parmley, 1995) however it is possible that this was due to the types of tasks for which the simulations evaluated were being used. It has been argued for example in the last decade or so that simulation is most useful as a learning device when the educational task at hand requires the student to learn the procedure for doing something e.g. how to prepare a will, how to negotiate a contract, how to manage a disciplinary procedure. Simulations appear to be best at supporting these sorts of procedural learning but are somewhat less effective when it comes to enabling conceptual learning (Mandl, Gruber & Renkl, 1994). Given the increasing amount of learning in higher education that does indeed involve procedures due to the increasing amount of taught masters and professional qualification courses that are hosted by universities and other institutions of higher education, along with the increasing enthusiasm for e-learning and the proliferation of systems that support its use, it is not difficult to see that simulations of this type might begin to become more commonplace in our universities. We are also at the point now, where given the proliferation of broadband and Web 2.0 technology, simulations can be richer in terms of the media that they can support and can now take place in non-fixed locations. That is to say that the participants do not have to be online or even within the environment at the same time for the interaction to proceed, which has implications for how we think about learning as a whole. Such

an approach is far removed from traditional class teaching, but opens up possibilities that traditional methods of teaching and learning have so far been unable to offer.

CURRENT THINKING ON DIGITAL SIMULATION IN EDUCATION

When thinking of simulation in an educational context, rich graphical environments such as Second Life might be what spring immediately to mind, however it is possible that simpler, less sophisticated environments might also confer educational benefits. Early work by Turkle (1995) and others, showed the power of text-based simulation interfaces for participants in virtual worlds. Later research by Gee, Squire, Schaffer, Steinkuhler and others demonstrated that 3D worlds are innately social spaces that have the potential to become specific learning spaces. There has also been a good deal of research into the educational potential of Massively Multiplayer Online Role-Playing Games (MMORPGs) and MultiUser Virtual Environments (MUVEs). Taking the well known social virtual worlds of Second Life and Habbo as examples, Book (2004) has identified the key features of such environments as follows:

- a space shared with many other users
- they have a graphical user interface either 2D or 3D
- users interact in the world, for example, building or creating objects
- immediacy of action
- persistence (i.e. the existence of the world is separate from the presence of the individual)
- socialisation in the communities.

The body of research on virtual worlds has shown clearly that textual simulations can create & sustain communities, and can to help build aspects of professional identity. Clearly, while

there are likely to be educational benefits to the individual from learning via simulation, it is currently beyond the scope of existing technology to simulate to a satisfactory degree the physical and other characteristics of human beings, however there are more straightforward ways in which digital technology can be harnessed in order to mimic real world experiences that the student will encounter when fully qualified in his/her profession. Much of what occurs in professional life is rooted in communication and interaction whether it be meeting face to face, composing and sending letters and emails, giving presentations, making phone calls and conducting interviews. Much of this communication takes place in the office environment. Could we not then digitally recreate an environment much like that the student will encounter when he/she enters employment? While it is not possible to easily recreate the physical walls and furniture of the office it is perfectly possible to allow the student to work in a digital space that allows many of the communications modes and channels that he/she would use when in the situation of doing their job 'for real'. There are in fact a number of educational projects that have attempted to do exactly this, that while not wholly immersive, do mimic aspects of the office environment of the professional that the student will one day become.

CASE STUDY #1: SIMPLE

SIMPLE (SIMulated Professional Learning Environment) is the digital simulation environment that has been used on the postgraduate diploma in legal studies at the former Glasgow Graduate School of Law (GGSL) at the University of Strathclyde since 2007. SIMPLE replaced an earlier simulation suite that the department had been using to teach a variety of modules on the diploma course since the early 2000s. The types of simulation run are generally adversarial, that is to say, they involve students negotiating against each other. This is done in the context of the negotiation of a legal case with students distributed between teams or firms, each student taking on the role of a lawyer within a simulated legal firm or practice.

Building Simulations

SIMPLE is innovative in two key ways. As well as being one of the first dedicated simulation environments, it has defined a unique approach to the building of simulations. In addition to providing a platform on which simulations can be run and played, SIMPLE includes a set of simulation construction tools that are designed with an educators' needs in mind. The SIMPLE tools are used by the educator to construct the simulation, which they then launch and run on the platform, while the other key game players, the students, are shielded from the inner workings of this aspect of the software, interacting only with the platform. Part of the motivation behind the development of the suite of simulation construction tools was to allow educators to have as close to full autonomy and ownership of their simulation projects as possible. A further motivation for the development of the tools was the desire to make it easier for educators to realize simulations that were closer to their image of them than was possible in the existing systems.

Traditionally, academics, unless they have a particular skill or affinity for using computer technology, have had to liaise with either university IT support staff or e-learning specialists in order to create and run e-learning projects, often with mixed results. In developing SIMPLE it was hoped that by creating an environment that would be easy and intuitive for any academic to use, this "middle man" aspect would be removed and the confusions that often arose from the language gap between academics and technologists would be removed. Clearly however, the designers had to be mindful that if these tools were to be successful some serious consideration would have to be given to the needs and characteristics of

Figure 1. The narrative event diagram (NED)

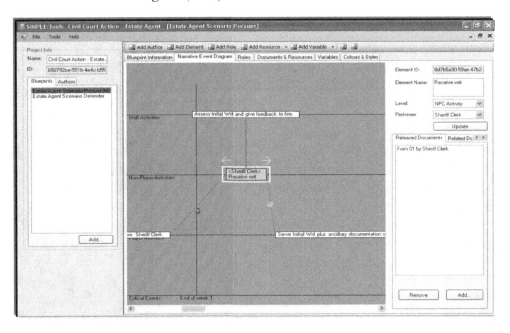

the eventual end users of the product. The tools were thus developed with a considerable amount of input from several educators from a variety of subject backgrounds. The further innovation of the SIMPLE developers was their development of the Narrative Event Diagram (NED) (Gould et al, 2008). The NED is a pictorial means of representing simulations in a manner that cannot be achieved as effectively using more familiar methods such as flow charts and UML diagrams. UML in any case is generally not a familiar language of description for a significant proportion of the academic community. The NED was the SIMPLE team's response to their acknowledgement of the differences in vocabulary between academics and software developers /e-learning technologists and was a unique and largely successful attempt to break down the barriers between both sets of e-learning content devisers in a way that had scarcely, if ever, been attempted before. Starting from the NED, the educator could use the tools to construct the simulation by defining all of the characters, roles, activities and necessary communications e.g. letters, memos that

are required by the transaction to be performed without recourse to the assistance of a technology specialist or IT professional.

Virtual Town

SIMPLE simulations take place in a virtual town called Ardcalloch that has been created to resemble an archetypal small town in the west of Scotland. A zoomable map of the town that employs Flash technology is provided, along with a directory of addresses of the various businesses and other entities in the town. All of these are entities with which the students may have to interact, for example public institutions such as a police station, doctor's surgery and courthouse and private entities such as car repair companies and mortgage brokers. Placing the entities in a physical location on the map, on roads with realistic names and assigning each of them a geographical albeit fictitious address as well as a website of their own that can be visited by anyone taking part in the simulation, is a simple and effective means of increasing the realism of the simulation by increasing the par-

Figure 2. Ardcalloch

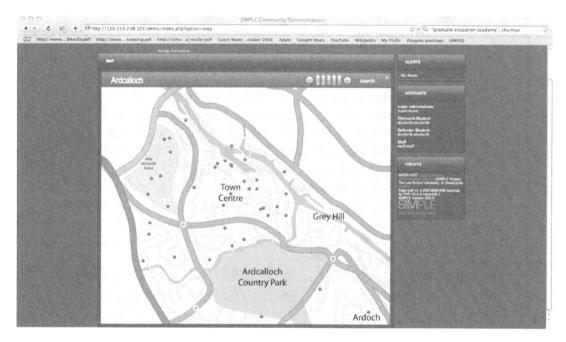

ticipants' sense of place and indeed time within the interaction environment.

Photographs of buildings and places of interest are also linked to from the map of Ardcalloch in order to enhance this sense of place. The websites of the various institutions are not uniform in style, rather they are designed in a way that reflects the diversity of web design that would be encountered in the real world. To add to the reality, the virtual town even has its own newspaper written by students (Owen & Maharg, 2007). The map is populated with photographs taken in towns in the area close to where the University is situated in order to give the student a sense of place with which they can identify. The style of the buildings in the photograph, as well as the quality of the light, the variety of types of structure and eras of buildings corresponds with what would be encountered in a real town.

Students have their own virtual 'office' that they share with the other members of the firm in which they are engaged in the transaction. They have a direct electronic means to communicate with any of the entities in the virtual town that does not require them to resort to email and can contact their opposing firm and their client for any information that they need regarding the case at hand. Encouraging the students within the simulation environment as much as possible is done with a view to enhancing the richness of the simulation and their engagement with it. The virtual office is designed as far as possible mimic the office management systems that are encountered by trainees when they reach law firms following graduation. Within the office environment there are also links to resources such as document databases and online catalogues, as is often the case with VLEs. The virtual office provides the student with a drafting area where the various pieces of communication necessary for the transaction can be created and amended either by one student acting on his own or by a team acting together.

Interaction Style

In a typical scenario, students take on the role of the professionals whom they are learning to be

Figure 3. SIMPLE office

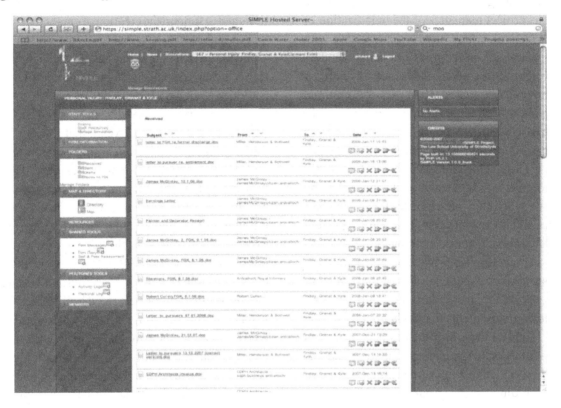

e.g. in the case of law students they will take on the role of solicitors. Members of staff may take on other roles within the simulation e.g. the senior partner of a law practice, a police officer, a court official, a crime scene surveyor or client. The nature of the simulation allows a staff member to take on more than one role if necessary and indeed allows for several staff members to take on the same role at different times, which can be useful from the point of sharing workload, dealing with staff absences etc. The nature of digital simulations means that the people interacting are shielded from each other by anonymity. Unless explicitly told, students generally do not know with whom they are really interacting, which leads to an interaction style that is very different from that which would be undertaken were the students consciously interacting with members of teaching staff. The anonymity leads to the emergence of interesting naturalistic behaviour

from the students and allows the staff in control of the simulation to take on roles or behaviour that would not normally be achievable in a classroom setting e.g. acting as a difficult client, abusive customer, deliberately being late with replies to mimic real life, using language that is candid and not necessarily what would be considered appropriate in normal dialogue between students and tutors for example.

Other Applications of SIMPLE

The use of SIMPLE simulations has not however been limited to the teaching of legal studies. Successful simulations that show the flexibility and ease of adaptability of the environment have been run at both undergraduate and postgraduate level in a number of other disciplines quite dissimilar to law, notably Management Science and Architecture. In the Management Science simulations,

teams of undergraduate students were called upon to act as project managers of the organization of a rock festival, which involved interacting with tutors who took on the roles of clients, vendors etc. Notably, this simulation was actually built by a senior undergraduate student with only minimal supervision from an academic member of staff, which is yet more evidence as to the ease with which simulations can be developed using this means. The Architecture simulation took place on a contract management module undertaken by students when they are close to the end of their studies and are at a stage in their learning where they have already gained experience of the workplace via a compulsory placement. Such placements and work experience are common in other subject areas too, particularly law, thus the need to create environments that authentically mimic those found in these workplaces becomes even more acute. For this particular simulation students had to work with contracts in a simulation of an entire building project (Agapiou et al, 2009).

Use of SIMPLE simulations has not been limited to the university where it was developed however. SIMPLE simulations have also been run in many other institutions to date, in a variety of legal jurisdictions (Scotland, England and Wales) and there are plans for further simulations of legal transactions to take place in the jurisdictions of the USA and Australia in the coming years.

CASE STUDY #2: CYBERDAM

Following the success of an early iteration of the SIMPLE environment, a similar piece of software was developed in the Netherlands to create a simulation environment for students to learn in. Cyberdam (2006) as it is now known, began life in late 2004 as Sieberdam (Holzhauer et al, 2004), a virtual Dutch town inspired by the Scottish virtual town of Ardcalloch. Along with the virtual town came an e-learning suite called ROCS that was used for the building of educational simulation

games (Holzhauer, 2004). The e-learning suite was designed to support the creation of games that were web-based and which were chiefly asynchronous, workflow-based games that involved the interaction of groups of players engaged in role-playing activities (Van der Hijden, 2007).

To give some idea of the scale of the Sieberdam project, during the 2 years that followed its initial release, 3 major e-learning projects were undertaken, with Sieberdam at their core. These projects ran in the Sieberdam environment at around 15 different educational institutions throughout the Netherlands, providing learning experiences in several subject disciplines at various levels of education. One of these projects was the Knowledge Development About and Through Online Simulations project (KODOS), which was managed by the Erasmus University of Rotterdam. KODOS had as its principal objective the validation of the use of online simulations in higher education. By developing and running six online simulation games in the Sieberdam environment the project's investigators were able to conduct systematic technological and user evaluations of the environment with a view to providing data to feed into the development of later iterations of the platform. The evaluations had several key findings regarding the experience and preferences of users of the system. Contrary to expectations, students were largely unfamiliar with online gaming outside of Sieberdam, however most appeared to like learning in this way and pointed to the improved student-tutor interaction that the platform allowed, particularly where face-to-face interaction was concerned (Bekebrede, 2007). Students were on the whole satisfied with their experience of using the platform but pointed to several areas that were in need of improvement. Regarding the experience of tutors, it emerged that the first generation of online games that they produced for Sieberdam were developed using only a limited set of the available functions. At the same time, it emerged that tutors would require a further set of functions in order to develop future

simulations in the way that they wanted. Aside from user considerations, Sieberdam itself turned out to be not particularly robust from a technical point of view (Bekebrede, 2007).

Thus it was clear that Sieberdam, while a promising concept, would require to undergo a substantial critical review and significant reconstruction were it to be used successfully in the future. Accordingly, a new version of the platform, Cyberdam (2007) was envisaged that would improve on the Sieberdam software and would allow the development of a substantial range of new games to be developed and played using the platform. The development was to be done as part of a project called Learning in a Virtual World (LIEVW, 2009).

Advantages and Consequences of Simulation Environments

Taking part in a simulation of a real life activity can force a student to think more about time management and organisation. The very act of working exclusively in a space with a particular structure not of their own defining, with every movement logged and time stamped can force students to think of their working practices in a new way. The educator can dictate in the physical design of the space how he/she expects the student to organise his or her work. The learner may begin to think about just how efficiently he or she is working which is important for those that will be working in professions in time-pressured environments. Evaluation carried out on several of the SIMPLE projects showed also that students developed their interpersonal skills as a result of taking part in a simulation and that many felt their communication skills, particularly in letter writing improved.

Keeping all of the communication in one place has several very important consequences for both the learner and the educator. Many institutions of higher and further education have recognised this by investing in Virtual Learning Environments,

and accordingly on many courses these days their use is mandatory rather than merely supplementary as was the case in the recent past. As is the case with VLEs, visibility and transparency are among the key benefits of a properly designed simulation environment. Educators can see exactly what information and other communications have passed between the various actors in the simulation and, where deadlines for particular tasks are concerned, can see the exact time information related to the sending or receipt of each piece of information relevant to the activity underway. The visibility and traceability is very useful from the point of view of assessing student work. Educators are also able, where necessary, to intervene when the students go down a 'blind alley' in their negotiations or when for example the simulation negotiation either breaks down because one student or group is either not responding quickly enough, or is responding in an appropriate way. Educators may also intervene for example, perhaps in the role of a senior manager, when the tone used in communication becomes overly hostile or when negotiations reach stalemate. Here it is important to keep a good balance between what would happen in real life and what will stop the simulation from becoming a futile, intractable exercise for the students involved.

Scenarios for Simulation

It is not an exaggeration to say that the possibilities for simulation are almost endless but in choosing a scenario to simulate careful consideration has to be given to certain aspects in order to ensure a simulation that has a good chance of reaching a satisfactory conclusion, moreover, one that will allow the students involved to achieve the learning objectives. This means a lot of testing of the scenario both offline and on before any students are allowed to take part. A typical scenario might be the negotiation of a sale or purchase, a personal injury scenario where a client has a fall or other accident that causes physical harm and to wants

Figure 4. Cyberdam

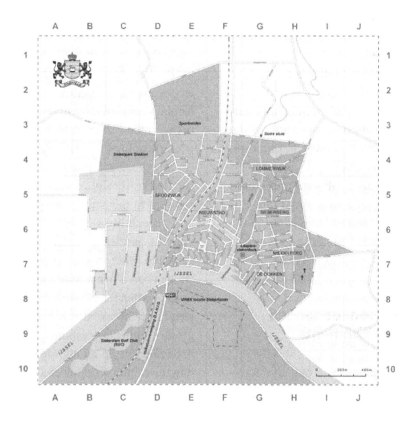

to sue the company or other body responsible for the damages incurred. Scenarios can be designed to last only a short time or can run over many weeks or months. Shorter scenarios can be used to build up a student's knowledge of a subject area cumulatively with short sequential scenarios building on the knowledge acquired during the performance of the previous one or several.

Successful Simulations and the Support Required To Build and Run Them

There is a dearth of data available on what makes a successful simulation or simulation engine. However, the SIMPLE software and the projects that ran on it were evaluated extensively following the first few years of use by students and tutors. Similar evaluations have taken place on Cyber-

dam as has already been reported. The findings of the evaluations of both simulation engines have informed much of what is discussed in the remainder of this chapter.

There is now over forty years of history of development and use of computer technology in education but very few instances of software or hardware that has had real staying power. Investment in something as sophisticated as a simulation environment can be costly in terms of money at the outset. While the simulation software available discussed in the two case studies is of course open source and therefore nominally free of financial cost, there are still potentially servers to be bought and maintained. Designing and running a simulation can also be time-consuming. It is important therefore that any effort can be rewarded by not needing to repeat the exercise next time a simulation is required. Reusability is key. Compatibility

with existing software also important, particularly where simulations involving the communication of documents in certain document formats is concerned. One of the biggest issues that those who are keen to implement simulation software in higher education face is the difficulty of getting central university information technology departments to support this 'alien' software. There are no big names in the market yet as far as simulation engines are concerned, nothing to compare to Moodle, WebCT et al in terms of penetration and reputation so it's going to be a challenge to get Higher education institutions to begin taking on software about which they know little.

Regarding the question of simulation design, there is a always the temptation to run the most elaborate simulation imaginable, however the SIMPLE evaluation showed that keeping simulation design as free from complexity as possible was often key to its success. More importantly, simplicity was key to the confidence of the people running and participating in the simulation. Educators can often confuse complexity with richness of experience when in fact sometimes even the most straightforward of simulation exercises can provide students with a very rich learning experience. Another key question is 'to what extent should the real life situation be modelled?' Is it really useful to have each person involved in the simulation represented by an avatar or other online character? The answer is probably not, particularly when communication means such as letters and email that are being mimicked require no use of such devices to enhance real life communication.

COMMUNICABILITY IN SIMULATION ENGINES

Designers of interactive systems that facilitate simulation face a complex task. Computer tools are cultural artefacts (Brown & Duguid 1992), which means that users must be able to understand the codes that designers use in order to appreciate the interaction possibilities that are available with the software. With this in mind, in order to maximise the usability and communicability of learning environments, Cipolla-Ficarra (2008) has identified several aspects that require attention from designers of interactive systems. All of these: localisation, age, ability, education, time, access to resources, time spent using and quality metrics, are as relevant to the design and evaluation of simulation environments, as they are to other interactive environments.

I propose adding a further 2 attributes that are specific to educational simulations: *authenticity*, and *feedback*. What little evaluation has been carried out with dedicated simulation engines has indicated that both of these attributes are instrumental to the success or failure of educational simulations. There is an additional aspect to *time spent using* that I think is worth exploring, which is *timetabling*, of which more later. In what follows I will discuss each of the attributes in turn in the context of an educational simulation.

- *Localisation* – A crucial aspect of educational simulations is defining the space where they take place as somewhere the student could imagine himself working. To take the SIMPLE simulations as an example, the virtual towns were designed in a way that would reflect the geographic characteristics of the area in which the students were studying. English universities had towns that were easily identifiable as English in terms of the place names and the landscape and character of the buildings, simulations at Welsh universities were based in virtual Welsh towns and of course Scottish universities used Ardcalloch, a recognizably Scottish town with a name derived from the Gaelic language and information about the town's place in Scottish history detailed on a website linked to from the map. As we have seen, the Dutch

project made use of an archetypal canal-based town called Cyberdam very different from anything used in the UK-based SIMPLE simulations. It's very important to recognise the difference that localisation can make to the user's sense of engagement with the system and to avoid any possible alienation by importing elements of what might be regarded as an alien culture.

- *Age* – Increasingly university students are drawn from a wider age spectrum than was the case in the past. In Scotland for example, university students can be as young as 16 years old and there are instances now of enrolled students graduating in their eighties, though admittedly this is a rarity. There are however an increasing number of mature students, that is to say those aged 25+ entering universities and this particularly the case in the UK at the present time due to the scarcity of work caused by the economic downturn. It's important to recognise this age spectrum and to design for it.

- *Ability* – Much consideration should be given to the abilities and needs of all potential users of the system. Is the system compatible with assistive technology for visually impaired users, for example? Can it be used with a screen reader? Does it provide a means to customise the interface in terms of colour, font face, size and background? Such considerations are often subject now to laws or at very least institutional regulations in order to ensure fairness for all learners.

- *Education* – Regarding education, it is not safe to assume that all students entering universities have come from similar educational backgrounds. There are multiple routes to university now that are not limited to school education, which means that there is a spectrum of experience in students arriving at university with resultant difference in attitude, expectations

and motivations. There is also a spectrum of experience regarding exposure to information technology and resultant skills that should be borne in mind by the designer.

- *Access to resources* – When designing simulation software that is to be available at all times to all users it is very important to consider the means by which the system will be accessed. Can we safely assume that all enrolled students will have access to a computer at home or should we ensure that there is sufficient capacity in terms of computer labs on campus for them to use? If students do have a computer at home will they have a broadband connection, and will the software be compatible with all operating systems, browsers etc that the student is likely to use? Given that many of the resources contained within the system are written in software programs such as Word and Excel, can we be sure that students will have the necessary and most recent versions of the software to enable them to download resources and also to create and upload them for others to see and use?

- *Time spent using* – Careful thought must be given to how much time students and their tutors will spend using the system and also to how often and at what times the users will make use of the system. Overload around the deadline of submission of assignments is a common problem to many LMS systems and one that the simulation environment designer should also be careful to avoid, which leads neatly on to the additional aspect of time that is *timetabling*. The timetabling aspect is often forgotten or at very least not given careful enough consideration when planning simulations. Managing simulations can often be labour intensive for educators in an unexpected way, especially when deadlines or particular milestones in the simulation or project are approaching. Managing

student's expectations is also extremely important. The ubiquitous, asynchronous aspect of the interaction will mean that students will often be interacting with the system at times when there is no-one available to answer their queries immediately, therefore it has to be made clear at the outset just what help will be available, when and for how long (per day, per week etc). It is not realistic that an educator will be able to be online at all times to respond to queries or to therefore it will probably be necessary provide extensive online help resources for when educators are not available to answer queries. It is however important to give careful consideration to the extent of the help available given that the simulation is intended to be as close to real life as possible. In few professional situations would one reasonably expect to receive a reply from a client or colleague in the middle of the night, for example, however urgent the need for a response might seem.

- *Resources* –The simulation 'script' itself is not enough. The props also need to be in place for each part of the scenario, for example, a letter from a client, a notice of intention to defend, a contractor's bill, or an eviction notice. ? Careful consideration must also be given to the human resources that might be required to play the various characters and roles in the simulation, and how will the simulation activities fit around resources such as lectures and tutorials? Should they still be used at all? All of these questions will require an answer at the design stage of both the simulation and of the engine itself.

- *Feedback* – Research, including that carried out on the SIMPLE project, has shown that in order to feel confident about the work in which they are engaged, particularly when they are working on a discrete piece of work for a considerable length of

time, students require to receive feedback as to their progress. This is particularly the case in a digital environment where the effect of interacting alone in the digital arena may be a dehumanising or alienating experience for some. Feedback can be provided by human intervention in the form of messages generated by tutors but also by automatic responses in the environment itself. On the other hand, withholding feedback can be used as mechanism to increase the realism of the task in which the student is engaged, and students themselves are often the first to acknowledge this. In the real world students know that they would not be able to rely on getting immediate answers, if any, about the quality or efficiency of their progress and the feeling of being 'dropped in at the deep end' is one that many of them will certainly experience when they first begin work. Arguably, working in a simulation under these circumstances can be good preparation for such situations.

- *Collaborative aspects* – Much of assessed university work is now undertaken on a group basis particularly where practical based projects are concerned. Simulation exercises are no exception to this. Simulations that are created to mimic what would be encountered in the workplace will often have to take account of the fact that professionals would normally be working on a case or other project as part of a team, thus any software developed to run simulations has to make it as simple as possible and indeed encourage students to work in and act as a team. The software must facilitate their effective collaboration by providing a space that they can all have access to simultaneously as well as individually and where they can immediately see the effects of the actions of any one of their number and add to or undo these

as and when appropriate. Transparency is extremely important in terms of individuals being able to see exactly what has arrived, and when, and being able to respond to communications in a timely fashion. Participants need reminders that they are not just acting as individuals within the space but that they have colleagues whom they are representing every time they send a message or otherwise respond via their shared space. It is important that the software is designed in a way that signposts this to them.

- *Quality metrics* – The usual quality metrics that apply to any interactive system are also important in a simulation environment. We have seen already the need to engage the user in order to avoid the simulation environment or exercise being abandoned therefore interfaces must be easy to use and easy to learn to use. System reliability must be excellent and remote access must be easily available. Regarding downtime, the system needs to be available at all times to avoid students abandoning it altogether and going back to using paper methods or simply not completing the exercise. The simulation environment is likely to need to interact with other existing software and hardware on campus that therefore some thought needs to be given to compatibility and interoperability.

- *Authenticity* – This is key to the success of a simulation environment. Given that our purpose in using simulation is to prepare in some way the student for the world of work in terms of imparting the skills that they need in order to carry out the necessary tasks in an appropriate and professional manner, there would be no point in trying to do this in an environment that did not contain many of the key attributes of practice as they will experience it later on. Furthermore if there are aspects of the

environment that simply seem false or inauthentic to the student, he or she is much less likely to engage with the task, which may result in a poorer learning experience.

TAKING SIMULATION FURTHER

We have seen already the features of human computer interaction that arise when students and tutors interact with a fairly basic simulated digital office environment, however in the future it is likely that simulations will become even more elaborate, making use of increasingly sophisticated software and allowing the integration of further multimedia technologies. Further development of existing software will allow participating students and tutors to take part in simulations remotely via mobile phones, Blackberrys, iphones and other devices used while on the move. Mobile technology will also facilitate the use of alerts that draw the participants' attention to the arrival of a new piece of information related to the scenario in which they are currently involved. It is anticipated that attempts to increase realism will mean that digital simulations will begin to include also the integration of phone calls and recorded phone messages between characters in the simulation. Furthermore, the use of streamed video of client interviews, court hearings, advertisements for example as well as a move towards allowing students to create their own content for upload beyond the word processed documents that they currently use as currency in the simulation. This might include their own video and audio files of interviews, photographs of evidence and photographs and video of crime scenes and other pertinent locations. Architectural simulations might in the future allow the integration of CAD drawings or other drawing/viewing software and medical simulations might allow the integration of case notes and x-ray photographs for example.

It is also likely in the future that educational simulations will take place over ever larger

geographical areas, crossing physical land and language borders, which will bring with it its own new set of user requirements. To date there has been one example of an international project, which was a simulation that took place in the Cyberdam environment in May 2009. 2 teams of Dutch law students negotiated an employment tribunal against 2 teams of Scottish students without the necessity of them having to meet physically, or pay for expensive international telephone calls. The project was a success, but was arguably only possible due to there being an English language version of the virtual environment available. Future projects involving other countries where neither Dutch nor English is spoken would require further translation of the site before simulation activities could proceed. Moving beyond simulation exercises that are confined to a particular subject area, there are plans at Strathclyde University for interdisciplinary projects that involve students studying for qualifications in various professions to interact with others studying for qualifications in professions with whom their future professional selves they might need to interact. For example one could imagine students of legal studies acting on behalf of architecture students who are themselves acting as project managers on a construction project. All of this of course adds to the richness of the educational experience and gives students a taste of the activities they might encounter when they reach the real world of work.

FUTURE WORK

The SIMPLE environment and associated tools and platform were developed using funding from JISC (Joint Information Systems Committee) and BILETA, the British and Irish Law and Education Technology Association. The SIMPLE team is now in the process of establishing what it calls the SIMPLE community (http://simplecommunity.org) in order to maintain the work that has been done over the past few years, and with the

intention of growing the number of users of the software. The software was always intended to be open source and accordingly the final SIMPLE environment release, source code and documentation, together with simulation blueprints are available from the community website. In the coming months several new SIMPLE simulations will get under way in locations as widespread as England, Australia and the USA. Cyberdam continues to run multiple projects in several universities across the Netherlands. Additionally, there are currently plans to make the SIMPLE platform mobile so that it can be accessed by students and tutors wherever they happen to be, using whatever device they have to hand, in recognition of the increasing preference for mobile access to educational resources. A forthcoming research project will investigate the collaborative authoring that takes place in mobile simulation environments, looking at both the human behaviour that occurs in such situations and the affordances of the system that are necessary to allow the collaboration to take place effectively.

CONCLUSION

As we have seen, simulations, when correctly devised and run in environments designed to support them, are a very powerful educational tool with the means to impart skills and knowledge in a manner that more traditional methods of delivery would fail to do as effectively. It is important when designing dedicated simulation environments that designers take heed of the needs of the students and tutors in a way that goes beyond the traditional usability guidelines of the web and web 2.0 because of the unique style of interaction that emerges from the use of a game or simulation for educational purposes, particularly a game that purports to mimic a real life experience or situation. We have seen that understanding the background and motivation of students is key to the successful engagement with and completion of a simulation

exercise. Additionally, it is clear that engagement is extremely important to ensure a good learning experience not only for the student himself but also for those other students with whom he/she interacts within the simulation. Also it has been established just how important the idea of realism is in such simulations. Adult humans are very good at sniffing out the phoney, the fake and the bogus and we must avoid developing systems that have features that negate this realism, otherwise we risk losing the trust of our learners and their tutors, and the rich learning experiences that digital simulation can afford will be lost. Adhering to the set of Communicability guidelines outlined here will go some way to ensuring that future simulation engines are a success and that the simulations they facilitate will be of the highest quality.

REFERENCES

Agapiou, A., Maharg, P., & Nicol, E. (2009). *Learning contract management and administration via a simulated game environment.* Presented at Viz 09, 13th International Conference on Information Visualisation July 2009, Barcelona.

Bangert-Drowns, R., Kulik, J., & Kulik, D. (1985). Effectiveness of computer-based education in secondary schools. *Journal of Computer Based Instruction, 12*(3), 59–68.

Barton, K., & Maharg, P. (2006). Situated learning and the management of learning: a case study. *The Law Teacher, 34*(2), 141–163.

Bekebrede, G. (2007). *Playing with multi-actor systems: Evaluation results of the Railway District online simulation-game in Sieberdam/ROCS.* Paper presented at the 38th Annual Conference of the International Simulation and Gaming Association (ISAGA), Nijmegen, The Netherlands.

Bevis, E. O., & Watson, J. (1990). *Towards a Caring Curriculum: A New Pedagogy for Nursing.* New York: National League for Nursing.

Book, B. (2004). *Moving beyond the game: social virtual worlds.* Retrieved from http://www.virtualworldsreview.com

Brown, J. S., & Duguid, P. (2000). *The Social Life of Information.* Boston: Harvard Business School Press, Boston.

Cipolla-Ficarra, F. (2008). *Communicability Design and Evaluation in Cultural and Ecological Multimedia Systems.* In Communicability MS 08' October 31 2008, Vancouver BC, Canada, (pp. 1-8). New York: ACM Press.

Cyberdam. (n.d.). Retrieved from http://www.cyberdam.nl

Ehman, L. H., & Glenn, A. D. (1987). *Computer-based Education in the Social Sciences,* (pp. 284 825). Bloomington, IN: Social Studies Development Center and ERIC Clearing house for Social Studies/Social Science Education, ED.

Gee, J. P. (2004). *Situated Language and Learning: A Critique of Traditional Schooling.* London: Routledge.

Gould, H., Hughes, M., Maharg, P., & Nicol, E. (2008). The narrative event diagram: a tool for designing professional simulations. In D. Gibson, (Ed.), *Digital Simulations for Improving Education: Learning Through Artificial Teaching Environments,* (pp. 111-114).

Holzhauer, R. W. (2004). *Sieberdam – Designing a Virtual Town for Academic Legal Education.* Retrieved from: http://oldwww.frg.eur.nl/lia/icto/projecten/rechtenonline/sieberdam.pdf

Jonassen, D. H. (2003). *Handbook of Research on Educational Communications and Technology.* Mahwah, NJ: Lawrence Erlbaum, Inc. *KODOS.* (n.d.). Retrieved from http://cps.tbm.tudelft.nl/node/95

Life, S. (n.d.). Retrieved from http://secondlife.com/

Maharg, P. (2006a). Authenticity in learning: transactional learning in virtual communities. *Innovating E-learning 2006: Transforming Learning Experiences*. Retrieved from http://www.jisc.ac.uk/elp_conference06.html

Maharg, P. (2006b). On the edge: ICT and the transformation of professional legal learning. *Web Journal of Current Legal Issues, 3*. Retrieved from http://wejcli.ncl.ac.k/2006/issue3/maharg3.html

Maharg, P., & Owen, M. (2007). Simulations, learning and the metaverse: changing cultures in legal education. *Journal of Information, Law, Technology, 1*. Retrieved from http://www2.warwick.ac.uk/fac/soc/law/elj/jilt/2007_1

Mandl, H., Gruber, H., & Renkl, A. (1994). Knowledge application in complex systems. In S. Vosniadou, E.D. Corte & H. Mandl, (Eds.), *Teachnology -based Learning Environments* (pp. 47-50). Berlin: Springer-Verlag.

Rieber, L. P., & Parmley, M. W. (1995). To teach or not to teach? Comparing the use of computer based simulations in deductive versus inductive approaches to learning with adults in science. *Journal of Educational Computing Research, 14*(4), 359–374.

Rystedt, H., & Lindwall, O. (2004). The interactive construction of learning foci in simulation-based learning environments: a case study of an anaesthesia course. *PsychNology, 2*(92), 168–188.

Satava, R. M. (2001). Surgical education and surgical Simulation. *World Journal of Surgery, 25*(11), 1484–1489. doi:10.1007/s00268-001-0134-0

Schaffer, D. W. (2004). Pedagogical praxis: the professions as models for post-industrial education. *Teachers College Record, 106*(7), 1401–1421. doi:10.1111/j.1467-9620.2004.00383.x

Schoen, D., & Bennett, J. (1996) Reflective Conversation with Materials. In T.A. Winograd (Ed.) *Bringing Design to Software* (pp. 171-184). New York: ACM Press.

SimPLE: Simulation Professional Learning Environment. (n.d.). Final project report. Retrieved from http://www.jisc.ac.uk/media/documents/programmes/elearninginnovation/simple_final_report.pdf

Squire, K. (2003). Video games in Education. *International Journal of Intelligent Simulations and gaming, 2*(1).

Squire, K. (2005). *Game-based learning: an emerging paradigm for instruction*. Academic ADL Co-Lab Initiative. Retrieved from http://www.academiccolab.org/initiatives/papershtml

Steinkuehler, C., & Williams, D. (2006). Where everybody knows your (screen)name: online games as 'third places'. *Journal of Computer Mediated Communication, 11*(4). Retrieved from http://jcmc.indiana.edu/vol11/issue4/steinkuehler.html.

Turkle, S. (1995). *Life on the Screen: Identity in the Age of the Internet*. New York: Simon and Schuster.

Van der Hijden, P. (2007). *Enabling Teachers in Higher Education to Develop their Own Simulations: The Virtual City of Cyberdam*. Berlin: Online Educa.

Windschitl, M., & Andre, T. (1998). Using computer simulations to enhance conceptual change: the roles of constructivist instruction and student epistemological beliefs. *Journal of Research in Science Teaching, 35*(2), 145–160. doi:10.1002/(SICI)1098-2736(199802)35:2<145::AID-TEA5>3.0.CO;2-S

KEY TERMS AND DEFINITIONS

Authenticity: The truthfulness of origins and attributions.

Collaboration: A process whereby two or more people work together to achieve common goals.

Communicability: The extent to which an interactive system successfully conveys its functionality to the user. The property of software that conveys to users its underlying design intent and interactive principles.

E-Learning: Technology enhanced learning.

Higher Education: University level education also known as tertiary education.

Narrative Event Diagram: A diagrammatic process used to elicit information about the structure of a scenario role within a simulation.

Professional Learning: The process of acquisition of knowledge for a particular vocation.

Simulation Environment: A piece of software that allows digital simulations to be run or created or both.

Virtual Worlds: Computer-based simulated environments intended for users to inhabit and interact via avatars.

Chapter 2
Venture to the Interior:
Virtual Object Lessons

Andreas Kratky
USC School of Cinematic Arts, USA

Juri Hwang
USC School of Cinematic Arts, USA

ABSTRACT

The question of how to design and implement efficient remote learning environments gains a new quality in the light of extensive digital education projects such as the One Laptop Per Child (OLPC) initiative. At the core of this consideration is not only the task of developing content for very different cultural settings but also the necessity to reflect the effects of learning processes that operate exclusively with digitally mediated content. This chapter outlines the design strategies of the project Venture to the Interior, an interactive experience that presents selected objects from the collections of the Museum of Natural History in Berlin, Germany, and displays them in a context reflecting the museum as an institution and the practices of collecting as knowledge constitution. The project investigates the role of objects as knowledge devices and the possibilities for a translation of the didactic effects of experiential learning into virtual environments.

INTRODUCTION

The recent announcement of a 10 Dollar computer by the Secretary for Higher Education in India as well as the announcement of a new computer series of the One Laptop Per Child initiative of the MIT for 2010 gives the discussion about virtual classrooms a new and strong impulse. These initiatives are designed to make educational resources available to children who do not have a regular access to them. Targeted for mass distribution in developing countries these networked computers will be used in areas with sparse infrastructure where the computer and the content available through this computer will often be the only contact with a wider range of learning possibilities. While many of the studies about the pedagogy and efficiency of virtual classroom settings have been conducted in areas where the technological platforms are generally available and where also other access channels to

DOI: 10.4018/978-1-61520-763-3.ch002

knowledge exist, the question of how to design and distribute educational resources for a situation where the codes and a basic familiarity with digital media is not developed poses a new challenge. At the same time this increasing demand for digital learning resources and remote learning is not limited to developing countries. Also in the industrialized countries the need for targeted and customized educational tools grows and an increasing number of institutions sees the need to provide information and educational content through digital channels such as the Internet and electronic publications.

With the project *Venture to the Interior* we are exploring several design strategies to address the question of how to communicate historic information outside of the scope of traditional classroom didactics and supporting resources such as libraries and museum collections. The aim of the project is to harness computer-based learning resources to create a flexible and engaging experience that can be explored in a hands-on way by the learner and that conveys the content with rich media. A special interest is to allow for widespread availability through network communication.

The subject of the project is a museum collection, namely the collection of the Museum of Natural History in Berlin, Germany. A set of selected objects is presented in connection with the information necessary to understand the role and character of these objects.

Choosing a natural history museum means that we are dealing with one of the paradigmatic institutions of the Enlightenment project of cumulative knowledge constitution. Starting in the Renaissance period with rather heterogeneous collections that attempted to gather all knowledge in one place, the museum is the center of an effort to collect material objects ranging from artworks to botanic samples, animals, minerals etc. as a way of constructing knowledge about the world. It accompanied the growing differentiation and specialization of knowledge domains and the rise of the scientific worldview throughout mo-

dernity. Thus this project allows us to reflect the transformations that this institution has to face in a culture that is dominated by electronically mediated communication and data storage. At the same time archives and museums are the places where our society stores 'history' and they are the places we turn to, when we want to get first-hand information about the past and examine or at least see historic pieces of evidence.

This focus on a museum collection raises a number of particular problems for the computer-based communication. The nature of the museum as a central location where material objects are collected and stored is the opposite of a ubiquitously available information resource. In the recent past more and more efforts to digitize the collections of museums in the idea to make them accessible in online databases for people in remote locations has changed this situation to some extent. But of course it is a tremendous task to create digital representations of the complete holdings of a museum. The collections of the Museum of Natural History in Berlin comprise approximately 30 million objects – a challenge for any kind of digitization project. Issues of quantity, though, are not the main focus of our project. We are more concerned with the questions regarding the contextualization of the objects, their didactic development, and the search for the most effective ways to communicate the corresponding knowledge domains to the learner. Generally the usage and navigation of these massive online databases is tailored for specialists while users who are interested but not familiar with the specific codes and terminologies are not provided the accessibility they need to make use of these resources. The database-tools often have a rather 'uninviting' user-interface that requires the user to have already specific questions and a notion of applicable search terms that guide their research with the database-tool. The novice user, who still has to acquire the knowledge necessary to make use of these tools and who has to develop a feeling for the boundaries of the domain, is more or less helpless in front of this information offer.

One of the aims of our project is to re-establish the context that makes the individual objects of the collection readable within a bigger picture. A second core aspect of the project is the translation of the specific individual characteristic of the material objects into a virtual, computer-generated environment.

The considerations leading to the particular design decisions made in the implementation of the project as well as the future research directions will be discussed in the remainder of this chapter.

EDUCATION WITH TANGIBLE OBJECTS

The motivations behind the current efforts to develop affordable computer technology to extend the availability of knowledge and education to areas where large parts of the society are excluded from the access to appropriate learning facilities bear parallels with earlier historic projects of this kind. The English social reformer James Silk Buckingham published in 1849 his ideas for a reformation of the society towards a more healthy and stable life. As a complement to the transformation of the inner attitudes of people he suggested a number of exterior improvements, among them "ready access to Libraries, Lectures, Galleries of Art, Public Worship, with many objects of architectural beauty, fountains, statues" (Benett 1995, p. 17). Buckingham was instrumental in introducing awareness for the role of culture into the agenda of British reform politics and promoted the establishment of municipal museums and libraries. The attempt for a general cultivation of people through "rational recreation" had the goal to make the society more disciplined, controllable, and efficient and to give people better access to education and future development. These motivations are not unlike those that are the driving force behind the ten Dollar computer in India, which is supposed to improve the skills of millions of students across the country and to build a more efficient and innovative layer of workers and future scientists. The same aim is behind the OLPC initiative, which has the goal to promote children to become an "educated and empowered resource" for countries whose "governments struggle to compete in a rapidly evolving, global information economy" (One Laptop Per Child 2009).

While the example of English reform politics is situated around the time when the museum acquired its modern form as a public institution the idea did not originate in this time. The German philosopher and mathematician Gottfried Wilhelm Leibniz formulated in 1669/70 the plan for an academy of the sciences and art, the *theatrum naturae et artis*, a plan which he promoted several times to different political leaders in Russia, Austria, France, and Germany. The idea was a combination of archive, museum, theatre and forum, open to all people to come together and admire new inventions and participate in discussions and various kinds of presentations. Leibniz mentioned that people of education should join forces with painters, sculptors, carpenters, and clockmakers to build machines and exhibits that have educative value. Further he imagined that mathematicians, engineers, architects, magicians, musicians, poets, librarians, typographers, and engravers would take care of documentation and distribution of what was treated in this theatre of nature and arts. Obviously this concept is a multi-disciplinary process that incorporates aspects of research and development as well as entertainment. Inspired by leisure and enjoyment this concept was supposed to popularize science and create an atmosphere of creative virtuosity. A particular role was attributed to the collection of tangible objects that conveyed the matters and results of the sciences to the visual and tactile senses and thus provided a basis for the "reform of economy, education, and the arts and crafts" (Bredekamp 2000, p. 14). The imagination of an educational 'theatre' was referred to as a new kind

of representation, which was not only comprising real objects but also mediated representations such as light projections using magic lanterns, an automaton-theatre, and various kinds of concerts (Bredekamp 2000, p.15).

All these examples do not only share a very similar motivation, they also have in common that they favor the practical and manifest interaction with objects as a suitable learning approach for a wide range of people who do not share the same educational background. In the historic examples it may be rather obvious that collections of objects of scientific enquiry are chosen as the vehicle to bring these sciences, their procedures and results to a mass of largely uneducated people because this was the state of the art of the sciences at that time. But the value of these tangible objects that speak to all senses is also confirmed by recent studies about the value of sensory stimulation for the development of the brain. "The brain uses the outside world to shape itself and to hone such crucial powers as vision, reasoning, and language. Not hard wiring but continual interaction with the external environments is now thought to produce even the most abstract kinds of cognition" (Stafford, 1999, p. 21).

This turn towards the object and its sensual stimulation was not only a form of Enlightenment entertainment where "bewitching arrangements of colorful rough stuff [...] piqued the curiosity of the public" (Stafford, 1999, p. 238), it was part of a general turn towards objectivity as a way to decipher and understand nature and the structure of the world. In his *Critique of Pure Reason* (1781/1787) Immanuel Kant places the human capacity to be affected by objects as a necessary precondition for any valid statements about the world. With the distinction between subjective opinion and objectively valid conviction he offers a paradigm that has influenced most modern philosophical discussions of the objectivity of mind. Operating with the term *communicability* Kant justifies objectivity "on the grounds that if a judgment can be communicated to other rational

beings, there is a solid (though not infallible) presumption that they are talking, and talking accurately, about the same object" (Daston/Gallison 2007, p. 262).

The particular value of tangible objects for learning purposes started to play a bigger role in the 19th century. The Swiss educator Johann Heinrich Pestalozzi was a pioneer of an educational practice based on the active manipulation of objects and the exposure to concrete phenomena in early childhood as the foundation for later complex learning. A student of Pestalozzi, Friedrich Fröbel, continued this didactic approach and founded in 1837 the first kindergarten in Germany. This development of reform pedagogics falls into the same timeframe as the development of the museum as a modern institution that is open to a mass audience. Besides their purpose of housing and ordering the collected artifacts Museums always served the purpose of representation and display of their holdings. In the growing urban centers of the 19th century in particular museums of natural history go through a phase of high popularity. The high time of colonial activities generates not only an increasing stream of new objects coming from foreign countries but also turns the attention to the museum as a place of representation of national power and the construction of several new buildings with particularly representative qualities is initiated. Ironically the history of the building of the Museum of Natural History in Berlin is a witness of the shifting debate between the museum as a research institute with access only for scientists and the museum as an institute for public education that is open for the general public. This discussion was ongoing on an international level. When the construction started in 1882, the plans for the new building of the museum in Berlin were to integrate the display part of the collection and the research part. All rooms were supposed to be accessible to the public. By the time the building opened, though, this plan had changed and the two parts of the collection were separated (Köstering 2003, p.46-53).

VIRTUAL OBJECTS OF KNOWLEDGE

A Consideration of Virtual Reality

How can the immediacy of the encounter with tangible objects that is the characteristic of the museum experience be translated into a digitally mediated context? It seems particularly valuable for the context outlined above, where education has to deal with significant cultural differences, to turn to this tangible immediacy to convey the desired information. Thus it is crucial to find an efficient translation of the real-world object encounter.

A technology that received a lot of attention in the 1990s was the idea of a computer-based Virtual Reality (VR), a space generated entirely through computer graphics and enhanced through immersive sound and other strategies like force feedback devices and sensors that were supposed to "talk" to the other senses beyond the visual sense. The user of such a system was to be immersed into the experience of an artificial world in which he could operate in a similar way as he would in the real world. He can navigate and interact with the space and objects in it. This concept of VR promoted ideas of tele-presence in remote places as well the possibility to create 'idea-spaces'. And the parallel between the theory of a multi-sensorial and tangible educational approach and some of the core ideas of VR is obvious. Even though the high-times of VR research are over, the idea still has currency. Several studies have been conducted on the use of Virtual Reality environments for educational purposes favoring the potential for high interactivity and a high degree of realism. Virtual Reality environments provide the possibility for the learner to explore and manipulate three-dimensional spaces that are displayed on a computer. As Michitaka Hirose points out, the most important contribution of this technology is "to visualize various objects that are difficult to understand intuitively" (Hirose 2006, p.31). This

evaluation goes along with several other studies finding VR environments capable of making "what is abstract and intangible to become concrete and manipulable" (Lee/Wong 2008 p. 233).

The area that benefited most from the VR research and the technologies stemming from it was the area of computer graphics. We now have very powerful systems, which deliver strong graphics capabilities at comparatively low cost. While the earlier applications needed dedicated and expensive hardware to deliver a responsive and esthetically compelling experience the necessary investment threshold is now significantly lower. Classically, VR environments operated with expensive immersive display technologies that were only suitable for a lab environment and due to their focus on an individual-centered perspective inhibiting the communication and interaction with other people and the immediate environment. In the combination of smaller, portable and more affordable computer hardware the use of digital VR technology seems to be on the track to move away from the costly and cumbersome hardware to become an easily available tool. The aspect of less intrusive devices and more mobility allows to bring some of the social aspects back into the experience that make learning and knowledge exchange effective and pleasurable (Cheok, Yang, Ying, Billinghurst, Kato 2002, p. 430).

These recent developments and applications suggest that VR technology provides possibilities to implement aspects of the immediacy and communicative value that was attributed to the real-world object in the earlier examples. At the same time it becomes conceivable to use Virtual Reality systems also for distance learning projects and virtual classrooms in technologically less developed areas thanks to affordable hardware and solid technology.

Obviously the focus on the graphics capabilities does not address the initial idea of a multi-sensorial immersion in VR. And even though the market has seen several alternative input devices that allow users to interact in more intuitive and

tangible ways with the computer it seems that this field is still more of a specialized domain with few products that enter the mass market and that are likely to see lower prices in the near future. The only exception to this may be the development of gestural interfaces as they recently have become popular through devices equipped with accelerometers and touch screens. While still far from the idea of force feedback that could make an actual touch-experience possible it is possible that touch-screen based interfaces may even be available in the next generation of low-cost computers of the One-Laptop-Per-Child initiative.

In the light of these developments a short consideration of the aspects of VR is useful that differentiates the high-technology ambitions of VR in the 90s and the affordances of current standard technologies. The aim driving the VR research is to create a sense experience with digital technology that would come very close to or – in the best-case scenario – that would equal the sense experience that viewers have in the real world. The success criterion for VR then is the degree to which the viewer takes the artificial reality presented by the system for real. The artificial reality therefore should create a strong feeling of presence in this other world; it should immerse the viewer into this world. The term 'immersion' is a central term in this approach and stands for the attempt to take over the viewer's sensory perception by delivering the visual experience through 3-dimensional stereoscopic images presented through e.g. a head-mounted display, and provide tactile experiences through data-gloves and -suits that can measure and feed tangible information to the viewer. The head-mounted display translates every movement of the head into the virtual world so that the view can be updated accordingly and the viewer experiences a seamless world where he has no visual clues anymore to differentiate the real and the virtual experience in terms of their visual appearance. There is no frame anymore that forms the border between the virtual and the real world. This similarity between the real and

the virtual world is the goal of VR research and the development of technologies that support this similarity. This kind of immersive Virtual Reality, though, is the exception, as Lambert Wiesing states in his book on artificial presence (Wiesing, 2005, p. 108). There are many examples of virtual worlds to which this idea of immersion does not apply. In the example of computer games, which are mostly set in a virtual environment that the player perceives rendered on a computer screen it is very well possible to distinguish between the reality and the virtual world. This leads us to distinguish two kinds of virtual reality – the immersive and the non-immersive implementation of it. In the light of this distinction it seems that only the first approach to VR, the technologically more complicated implementation that involves besides the visual also tactile information is in the position to deliver the multi-sensorial experience we stated earlier. The visual perception in this first approach is such that it produces a perceptual experience of the virtual environment that equals or is very similar to the sensual perception of reality. The viewer has in both situations an experience that implies that what he sees exists in reality and is present in front of his eyes. In this way the first approach relates an ontological quality of perception and can convey the sense of tangibility such that, if the viewer extended his arm, he could touch the object he is looking at.

The second case, the non-immersive VR approach, is more similar to the experience of looking at an image depicting some object or scenery. The viewer knows that he is looking at an image since he can distinguish it from his perception of reality and therefore does not believe that this object or scenery were really existent in front of him. He still sees what is depicted and his intention may be directed towards it but he does not take the image for real. Wiesing uses the following comparison: The viewer has an experience that is an intermediate between imagination and direct sense perception. It has the quality of sense perception, because the viewer believes he can see it, and at

the same time it has the quality of imagination because the viewer does not take it for really existent (Wiesing, 2005, p. 112). The fact that the image is computer-generated and interactively manipulable makes this experience different from the experience of looking at a normal image. Through his deliberate interaction with the depicted objects or sceneries the virtual world assumes some of the qualities that Jean-Paul Sartre attributes to the thought image. While the perception image has to be explored and synthesized from many individual perspectives and the mind cannot deliberately act on the image, the thought image is a concept that exists only in mind and is 'at once' and can be manipulated according to the will of the viewer: "I am at the center of my idea, I apprehend its entirety in one glance. Naturally, it is not to say that my idea does not need to be completed by an infinite progression." (Sartre, 2006, p. 8). The virtual reality image shares qualities of both the perception image and the thought image. The image is given visually to the perception of the viewer but the viewer can deliberately influence the image and change it. He cannot do this, though, with the same flexibility and 'at-once-ness' as it is possible with the image that is purely given as a mental concept. This intermediate position is supported by the characteristic of the non-immersive virtual reality. Since in this approach the virtual world cannot be confounded with reality because they are clearly different the status of the abstract, mental quality of the virtual world is underlined. This consideration shows that the non-immersive VR technology provides some desirable aspects for the application in a learning environment.

Translation Artifacts Between Real and Virtual

Even though the tangibility and material presence of the observed objects is not given in the same way, the intellectual quality to establish a reflective position towards the observed is very interesting and may be more efficient than a mere 'duplication' of reality. Compared to many actual museum-settings this delivers already more tangibility and freedom of observation than the real museum exhibit. For reasons of preservation the objects are often presented behind glass so that viewers can only approach them up to a certain distance and not see them from all sides. The possibility to bring the image close to the eye, to enlarge the view and navigate it freely provides in this sense a closer observation than the reality.

With these considerations in mind we decided to use a virtual space in which to present the selected objects of the museum. The viewer can explore this space according to two different orientation systems, which are superimposed in the application. The first orientation system is the museum geography itself. The architecture of the museum is replicated in an abstract way just sketching the outline and floor-plans of the building to allow for an intuitive spatial navigation. A second alternative navigation system has been implemented that follows contextual connections between certain objects and knowledge domains. The implementation was done using a 3D game engine suitable for fast and robust development. The decision to go with a game engine implies that we are not aiming for an immersive virtual world but a non-immersive representation. Besides the qualities described above this also provides a wider range of delivery channels, which will be explored in the future research.

One of the strongest reasons informing our decision to go for a virtual space was the possibility to embed the objects into a coherent space that provides the possibility for an easy and intuitive navigation by amateur users. They do not have to have preexisting knowledge of the domain in order to start their navigation of the database of objects that the application contains.

Since every user has knowledge of how to navigate and orient himself in a normal geographic space that is bounded by walls and obeys normal physical laws such as gravity, up and down, the only learning process that needs to occur to enable

users to navigate the place is to acquire familiarity of the controls for forward and backward movement and viewpoint control. The controls for these functions are consistent with the majority of established products and should not provide a significant strain on the user.

The implementation of the spatial orientation systems further has the effect to provide context for the individual objects. It is in the nature of museums that they take the objects of their collection out of their normal context. The desire for an efficient organization and storage of the objects makes this decontextualization necessary. It is for example impossible to show each animal within its normal environment, the scientific classification and an efficient work organization in the museum demand a structure that follows scientific criteria such as lines of evolutionary development etc. For the amateur user these criteria are often of little help and do not communicate a holistic picture of the natural environment of an animal. Moreover the normal ordering systems in museums do generally not convey information about the historic development of the field. Specialized departments or exhibits provide this information in a different context that splits these components, which are aspects of the same object complex into completely separated discourses. The separation of the research part and the display part of the collection for example made it possible to install dioramas which present a model of an excerpt of a complete ecosystem and thus provide the context to the visitors that is missing in the scientific collection – but at the same time it takes the objects on display out of their embedding in the scientific systematic. In the virtual environment these components can be superposed and integrated into one experience that has several layers between which the user can navigate seamlessly. In this way the intertwined perspectives on the object can be communicated in an integrated way where not one aspect has to be eliminated in order for the other to be present. Such an approach, though, poses again new didactic challenges. A problem

that we know from various hypertext implementations is the cognitive load that is put on the reader of the hypertext to negotiate the different argumentative threads and knowledge areas that are brought together though links between them. It has often been criticized about hypertext that the reader, after following a hyperlink, is put into a completely different context that is thematically related but formulating a different argument then the text he was originally reading. Often termed as 'lost in hyperspace', this problem has continued to haunt authors and readers of hypertexts. Another problem of such a multi-layered approach is to find the right measure in respect to the depth in which the different aspects should be covered to control the cognitive load on the viewer. It is necessary to establish the right balance and avoid an oversimplification of the matter and an overly challenging and thus discouraging depth of information.

We are using two main strategies to respond to these challenges. The sense of being lost after following a contextual link is mitigated by our use of a geographic organization system, which allows the user to use his experience with spatial navigation in order to adjust his orientation. The contextual thematic displacements have actual position changes and distances in the virtual geography associated with them making the displacements more easily readable. A map overview helps to trace the path that the user follows while traveling through the virtual space.

Starting inside the virtual representation of the museum the users can follow contextual links the lead them to secondary spaces, which can be explored in order to learn about a particular aspect linked to an object that they encountered inside the museum space. These contextual spaces provide access to historical documents, additional information about expedition journeys together with photographs etc. In this way the user can for example follow the route of a particular expedition and learn where and under which circumstances the objects that he sees now as taxidermies in the

Figure 1. The museum space as an abstract rendition of the architecture is the central hub in the experience. From here the viewers can explore several contextual spaces

museum were found and which role they played in the scientific interpretation. Specific objects serve as connectors between these spaces. Since the objects are nodes in which the thematic lines of the different discourses intersect – for example the discourse of the historic interpretation and

the role of an object in the current scientific research – the objects serve as the gateways or links between the central museum space and various contextual spaces.

In our first implementation we found that the particular quality of the rich and textured objects

Figure 2. Screenshot of a contextual space. The depicted space allows the user to learn about the first German deep-sea expedition of 1898-1899

and the museum space itself were not conveyed in the virtual environment. The sensation of tangible reality of the encounter with real objects was impossible to achieve with a pure computer graphics-based approach. The use of computer-generated models and of a space that is suitable for real-time rendering does not convey the aspect of reality and individuality of these objects. In reality we use a whole range of cues to understand and interpret the material structure of objects that we see. Just from looking at it we can infer what the surface and materiality of an object will feel like. The computer graphics are not in the position to deliver this degree of detail and realism so that we always perceive them as artificial pointers that stand in for the real object. With computer graphics we thus cannot transmit the pungent feeling that the object on display actually is a real animal, maybe a sample of a species that used to live on earth and that now is extinct. The particular power of realizations from this reality-encounter and its pedagogic values were not communicable in the VR environment.

Geoffrey C. Bowker points in his book *Memory Practices in the Sciences* to the inherent difference between the two devices, the museum collection and the computer-based collection, as two different memory regimes. We can either be "acting as archives commissioners or conjuring the world into a form that can be represented in a universal Turing machine whose past has been evacuated in order to render its future completely controllable. Integrally associated with each are two symbolic realms: memorializing difference and secular time through classification and hermeneutics, or memorializing sameness and circular time through abstraction and analysis" (Bowker 2005, p.109). Bowker sharpens our understanding of how the encoding of information into a particular memory practice shapes the information that is being encoded and produces distortions and translation artifacts. We perceive the computer-generated images as the idealized result of an abstraction, as the result of a com-

plicated but nevertheless formulaic description rather than as individual real objects of which only this one singular entity exists. Despite the qualities of the VR environment stated above this particular aspect of individuality and historicity of the presented objects was missing.

A Mixed Reality Environment

In order to preserve the quality of object representations, which we considered very important for our project, the decision was to create a mixed reality environment using a combination of computer-generated space and photography. The use of photographic images allowed us to re-establish at least part of the rich and individual quality of the space and the objects. Photographically derived images capture exactly all these small cues that we use in order to determine realness and materiality of an object. In this way we were able to fill in the aspect that seemed missing in the pure computer graphics solution and make clear that the viewer is looking at specific objects that have 'their own life', their stories and their past, which is part of their role of scientific knowledge devices. The collection that is the center of our project contains a large number of so called type-objects, objects which are the one particular individual that was used to describe a species. It is this object that scientists have to come back to when they found a new species that they want to establish in distinction to an existing one. This means that the aspect of individuality of the objects plays an important role in the perception of the collection.

In holding with Roland Barthes' considerations of photography we use the aspect that a photograph makes "it possible to recover and print directly the luminous rays emitted by a variously lighted object. The photograph is literally an emanation of the referent" (Barthes 1981, p. 80). According to Barthes a photograph has the ability to conjure the presence of an object or person even when it is the image of a corpse: it is the living image of a dead thing.

Figure 3. Screenshot of the central space and one object of the mixed reality environment. Both are represented with photographs posed in the space of the virtual museum

We used photography in several ways to depict the museum space as well as the objects that we are presenting. For the object representation we used a motion control camera to take a series of photographs from all perspectives of the objects in 10-degree steps and texture-mapped these images on planes in the virtual space. This enables the viewer to manipulate the virtual representation of the objects and turn them around in all directions in front of him. This technology allows him to examine the highly realistic rendition of the object as if he could take it into his own hand – he can examine it thus in a way that would even be impossible with the real object in the museum. This is a great step towards enhancing the immediacy and tangibility of the matter for the learner. The images were photographed in a light tent in front of a defined background in order to be able to mask them to fit seamlessly into the virtual space.

For the rendition of the museum space we shot still images from various perspectives in the space and placed them inside the virtual space in correspondence to the position where they were shot in reality. As the viewer navigates through the space the images appear in front of him revealing the perspective of the building from this point of view. As he continues new images appear while the others fade away. The building is thus communicated as a series of highly realistic perspectives that form as a sum effect an impression of the space. Rather than creating one seamless and coherent appearance of the building we decided to use this additive approach that lets the viewer appreciate the building as the result of exploration. If the viewer stands still the space appears empty. It will only be filled through the active navigation of the viewer. The posing data for the images were gathered with the help of laser distance measuring and inclination measuring using accelerometers attached to the camera.

In addition to the still images we shot video footage of trajectories through the space. In a combination of track-shots and steady-cam shots we produced a number of displacement sequences that deliver an animated and seamless depiction of different paths through the building. As the viewer navigates through the space these images appear and start to move along their path. The fading behavior of appearance and disappearance is similar to the still images, but the video sequences 'fill

Figure 4. Screenshot of one of the mixed reality objects consisting of a regular matrix of photographic images from different perspectives on the object

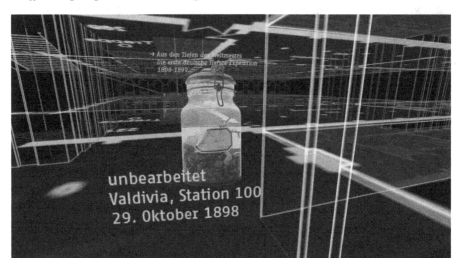

in' the gaps between the still images and deliver a continuous perspective. Nevertheless the video image is restricted by the borders of the frame and equally delivers only one point of view, one excerpt of 'reality'. The video-trajectories are posed in the space in the same way as the still images.

In order to support the notion of discontinuous perspectives that is formulated with the still and moving imagery we added a third kind of photographic rendition in the form of spherical panoramas. The panoramas depict full spherical views (360 degrees of horizontal and 180 degrees of vertical field of view) around one defined point of view. These spheres are distributed in the exterior space around the museum. They deliver a coherent full panoramic view but do not allow for any displacement in space. In particular the spherical panoramas render the epistemological quality of the collection of individual samples evident, which is the basic epistemic form in many of the research approaches of natural sciences. One of the clear examples for this is the exploration of the ground of the sea by a series of soundings that only measure one small point of the ground but in a massive density give us an image of the relief of the bottom of the ocean.

The design approach we followed in our project does not aim for photorealism instead we are underlining the fact that each photograph is just one perspective from one particular point of view inside an abstract constructed space. By navigating through the museum space the viewer moves in and out of these vantage points and experiences an impression of a space reminiscent of cubist paintings that combine multiple perspectives into one picture. This appears as a good translation of the notion expressed by Jean-Paul Sarte that was mentioned earlier which describes the perception of reality as a succession of views where the object is never given as a whole (Sartre 2006, p. 8).

The same principle applies to the objects which can be seen from all sides by navigating around them as if they were three dimensional objects but it is still clear that each individual perspective is given by one flat image. We intentionally made the cuts from one perspective to the next obvious in order to highlight the changes between perspectives rather than smoothly cross-fading them. Our motivation for this design is that we want to heighten the awareness for perspective dependency rather than creating a coherent illusory space. Through the decision not to create

Figure 5. Screenshot of the panoramic spheres surrounding the museum space

a virtual environment that strives for immersion by means of extreme realism of the experience we are able to create a hybrid space that combines highly realistic aspects with abstract aspects. The reduction of the museum building to its floor-plan and elevation outlines clearly does not give the viewer the idea that he is navigating a more or less perfect computer-generated likeness of the real museum. Instead, the use of visual abstraction rather directs his attention to the functional principles of the museum space. He sees the building as an abstract ordering system that defines numbered compartments in which the objects are categorized and stored. The floor-plan with the room numbers and section names becomes thus an allegorical representation of one of the core functions that the museum fulfills as an institution. In all parts of the experience we attempted to create this kind of functional analogy between the virtual space and the real entity that it represents.

We refer to the virtual environment of our project as a mixed reality environment. The term

Figure 6. Singular point of view of a spherical panorama

mixed reality has been used to refer to the combination of different modes of representation within one display environment. These are generally a combination of computer-generated artificial representations with 'real' representations, which are mostly photographically derived. In many implementations of mixed reality environments we see virtual objects placed in a 'real' space. This 'real' space is mostly rendered by a video camera view that is composited in real time with the virtual object to form a seamless compound. A similar system can be found in displays that overlay abstract data representations over a real or photographically rendered space. Our approach in *Venture to the Interior* is the opposite as it inserts 'real' objects in their photographical depiction into an abstract virtual space. We are writing 'real' here in apostrophes since it is philosophically contestable to speak of a photographical rendition of an object as 'real' – but for the ease of the argument we are following the established usage of the word in distinction to the computer generated, artificial renditions. As explained at the beginning of this chapter we are concerned with the communication of the tangible aspects of the museum objects in this project. This is the reason why we went to this kind of inverse implementation of mixed reality that allows us to convey an aspect of high realism in the rendition of the objects while placing them in a space that is focusing on the metaphorical communication of the abstract functional principles of the museum as an institution of knowledge constitution.

The idea of a space that does not convey the notion of seamlessness and coherence also serves us to address another concern. Even though the creation of a consistent and complete system of knowledge is along the lines of the scientific worldview inspired by the ideas of Enlightenment, we wanted to direct the attention to the fact that the knowledge comprised in a system like the museum can never be complete and proceeds only from one position to another. By highlighting the gaps between the different positions and making the transition from one view to the next discontinuous and noticeable we support the awareness of the vanity of the project of collecting with the implication of completeness – and direct the attention more towards the research methodology and the museum as an institution in general rather just giving a realistic depiction of one particular museum. With this consideration we are closing the circle to the ideas of Gottfried Wilhelm Leibniz who we quoted earlier with his idea of a public forum of education and entertainment. In his work *Monadology* he describes a similar concept of a worldview consisting of a dense assembly of individual and discreet perspectives. "And so the same town, looked at from various sides, appears quite different and becomes, as it were, perspectivally numerous; it happens in the same way that, because of the infinite number of simple substances, it is as if there were so many different universes, which are nothing but perspectives of a single universe, according to the special view of each Monad." (Leibniz, G. F. quoted after Jones, 2006, p. 208). Leibniz uses the concept of a great number of individual perspectives that can theoretically be extended towards infinity first as a mathematical concept to formulate a solution to the problem of the quadrature of the circle and his invention of the infinitesimal calculus. Later he extends this concept to comprise perspectives in a more universal sense: "There are as any mirrors of the universe as there are minds; for every mind perceives the entire universe, but confusedly." (Leibniz, G. F. quoted after Jones, 2006, p. 208).

FUTURE RESEARCH DIRECTIONS

The *Venture to the Interior* is a first implementation of a virtual learning and entertainment application, which allowed us to develop design strategies that address questions relevant to several fields. As stated in the introduction of the chapter we see an increasing demand for virtual

learning environments for public education made available through computer networks. These applications will have to address various levels of learner expertise ranging from young students at school entry level to older students and eventually adults who need additional schooling. The use of computer-based applications for remote learning has received growing attention and in particular the area of serious games as an educational tool acquired recognition over the past years. Translating the sources and principles of player motivation into the realm of learning applications has a very compelling promise. The main discursive mode of games is a form of simulation as the game theorist Gonzalo Frasca outlines (Frasca 2003, p. 233). He describes games as instances of simulation, which are constituted by a set of states and transformation rules that models the behavior of a system that is the subject of this simulation or the topic of the game: "to simulate is to model a (source) system through a different system which maintains (for Somebody) some of the behaviors of the original system. The key term here is 'behavior' (Frasca 2003, p 223). The focus on the behavioral modeling is what Frasca highlights as the main distinction to the 'classical' representational media. It is clear that there is great didactic value in the creation of a system in which the player – or the learner – can play through different scenarios and find out how a certain behavior influences the system as a whole. This approach has the benefit that learners can determine in an experimental way what the 'best' solution in a given situation would be and they can find answers for example to questions of the type *'what would have happened if?'*. They can arrive at this conclusion in a self-guided way and have potentially good retention of the results due to their experiential involvement. The downside is that the actual historic development becomes a contingency of the simulation process. As one version among many other possible outcomes the actual historic scenario is weakened in its role and not at the center of the investigation. Instead

of directing the focus on historical evidence and why things happened the way they happened, it is directed to the modeling aspect of the experience. The implementation of the mechanisms that model the situation are an abstraction based on prior analysis and therefore present the result of this analysis for the investigation through the learner rather than giving him the possibility to engage into the analysis himself. In our approach in the *Venture to the Interior* project we direct the focus towards the historical component of the museum collection and the shifting interpretations of scientific objects. All information is conveyed through actual historic documents and interviews. The photographic presentation strategy of the objects discussed above extends to the other documentation materials as well. The interaction principles of our application turn away from simulation towards exploration. Nevertheless, the metaphor of spatial exploration is pertinent to the activity of scientific exploration and collecting and therefore does not move away from a correspondence between the principles pertinent to the subject matter and the interaction principles. With this shift towards a documentary approach we are moving in a direction that has been sparsely explored so far but seems very promising and relevant for educational purposes (Bogost, Poremba, 2006, p. 2). In order to enable an efficient assessment of the educational efficiency of applications implementing this documentary paradigm it will be necessary to develop an appropriate evaluation methodology. This methodology will inform the design process of balancing the components of representation and simulation within such an application. It will equally guide further research into other usage and distribution scenarios. It seems that this form can be equally useful as an application for remote learning experiences as for onsite enhancement of existing museum exhibits. The possibility to deploy such an application as a fixed museum installation with custom interface technology, as an online component that is distributed over the internet or even as an application that can be

deployed on portable devices makes this project a very rich platform for further investigation. In particular the possibilities of current mobile devices that combine versatile communication capabilities with powerful computer graphics open a new range of applications in the context of spatial exploration. Both the onsite museum exhibit as well as the remote applications can benefit from the possibility to explore the museum space with the support of small portable handheld.

CONCLUSION

The project *Venture to the Interior* gave us the opportunity to reflect questions linked to the representation of real historic objects in a computer-based simulation environment. The particular setting of the project made it obvious to consider these issues between the pole of the classic natural history museum as a collection of tangible objects and the pole of digital data-collections communicated through electronic networks. Of special interest was the possibility to translate the didactic values that the encounter with real-world objects provides for a learning experience into a digitally mediated environment. We found that a mixed reality approach provides particular advantages to integrate the high degree of interactivity and flexibility of a virtual environment with the reality reference of photographic media. This combination allows to create a learning experience that is engaging and has the advantages of easy and widespread distribution through electronic networks enabled by the digital format while still communicating a feeling of groundedness in reality. The aspect of immediacy and experiential directness provides great potential for the use in communicative situations spanning vastly different educational levels and cultural backgrounds. Further experiments based on this model will be developed to further investigate this potential.

The current implementation allows us to see how the project is suitable to serve as a versatile and strong learning tool. At the same time it becomes a means of communication for a museum that can use it to satisfy its preservation needs to protect the collection objects while still making them available to the public in a mediated hands-on experience.

In our particular case the project served also to make parts of the collection available to the viewers that are normally not part of the display collection. By 'opening' the scientific collection, the storage area of the museum is accessible for the virtual exploration through the viewers, which is a reversion of the historical decision to separate the two parts of the collection without compromising workflow and conservational demands.

REFERENCES

Barthes, R. (1981). *Camera Lucida.* New York: Hill and Wang.

Benett, T. (1995). *The Birth of the Museum.* London: Routledge.

Bogost, I., & Poremba, C. (2006). (Forthcoming). Can Games get Real? A Closer Look at 'Documentary'. *Digital Games.*

Bowker, G. C. (2005). *Memory Practices of the Sciences.* Cambridge, MA: MIT Press.

Cheok, A. D., Yang, X., Ying, Z. Z., Billinghurst, M., & Kato, H. (2002). Touch Space: Mixed Reality Game Space Based on Ubiquitous, Tangible, and Social Computing. *Personal and Ubiquitous Computing 6.* London: Springer Verlag.

Daston, L., & Gallison, P. (2007). *Objectivity.* New York: Zone Books.

Frasca, G. (2003). Simulation versus Narrative – Introduction to Ludology. In Wolf, M. J. P., & Perron, B. (Eds.), *The Video Game Theory Reader.* New York, London: Routledge.

Hirose, M. (2006). Virtual Reality Technology and Museum Exhibit. *The International Journal of Virtual Reality*, 5(2), 31–36.

Horst, B. (2000). Leibniz' Theater der Natur und Kunst. In Bredekamp, Brüning, Weber, *Theater der Natur und Kunst,* (pp. 12-19). Berlin: Henschel Verlag.

Jones, M. L. (2006). *The Good Life in the Scientific Revolution.* Chicago: University of Chicago Press.

Köstering, S. (2003). *Natur zum Anschauen.* Köln, Germany: Böhlau Verlag.

Lee, E. A.-L., & Wong, K. W. (2008). A Review of Using Virtual Reality for Learning. In Pan, Z. et al. (Eds.), *Transactions on Edutainment I,* (LNCS Vol. 5080). Berlin: Springer Verlag.

One Laptop Per Child. (2009). Mission Statement. *One Laptop Per Child.* Retrieved February 28, 2009, from http://laptop.org/en/vision/mission/index2.shtml

Sartre, J.-P. (2006). *The Imaginary.* Abingdon, UK: Routledge.

Stafford, B. M. (1999). *Artful Science.* Cambridge, MA: MIT Press.

Wiesing, L. (2005). *Artifizielle Präsenz.* Frankfurt am Main, Germany: Suhrkamp.

KEY TERMS AND DEFINITIONS

Distance Learning: A learning environment designed to be used outside of the normal classroom setting in a self-controlled manner. Generally distance-learning systems are implemented for remote access through electronic communication.

History: A chronological account of events that happened in the past.

Mixed Reality: An environment comprising different kinds of renditions in the same display context such as a combination of computer-generated imagery combined with photographically derived images.

Realism: A concept describing a representation of an entity that is assumed to exist in the world that is in strong similarity to our perception of this entity. The concept is often used in the context of photo-realism referring to the 'realistic' – life-like quality of photographic depictions.

Serious Games: A game that is designed to serve a purpose that is not primary entertainment but for example education or training etc.

Virtual Museum: A collection of artifacts of non-material character. Generally used for digital representations of artifacts that can be accessed in a computer-based environment.

Virtual Reality: A computer application that allows the user of this application to interact with a computer-generated simulated environment.

Chapter 3
The Anatomy of Web 2.0:
The Web as a Platform to Promote Users' Participation and Collaboration

A. Bellucci
Universidad Carlos III, Spain

A. Malizia
Universidad Carlos III, Spain

P. Diaz I
Universidad Carlos III, Spain

Aedo
Universidad Carlos III, Spain

ABSTRACT

In the last 20 years we have assisted to the birth and growth of the World Wide Web. It rapidly changed from a tool conceived for scientists at CERN, into a global information network, populated by billions of users. Currently, we are experiencing another change within the Web paradigm, where the Web is viewed as a read/write tool enhancing users' collaboration and participation in information creation, consuming and sharing. Web 2.0, intended as a second step in the Web's evolution, is a complex topic and therefore it is difficult to clearly define it. It concerns viewing the Web as a platform for the development of Rich Internet Applications that go beyond the page metaphor of Web 1.0. It lies on the ideas of 1) users' participation; 2) users production of content and; 3) data remixability, so that Web applications and services can be employed as social tools allowing mass users collaboration and information sharing. The authors describe in this chapter, the main concepts behind the Web 2.0 paradigm, together with the technological aspects and design patterns that demonstrate this new way to use and perceive the Web. In second stance, they highlight future directions and research trends which are leading to the next Web's evolution phase: the Social Semantic Web.

DOI: 10.4018/978-1-61520-763-3.ch003

INTRODUCTION

The Web was initially conceived as a standard to link static hypertext documents by means of the HTML language. This approach is known as the 1.0 stage of the Web. With the advent of the first data memorization systems and server-side languages, we assisted to the birth of dynamic Web sites, like on-line bulletin boards or forums. This brought many advantages both to the developers (who can easily manage the contents of their Web site) and to the users (who can make use of always up-to-date contents, with more possibility of interaction and data filtering). Moreover, client-side languages and Cascading Style Sheets (CSS) enabled the creation of Web applications which have functionalities that are similar to the corresponding desktop applications. Web 2.0 is the term adopted to identify this kind of evolution, where the increment in the version number (from 1.0 to 2.0) does not refer to an updating of the technical aspects of the World Wide Web, but to a different use of the Web platform by developers.

It was mainly in 2004 that the diffusion of this new term associated with the Internet began to take place. Web sites like Flickr[1], Youtube[2] and Wikipedia[3] started to influence the form users search, consume and share information. It is important to notice that most of these users did not even know the term Web 2.0, testifying that the level of adoption of a certain technology by users is not necessarily bound to its name. As stated by Tim Berners Lee (2006) during an interview, *"Web 2.0 is of course a piece of jargon, nobody even knows what it means"*.

The salient characteristics of Web 2.0 are: *1)* the users' participation in generating information and the consequent development of a collective intelligence; *2)* the Web as an environment where developing Web sites and applications that put the control of contents in the hand of its final users; *3)* the user-centered design and the rich user experience.

BACKGROUND

Starting from 2004 we are assisting to an evolution of the Web due to the birth of new services and applications that are changing the habits of Internet users. The term Web 2.0 was coined during a conference brainstorming session during FOO Camp[4] (a conference at O'Reilly Media) where Dale Dougherty, vice-president of O'Reilly, stated that the Internet was going through a phase of growth and innovation that cannot be ignored. It is not possible to give a unique and synthetic definition of what the Web 2.0 is, mainly because not all the people agree on the point that it really is an innovation or a mere evolution. In any case, it is possible to refer to this compact definition of Tim O'Reilly (2006) in order to catch some of the most important aspects of Web 2.0: *"Web 2.0 is the business revolution in the computer industry caused by the move to the Internet as platform, and an attempt to understand the rules for success on that new platform. Chief among those rules is this: Build applications that harness network effects to get better the more people use them"* (O'Reilly, 2006).

It appears clear from this definition that one of the cardinal points of the Web 2.0 is the possibility to view the Web as a platform for developing new applications that no longer reside on users' machines. The same fact of labeling with a version number this new stage of the Web can be viewed as an analogy with the classical desktop application we are used to. This process is mainly guided by the fact that the user no longer accepts to passively use this communication medium but otherwise to actively participate in its growth. Therefore, it should be an error to consider this *second stage of the Web* only from a technical point of view.

Skeptics support the thesis that the Web 2.0 term does not have its own meaning because it rests mainly with the meaning each promoter decides to assign to it. As stated by Russell Shaw (2005): *"[...] But Web 2.0 does not exist. First of*

Table 1. Main differences between Web 1.0 and Web 2.0 (Partially extracted from (O'Reilly, 2007, p. 18)

WEB 1.0	WEB 2.0
Publishing	Participation
Personal Web sites	Blogging services
Taxonomies (directory)	Folksonomies (tagging)
Stickiness	Syndication
Content Management Systems (CMS)	Wikis

all, Web 2.0 is a marketing slogan". In any case, all the researchers in this area agreeing that Web 2.0 is concerned with the users and developers' consciousness to exploit communication media like the Internet, by taking advantage of active users' participation in creating and sharing information. This new form of participation breaks with the hierarchical conception of the Web as an administrator-user model and establishes new rules in the creation of novel communication models.

From Web 1.0 to Web 2.0

It is easy to perceive that, from a pure technological point of view, there are no substantial differences from Web 1.0 and Web 2.0 because they share the same fundamental communication protocols like TCP/IP and HTTP. The concept at the base of the relationships between contents is still the hypertext, allowing to define a semantic structure for the hypertextual documents.

During the brainstorming at the O'Reilly Media's conference (O'Reilly, 2006), the main differences between the two Web paradigms have been highlighted. These differences are summarized in Table 1.

The design and development of a personal Web site has always required time as well as technical skills and knowledge. As an example, to build her own Web page, a user had to know several languages including: *1)* languages to describe the structure of the information within a document (like HTML) or its look and formatting (like CSS); *2)* server-side languages (like PHP or ASP); *3)* languages for querying databases (like SQL). These requirements can be considered as a serious obstacle for all that users who would like to build their personal page, but who did not have the adequate technical skills. The birth of blogging services provided a new impulse in the creation of personal pages by the user, due to the ease and simplicity in subscribing to these services and starting to publish and share any kind of information.

The Wiki technology represents the natural evolution of the Content Management Systems, implementing all its paradigms: it allows the users to add new contents and at the same time to modify existing content, as inserted by other users.

The term stickiness refers to the kind of content employed in a Web site to make the user return to visit it, creating a sort of community. On the other hand with the syndication technique, the user is no more forced to visit again the Web site to visualize its contents, but Web site material is made available to multiple other sites. Most commonly, *Web syndication* refers to making Web feeds available from a site in order to provide other people with a summary of the Web site's recently added content (for example, latest news or forum posts).

Data, information and concepts can be classified and categorized following a taxonomic scheme. In a taxonomy concepts ar organized in a hierarchical structure so that each concept is related to others by means of previously defined

Figure 1. Meme map of Web 2.0 that was developed at a brainstorming session during FOO Camp.
Source (O'Reilly, 2005)

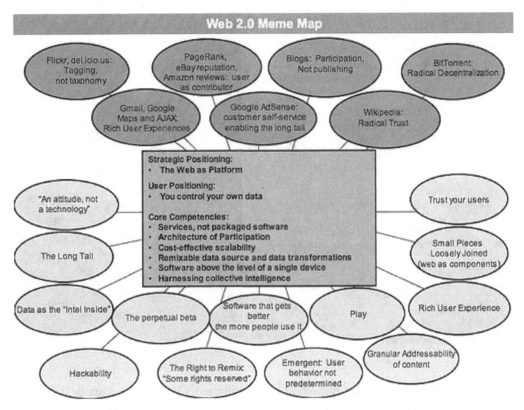

categories/subcategories. In a participative context like the Web, this lack of flexibility can be a problem. The term folksonomy refers to a different kind of content classification that exploit users' collaboration. A folksonomy is a user-generated taxonomy, in which users are collaboratively creating and managing keywords (*tags*) to annotate and categorize content. In contrast to traditional taxonomies, metadata is generated by creators and consumers of the content, employing freely chosen keywords.

FOUNDATIONS OF WEB 2.0

Figure 1 and Figure 2 provide two different mind maps regarding the main concepts that characterize the Web 2.0. Mind maps turn out to be really helpful to represent words, ideas, tasks, or other items linked to and arranged around a central key word or idea. As we can see, there exist a multitude of terms related to the Web 2.0 demonstrating that Web 2.0 is a complex topic and it is difficult to clearly define it.

In the next paragraphs we present some of the fundamental ideas behind the Web 2.0 paradigm: *1)* the *architecture of participation*, or the idea of bringing together various technologies and activities designed to facilitate and promote participation, communication and the active production of meanings and knowledge; *2)* the *user-generated content,* referring to that kind of multimedia content produced by users, that are publicly available for others to consume; *3)* the value of the *power of the crowd* and the *collective intelligence,* based on the concept expressed by Bennis and Biederman (1998) that *"none of us is as smart as all of us"*; *4)* consider the *Web as a platform* for the development and deployment of new Web applications, that have to be delivered

Figure 2. Markus Angermeier's Web 2.0 mind map. Source (Angermeier, 2005)

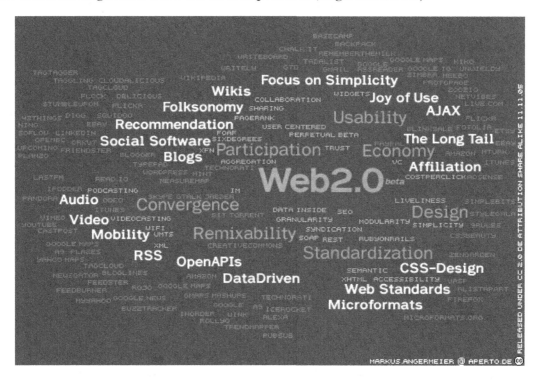

as frequently-updated services that, following the open source philosophy, get better the more people use them and; *5) the network effect*, concerning the benefits related to the effect that one user of a service has on the value of the service to other people.

ARCHITECTURE OF PARTICIPATION

The architecture of participation is quite a subtle concept, which is confirming the diffusion of the Web 2.0 paradigm. The key intuition resides on the ideas of collaboration and user production of content, so that Web services can be employed as tools allowing mass user collaboration and information sharing. At a higher level, we can identify the presence of the architecture of participation in the process involving user interactions with an application or service as a means to improve the application or the service itself. In fact, new

multimedia Web systems are designed following development and fruition procedures near to the Open Source's models, where the user interaction is not only an effect produced by a service, but a possible source for the improvement of the system. Referring to the idea exposed by O'Reilly in his work, the Bittorrent network is a clear example to demonstrate the Web 2.0 principle of architecture of participation. He stated that *"the service automatically gets better the more people use it"* and that this process confirms the presence of *"an implicit 'architecture of participation', a built-in ethic of cooperation, in which the service acts primarily as an intelligent broker, connecting the edges to each other and harnessing the power of the users themselves"* (O'Reilly, 2005, p. 2).

The hyperlinking, which represents the base of the Web, can be employed to take advantage of the *collective intelligence* and promote architecture of participation: for example, users can generate new documents, which will be added to

the Web structure and subsequently discovered by other users (these latter can further spread such information by creating new hyperlinks). Therefore, connections over the Web grow as a result of user's participation. Such connections can be exploited by Web search engines as a *popularity measure* in order to create a hierarchy and supply better search results. As an example PageRank (the well-known link analysis algorithm used by the Google search engine) (Brin and Page, 1998) assigns a numerical weight to each element of a hyperlinked set of documents, to *measure* its relative importance within the set. Briefly, the PageRank for a Web site results from a voting process among all the other pages on the World Wide Web. A hyperlink to a page counts as a vote of support. Sites with a high PageRank value are considered as *authorities*, so that their vote is more influential in determining the PageRank of linked sites.

Twitter's[5] social network is an example of architecture of participation on a micro scale. Twitter is essentially a free micro-blogging service that enables its users to send and read other users' updates known as *tweets*. Tweets are text-based posts of up to 140 characters, which are displayed on the user's profile page and delivered to other users who have subscribed to them. Twitter's micro-blogging platform supports the architecture of participation in the way it allows users to share links to multimedia resources as developers to create open source tools for the community.

In any case, when considering the architecture of participation, we have to take into account the concept of *Participation Inequality* exposed by Jacob Nielsen (2006). He stated that: *"In most on-line communities, 90% of users are lurkers who never contribute, 9% of users contribute a little, and 1% of users account for almost all the action"* (Nielsen, 2006). Participation over the Web follows this 90-9-1 rule: 90% of users only read or observe, but do not contribute; 9% of users contribute from time to time, but contributing does not represent their main priority and; 1% of users

are responsible for the mayority of contributions: it seems as if they do not have real lives as they often post a comment just minutes after an event occurs. A direct consequence is that the set of active users is not representative of the totality of the users and this, for example, can negatively affects customer feedback studies.

Designer's aim should not lie in eliminating this participation inequality, but in reducing the existing gap, so to involve that part of users oriented to participate (the 9% of the formula). Nielsen (2006) highlighted some guidelines to overcome the inequality among which:

- Facilitate users' collaboration by making it easier to contribute;
- Automate relationship mechanisms by exploiting available data. A clear example is the Amazon's *recommendation* engine, an item-to-item collaborative filtering algorithm using input about a customer's interests to generate a list of recommended items;
- Promote quality users by introducing mechanisms to evaluate their reputation. An example is eBay's feedback policy. Feedback is made up of comments and ratings left by eBay members who have bought from and sold to the member who they evaluate. These comments and ratings are then employed as indicators of user's reputation as a buyer or seller on the eBay platform.
- Incentive participation by rewarding people for contributing. Several prizes besides money to reward contributors can be taken into account, such as preferential treatment or use special symbols in users' profiles that indicate their level of participation. An example is the *Duke Stars Program* on the Sun Microsystems Forum[6], where forum users can earn Duke Stars by answering questions posted by fellow developers and receiving points from the question owner.

User-Generated Content

The architecture of participation of the Web is deeply influenced by the growing presence of Web services that encourage users to collaborate, contribute and share multimedia content. It is common to refer to this kind of content publicly available on the Web, which is produced by end-users, with the term *user generated content* (UGC) or *consumer generated media* (CGM).

Despite UGC is a topic frequently referenced by media and experts, when discussing about Web 2.0 concepts and technologies, it does not really exist a widely accepted definition of it. Wikipedia, for example, refers to it as *"on-line content that is produced by users [i.e. non-media professionals (i.e. "ordinary people")] as opposed to traditional media producers such as broadcasters and production companies. [...]"*.

OECD (Organization for Economic Co-operation and Development) (Vickery *et al.*, 2006) has identified three main aspects that characterize UGC. The first aspect deals with the publication of content. In fact, only such content that is been published in some context and is of public access over the Web (e.g. on blogs or social network sites) can be considered as UGC. This characteristic allows to exclude from UGC email messages, two-way instant messages and similar. The second aspect regards the creativity effort behind UGC. The production of this kind of content always involves user's creative power, whether she is generating new content or adapting existing works to produce a new original one. In any case, users must add their own value to the work, which can also be generated from a collaborative effort, as in the case of Web sites allowing users to collaboratively edit information. Lastly, UGC is the result of a process generally led outside an institutional or commercial market context and it is generated by non-professional users without the expectation of any economical profit. As a matter of fact, there exists a variety of motivations that leads users to produce content which include:

social rewards like fame, notoriety and reputation within a group of people (Anderson, 2006), the possibility of connecting with other users and the opportunity to express one's own ideas. UGC has also been characterized as a two-way process which encourages the publishing of one's own content and commenting on other people's, in contrast to the classical one-way distribution of the information.

In any case, the conjunction element of all the definitions concerning UGC seems to involve *self/personal publishing* (Downes, 2004) and *self expression* as the new media and technologies that allow its production. New media as digital, computerized, or networked information and communication technologies, in fact, can be considered the optimal vehicle to generate, spread and share such kind of materials. Particularly, digital media technologies, blogging and podcasting services, mobile phone photography, wikis and social network sites are significant. As an example, the widespread use of Web sites and services hosting UGC constituted a great incentive for its creation, for not every user had available server space or the required skills to publish her work.

Journalist Dan Gillmor (2004) analyzed the implications of the Web together with the proliferation of cheap and high quality digital cameras, videos, mobile and smart phones in the rise of the so called *citizen journalism* (also known as *grassroots* or *participatory journalism*). This term refers to the concept of members of the public *"playing an active role in the process of collecting, reporting, analyzing and disseminating news and information"* (Bowman and Willis, 2003). As a result, many media organizations, like newspapers or television companies, are carrying out new forms of information generation by taking into account public involvement in newsgathering. For example, as reported by Anderson (2006), the Sun newspaper allows his readers to submit photos by providing a dedicated mobile phone number.

The Power of the Crowd

Wisdom of the crowd refers to a concept exposed by James Surowiecki (2004). In his book, Suruowiecki wrote about information generated or aggregated by groups of people. The main idea behind this concept is that the result is generally better than what could be achieved by a single member of the group. In this work three different types of disorganized decision processes have been classified (*cognition, coordination* and *cooperation*), where group judgments result in a more effective solution of a problem. Nevertheless, Surowiecki pointed out that not all the crowds are wise and there exist four elements that characterize wise ones: *1)* diversity of opinion; *2)* independence; 3) decentralization; and; *4)* aggregation. Conversely, the wisdom of crowds fails when: *1)* decision making is too centralized; *2)* decision making is too divided and; *3)* decision making is imitative (Surowiecki, 2004).

Tim O'Reilly (2005) has exposed clearly the extent in which the idea of the Wisdom of the Crowd has influenced the Web 2.0 philosophy. He discussed the usage of users collaboration to enhance email spam filtering systems by reporting that "*the individual decisions of email users about what is and is not spam, outperform[ing] systems that rely on analysis of the messages themselves*" (O'Reilly, 2005, p. 2). This demonstrates that, in certain situations, it is possible for a group of people, acting in an independent but collective way, to perform better that any one individual.

In any case, it is necessary to point out that the original definition of W*isdom of Crowds* as expressed by Surowiecki did not directly address Web systems. In fact, examples like the collaborative filtering, which supposedly have to express the positive implications of the *wisdom of the crowds* within the Web 2.0 paradigm, are really more related to collaborative content authoring and sharing than to a proper collective wisdom.

The key point in the success of the most important Web 2.0 companies relies on their usage of the Web platform and technologies to take advantage of this *collective intelligence* (O'Reilly, 2005) that arises from users as they begin to communicate. In order to harness collective intelligence: *1)* information must be freely produced and disseminated and; *2)* it must be a harnessing process that generates some knowledge from the collection of information. One of the best examples of this phenomenon is the online encyclopedia Wikipedia. Millions of people contribute to the collective wisdom of Wikipedia, making it one of the most popular information Web sites. Collective intelligence also applies to democratic journalism (Baase, 2007) in that a group of non-experts determine what news is important, and then people outside the group can view the news based on those rankings. The social news sites Digg[7] and Newsvine[8] both fall into this category and rely heavily upon collective intelligence in creating their content.

Web as a Platform and the *Perpetual Beta*

Another important facet that characterizes the 2.0 approach, is considering the Web as a development and deployment platform for new applications. It was Google[9] who firstly introduced this new manner of dealing with the Web, by breaking the old software paradigm of desktop application sold or licensed to the users. Google in fact, as appeared, imposed the new paradigm of native Web applications delivered as Web services.

W3C defines a Web service as "*a software system designed to support interoperable machine-to-machine interaction over a network*" (W3C, 2004). Generally the term refers to a client-server architecture in which communication takes place by using the HTTP protocol. It is possible to classify Web services into two main classes: *1) Big Web services,* which make massive use of the Extensible Markup Language (XML) as message format and which follow the Simple Object Access Protocol (SOAP) as message negotiation and transmission protocol and; *2) RESTful Web*

Services, which follow the REST principles. In a RESTful Web service, in fact, application state and functionality are abstracted into resources, which are uniquely addressable using a universal syntax to employ in hypermedia links, to achieve better integration with the HTTP protocol.

The characteristic of Web 2.0 applications being delivered as a service and not as a product represents the key aspect of the *Web as a platform* idea, and leads to a number of related implications. First of all, as highlighted by Tim O'Reilly (2007), *"the users must be treated as co-developers, in a reflection of open source development practices"*. Web 2.0 applications, in fact, embraced the open source philosophy of *release early and release often,* impulsing the creation of an environment in which constant updates are the foundation for the development of a service. O'Reilly (2007) defined this concept as the *Perpetual Beta, "[...] in which the product is developed in the open, with new features slipstreamed in on a monthly, weekly or even daily basis. It's no accident that services such as Gmail, Google Maps, Flickr, del.icio.us, and the like may be expected to bear a 'Beta' logo for years at a time".* This highlights that Web 2.0 applications have a development and deployment cycle completely different from the desktop applications of the client-server era.

Another aspect to be considered is that Web services frequently configure themselves as an Application Programming Interface (API), which can be accessed over the Web and executed on a remote system that hosts the requested services. The API concept mainly refers to a set of procedures, data structures, and protocols made available to developers in the form of libraries or operating system services in order to support the implementation of software applications. A simple example of API is the abstraction between the hardware and the programmer who can read/write on a storage device using the procedures of the available interface, without knowing what micro-operation are carried out by the hardware.

The software that provides the functionality described by an API is said to be an *implementation* of the API.

The employment of API changed the way in which Web companies interact on the Internet allowing developers (skilled as well as occasional) to combine data from several sources, like Amazon[10], eBay[11], Google and Yahoo![12] in innovative ways and to build novel applications relying on such data. Therefore, the presence of a huge amount of user-generated data, together with the availability of such open APIs, has helped Web 2.0 services to develop rapidly and has facilitated the creation of mashup applications that exploit the synergy of different data sources, integrating a variety of contents (Zang and Rosson, 2008).

Treating the Web as a platform and the user as a co-designer, together with the availability of a huge amount of information, also generates new strategies for the design of Web applications. As an example, Web applications are designed to support *remixability*, defined as the users and developers' needs to use and share public information present on the Internet, in order to build new original work by composing, elaborating and modifying the available material.

Creative Commons is a no-profit organization that increases sharing and improves users' collaboration by promoting the wide distribution of creative works available for others to build upon legally and to share. During the last years, this organization has released several licenses which allow creators to communicate which rights they reserve and that are characterized by a combination of four conditions: *1)* Attribution; *2)* Non-commercial; *3)* No derivates and; *4)* share-alike. As an example, the "Attribution non commercial share-alike" license means that users are free to publish and modify the work of other users only if they clearly attribute the paternity of the work in the ways as defined by the author, they do not use it for commercial purposes and they share the work with the same original license. With these

Figure 3. Google Docs

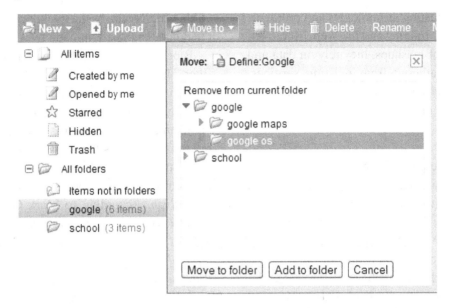

licenses it is easy to establish in what manner a work can be distributed on the Web.

Lastly, the Web can be considered as a platform in the sense that, thanks to new development technologies and frameworks such as Asynchronous Javascript and XML (AJAX), Adobe Flex, Java enabled technologies like JavaFX and JavaServer Faces (JSF) and Microsoft Silverlight, Rich Internet Applications (RIA) to mimic classical desktop applications. For example, Google Docs[13] (Figure 3) offers the functionalities of a word processor, spreadsheet and slide-show presentation in a single Web application with rich user interaction. It also supports collaborative features by allowing users to create and edit on-line documents while collaborating in real-time with other users.

Network Effect

When applied to the Web, this economic term, is employed to demonstrate that, as more people start to use a service in which there is some form of interaction among users, there is an increase in value to the existing users (Klemperer, 2006). As the number of users increases, the system be-

comes even more valuable and is able to attract a wider user base. For example, as stated by the creator of del.icio.us[14] Joshua Schachter (2006): *"For a system to be successful, the users of the system have to perceive that it's directly valuable to them"*, and *"If you need scale in order to create value, it's hard to get scale, because there's little incentive for the first people to use the product. Ideally, the system should be useful for user number one"*.

Social networking sites are also good examples of network effect. The more people register onto a social networking Web site, the more useful the Web site is to its registrants.

SERVICES AND TECHNOLOGIES OF THE WEB 2.0

We describe in this Section technologies, Web services and applications that demonstrate the foundations of the Web 2.0 paradigm including: blogs, wikis, collaborative tagging systems and folksonomies, content syndication, social networking sites and mashup applications. Notice that

these are not really new technologies, since they make use of existing technologies and protocols constituting the Internet and the Web. Moreover, as in the case of mashups, they rely on data and information gathered from existing services, combining them to build new applications.

Blogs

The term blog refers to a Web site where a user (the author who maintained the blog, called *blogger*) writes articles (the blog *entries* or *posts*) in terms of commentary on a particular subject, descriptions of event or personal diary entries, combining text, graphic content, and links to other blogs, Web pages, and other media related to the topic. Blog entries are generally displayed in an inverse chronological order (from the most recent to the oldest one), reflecting an on-line journal style (Doctorow *et al.*, 2002). Most blogs also allow visitors to add a *comment* below a blog entry.

The blog structure is built by means of a dedicated publishing application, which guides the user in the blog creation process. This structure is generally composed by a set of Web pages corresponding to the articles to be published. To each page a *permalink*, which is a link directly pointing the related article, is associated. A permalink is formed by a string of characters representing the date and the hour of the insertion plus some other system's identification codes. If an article has been modified, renamed or moved, its permalink remains the same, so that if the content of the article has been cited by other blogs or Web sites, such links are not to be altered.

Trackback is another typical mechanism of a blog platform, allowing communications and notifications between two users. Supposing the author of a blog is referring to a post written by the author of another blog: the former can inform the latter by executing a trackback to the cited blog. Trackback works as follow: *1)* the user *A* reads a post in a blog *B*; *2)* *A* writes a post in her blog, inserting the trackback to the address of the post in

B she wants to refer to; *3)* once the post has been published, *B* receives the trackback informing on the related publication made by *A*.

Blogs employ the collective intelligence as a filter. The blog community is self-referential and the same bloggers are who augment the visibility or ratify the popularity of a blog. The ease in publishing articles, as well as inserting comments by users, promotes the creation of communities committed to share information and reflections on different topics. This process also promotes *citizen journalism*. According to Mark Glaser (2006): *"The idea behind citizen journalism is that people without professional journalism training can use the tools of modern technology and the global distribution of the Internet to create, augment or fact-check media on their own or in collaboration with others"*. Moreover, *"blogs enable individuals to write to their Web pages in journalism time – that is hourly, daily, weekly – whereas the Web page culture that preceded it tended to be slower moving: less an equivalent of reportage than of the essay"*(Benkler, 2006, p. 217).

Wikis

A wiki is essentially a Web site that allows users to modify its content (as well as to add new content) (Ebersbach *et al.*, 2006). Such system is highly collaborative, due to the fact that it strictly implies people's participation in generating and updating content. Many public wikis do not require mandatory registration to the service, still providing method to limit write access. Moreover, some wiki engines allow inhibiting users' write access, for example, by checking their IP address or their username, when available. Restricted access wikis are often used for professional purposes (Cych, 2006).

Within traditional wikis, there exist three different representations for each page: *1)* the HTML code; *2)* the page displayed by the Web browser (as the result of the HTML code parsing) and; *3)* the source code which can be modified by users and

from which the system produces the corresponding HTML code. This latter format, called *wikitext*, is written by means of a simplified markup language and its style and syntax vary, depending on the different implementations.

There are many factors that contributed to the success of the wiki platform, among which: ease in creating, modifying and deleting information, extreme flexibility and open access (no software installation is required) (Ebersbach *et al.*, 2006; Lamb, 2004). Nevertheless, there are problems for systems that allow such a level of users' collaboration and participation. Such systems, in fact, suffer from problems of malicious editing and vandalism, allowing users to write whatever they want (although under the supervision of other users).

Wikipedia, the most famous wiki community, offers an example of both the benefits and the problems of the wiki approach. Wikipedia is a free, multilingual and open content on-line encyclopedia, created through the collaborative effort of a community of users: anyone registered on the site can create an article for publication (registration is not required to edit articles). The trustworthiness of information inserted by users is guaranteed by the same users. Nevertheless, in many occasions Wikipedia's content has been object of jokes and acts of vandalism (Stvilia et al., 2005). However, thanks to the huge numbers of users involved in the self-moderation processes, these acts of tampering and mistakes are often rectified quickly. A tool, WikiDashboard[15], for improving trustworthiness of Wikipedia articles, along with their interpretation and communication, has been developed at the Palo Alto Research Center (PARC) (Suh *et. al*, 2008). Suh *et. al* (2008) investigated how to provide attribution of work to individual users on Wikipedia, for example who edits how many revisions for an article, could affect users' trust and interpretation of Wikipedia's entry.

Folksnomies and Collaborative Tagging Systems

By means of the collaborative tagging process, users add metadata to community-shared material employing descriptive terms known as *tags*. This kind of non-hierarchical labels allows classifying or categorizing content for future navigation, filtering or search. The tags are usually chosen informally and personally by the creator of a document.

In document repositories, digital libraries or other systems of content organization, metadata creation belongs to the domain of dedicated professionals, such as librarians, or in other cases the classification of the documents derives from additional material supplied by the authors (Golder and Huberman, 2006; Mathes, 2004).

Collaborative tagging systems, such as del.icio.us or bibsonomy[16], are popular examples of such tools, which allow users to conceptualize, describe, and share resources. Users can assign a set of tags simplifying the search of resources by providing indications to other users. Nevertheless, there is actually not an effective usage of tags. They are typically applied just for a personal consumption and people associate different meaning to the same tag; tagging systems are not based on well defined vocabularies, and so many tags do not provide any help to a user.

Collaborative tagging is one of the most important phenomenon impulsing Web 2.0 because it promotes the organization and categorization of the vast amount of information currently present on the Web, in an environment where there can not exist a single *content classification authority*. As a matter of fact, these systems represent an interesting research domain as an alternative or a complement to the semantic Web approach for building ontologies (Gendarmi and Lanubile, 2006). In this latter case, the knowledge base is built by domain-field experts in agreement with the community and found through a predeter-

mined relationship among keywords while, in a collaborative tagging system, content indexing develops as a natural process.

One of the most important outcomes of social and collaborative tagging practices is the birth of *folksonomies* (short for *folk taxonomy*) (Mathes, 2004): a taxonomy generated by users' participation. Folksonomies are generally classified as: 1) the *broad* folksonomies and 2) the *narrow* ones (Van der Wal, 2005). A broad folksonomy is the result of one item being categorized by many people (e.g. del.icio.us) while a narrow folksonomy is the result of one person categorizing one item (e.g. Flickr).

Drawbacks can be identified in using folksonomies such as: *1)* none of the current implementations provides synonyms control; *2)* there is a lack of precision in using simple one-word tags and; *3)* there is no hierarchical structure in the tagging process (Farooq et al., 2007).

Examples of systems relying on users' tagging activities are: del.icio.us, a site allows you to bookmark, categorize and share sites of interest and Flickr, a service giving the possibility to users to tag photographs they own.

Two Examples: del.icio.us and Flickr.

The del.icio.us Web site, as defined by its creator J. Schachter, is a social bookmarking Web service for storing, sharing and discovering Web bookmarks. The system is based on a non-hierarchical keyword document categorization, where users may tag each of their bookmarks with any number of freely chosen words. Del.icio.us is considered *social* since a user not only stores his own bookmarks, but can also see other users' bookmarks.

Del.icio.us also represents an example of the *enlightened selfishness* characterizing users' contribution in this kind of systems. Within collaborative tagging systems, in fact, the process of content generation is driven by the philosophy that personal value comes before network value (Porter, 2006). No one can contribute to a community with value if he has not found something valuable for himself before. In the case of del.icio.us, this value is represented by storing personal bookmarks: all other utilities are subsidiary. We may consider the tagging activity as secondary, and performed for personal benefit.

If we look at motivations and contribution behavior in social bookmarking systems we can observe, from a study conducted by Raquel Benbunan-Fich and Marios Koufaris (2008), that there are two different motivations driving the tagging of resources on the web: self-oriented motivation to store and tag bookmarks for personal use, and other-oriented or altruistic motivation associated with the quality of contributions. This study demonstrated that people are more selective when sharing tags for others than when saving tags for their purposes and this increases the overall quality of the collaborative tagging system.

Flickr is a photo management Web sites and an on-line community platform. It allows users to store and share personal photographs; furthermore the service is widely used by bloggers as a photo repository.

Flickr was the first service introducing a tags visual representation called *tag cloud* (see Figure 4). A tag cloud is a list of tags where each tag size is proportional to the number of times such tag has been employed, so that tags with higher frequency of use are displayed in a larger text. As an example, in a tag cloud of a blog, tags associated to many posts are bigger, with respect to less frequent tags.

RSS and Syndication

RSS (commonly known as *Really Simple Syndication*) is the standard *de facto* for exporting Web contents. It allows to easily distributing the contents of a site by presenting them on different forms. Particularly, RSS promotes Web syndication making available Web feeds (and material from a site) to provide other people with a summary of the Web site's recently added content.

Figure 4. Flickr's tag cloud

Explore / Tags /

Hot tags

In the last 24 hours
烟火, thanksgiving2006, decompression, firework, cbgb, nebel, zd, thebiggestgroup, emailed, canoneos350d, alentejo, 台灣, animaladdiction, columbusday, chicagoist, e1, thanksgiving, 台北, xti, hotairballoon

Over the last week
hardlystrictlybluegrass, fleetweek2006, thanksgiving2006, upcomingevent109550, utatathursdaywalk25, tallstacks, openhousenewyork, worldcantwait, columbusday, buchmesse, ohny, fundamentosweb2006, fundamentosweb, fleetweek, 中秋節, msh1006, nlds, aids, ceatec, sukkot

Jump to: [   ] GO

All time most popular tags

06 africa amsterdam animal animals april architecture art august australia baby barcelona beach berlin birthday black blackandwhite blue boston bw california cameraphone camping canada canon car cat cats chicago china christmas church city clouds color concert day dc dog england europe family festival film florida flower flowers food france friends fun garden geotagged germany girl graffiti green halloween hawaii hiking holiday home honeymoon hongkong house india ireland island italy japan july june kids lake landscape light live london losangeles macro may me mexico mountain mountains museum music nature new newyork newyorkcity newzealand night nikon nyc ocean

RSS format was firstly introduced by Netscape who used it to publish links and news that might be useful to the community. Later, the blogger community started to employ RSS for providing users with frequently updated content and allowing the exportation of blog posts. The popularity of RSS data format as a Web feed technology is strictly related to the widespread use of blogs: users started to generate content in the RSS format and, at the same time, Web sites and desktop applications able to collect selections of these posts appeared. In order to be able to view a feed, a user must: *1)* decide which RSS feeds they want to receive and; *2) subscribe* to them by employing an *aggregator* or a *feed reader* system. In fact, as to navigate a Web site a browser is needed, to read a RSS feed a special tool is required that can parse the structure of the feed, gathering all its contents to be offered to the users. Such applications periodically check for updates to the RSS feed and keep the user informed of any changes.

From a technical point of view, RSS is an XML dialect, created with the aim to represent a simplified form of content diffusion over the Web. It was born with the aim to rapidly collect up-to-date content from different sources, without checking each site individually but simply verifying a list of published contents. This list (the RSS feed) provides all the fundamental data to notify the users for new contents.

Another example of a syndication standard is Atom, which was developed as an alternative to RSS. Atom refers to an XML language used for Web feeds (*Atom Syndication Format*) as to a protocol for creating and updating Web resources (*Atom Publishing Protocol*). The Atom Syndication Format was designed to overcome RSS limitations and flaws, such as lack of on-going innovation and its necessity to remain backward compatible.

Mashups

A mashup is a Web application that combines data or functionality from different sources or services into a single integrated tool (Zang and Rosson,

2008). The term mashup implies easy and fast integration of existent services, most of the time achieved by access to open APIs and data sources to produce results that were dissimilar from the reason for producing the original information source. As a matter of fact, the widespread use of such mashup applications is a direct result of the availability of open APIs offered by different Web services (such as Google, Yahoo!, eBay, Amazon and so on) and because they are publicly available in principle anyone can built his own Web mashup.

For example one could use cartographic data from Google Maps[17] to visualize georeferenced information, such as weather forecasts data as in weatherbonk.com or house rental listings (crawled from the CraigList[18] community Web site) as in housingmaps.com, thereby creating a new and distinct Web service that was not originally provided by either source. For the final user, in fact, it results in a more efficient and useful solution to see directly in the map all the available rentals, rather than having to search in text listing and then having to insert each address into a separated map service.

ProgrammableWeb.com drew up a ranking of the most employed API to build mashup applications, where the preponderance of the Google Maps APIs can be noticed (Figure 5). While mashups can be categorized as *mapping, search,* *mobile, messaging, sports, shopping and movies,* it results that more than 40% of them are mapping mashups (Van der Vlist *et al.,* 2006).

Actually, considering the facets impulsing the Web 2.0 philosophy, mashups are more than Web sites that combines functionalities of two or more services (Wong and Hong, 2008). Leaving out technical aspects, the migration from the concept of application to the one of a service developed and used in a shared and collaborative mode by the users can be recognized. Moreover, mashups and tools supporting their rapid design and development are important in the way they represent an expression of how users exploit existing technologies and services to produce new original works. Mashups are also important to the development of end-user programming (Myers and Burnet, 2006), because they allow even non-professional developers to build their own Web application, taking advantage of the tremendous amount of Web content available (Wong and Hong, 2007).

A Real Example: Mashups in Emergency Management

Mashups are important during emergency situations as they can be created very quickly to summarize and disseminate useful information. In a short amount of time it is possible to create applications to collect information on the status of an

Figure 5. All time top APIs for mashups. Source www.programmableweb.com (06-02-09)

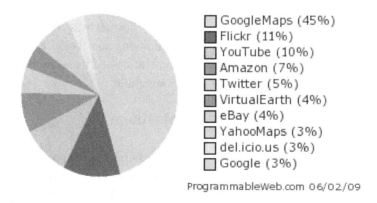

GoogleMaps (45%)
Flickr (11%)
YouTube (10%)
Amazon (7%)
Twitter (5%)
VirtualEarth (4%)
eBay (4%)
YahooMaps (3%)
del.icio.us (3%)
Google (3%)

ProgrammableWeb.com 06/02/09

Figure 6. Web site mashup generated with the Ushahidi platform

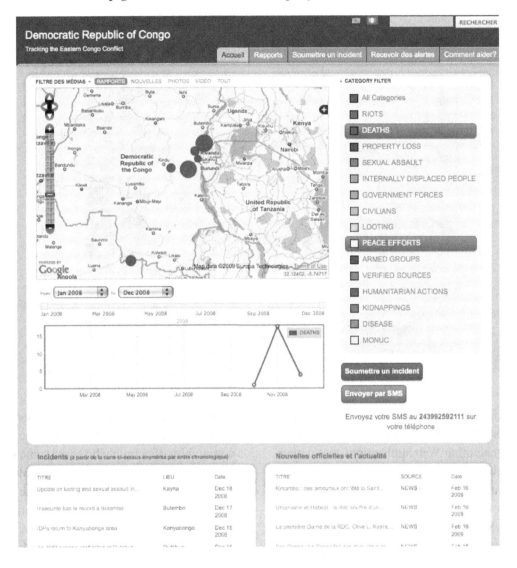

emergency situation (damaged buildings, people got wounded, etc.), which can be distributed to a very wide audience.

Mashups are relevant because they can be created by citizens. In fact, it is likely that in any serious disaster, private citizens develop their own mashups, in order to organize among themselves and share information exploiting existing technologies. There exist many examples of quick mashups created during crisis situations (Liu and Palen, 2009). They mainly exploit mapping services, like the one offered by Google Maps, in order to connect multimedia content over the

Web through locations metadata and integrate such georeferenced content into an existing digital map.

One of the clearest examples of such mashups is the ChicagoCrime.org Web site which integrates crime data from the Chicago Police Department's database with cartographic data from Google Maps. Another simple example is the Hurricane Digital Memory Bank Web site, a project to collect and share users' digital contributions on the hurricanes Katrina and Rita.

Ushahidi[19] (Figure 6), which means *testimony* in Swahili, is an example of a spatiotemporal

Figure 7. The user interface of eStoryS

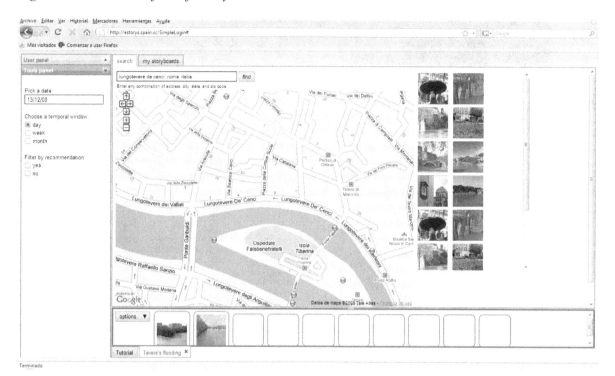

mashup for emergency management purposes. The aim of Ushahidi is to create an environment for quickly generating Web applications that gather and visualize on a map real-time reports from the general public via mobile phone, email and Web syndications.

eStoryS[20] (Figure 7) is another example of a visual system providing a combination of tools that result to be effective during crisis situations such as: spatio-temporal search features, storyboards authoring, content recommendation and filtering (Malizia *et. al*, 2009).

Social Network Sites

A social network site (SNS) is essentially a Web site that allows a user to *1)* build her public or semi-public personal profile within the system; *2)* manage a list of other users with whom she is connected to and; *3)* explore the list of connections of her contacts, as well as those of others users in the social network (Boyd and Ellison, 2007). Therefore, a social network site aims on creating a community of people who share same interests or activities, or who are interested in exploring the interests and activities of others. These services usually provide a variety of communication tools, in the form of encapsulated services for users to interact, such as e-mail and Instant Messaging, blogging features, photo and video sharing and mobile connectivities. Noteworthy examples of popular SNSs are: Facebook[21], Myspace[22], Twitter and Youtube[23].

While SNSs can vary in their scopes and technical implementation, their main feature consists on the possibility to create a personal profile and displaying a list of *friends,* who are also users of the system, together with a description of their activities. By joining an SNS, a user can generate her profile by answering to a form containing a series of questions, which include descriptors such as age, location, interests and so on. Most

sites also encourage users to upload a profile photo. Some sites allow users to enhance their profiles by adding multimedia content, including third-party applications (as the case of Facebook's modules).

During the last years, SNSs are being used by millions of people as part of their daily practices and has encouraged new ways to communicate and share information. As an example, information posted on MySpace and Facebook has been used in legal and criminal investigations (Snyder *et al.*, 2006). In May 2009, a Twitter user (Jean Ramses Anleu Fernández, known in the micro-blogging platform as *Jeanfer*) was jailed with the charge of inciting financial panic. He posted on Twitter a commentary (see Figure 8) that invited people to withdraw all the funds from their accounts at the Banrural (a bank of Guatemala), following up the events involving Álvaro Colom Caballeros, President of Guatemala, in the murder of the lawyer Rodrigo Rosenberg Marzano.

There also exist examples of the use of SNSs during emergency situations because they allow users to both quickly produce and consume information about a disaster. In the 2007 wildfires in California, Twitter was employed by local citizens and organizations to provide updates about the fires situation in the region (Sutton *et al.*, 2008). Communication tools provided by Facebook can be used to trace on-line users' activities and to determine whether people are safe or not. As reported by Hughes *et al.* (2008) users can deduce relatives or friends current condition by simply interpreting their activity on the Facebook Web site. They could infer that a friend is OK because she just posted a message on her account.

Development Approaches

Within the existing approaches to build Web 2.0 applications providing rich user interaction, three holds a great importance: Asynchronous Javascript and XML, Adobe Flex and approaches based on the exploitation of toolkit, like the Google Web Toolkit[24] or visual editors, like Yahoo! Pipes[25].

AJAX

The term AJAX identifies a set of Web development techniques employed to build interactive Web applications. The main advantage and innovation of this technology reside in the possibility for applications to retrieve data from a server in an asynchronous way so that data exchange can take

Figure 8. A post on the Twitter platform: its author was charged of inciting financial panic

place in the background, without user interaction interfering with the displayed Web page. Data is retrieved by means of the XMLHttpRequest object, which can be invoked employing a scripting language such as Javascript in order to send an HTTP request to a Web server. As a result, the server response data are loaded back directly into the scripting language. In this way, by exchanging small amounts of data with the server, the entire page does not need to be reloaded each time a user interacts with it.

When firstly explained the AJAX philosophy, Jasse James Garrett (2005) pointed out that AJAX represented a group of existing technologies coming together to implement asynchronous communication between client and server, rather than a single new technology. Particularly it included: *1)* XHTML and CSS for presentation; *2)* the Document Object Model for display and interaction with data; *3)* XML and XSLT for the interchange, manipulation and display of data, respectively; *4)* the XMLHTTPRequest object for asynchronous communication; *5)* the Javascript language to bind all these technologies.

Although the AJAX acronym mentions Javascript and XML, their use is not actually required, nor do the requests need to be asynchronous (Ullman and Dykes, 2007). There exist, in fact, other client side scripting language instead of Javascript that can be used to implement AJAX functionalities, such as VBScript. Also data exchange does not necessarily require XML. For example, the JavaScript Object Notation[26] (JSON) is often used as an alternative format.

Thanks to the advantages introduced by the usage of the XMLHttpRequest object, AJAX has lead to an improvement in Web page's interactivity, speed and usability (Murugesan, 2007). This development approach has facilitated building rich Web applications and has increased the quality of existing Web services.

Flex

Like AJAX, Adobe Flex is a collection of technologies for the development of Web applications that provide rich user interfaces. It was released by Adobe Systems and it is based on Adobe Flash. It was mainly designed to overcome the problem programmers encounter in adapting to the animation metaphor typical of the Flash platform.

Flex provides a standards-based language and a programming model that supports common design patterns. Graphic user interfaces, for example, can be designed and laid out by means of an XML-based language while the interactivity is achieved through the employment of the Flash's ActionScript language.

Another interesting aspect of the Flex approach is that it comes with a SDK including a visual IDE that allow user to build interfaces by simply selecting components in a list. UI components include buttons, list boxes, trees, data grids, several text controls, layout containers, charts and graphs. By means of the Flex SDK users can also create Web services or provide their application with drag and drop functionality, animation effects or form validation.

Like the AJAX approach, Flex and Flash Player provide many useful ways to send and load data to and from server-side components without requiring the client to reload the view, so that significant changes to the view do not require loading a new page.

Although Flex is establishing as a rich internet application development environment, the analyst Tony Byrne (2009) pointed out some critics to the use of Flex for enterprise application user interfaces.

Toolkit-Based and Visual Editors Approaches

Google Web Toolkit (GWT) is an open source Java framework created to help Web developers in building and debugging applications that rely

Figure 9. Yahoo! Pipes

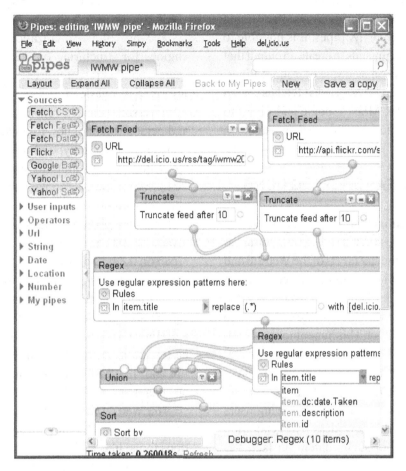

on complex Javascript code, by exploiting the Java programming language. GWT allows programmers to develop their application in Java, exploiting development tools of their choice. As it can be read in its mission statement *"GWT's mission is to radically improve the Web experience for users by enabling developers to use existing Java tools to build no-compromise AJAX for any modern browser"* (Google, 2009).

It provides a compiler to translate Java code to browser compliant code, exploiting Javascript and HTML for the deployment. The toolkit also provides widgets to rapidly build the user interface by employing elements that provide AJAX functionalities. GWT aims to overcome challenges rising when developing AJAX applications, by using reusable and efficient solutions.

Mashup frameworks as well as mashup editors (Yahoo! Pipes, see Figure 8, Google Mashup Editor[27]) have recently become very popular, allowing users to easily create their mashup application regardless of their technical skill level. Note that mashups rely on standards (SOAP, REST, RSS, JSON), since only standard protocols allow easy adaptation of content according to the change of context.

Yahoo! Pipes is a tool to aggregate, manipulate and mashup content from different sources around the Web, by remixing popular feeds types. It provides a graphical user interface and a visual language for creating data mashups that can combine feeds, Web pages and information from other Web services. Basically, Yahoo! Pipes allows users to literally *pipe* information from various sources

and to define rules for the content to be retrieved and visualized (e.g. filtering rules). The main idea is that, like for UNIX pipes, it is possible to combine simple commands to create an output that meets users needs. An example of Yahoo! Pipes' usage is PeopleSearch[28], a tool that fetches search results from yahoo, MSN, Google and Flickr to find any people entered with a certain name.

FUTURE RESEARCH DIRECTIONS

In an effort to highlight the aspects that will characterize the future research trends, it is important to focus in the fundamental facets of the Web 2.0 and to frame the overall development directions.

First of all the importance of user-generated material, publicly available on-line for others to use has been pointed out. This huge amount of multimedia content, of course, will continue growing, as a consequence of the presence of Web applications that facilitate the aggregation, consuming and sharing of such information, allowing users to explore and develop new ideas. The generation and dissemination of such content, in fact, has become more easy, thanks to the widespread use of digital devices, such as digital cameras, and mashup applications (Cerf, 2007). The scale of this will grow through the network effect as more people come online and existing users increase their use of Web 2.0 services. Nevertheless, this growth in the production of multimedia content may raise problems of information overload. For example, the presence of many different ways of accessing information (blogs, wikis, RSS feeds etc.) may cause a sense of anxiety as people worry that they do not understand or use all of these forms. A research trend can be detected which aims to the creation of environments that support end-users in the generation of mashups (Wong and Hong, 2007). Available content is not always in a form that best supports users' needs and tools that help the end-user in the creation of applications that repurpose and combine existing

Web data and services in order to accomplish their goals are necessary.

The use of personalization techniques and engines for structuring online interactions with users is another research area that aims to face this information overload. It focuses in the creation of more sophisticated recommendation systems and personal catalogues. Recommender systems represent a specific type of information filtering technique that attempts to suggest information items (movies, music, books, news, images or Web pages) by taking into account users' preferences and interests (Adomavicius and Tuzhilin, 2005). This systems can be useful in the generation of a personal catalog of a user, a digital collection containing all its preferences in term of music, photographs, videos, books, trips and so on, which can be also considered as a personal archive of a lifetime (Anderson, 2007). Such collection can be treated as an on-line manifestation of a user life and, like any other content on the Web, can be shared and exchanged (Beagrie, 2005).

The Web 2.0 it is deeply characterized by the presence of social communication and collaborations tools, like wikis, blogs and social networks sites. These technologies have changed the way users interact among them in various situations, fostering the creation of communities in which information is shared (Shadbolt, 2006). Research practices addressing the social aspect of Web's topological interconnectedness are becoming increasingly important. For example, in the emergency management domain, recent studies analyzed the nature of social practices around photographic content during the response to a disaster situation, taking into account the prominent role of the Flickr photo-sharing website (Liu *et al*, 2008).

In any case, more than the exposed trends, what it really seems to depict is the future development of the Web in what, as analogy, it can be called the Web 3.0 stage, which is the combination of the social aspect of the Web 2.0 with the vision of a *Semantic Web*, expressed by Tim Berners

Lee *et al.* (2001, 2006). The aim is exploiting the collective human intelligence to make computers and the Web more intelligent and interoperable, focusing on machine-processable semantics. So, while social systems such as Wikipedia, Facebook, or LinkedIn[29] are known for fomenting on-line data production via their network effect, the new Web 3.0 applications, driven by semantic Web technologies such as RDF, OWL and SPARQL, will offer powerful data organization, combination, and query capabilities.

WEB 3.0: TOWARD A SOCIAL SEMANTIC WEB

In the original idea of Tim Berners Lee *et al.* (2001, 2006), the Semantic Web represents an extension of the World Wide Web, conceived as a medium for data, information and knowledge exchange, in which the semantics of data and services is defined, making it possible for Web applications to understand and satisfy users' requests and for machines to exploit user-generated Web content.

It is possible to view the Semantic Web as the conjunction of Web technologies and knowledge representation, a specialization of Artificial Intelligence in which models enabling formalized reasoning about objects within a chosen domain can be constructed and maintained (Lassila and Hendler, 2007). As Lassila and Hendler (2007) stated, the failure in the stand-alone approach to Artificial Intelligence constituted a useful lesson, teaching that technologies like reasoning engines have sense and work only when embedded within other systems, for example current Web applications.

The Social Web and the Semantic Web complement each other due to their different approaches in content generation and organization. From one side, social Web applications are not able to preserve the semantics in user-submitted content typically limiting themselves to user tagging and basic metadata. Therefore they offer only limited features for users to find, customize, filter and reuse data. On the other hand, semantic Web applications, employ powerful reasoning and data handling technologies and formats, but lack the kind of scalable content production and information aggregation found in social Web applications. As a result, semantic Web applications are typically of limited scope and impact. Web 3.0 aims at a new generation of applications that exploiting the symbiosis of knowledge representation and collective intelligence, can combine the strengths of these two approaches: the data flexibility and portability of the semantic Web, and the scalability and authorship advantages of the social Web.

A first step toward a Social Semantic Web is the standardization of the various formats for data representation. Information is published on the Web in different formats such as XML, RDF or employing microformat, but they all should be transformed in a single format suitable for Semantic Web agents to process. SPARQL, an RDF query language, represents an approach to define a standardized language and an API to perform searches within different on-line databases. This will allow to reach a new level in data integration and interoperability, by making structured data accessible and allowing to embed them into existing Web resources, employing an RDF format. Thanks to the advances in data standardization and interoperability it will be possible to develop Web applications founded in logic description and intelligent agents. These applications can be able to accomplish logical inferences by employing rules that express logic relationship between concepts and information available on the Web. Nevertheless, it has not yet been established if the real power of the new Web 3.0 will reside in intelligent systems or if the intelligence will be gathered directly from the users, taking advantage collaborative services such as del.icio.us, Flickr or Digg.

As part of this process there exist research areas where it has been started to consider the combined

development of social systems that exploit the Semantic Web approach, such as semantic wikis and semantic blogs (Anderson, 2007). Semantic wiki is concerned with efforts in allowing users to annotate classical wiki pages with semantic information using formal languages such as RDF and OWL (Oren *et al.*, 2006). Examples of engines allowing this process are Platypus[30], SemperWiki[31], OntoWiki[32] and SweetWiki[33] (Buffa *et al.*, 2009). Semantic blogging, instead, refers to the development of new information management systems by exploiting Semantic Web capabilities with the ability of blogging platforms to generate machine-readable RSS and Atom feeds, in order to facilitate the aggregation of information from a number of sources.

CONCLUSION

In this chapter we have analyzed the fundamental aspects, technologies and design patterns that characterize the Web 2.0 paradigm. While the Web 1.0 was concerned with the fruition of contents by the users, the Web 2.0 can be viewed as an evolution to a read/write stage, in which users become producers, more than consumers of contents. New technologies and Web applications allow the users to perform an active role in content generation and dissemination, shifting the Web paradigm from a publishing medium to a medium promoting user's interaction and participation.

It has been pointed out that Web 2.0 is far from being only a collection of technologies, though some of these can play a preponderant role in its development. The Web 2.0 concept rather focuses on some ideas that changed the way people perceive and use the Web medium. Firstly, an architecture that promotes users' participation and fosters the adoption of procedures near to the Open Source's models, where the user interaction is not only an effect produced by a service, but a possible source for the improvement of the system itself. The architecture of participation of the Web

is deeply influenced by the growing presence of Web services that encourage the consuming and sharing of multimedia content produced by end-users. Secondly the crowd, and its power, that becomes more important as the Web facilitates the creation of new communities and groups. Lastly, the role of the Web as a platform, which breaks the paradigm of desktop applications sold or licensed to the users, imposing the new paradigm of native Web applications delivered as Web services.

Several technologies and services that demonstrate the foundations of the Web 2.0 paradigm has been deeply analyzed, such as: blogs, wikis, collaborative tagging systems and folksonomies, content syndication, social network tools and mashup applications.

Lastly, current research trends in the field of the Web science have been illustrated and the concept of Web 3.0 has been defined as the conjunction of the social feature of the Web 2.0 with the Semantic Web approach. This results in a new Web environment where the read/write paradigm could be enriched by the possibility to automatically generate logical relationships between Web sites content.

ACKNOWLEDGMENT

This work has been partially supported by research project urThey "Building citizens emergency preparation and response capacity through web 2.0 tools" (TIN2009-09687).

REFERENCES

W3C. (2004). *Web Services Glossary.* W3C Working Group Note 11 February 2004. Retrieved on May 21, 2009 from http://www.w3.org/TR/ws-gloss/

Adomavicius, G., & Tuzhilin, A. (2005). Toward the Next Generation of Recommender Systems: A Survey of the State-of-the-Art and Possible Extensions. *IEEE Transactions on Knowledge and Data Engineering, 17*(6), 734–749. doi:10.1109/TKDE.2005.99

Anderson, C. (2006). *The Long Tail: How endless choice is creating unlimited demand.* London: Random House Business Books.

Anderson, P. (2007). What is Web 2.0? Ideas, technologies and implications for education. *JISC.*

Angermeier, M. (2005). *The huge cloud lens bubble map Web2.0.* Retrieved May 8, 2009 from http://kosmar.de/archives/2005/11/11/the-huge-cloud-lens-bubble-map-Web20/

Baase, S. (2007). *A Gift of Fire: Social, Legal, and Ethical Issues for Computing and the Internet* (pp. 351). Upper Saddle River: Prentice Hall.

Beagrie, N. (2005). Plenty of room at the bottom? Personal digital libraries and collections. *D-Lib magazine, 11*(6). Retrieved from http://www.dlib.org/dlib/june05/beagrie/06beagrie.html

Benbunan-Fich, R., & Koufaris, M. (2008). Motivations and Contribution Behaviour in Social Bookmarking Systems: An Empirical Investigation. *Electronic Markets, 18*(2), 150–160. doi:10.1080/10196780802044933

Benkler, Y. (2006). *The Wealth of Networks: how social production transforms markets and freedom.* New Haven, CT: Yale University Press.

Bennis, W., & Biederman, P. W. (1998). None of Us Is As Smart As All of Us. *IEEE Computer, 31*(3), 116–117.

Berners Lee, T. (2006). *developerWorks Interviews*, 22nd August, 2006. Laningham (ed.).

Berners-Lee, T., Hall, W., & Shadbolt, N. (2006). The Semantic Web Revisited. *IEEE Intelligent Systems, 21*(3), 96–101. doi:10.1109/MIS.2006.62

Berners-Lee, T., Hendler, J. & Lassila, O. (May 17, 2001). The Semantic Web. *Scientific American Magazine.* Retrieved on 2008-03-26.

Bowman, S., & Willis, C. (2003). We Media: How Audiences are Shaping the Future of News and Information. *The Media Center at the American Press Institute.*

Boyd, D. M., & Ellison, N. B. (2007). Social network sites: Definition, history, and scholarship. *Journal of Computer-Mediated Communication, 13*(1).

Brin, S. & Page, L. (1998). The Anatomy of a Large-Scale Hypertextual Web Search Engine. *Computer Networks and ISDN Systems, 30*(1-7), 107--117.

Buffa, M., Gandon, F., Ereteo, G., Sander, P., & Faron, C. (2008). SweetWiki: A Semantic Wiki. *Web Semantics, 6*(1), 84–97.

Byrne, T. (2009). *The case against Flex-based application UIs.* CMS Watch. Retrieved on May 15, 2009 from http://www.cmswatch.com/Trends/1492-The-case-against-Flex-based-application-Uis

Cerf, V. (2007). An Information Avalanche. *IEEE Computer, 40*(1).

Csikszentmihalyi, M. (1996). *Creativity-flow and the psychology of discovery and invention.* New York: Harper perennial.

Cych, L. (2006). Social Networks. In *Emerging Technologies for Education, BECTA* (ed.). Coventry, UK: Becta ICT Research.

Doctorow, C., Dornfest, F., Johnson, J., & Powers, S. (2002). *Essential Blogging.* Sebastol, CA: O'Reilly.

Downes, S. (2004). Educational Blogging. *EDUCAUSE Review, 39*(5), 14–26.

Ebersbach, A., Glaser, M., & Heigl, R. (2006). *Wiki: Web Collaboration*. Berlin: Springer-Verlag.

Farooq, U., Kannampallil, T. G., Song, Y., Ganoe, C. H., Carroll, J. M., & Giles, L. (2007). Evaluating tagging behavior in social bookmarking systems: metrics and design heuristics. In *'GROUP '07: Proceedings of the 2007 international ACM conference on Supporting group work,'* (pp. 351—360). New York: ACM.

Fischer, G. (2006). Distributed intelligence: extending the power of the unaided, individual human mind. In *AVI '06: Proceedings of the working conference on Advanced visual interfaces*, (pp.7-14). New York: ACM Press.

Garrett, J. J. (2005). Ajax: a new approach to Web applications. *AdaptivePath.com*. Retrieved on May 15, 2009.

Gendarmi, D., & Lanubile, F. (2006). *Community-Driven Ontology Evolution Based on Folksonomies, On the Move to Meaningful Internet Systems 2006: OTM 2006 Workshops*, (pp. 181—188).

Gillmor, D. Noren, A., (eds.). (2004). *We the Media: Grassroots Journalism by the People, for the People*. Sebastopol, CA: O'Reilly Media, Inc.

Glaser, M. (2006, September 27). *Your Guide to Citizen Journalism*. Public Broadcasting Service. Retrieved on May 9, 2009.

Golder, S., & Huberman, B. A. (2006). The Structure of Collaborative Tagging Systems. *Journal of Information Science, 32*(2), 198–208. doi:10.1177/0165551506062337

Google. (2007). *Google Web Toolkit Mission Statement*. Retrieved on May 15, 2009 from http://code.google.com/Webtoolkit/makinggwtbetter.html#introduction

Hughes, A. L., Palen, L., Sutton, J., Liu, S. B., & Vieweg, S. (2008), Site-seeing in disaster: An examination of on-line social convergence. In *Proceedings of the 2008 ISCRAM Conference*, Washington, 2008.

Klemperer, P. (2006). *Network Effects and Switching Costs: Two Short Essays for the New Palgrave*. Working Paper series, Social Science Research Network. Retrieved on May 21, 2009 from http://papers.ssrn.com/sol3/papers.cfm?abstract_id=907502

Lasica, J. D. (2003, August 7). What is Participatory Journalism? *Online Journalism Review*. Retrieved on May 9, 2009.

Lassila, O., & Hendler, J. (2007). Embracing Web 3.0. *Internet Computing, 11*(3), 90–93. doi:10.1109/MIC.2007.52

Liu, S. B., Palen, L., Sutton, J., Hughes, A. L., & Vieweg, S. (2008), In search of the bigger picture: The emergent role of on-line photo sharing in times of disaster. In *ISCRAM '08: Proceedings of the 5th International ISCRAM conference*, (pp.140–149).

Malizia, A., Bellucci, A., Levialdi, S. G., Diaz, P., & Aedo, I. (2009). A visual Storyboard System to support back-channel communication for emergencies. Submitted to *Journal of Visual Languages and Computing (JVLC)*.

Mathes, A. (2004). *Folksonomies --- Cooperative Classification and Communication Through Shared Metadata*. Technical report, Computer Mediated Communication (LIS590CMC), Urbana-Champaign, Illinois.

Murugesan, S. (2007). Understanding Web 2.0. *IT Professional, 9*(4), 34–41. doi:10.1109/MITP.2007.78

Myers, B. A., Ko, A. J., & Burnett, M. M. (2006). Invited research overview: end-user programming. In *CHI '06 Extended Abstracts on Human Factors in Computing Systems,* Montréal, Québec, Canada, April 22 - 27, 2006, CHI '06, (pp. 75-80). New York: ACM.

O'Reilly, T. (2005, September 30th). *What is Web 2.0: Design Patterns and Business Models for the next generation of software.* Sebastol, CA: O'Reilly Media Inc. Retrieved 08/05/09 from http://www.oreillynet.com/pub/a/oreilly/tim/news/2005/09/30/what-is-Web-20.html

O'Reilly, T. (2006, December). *Web 2.0 compact definition: Trying again.* Retrieved from http://radar.oreilly.com/archives/2006/12/Web-20-compact.html

O'Reilly, T. (2007). What is Web 2.0: Design Patterns and Business Models for the Next Generation of Software, Communications & Strategies. *International journal of digital economics, 65,* 17-37.

Oren, E., Breslin, J., & Decker, S. (2006). How Semantics Make Better Wikis. In *Proceedings of WWW2006,* May 23-26, 2006, Edinburgh, Scotland. New York: ACM Press.

Porter, J. (2006). *The del.icio.us lesson.* Retrieved May 11, 2009 from http://bokardo.com/archives/the-delicious-lesson/

Schachter, J. (2006), TR35 2006 Young Innovator: Joshua Schachter, 32 (Del.icio.us [Yahoo)]". *Technology Review.* Retrieved on May 21, 2009.

Shadbolt, N. (2006). Private conversation at *Memories for Life: the future of our pasts* event. British Library, London, Dec. 12th 2006.

Shaw, R. (2005). *Web 2.0? It doesn't exist.* Retrieved from http://blogs.zdnet.com/ip-telephony/?p=805

Snyder, J., Carpenter, D., & Slauson, G. J. (2006). *Myspace.com: a social networking site and social contract theory.* Dallas, TX: ISECON 23.

Stvilia, B., Twidale, M. B., Gasser, L., & Smith, L. C. (2005). *Information quality discussions in Wikipedia.* Technical Report, Florida State University. Retrieved May 11, 2009 from http://mailer.fsu.edu/~bstvilia/

Suh, B., Chi, E. H., Kittur, A., & Pendleton, B. A. (2008). Lifting the veil: improving accountability and social transparency in Wikipedia with wikidashboard. In *Proceeding of the Twenty-Sixth Annual SIGCHI Conference on Human Factors in Computing Systems,* Florence, Italy, April 05 - 10, 2008, CHI '08. New York: ACM, New York.

Surowiecki, J. (2004). *The wisdom of crowds: Why the many are smarter than the few and how collective wisdom shapes business, economies, societies, and nations.* New York: Doubleday Books.

Sutton, J., Palen, L., & Shklovsky, I. (2008). Backchannels on the front lines: Emergent uses of social media in the 2007 southern california wildfires. In *Proceedings of the 2008 ISCRAM Conference,* Washington.

Ullman, C., & Dykes, L. (2007). *Beginning AJAX (Programmer to Programmer).* Hoboken, NJ: Wrox.

Van der Vlist, E., Ayers, D., Bruchez, E., Fawcett, J., & Vernet, A. (2006). *Professional Web 2.0 Programming (Wrox Professional Guides).* Wrox.

Van der Wal, T. (2005). *Explaining and showing broad and narrow folksonomies.* Retrieved on May 11, 2009 from http://www.vanderwal.net/random/category.php?cat=153

Vickery, G., & Wunsch-Vincent, S. (2007). *Participative Web And User-Created Content: Web 2.0 Wikis and Social Networking.* Organization for Economic.

Wong, J., & Hong, J. (2008). What do we "mashup" when we make mashups? In *Proceedings of the 4th international Workshop on End-User Software Engineering,* Leipzig, Germany, May 12 - 12, 2008, WEUSE '08, (pp. 35-39). New York: ACM.

Wong, J., & Hong, J. I. (2007). Making mashups with marmite: towards end-user programming for the Web. In *Proceedings of the SIGCHI Conference on Human Factors in Computing Systems,* San Jose, CA, April 28 - May 03, 2007, CHI '07, (pp. 1435-1444). New York: ACM.

Zang, N., & Rosson, M. B. (2008). What's in a mashup? and why? studying the perceptions of Web-active end users. In *Visual Languages and Human-Centric Computing, 2008. VL/HCC 2008. IEEE Symposium on,* (pp. 31-38).

KEY TERMS AND DEFINITIONS

AJAX: A set of interrelated web development technologies employed on the client side to obtain rich user interaction with web applications.

Blog: A web site maintained by an individual with regular entries of commentary, descriptions of events, or other material such as graphics or video.

Folksonomy: It refers to the practice and method of collaboratively creating and managing tags (keywords) to categorize content. It is also known as collaborative or social tagging.

Mashup: A Web application that combines data or functionality from different sources or services into a single integrated tool.

Semantic Web: An evolution of the web based on the idea of adding semantic information to web content, making it possible for machines to understand and satisfy the requests of people.

Social Network Site: A web site to build online communities of people who share interests and/or activities, or who are interested in exploring the interests and activities of others

User-Generated Content: An on-line content that is produced by users (i.e. non-media profes-sionals) as opposed to traditional media producers such as broadcasters and production companies.

Web Feeds: A data format for presenting to users frequently updated content, related to a web site.

Web Syndication: A form of content broadcasting in which web site material is made available to multiple other sites by means of web feeds.

Wiki: Web site allowing users to easly edit its pages by means of a web browser. With the software provided by the wiki platform, users can collaboratively edit a shared text.

XMLHttpRequest: An API used within a web browser scripting language to send HTTP requests directly to a web server and load the server responses data directly back into the scripting language.

ENDNOTES

1. http://www.flickr.com/
2. http://www.youtube.com/
3. http://www.wikipedia.com/
4. http://wiki.oreillynet.com/foo-camp/index.cgi
5. http://www.twitter.com/
6. http://developers.sun.com/forums/duke-stars/index.jsp
7. http://www.digg.com
8. http://www.newsvine.com
9. http://www.google.com
10. http://www.amazon.com
11. http://www.ebay.com
12. http://www.yahoo.com
13. http://docs.google.com
14. http://del.icio.us
15. http://wikidashboard.parc.com/
16. http://www.bibsonomy.org/
17. https://maps.google.com
18. http://www.craigslist.org/about/sites
19. https://www.ushahidi.com
20. http://estorys.spain.sc/
21. http://www.facebook.com/

22   http://www.myspace.com/
23   http://www.youtube.com/
24   http://code.google.com/intl/en-EN/webtool-kit/
25   http://pipes.yahoo.com/
26   http://json.org
27   http://code.google.com/intl/en-EN/gme/
28   http://pipes.yahoo.com/pipes/pipe.info?_id=XgRo96h13BGtJWvS8SvLAg
29   http://www.linkedin.com
30   http://platypuswiki.sourceforge.net/
31   http://semanticweb.org/wiki/SemperWiki
32   http://ontowiki.net/Projects/OntoWiki
33   http://sweetwiki.inria.fr/wiki/data/Main/MainHome.jsp

Chapter 4
Accessibility and Usability of Web Content and Applications

Maria Claudia Buzzi
IIT-National Research Council, Italy

Marina Buzzi
IIT-National Research Council, Italy

Barbara Leporini
ISTI-National Research Council, Italy

ABSTRACT

Accessibility is essential for every system or product in order to guarantee equal opportunity for access and use to all, including the differently-abled. Thus it is crucial to remove any technological barriers for special needs users, who explore the Internet by assistive technologies. However, ensuring efficient and satisfactory (in other words, usable) interaction with user interfaces (UIs) of products or services must occur in the design phase, in order to produce UIs that are universally simple to understand, rapid and easy to use. Applying accessibility and usability criteria from the very beginning of the design phase is much less costly than introducing it later, so specific guidelines should be followed from the earliest stages of the design process. In the long run, creating accessible and usable Web UIs will improve overall efficiency and effectiveness of interaction for any individual and organization.

INTRODUCTION

Every day the Internet brings new communication, informational and learning experiences to rapidly expanding user communities. Interactive and hypermedia applications are increasingly applied in contexts ranging from news and thematic blogs to on-line libraries and structured educational content.

Furthermore, new Web 2.0 applications such as Wikipedia or Facebook encourage the active participation of users worldwide, in a collaborative and cooperative way. This opens extraordinary vistas for the differently-abled, provided that interactive systems and content are properly designed and delivered.

Accessibility is a basic requirement for every system or product in order to guarantee equal access, opportunity and use to all, including the

DOI: 10.4018/978-1-61520-763-3.ch004

differently-abled. An accessible Web also helps people with disabilities to participate more actively in society. "The Web is an opportunity for unprecedented access to information for people with disabilities. That is, the accessibility barriers to print, audio, and visual media can be much more easily overcome through Web technologies" (World Wide Web Consortium [W3C], 2005). Thus it is crucial to remove any technological barriers for special needs users, who explore the Internet and interact with multimedia content by assistive technology, i.e. HW and SW that allow one to operate computers and applications.

The type of assistive technology used varies according to disability. For instance, the visually-impaired use screen readers (with voice synthesizer and/or Braille display) or magnifiers (for low-vision users). Motor impairment requires the use of special input devices, and so on. An accessible user interface must consider all of these needs in order to allow universal access. Thus, developers can only implement good design by becoming aware of all the obstacles encountered by users aided by assistive technologies.

Likewise, making interaction with the user interfaces (UIs) of products or services effective, efficient and satisfactory (in other words, usable (International Standard Organization [ISO], 1998) is another pillar of the design phase (Nielsen, 2001; Norman, 2004).

When designing for the differently-abled, who have reduced sensorial abilities, it is necessary to consider the three main interacting subsystems of the Model Human Processor: the perceptual, motor and cognitive systems (Card, Moran & Newell, 1983). Since websites and hypermedia applications have increasingly complex UIs containing embedded movies, audio, and graphics, the main goal is to provide mechanisms for delivering content according to user ability.

Applying accessibility and usability criteria from the very beginning of the design phase is much less costly than introducing it later, so specific guidelines, such as Web Content Accessibility Guidelines - WCAG 2.0 (W3C, 2008c), should be followed from the earliest stages of the design process. In the long run, creating different ways of delivering multimedia content according to user ability will increase efficient and effective interaction for any individual and organization, regardless of time, place or pace.

The chapter is divided into five sections. A brief introduction highlights the content and objectives. In the second section, user disabilities and assistive technologies are introduced and explained briefly. Next, we focus on accessibility and usability definitions, principles and general guidelines. Since the range of different abilities is vast and techniques are very specific and depend on individual characteristics, we then focus on the needs of totally blind users, since they are more disadvantaged and because we are thoroughly familiar with this field. Specifically, problems regarding different application domains will be explored since usability principles depend on the goal of the user and the type of application (e.g., the procedure for accessing a wiki system is different from that for using a search engine). Next, practical examples of technology use are given, to illustrate the potential of new emerging standards and help designers to enhance usability for the blind. Last, the chapter concludes with a discussion.

BACKGROUND

Accessibility is a basic requirement for any system or product in order to guarantee access and use to all. Therefore, considering the different types and range of user abilities, there should be more than one way to deliver the same content (text, audio, video, etc.) to accommodate user preferences or needs. In the following we introduce the needs of users with different abilities, and related assistive technologies.

Users with Special Needs

In 2001, the World Health Organization (WHO) produced the International Classification of Functioning, Disability and Health (ICF). The ICF comprises the following broad categories (World Health Organization, 2001):

- Body functions (physiological functions of body systems, such as mental functions, voice and speech functions, etc.) and structures (parts of the body, such as the nervous system, eye, ear and related structures, the cardiovascular, immune and respiratory systems, etc.);
- Activities, related to tasks and actions performed by an individual, and participation (involvement in a life situation): learning and applying knowledge, communication, mobility, self-care, etc.;
- Additional information on environmental factors (support and relationships, attitude, etc.).

Functioning and disability are viewed as a complex dynamic interaction between the individual's health and the contextual factors of the environment, as well as personal factors.

It is important to note that some people are only temporarily disabled; their disabilities (resulting from illness/disease, accidents, surgical intervention, etc.) last for only a limited time in their life.

Previous studies classified disabilities by categories (Brewer, 2005), (Foraker Design, 2005):

- Visual disabilities
  - Blindness: no visual perception whatsoever of light and form
  - Low vision/partially sighted: people with reduced vision
  - Color blindness: the inability to perceive differences between certain colors that others can distinguish.

- Hearing impairments
  - Deafness: impaired hearing in both ears, inability to detect or understand sounds
  - Hard of hearing: decreased ability to detect or understand sounds.
- Motor disabilities: Motor impairments are a loss or limitation of function in muscle control or movement or a limitation in mobility. They can include weakness, pain that impedes movement, limitations of muscular control or sensation, joint problems, or missing limbs. These conditions can affect hands and arms as well as other parts of the body.
- Speech disabilities: difficulty speaking due to vocalization or articulation impairments or to neurological language disorders.
- Cognitive and neurological disabilities, such as:
  - dyslexia and dyscalculia
  - attention deficit disorder
  - intellectual disabilities
  - memory impairments
  - mental health disabilities
  - seizure disorders.
- Multiple disabilities, involving various degrees (severe, mild, moderate) of degradation of perceptual, motor and cognitive systems.
- Aging-related conditions are often similar to multiple disabilities: hearing, visual, motor, cognitive or neurological impairments can be involved.

Assistive Technologies

Like a computer, the human mind is a system for storing and processing information (Card, Moran & Newell, 1983). To aid our understanding of human/computer interaction Card et al. proposed a model, the Model Human Processor, which is still considered the main reference point today. The Model Human Processor comprises the perceptual,

motor and cognitive systems. When a user navigates an interface, all of these systems are involved in the interaction, thus the time required to complete a task depends on these three systems.

When perception is impaired (as with blind or deaf users), less information is communicated to the brain. The cognitive part of the interaction depends on the perception received and takes one or more cycles to process the information. Thus a disabled person may develop a different mental model of both the interaction and the learning processes. Next, the motor cycle(s) allows the user to interact with an interface (for instance, to push a key, move a mouse, or speak a command).

Assistive technologies helps people with disabilities interact with the environment. Specific assistive technologies are designed to allow and simplify interaction with computers, PDAs, cell phones, etc. Some accessibility solutions are embedded into the operating system or browser, such as the ability to zoom the content or change the style properties. Furthermore specific adaptive strategies may be adopted by people with disabilities to make interaction more satisfying: for example a blind user may tab through a Web page to skip content (Brewer, 2005).

The type of assistive technology used varies with the disability, to provide a different way to access content. In the following we present some technologies used for different kinds of disabilities, with special focus on visual disabilities.

Visual Disabilities

The visually-impaired generally use screen readers or screen magnifiers. A screen reader is an assistive technology used by the blind to interact with a computer or other electronic devices, such as mobile phones. The screen reader mediates between the user and the operating system, assisting individuals by interpreting the user interface which is read aloud sequentially (word by word and line by line) by means of a voice synthesizer, or written using a Braille display. However, Braille output is

extremely slow while working with the Internet, so the vocal synthesis is more common.

Technically, a screen reader is SW that identifies and interprets what is being displayed on the screen (or, more accurately, sent it to a standard output device whether a video monitor is present or not). This interpretation is then re-presented to the user with voice synthesizer, text-to-speech, sound icons, or a Braille output device (as refreshable Braille display) (Thatcher, 2006). Several screen readers have been developed over the last few years, including: Jaws for Windows (http://www.freedomscientific.com/), Windows Bridge (http://www.synthavoice.on.ca/), Windows-Eyes (http://www.gwmicro.com/) and Hal for Windows (http://www.dolphincomputeraccess.com/). These screen readers are used by more than 95 percent of blind users on the Web (Thatcher, 2006).

A screen magnifier is software that interfaces with a computer's graphical output to present enlarged screen content; it is often used by low-vision people. Screen magnification software uses standard display monitors. It increases the size of everything in the display, including text and images in a web page. Screen magnification software provides various degrees of magnification, typically from 1.5x to 32x. Due to the physical limitations of the monitor, the greater the magnification, the smaller the amount of content shown. Screen magnifiers provide multiple settings for magnification. Some also provide a split screen that shows both the magnified page and a non magnified page. Examples are iZoom, MAGic, Magical Glass, Magnifixer, Zoomtext, and Lunar.

There are other tools that can be used in place of or in addition to screen readers and magnifiers (Foraker Design, 2005):

- text-to-speech system: software that takes written text and speaks it using some kind of speech synthesizer
- auditory feedback: sounds in response to user activity, such as a "click" after a keypress, "whoosh" accompanying opening

and closing windows, or "klunk" when a file is deleted. Useful as redundant reinforcement of activities and for those who are visually impaired

- tactile interface: a user interface that uses touch for input and/or output, such as a Braille reader.

Last, text browsers such as Lynx are an alternative to graphical user interface browsers.

Hearing Impairments

Sensorial-neural hearing loss may vary in degree (profound, mild, and moderate) and type (unilateral, bilateral). Furthermore, depending on age at disability onset (birth, childhood, elderly), rapidity in correcting hearing loss, association with other disabilities (autism, etc.), hearing loss may also impact on cognitive ability. For these reasons, it is also necessary to provide different ways to vehicle audio information, such as:

- visible alerts that accompany any audio alerts (some operating systems offer this possibility as an alternative feature)
- captions/subtitles or transcripts of audio on the web
- additional Sign Language (SL) video to describe main content
- speech-to-text system: a type of voice-recognition system that converts spoken language to text.

It is fundamental to reduce user cognitive effort by:

- providing a clear navigation mechanism
- using a clear and simple language.

Motor Disabilities

Motor impairment people may require the use of special input devices, such as (Brewer, 2005; Foraker Design, 2005):

- Alternative keyboards, for instance with extra-small/large key spacing, enabling options such as: a) Sticky Keys (modifier keys, such as Shift, Control, etc., will "stick" down and apply to the next keystroke, to press only one key at a time) or b) slow keys (feature that prevents keystrokes from registering until a key has been held down for a certain period of time)
- hardware or software specialized devices such as mouth-stick (for browsing with the keyboard), blow-suck tube, tongue-activated joystick, foot-controlled devices, head-mounted input devices, eye-tracking systems
- speech-to-text system: a voice-recognition system that converts spoken language to text and commands (such as *Dragon)*. Some browsers use speech (or voice) recognition as an input method
- scanning software, that allows one to move (and select) through a set of options (usually automatically) by hitting a switch when the desired item is highlighted or announced.

Speech Disabilities

When motor impairments are the source of speech difficulties, it is possible to use non-vocal means to specify a phrase and provide speech synthesis as output. Some people may only be able to enter single keystrokes very slowly. Letter and message prediction systems anticipate the most likely next letter, word, or phrase to be entered and make them easier to access (Foraker Design, 2005).

People with little or no functional speech may also be using Augmentative and Alternative Communication (AAC), which aids people who find it hard to communicate by speech or writing. AAC includes traditional signing and gesture, picture charts, books, special computers, etc. For example, Web content can be displayed/explained with symbol systems (such as Bliss, PCS or Re-

bus symbols) which can facilitate understanding of certain information (International Society for Augmentative and Alternative Communication, n.d.)

Cognitive and Neurological Disabilities

The spectrum of cognitive and neurological disabilities is broad and requires several different strategies and technologies depending on the disability, which can be Down Syndrome, autism, Traumatic Brain Injury, dementia, attention deficit disorder (ADD), dyslexia (difficulty reading), dyscalculia (difficulty with math), etc. For example a dyslexic user may have difficulty with spatial orientation and prefer changing colors and using text to speech software; people with memory impairment may rely on a consistent navigational structure throughout the site; people with seizure disorders may need to turn off animations, blinking text, or certain audio frequencies (Brewer, 2005).

ACCESSIBILITY AND USABILITY OF WEB USER INTERFACES

To make a product universally easy to use for all, accessibility and usability principles should be taken into account during the design and development phases, and it is crucial for the development team to keep in mind what those principles will mean in practice. In this section we will discuss the accessibility and usability of Web User Interfaces (UIs).

Usability and accessibility are important concepts for general user interfaces as well as websites. Usually, we can make a distinction between WIMP (Windows, Icons, Pointer, and Mouse) interfaces and Web interfaces, partly because the nature of these interfaces differs and partly because often usability methods have only been applied to one type or the other in the literature. Generally speaking, we use the term WIMP to refer to applications,

such as programs written in Java, C++, Delphi, etc. We use the term Web to refer to Web pages, sites or applications; in general we can speak of Web interface. Web interface features differ from those of classical WIMP user Interfaces, mainly regarding (Scapin et al., 2000):

- The structure of the Web site (e.g., number of pages, links between pages) is directly related to the information available on the Web site (amount, type, etc), while the structure of WIMP user interfaces is usually static;
- Web applications are usually modified frequently and without any notice to the user, so can be considered more unpredictable;
- Moving from one Web site to another is like switching from one application to another, but no guidelines are provided for ensuring inter-application coherence.

When considering accessibility and usability issues for Web or WIMP interfaces, we should keep in mind the eventual tasks that will be performed by the users. A task is an activity performed to accomplish a goal. Tasks can involve different abstraction levels, ranging from certain high-level tasks (such as retrieving information on film projections available today) to very low-level tasks (such as selecting a button on the screen) (Paternò, 1999). Depending on the task, accessibility and especially usability principles can make interaction easier and much more satisfying.

The number of Web sites (and their users) is constantly expanding, so their information, as well as the interactive hypertext applications, should be made easily available to all. More precisely, the age range of the user population is expanding (from younger users to the elderly), as are the range of expectations (from private entertainment to professional use), of information needs (from simple information to compound multimedia resources), task types (from basic text searches to complex problem-solving methods), and user

abilities (from the able-bodied to anyone with special needs, such as for motor-, hearing- or visually-impaired persons). These concepts can be summed up in the phrase "anyone, anywhere". We will discuss several basic concepts regarding accessibility and usability.

Accessibility

Many users may be operating in a vastly different context from that of the average user: they might not be able to see, hear, move, or process some types of information easily (if at all); they may have difficulty reading or comprehending text; they may not have or be able to use a keyboard or mouse; they may be using a text-only screen, a small screen, or a slow internet connection; they may not speak or understand well the language in which the document is written; they may be in a situation where their eyes, ears, or hands are busy or distracted (e.g., driving to work, working in a noisy environment, etc.); they may have an early version of a browser, an entirely different browser, a voice browser, or a different operating system.

Accessibility is a general term used to describe the degree to which a system can be used by as many people as possible. A system (Web site or application) is accessible if it can be used by everyone, including people with disabilities.

For example, in addition to people with disabilities who explore Web pages with the help of common assistive technology, we can include those using low-bandwidth technology such as cellular phones, black and white screens, speaking browsers via telephone, etc.

Inaccessibility results from "technical barriers" to accessing a product or information. An accessible (Web) user interface means that potential technical barriers have been removed, and thus anyone can interact with it.

Content developers must consider all these different situations during Web page design. While there are various situations to consider, each accessible design choice generally benefits several disability groups at once and the Web community as a whole.

Web Barriers

To better understand the problems that special-needs people might encounter when accessing Web content and applications, the W3C Web Accessibility Initiative (WAI) group illustrates basic obstacles encountered by differently-abled persons with the following impairments, as summarized in Table 1 ((Brewer, 2005)):

Usability

Usability was defined by Lindgaard (1989) as "...a quantitative, or quantifiable, statement of the ease with which users can accomplish tasks for which a given computer system was designed".

Usability of a Web site is determined by user satisfaction, ease of learning and remembering its organization and functionalities, efficiency and likelihood of errors while performing tasks (like finding sought-for information or completing e-commerce operations). However, of the many definitions, we prefer referring to the standard ISO 9241 (1998), which defined usability as "the effectiveness, efficiency and satisfaction with which specified users achieve specified goals in particular environments" (as cited in Koivunen, 2002). According to this definition:

- Effectiveness means "the accuracy and completeness with which specified users can achieve specified goals in particular environments";
- Efficiency means "the resources expended in relation to the accuracy and completeness of goals achieved";
- Satisfaction means "the comfort and acceptability of the work system for its users and other people affected by its use".

Table 1. Obstacles encountered by different special-needs users when navigating the Web (Source W3C)

VISUAL DISABILITIES
Blindness:
- images without alternative text
- graphical alert without alternative text/advice
- complex images (e.g., graphs or charts) inadequately described
- video without text or audio description
- video subtitles not announced by screen reader
- tables that do not make sense when read serially (in a cell-by-cell or "linearized" mode)
- frames without "NOFRAME" alternatives, or without meaningful names
- forms that cannot be tabbed through in a logical sequence or that are poorly labeled
- browsers and authoring tools that lack keyboard support for all commands
- browsers and authoring tools that do not use standard application programmer interfaces for the operating system on which they are based
- non-standard document formats that may be difficult for their screen reader to interpret

Low vision:
- Web pages with absolute font sizes that do not change easily
- Web pages with inconsistent layout that are difficult to navigate when enlarged, due to loss of surrounding context
- Web pages, or images on Web pages, that have poor contrast, and whose contrast cannot be easily changed through user override of author style sheets
- text presented as images, which prevents wrapping to the next line when enlarged
- many of the barriers listed for blindness (above) depending on the type and extent of visual limitation

Color blindness:
- color that is used as a unique marker to emphasize text on a Web site
- text that inadequately contrasts with background color or patterns
- browsers that do not support user override of authors' style sheets

Hearing impairment:
- lack of captions or transcripts of audio on the web, or Sign Language video translation
- requirements for voice input on Web sites
- difficult reading content for lack of clear and simple language
- lack of content-related images in pages full of text which can slow comprehension for people whose first language may be a sign language (stronger image and video- oriented content or additional glossary in Sign Language might be useful).

Motor disabilities affecting the hands or arms:
- Time-limited response options on Web pages
- Browser and authoring tools that do not support keyboard alternatives for mouse commands
- Forms that cannot be tabbed through in a logical order

Speech disabilities:
- websites that require voice-based interaction and have no alternative input mode

COGNITIVE AND NEUROLOGICAL DISABILITIES
Attention deficit disorder:
- distracting visual or audio elements that cannot easily be turned off
- lack of clear and consistent organization of Web sites

Intellectual disabilities:
- use of unnecessarily complex language on Web sites
- lack of graphics on Web sites
- lack of clear or consistent organization of Web sites

Memory impairment:
- lack of clear or consistent organization of Web sites

Mental health disabilities:
- distracting visual or audio elements that cannot easily be turned off
- Web pages with absolute font sizes that do not enlarge easily

Seizure disorders:
- use of animations, blinking text, or generally of visual or audio frequencies that can trigger seizures

MULTIPLE DISABILITIES
- visual and auditory perceptual disabilities:
  - o lack of alternative modalities for information on Web sites, for instance lack of alternative text that can be converted to audio to supplement visuals, or the lack of captions for audio
- other

Important properties for Web site usability concern navigability as well as interaction. Five usability criteria were proposed by Nielsen (Nielsen, 1993): Efficiency, Errors (few and easily recoverable), Satisfaction, Memorability (of visited items and functions) and Learnability, the ability to be proficient quickly, which impacts on performance of novice users.

Some other fundamental characteristics of Web site usability are (Fleming, 1998):

- Consistency of presentation and controls across the site or application, natural organization of information (clear structure, systematic labels, clear and meaningful labels)
- Contextual navigation, in terms of environment, "type" of users, particular devices, etc; someone often considers also how much information is available for providing a context for the user (where is he, where he can go, and so on).

Regarding page layout Nielsen and Loranger highlighted common mistakes:

- "Page not structured in prioritized order
- Interaction overly complex and don't offer guidance
- Related areas not grouped in close proximity
- Elements not places where people expect
- Too many elements on page" (Nielsen & Loranger, 2006, p.322).

These principles are very general and need to be applied concretely and expanded into more specific and detailed guidelines that can be assessed in a simpler and perhaps more standard way, to be rapidly applied. For instance, focusing on the differently-abled, Pernice and Nielsen (2001) defined specific guidelines derived from user testing with a large group of visually- (including totally blind) and motor-impaired persons. The 75 guidelines are very useful but need to be updated as technologies evolve, especially multimedia (such as Adobe Flash presentations or dynamic applications such as AJAX, Asynchronous JavaScript and XML (Mozilla Developer Center, n.d.).

Usability is not the only important aspect of the site: obviously its contents/functions, and its popularity contribute even more to a site's success. However, if users can perform the same task with two different sites, they will choose the one that is more effective, efficient and satisfactory (Nielsen, 2001).

Integrating Usability and Accessibility of Web UIs

To use Web sites and applications effectively, accessibility alone is not enough; usability should be addressed as well. Accessibility is aimed at removing "technical barriers" which could prevent use of or access to a certain on-line service or application. Usability is a multidimensional concept, since it can refer to several aspects whose importance depends on the application domain and user context. Indeed, although they are strictly correlated, accessibility and usability are frequently addressed as two separate aspects, but users with disabilities need to have applications that are both accessible and usable. Thus, if they are not properly integrated, the UI may turn out to be accessible but barely usable, or usable but barely accessible: in either case navigation by users with disabilities is likely to be seriously compromised, since they may not be able to access the desired information (i.e., "not accessible") or may have difficulty arriving at their goal ("not usable").

Usability principles are particularly important even in an educational context, where the student should be able to concentrate on the learning process rather than wasting extra time and effort orientating themselves on the user interface. Therefore, accessibility alone might be too restrictive

for the main goal; and usability should improve interaction, regardless of the user's abilities. In this perspective, it is important to establish the users' requirements as well as the "specified" context.

Designers should be aware of both usability and accessibility issues in the decisions they make, in order to avoid inconveniencing or excluding a wide range of potential consumers.

General Guidelines

To permit universal access, an accessible and usable user interface must consider all possible user needs. Thus, developers can only implement good design by being aware of all the obstacles encountered by users aided by assistive technology. Information should be complete, quick to find, and easy to understand for everyone.

The Web Accessibility Initiative (WAI) WCAG 2.0 Guidelines are high-level criteria for making Web content more accessible and usable to a wider range of people with disabilities (W3C, 2008c). They are organized in four categories relying on perception, interaction, comprehension and robustness (consistency, inter-operability) as shown in Table 2.

It is remarkable to observe that this new version of the WCAG completely changes its approach with respect to version 1, which was widely criticized (Sloan et al., 2006; Leuthold, Bargas-Avila & Opwis, 2008) because accessibility alone does not guarantee a satisfactory interaction. Indeed the new WCAG version focuses on the full interaction paradigm (perception, cognition, interaction) considered as a whole (not only on accessibility), thus also including usability features (effectiveness, efficiency, satisfaction).

In this chapter we do not discuss the details of the WCAG 2.0 Guidelines, available online (W3C, 2008c). Each guideline is general and applicable to more than one element. To conform to WCAG 2.0 developer should refer the "Techniques for WCAG 2.0" document (W3C, 2008a), which con-

tains techniques and failures (for non-proprietary technologies) grouped by:

- General Techniques (applicable to any technology)
- HTML and XHTML
- CSS
- Client-side Scripting
- Server-side Scripting
- SMIL
- Plain Text
- ARIA.

The Accessible Rich Internet Applications (WAI-ARIA) Suite (W3C, 2008b) was developed by the World Wide Web Consortium (W3C) within the framework of the Web Accessibility Initiative (WAI) to enhance navigation via screen reader and interaction via keyboard, and specifically for making dynamic Web content and Web applications (AJAX, DHTML, etc.) accessible.

There are also more specific W3C guidelines, such as:

- Authoring Tool Accessibility Guidelines (ATAG) for software that creates Web sites
- User Agent Accessibility Guidelines (UAAG) for Web browsers and media players, and relating to assistive technologies
- Accessibility Information for Specific Technologies, as XML, SVG, SMIL, and others.

The details of these guidelines and the description of WAI activities are available at http://www.w3.org/WAI/.

Some countries have enacted specific accessibility (and usability) guidelines. For example in the USA, Section 508 of the Rehabilitation Act contains a set of standards required of Federal agencies in order to make their electronic and information technology accessible to people

Table2. WCAG 2.0 Guidelines (Source W3C)

1. Perceivable
   - 1.1 Provide text alternatives for any non-text content so that it can be changed into other forms people need, such as large print, Braille, speech, symbols or simpler language.
   - 1.2 Provide alternatives for time-based media.
   - 1.3 Create content that can be presented in different ways (for example simpler layout) without losing information or structure.
   - 1.4 Make it easier for users to see and hear content including separating foreground from background.
2. Operable
   - 2.1 Make all functionality available from a keyboard.
   - 2.2 Provide users enough time to read and use content.
   - 2.3 Do not design content in a way that is known to cause seizures.
   - 2.4 Provide ways to help users navigate, find content, and determine where they are.
3. Understandable
   - 3.1 Make text content readable and understandable.
   - 3.2 Make Web pages appear and operate in predictable ways.
   - 3.3 Help users avoid and correct mistakes.
4. Robust
   - Maximize compatibility with current and future user agents, including assistive technologies.

with disabilities (http://www.section508.gov/). A group of these standards is related to Web-based intranet and internet information and applications (1194.22).

Also the European Union with the Communication "Towards an accessible information society" (2008) declared it urgent to achieve a wider and more effective approach to e-accessibility, and in particular web accessibility, favoring the adoption of the WCAG 2.0 in Europe, with a set of key actions (publishing updated technical guidance, translating relevant W3C specifications, etc.). The objective is to achieve 100% accessibility of member states' public websites by 2010.

Accessible Rich Internet Applications

Accessibility deficiencies in (X)HTML may render dynamic web applications unusable by people who use assistive technologies (AT) or who rely on keyboard navigation (W3C, 2008b). ARIA, developed by the World Wide Web Consortium, aim at making dynamic content such as AJAX (Mozilla Developer Center, n.d.), (X)HTML, JavaScript, and related technologies more accessible to the differently-abled persons, such as people interacting via screen readers (W3C,

2008b). ARIA defines roles (toolbar, button, listbox, etc.), states and properties of (X)HTML objects. In this way changes in the user interface may be communicated to the assistive technology and thus to the user.

When using the screen reader or a vocal browser, the use of ARIA would enhance web application usability in many ways, as explained and exhaustively illustrated by the ARIA best practices document (W3C, 2009). Specifically advantages include:

- reducing user overload, since it is possible to select the sections be announced (decreasing the amount of unnecessary text announced). Specifically, the use of an (X) HTML element (such as a table) as layout may be silently ignored by the screen reader if the table is tagged with the "presentation" role.
- using ARIA regions the user is able to get a page overview ("Ctrl+Ins+;" command in JAWS v.10). The use of landmarks/regions also allows simplifying navigation via keyboard since the user may jump from one region to the next by pressing a key (in JAWS v.10 the ";").

Furthermore, the developer using the attribute "flowto" defines the order in which regions should be visited. For example, considering the Wikipedia Editing page, we would create the "Editing Content" and "Save&Preview" regions (<div role="region" title="Editing Content" flowto="Save&Preview">).

- facilitating page navigation. Using only standard (X)HTML code, the usability of keyboard navigation is reduced so blind users are forced to use tabbing for accessing active elements (form elements and links). To simplify interaction and allow easy jumping to main interface regions, developers usually rely on creating a link to the main content or use heading levels to structure the page (since the screen reader gives a table of headings). However the use of headings to mark sections is not consistent across web sites (W3C, 2008b). ARIA instead allows marking sections with standard specifying XHTML landmarks (main, navigation, search, banner, contentinfo, etc.) or defining customized regions, if they do not appropriately reflect the aim of the region (f.e.: <div role="main" title="Math Module">).

Accessibility Issues with Multimedia Objects

In the previous section we addressed web accessibility and usability concepts, without taking into account multimedia contents i.e. objects such as Adobe Flash components, applets, movies. When considering accessibility and usability for hypermedia interfaces, we need to address multimedia components as well.

A possible definition of hypermedia is "The use of text, data, graphics, audio and video as elements of an extended hypertext system in which all elements are linked so that the user can move between them at will" (Wikipedia, n.d.).

Sometimes a multimedia object is the best way to convey the message to a target audience, but it is necessary to keep in mind users who could potentially have accessibility issues with multimedia objects. For instance, hypermedia systems allowing one to assemble multimedia components (Learning Objects) are increasingly used to prepare learning contents and lessons (Engelhardt, Hildebrand, Lange & Schmidt, 2006). If multimedia components are not appropriately designed and developed the user could not obtain the intended information. This is particularly crucial for e-Learning platforms in which missing a multimedia content could mean not being able to receive important learning content. Consequently, including multimedia components requires special attention in order to assure their accessibility.

Equivalent Information

The first guideline recommended in the Web Content Accessibility Guidelines 2.0 (W3C, 2008c) is on the equivalent alternative content (see Table 1): "Provide text alternatives for any non-text content so that it can be changed into other forms people need, such as large print, Braille, speech, symbols or simpler language".

One the major problem in making accessible and usable non-textual content is that few developers are providing appropriate equivalent information for the multimedia they include in their pages, probably because it is not so simple to provide an appropriate and meaningful equivalent text. Content is "equivalent" to other content when both fulfill essentially the same function or purpose upon presentation to the user. For example, consider a repeating animation that shows cloud cover and precipitation as part of a weather report. Since the animation supplements the rest of the weather report, which is already presented in natural language i.e. plain text, a less verbose description of the animation is necessary. However, if the animation appears in a classroom setting where students are learning about cloud formations in

relation to land mass, then the animation ought to be described for those who cannot view the animation but also want to learn the lesson. Note that equivalent information focuses on fulfilling the same function. An equivalent text may involve a description of that content (i.e., what the content looks like or sounds like). For example, in order for users to understand the information conveyed by an interactive chart, developers should describe the visual information in the chart. To provide accessibility to graphs Ferres, Verkhogliad, and Boucher (2007) developed iGraph, a system that provides short verbal descriptions of the information depicted in graphs and a way of also interacting with graphical information.

Since text content can be presented to the user as synthesized speech and Braille, as well as visually-displayed text, equivalents must be written so that they convey all essential content. Non-text equivalents (e.g., an auditory description of a visual presentation, a video of a person telling a story using a sign language version of a written story, etc.) also improve accessibility for people who cannot access visual information or written text, including many individuals with blindness, cognitive disabilities, learning disabilities, and deafness. What is crucial is the quality of the equivalent content provided. This is not a technical issue, but requires a certain quality in preparing and providing adequate and effective equivalent alternative information for those users who are not be able to obtain the content from the original multimedia component. Equivalent information may be provided as:

- Alt attribute, longdesc attribute, and "D" links (description links) as part of element content or as part of the document's prose;
- text transcripts, captioning, or auditory description for video components.

A text transcript is a text equivalent of audio information that includes spoken words and non-spoken sounds such as sound effects. Captioning is a text transcript for the audio track of a video presentation that is synchronized with the video and audio tracks. Captions are generally rendered visually by being superimposed over the video, benefitting people who are deaf and hard-of-hearing, and anyone else who cannot hear the audio. Depending on the complexity of the content, often it may be necessary to combine techniques.

One example of a non-text equivalent is an auditory description of the key visual elements of a presentation. The description is either a pre-recorded human voice or a synthesized voice (recorded or generated on the fly). The auditory description is synchronized with the audio track of the presentation, usually during natural pauses in the audio track. Auditory descriptions include information about actions, body language, graphics, and scene changes.

It is fundamental to provide the "key information" that is crucial for understanding the main meaning of the component. In this sense, providing equivalents for multimedia objects can be a lot of work but it can be crucial.

Flash Content

Adobe Flash is increasingly used for Web and standalone applications due to the multi-media features and opportunities it offers (http://www.adobe.com/). With Flash several enhancements can be made available through hypermedia and multimedia objects: toolbars, animations, interactive games, etc. Thus, it is important that Flash applications be accessible to all users, including those who have to interact through assistive technologies. Several years ago Flash was criticized for the difficulties it raised for users with disabilities for various reasons, such as for lack of alternative textual descriptions. However, in recent years Flash has improved in this respect, aiming to provide support for accessibility (Adobe, n.d.).

Although best practice guidelines on how to make a Flash multimedia application accessible for assistive technologies are available, problems still exist, especially for more complex and structured multimedia applications. Leporini,

Paternò, and Spano (2009) investigated on the real Flash accessibility features for blind users. A case study for testing effectiveness and concrete accessibility features has been taken into account. The application considered describes the tactile room in the Museum of Natural History (Calci, Italy), and has been entirely developed with Flash technology.

Even if accessibility support made available by the Flash environment (i.e. versions 8 and 9, through the Accessibility panel) was used when developing the application, the resulting UI has not been found to be completely accessible by screen reader.

In short, the main accessibility problems are related to "content reading order" -- i.e. text, buttons and so on are mixed -- especially when contents are built in a dynamic way; to "Images", which are correctly loaded in the text area, but for which the screen reader does not read the alternative description. Links are displayed but the screen reader cannot list them. Buttons do not present particular accessibility problems, but a strange problem occurs for some buttons inexplicably detected by the screen reader as unlabelled (e.g. six button, nine button, etc.). And even if "Shortcuts" are assigned to buttons or links, they cannot be used. These issues do not occur for simpler Flash objects, such as a navigation bar or non- complex Flash movies or videos.

This study confirms that Flash technology should just be used for certain components of the page, such as the navigation bar -- which is composed of buttons -- or for those objects requiring graphical animations. Thus, if Flash objects are only used for small components it is possible to develop accessible applications.

A CASE STUDY: WEB INTERACTION OF TOTALLY BLIND PERSONS

Numerous user studies suggest that the totally blind encounter more difficulty than those with other sensorial disabilities (such as low vision, motor or hearing impairments) when executing specific tasks (Petrie, Fraser & Neil, 2004; Craven, & Brophy, 2003; Ivory, Yu & Gronemyer, 2004). Petrie et al. presented the results of accessibility testing of 100 websites with users with visual, motor and perceptual disabilities, showing that websites that are accessible for differently-abled users can also be visually pleasing. Specifically, 100 websites spread out over five sectors were tested with automated verification and user testing, involving 51 differently-abled users, including 10 totally blind users. Results showed a mean task success rate of 76% that goes down to 53% considering only the totally blind (the lowest score of all the user categories). Likewise, regarding user satisfaction, the authors recorded that the blind encountered more difficulty than other differently-abled users (4.2 on an 1..7 Likert scale, the lowest score of all the user categories). Researchers at Manchester Metropolitan University (Craven & Brophy, 2003) highlighted issues of non-visual access by studying a sample of blind and visually-impaired users who performed four information-seeking tasks, including the use of search engines. Visually-impaired users searching the Web for a specific piece of information took an average of 2.5 times longer than sighted users. The efficiency gap was further quantified by Ivory et al. (Ivory et al., 2004); when blind subjects executed a set of tasks, they took twice as long as sighted users to explore search results and three times as long to explore the corresponding web pages. Leuthold, Bargas-Avila and Opwis (2008), extending the only three non-technical WCAG 1.0 guidelines, defined nine specific guidelines for building enhanced text user interfaces (ETI). The authors demonstrated that the ETI guidelines enhance usability, by evaluating efficiency, errors and user satisfaction of a web user interface developed according to these specific guidelines regarding GUI conformance to standard (WCAG 1.0 guidelines); the study involved 39 blind users who were asked to carry out two tasks (Leuthold et al., 2008).

Considering that the range of different disabilities is so vast and the techniques are quite specific, in the following part of this chapter we limit our discussion to visual impairment, and specifically on the needs of the totally blind, being thoroughly familiar with this field.

A screen reader is essential software for blind people who interact with computers. When navigating the Web, a screen reader and voice synthesizer allow vocal conversion of all the information in the pages visited, following a linear scan from top to bottom and from left to right. They also provide some support to access specific elements in the Web pages. Thus, a certain expertise in screen readers and browser commands is useful, and orienting oneself within the page content can require considerable effort. Blind users rarely use the mouse functions (i.e. pointing, scrolling, selecting, etc.) for moving around the page. In fact, although the mouse functions can be emulated by the keyboard, all such movements require a great deal of effort of a blind user. They prefer to move via keyboard: by arrow keys, via Tab key, and access keys.

A user interface with some interactive elements that cannot be activated through the keyboard (or that cannot receive the focus) is not usable. Thus, developers should take this into account and build user interfaces that are fully accessible by keyboard.

Even when Web sites apply accessibility recommendations, users can still encounter navigational problems. This is partly due to the fact that Web pages are increasingly designed for parallel or non-serial navigation, offering a variety of options within one page (frames, tables, drop-down menus, etc). Complex Web pages can cause problems for users who are navigating the site using assistive technologies, which force them to follow a serial route, for example when a screen reader reads out each hypertext link on a page, one by one.

In brief, the main problems for a blind person navigating by screen reader are:

- Information overload due to excessive sequential reading – static portions of the page (links, frames with banners, etc.) may overload the reading process, since the user has to read every single thing almost every time, significantly prolonging navigation time. Thus, it is important to introduce mechanisms to facilitate the identification of precise parts within the page. For example, at the top of the result pages generated by a search engine the user usually finds several links, advertisements, search fields, buttons, etc., that the user should be able to skip to go directly to the search results listed below. As a consequence, blind users often have to stop the screen reading at the beginning, and they prefer to navigate by Tab Keys, from link to link, or explore the content row by row, via arrow keys.

- Lack of page context – the user may lose the overall context of the current page when navigating by screen reader, since they can read only small portions of texts at a time. For example, the blind user who is skipping from link to link with the tab key will read the text associated with a link on the Braille display or will hear it from the synthesizer (e.g. ".PDF", "more details", etc.) but she/he does not know what is written before and after. Thus it may be necessary to reiterate the reading process.

- Content and structure mixing. The screen reader announces the most important interface elements such as links, images, and window objects as they appear in the code. For the blind user, these elements are important for figuring out the page structure. However, the actual reading process can overload the user, requiring considerable cognitive effort

- Lack of interface overview. Blind persons do not perceive the overall structure of the interface, so they can navigate for a long time without finding the most relevant contents.

- Difficulty understanding UI elements. Links, content, and button labels should be context-independent and self-explanatory.
- Difficulty working with form control elements.
- Last, the blind person is unable to access visual content (such as video streaming, video conferencing, and captioning) so a text alternative is crucial for effectively delivering the same content.

For users interacting by means of assistive technologies, user interface layout and structure are crucial. Traveling around the Web (or operating with a stand-alone application) is difficult for visually-impaired users since the Web pages (or program windows) are designed for visual interaction (Goble, Harper & Stevens, 2000). In contrast to sighted users, screen reader users cannot see the implicit structural and navigational knowledge encoded within the visual presentation of Web pages (Yesilada, Harper, Goble & Stevens, 2004). Therefore when navigating by screen reader the user's perception of windows or page content may differ greatly from what is actually shown on the screen. These differences can cause considerable frustration. Page layout may result in confusing screen reader feedback, poorly designed or unlabeled forms can make navigation very difficult, the lack of alternative text for pictures can be mystifying, and so forth (Lazar, Allen, Kleinman & Malarkey, 2007). To resolve or reduce these inconveniences, developers should be aware of how the content is perceived when interacting via screen reader so that they can design user interfaces appropriately.

Organizing a page in logical sections enhances the experience of the blind user when navigating a page in two ways: it provides a page overview, and offers the possibility of jumping from section to section. Specifically, heading levels may improve navigation since screen readers have special commands for moving from one heading to another. Brudvik, Bigham, Cavander, and Ladner (2008)

presented an interesting study on how sighted users associate headings with a web page, observing very different results depending on factors such as whether the page has a hierarchic structure, how users identify sections, etc. Furthermore, authors applied techniques of information retrieval (i.e. training data and a classifier), developing a system for automatically inferring from the context (font, size, color, surrounding text, etc.) whether a phrase "works semantically" (and may function) as a heading, and dynamically adds the heading level using Javascript. The system called HeadingHunter was evaluated using human-labeled headings gathered from the study and showed high precision (0.92 with 1 the max). Most common website usability factors involve meeting business objectives while providing a satisfying user experience. Therefore, accessibility should be seen as a challenge to designers and implementers, rather than as a constraint.

General Guidelines for Simplifying Interaction via Screen Reader

It is important to remember that totally blind persons using screen reader and voice synthesizer do not interact by mouse or other pointing devices, but perceive the page content vocally and navigate only via keyboard. In the following examples we refer to the Jaws for Windows screen reader.

As previously discussed, due to the reduced visual perception the blind may develop a different mental model of the user interface. Furthermore, the cognitive part of the interaction, which also depends on personal factors such as the age at which an individual lost his/her sight, and on whether the person has experienced visual knowledge of the real world or has only figured it out in other ways (i.e., has been blind since birth), is very important. Regarding the interaction with the interface, a simple and rapid interaction via keyboard should be assured, as discussed in detail in the following.

Thus, when designing a UI for the blind, it is crucial to:

- provide alternative ways to deliver the same content (included aural feedback)
- reduce the user's cognitive effort (i.e., to provide an overview of the system and contents)
- provide ways to access important content rapidly.

As previously mentioned, a screen reader reads the contents sequentially, as they appear in the HTML code, and also announces the most important interface elements such as links, image and window objects. This process can be time-consuming and annoying, especially when the content is not well organized and the same parts of the interface, such as the menu and/or the navigation bar, are repeated on all pages. Blind users often stop the screen reading at the beginning, preferring to navigate by Tab keys jumping from link to link, or explore contents via arrow keys. However jumping from link to link is effective only if the description (and link title) is meaningful and does not depend on the context.

Some general features for simplifying interaction via screen reader are:

- Logical sections (as with landmarks and ARIA regions): allow an overview of the UI features (e.g., main, search, navigation bar, footer, etc.). The first problem to address is that the blind person does not perceive the overall structure of the interface, so they can navigate for a long time without finding the most relevant contents. To reduce this gap, the HTML source code has to be structured defining logical sections of the interface. Specifically, sets of homogenous text and elements were grouped and structured by ARIA landmarks and regions, in order to give the user an immediate idea of the interface, and allow him/her to rapidly move from one section to another.
- Positioning the relevant content at the top of UI (source code): important for novice users since it allows immediate access to the main

part, related to the main goal to be accomplished. The use of ARIA presumes the user is able to use the command for visualizing and moving between landmarks/regions, so no action is required the user to access the main of the page.

- Shortcuts: useful for faster navigation
- Enable the visiting order according to importance of UI elements increases efficiency (rapidity) in exploring the interface
- Aural feedback: crucial for immediate perception of important events
- Hidden labels: useful for better user orientation
- Help page: a non-intrusive help page on accessibility features and invisible link to it can be very useful.

Application Domains and Specific Guidelines

General criteria for simplify navigation and interaction must be merged with the context and characteristics of a specific application domain, to provide more specific guidelines for web designers. As a case study we recall two examples of guidelines for two application domains for simplifying interaction for the blind: search engines and wikis. The first example was tracked by analyzing the Google UI (Leporini, Andronico, Buzzi, & Castillo, 2008), and the second one is derived from a study on Wikipedia, the on-line encyclopedia (Buzzi M.C., Buzzi M., Leporini, & Senette, 2008).

Search Engine

In the following we report the results of the general guidelines applied in the search engine domain (Leporini et al., 2008). The resulting criteria can be summarized thus:

- Make the main content of the UI immediately accessible, in one of two ways:

1. Place the most important elements of the interface at the top of the source file. For search engines the most important elements are: search box and button, and query results. To place an object in a specific position of the visual layout, use the "position" property in the style sheet.
2. Use ARIA regions, so the user can immediately jump to the main section.

- Facilitate user orientation in the interface:

Be careful to correctly match <label for> with input elements, and place labels above or to the left of the input element, rather than below.

- Navigating faster. Assign a scale of importance (i.e. by tab index attribute) to important elements so users can reach the most important parts quickly. On the search page, higher values should be assigned to edit field and search options; whereas in the result page the higher values should be given to result links. A lower value should be assigned to secondary links if present (such as "cached" or "similar pages"). Furthermore, shortcuts may be associated with search elements (text boxes, buttons) and with links to pages of results (e.g. access key="1" for the first page, or "2" for the second, etc.).
- Alerting by sound. When using interactive elements, different sounds should be associated with different events in order to rapidly provide feedback to blind users. For instance, two different tones may be used to indicate the success (at least one result) or failure (no result) of the search.
- Easy interaction with form elements (edit field and search options), i.e easy location and labeling. Avoid secondary elements (links, texts, banner frames, etc.).
- Highlighting the search result. Use a heading level (i.e. <h1> or <h2>...<h6>) at the beginning of the result list. If a table is used to format results, a summary attribute such as "Results of the research: xxx results found" or "No results found" should be assigned. In addition, the number of the current page vs the total number of pages should be clearly indicated (e.g. x of y result pages).

- Arranging the results in numbered lists. Put the list of the result links with their summary, just after the search result notification (nothing else should be located in the middle). Create a list by applying <ul> or <ol> elements; each item on the list must be a single result; it is possible to make the numbering invisible by using hidden labels. With this feature, the screen reader informs the user of the number of items; the user is then able to skip quickly from item to item. Besides, each page result should not contain too many results; an appropriate number would be ten items.
- Recognizing sponsored links. Keep sponsored links separate from the other results in the HTML code, not only in the visual layout. Put them in a clearly labelled table (e.g. "sponsored links" summary attribute), and insert the table code after the results list in the page source; to locate sponsored links on the right side – or in another specific place – use the CSS (Cascading Style Sheets) properties.
- Adding navigation and help links. Place links pointing to result pages at the end of the list (not before). This allows users to read the current results (summaries and links) first and then read the pointers to the next group of results; this is important when users move by arrow keys (i.e. in a sequential manner).
- Last, applying standards also assures interoperability. For instance, use XHTML and CSS to separate content from rendering and structure the page. Web designers

should use aural style sheets provided by CSS2 specification for making web content more usable by and accessible to blind people. At the same time, browsers and screen readers must be able to interpret aural CSS.

Wikis

Wikis and eLearning systems are multiplying rapidly. Although these guidelines were derived from studying Wikipedia, they are general and thus apply to all Wikis (Buzzi et al., 2008):

- Make it easy to identify the separate content parts.

Usually a wiki page is split into several logical sections: navigation bar, header, footer, main content, etc. Each area should be clearly identifiable, both visually and via screen reader, offering a blind user a rapid overview of the main macro topics available on the page. Using ARIA roles to define landmarks and regions (corresponding to logical page sections) the screen reader can provide a list of all regions on the page, (i.e. the page overview) to which the user can jump easily and rapidly. Previously this overview was obtained with heading levels, but this was not consistent with the meaning of heading levels in the websites (W3C, 2009). Furthermore, regions make the main content immediately accessible in aural exploration.

- Make the search box clearly and quickly identifiable.

The search function is one of the most important features of a portal, so it is essential to find it very easily. Search edit field and buttons should be located at the beginning of the logical flow of the page's main content. Its location early in the content flow should ensure that the screen reader (and thus the user) can identify that important main area almost immediately.

The search box should be easily identifiable and clear labels should be used for edit field and search buttons. Moreover, terminology on the page should be consistent.

- Keep the Editing function simple.

The Editing function is very important in a Wiki system, as in any collaborative environment. Consequently, the Editing commands as well as the Editing page should be easy for anyone to use, independent of the interaction modality used. We offer several suggestions regarding the Editing function:

- Use a separate page for the Editing function.
- Provide a quick way to use formatting functions via keyboard. For instance, if using a graphical toolbar make it accessible via ARIA.
- Provide an alternative textual input that could facilitate formatting for skilled users. To facilitate this modality, two possible suggestions are (1) provide a help page listing all commands with their textual alternative input modalities (2) a very similar HTML syntax could might also facilitate the input process for users who have some experience with HTML.
- Concerning special symbols, two suggestions may be useful:
- provide a quick and compact way to select a special symbol. Since a great number of links makes interaction via screen reader too difficult, a more effective way should be developed. A list on a separate Web page, or a compact combo-box containing descriptions of all available symbols, are possible solutions.
- associate a clearer symbol description. Many special chars and symbols are not recognized by the screen reader. A descriptive text would overcome this problem; for instance 'a with circumflex accent' is

clearer than the corresponding character (e.g. 'â' is announced by JAWS as 'a').

- Control the edit focus. As in the Editing procedure, the focus is very important and it is necessary to ensure that when interacting with formatting commands or choosing special symbols, the focus goes back to the editing cursor. This feature is fundamental for facilitating the Editing process when using a screen reader -- otherwise, the user risks losing the Editing position, which makes the composing process difficult or impossible.

Examples

An important usability issue for the blind who interact via screen reader is the lack of a general view of the content. Thus it is crucial that the text associated with links, frame names, table summaries, heading levels (for structuring the content), etc., are meaningful and context-independent, to better orientate users. Furthermore, adding "hidden labels" makes the content clearer, enhancing experience of the page navigation.

One important principle for making a web page easily and rapidly navigable is dividing the page content into logical sections (Leporini et al., 2008). In fact, when a page contains a great deal of content it is perceived as very long due to the sequential access (via arrow keys), so navigation becomes tedious and requires considerable effort. As previously mentioned, a useful method for logically organizing a UI is to use appropriate heading elements. In fact, several screen readers have special commands to list the headings in the page, so that with a general overview the user can understand the content of the page, and can reach the desired information more quickly. In addition, users can skip quickly from one section to another.

For example to catch the last section of a long page a user has to read through a lot of content. In addition, to get an overview of the page content in order to understand the main information, it is necessary read the entire page. In this case the page is accessible because the screen reader detects all the content, but a blind user navigating sequentially may have a cognitive overload and a sense of frustration due to the long time needed to read the information.

Let us consider as an example the Pisa airport home page available at http://www.pisa-airport.com/index.php?lang=_en, as accessed with JAWS. This page is an example of a well- structured UI: the page content is divided by using heading levels assigned to each section title. The user can get an overview of the page content simply through a special screen reader command (with JAWS, "Insert+F6") that lists all headings available on the page (See Figure 1). In this case finding one of the last sections of the page, such as "Weather information" is easy: the blind user can list all headings (with the "Insert+F6" JAWS command) and explores the section titles via "down" arrow key. When the focus is over the "Weather forecast" section, by pressing the enter key, the focus moves to that section so the user can read it. To move more quickly, when the user navigates the page frequently, he/she can pick up the "Weather forecast" title just by pressing the letter "w" when the headings are listed. This way it is not necessary to explore all headings shown in the list.

A user who cannot see the screen often uses the Tab key to search the page for the desired link without having to read the entire content. Another way to select a specific link is to use a particular screen reader command to open the link list. In both cases, the user reads only the text of the links, so a meaningful text is important. It is necessary to avoid links that are not self-explanatory, such as "click here", ".pdf" or "go to the paragraph", which are not very useful. Often the link text refers to a specific context, so that if the links are considered separately, it is difficult to understand the related content.

For example, on the Pisa airport home page for each section there is a short introduction to

Figure 1. Pisa airport home page: headings listed by the JAWS command "Insert+F6"

the related content; to read a deeper description a link "Enter" pointing to a second level page can be clicked (this mechanism is common in Content Management Systems, that apply general labels by default). Unfortunately, all these links have the same label: "Enter". This leads to a list of available links that are unclear and confusing out of context. If a blind user lists all links available on the page, several links are named "Enter". Thus the user has no idea what kind of information they are related to. Figure 2 shows the list of links on the Pisa airport home page.

In the following we offer two examples of using technology to improve interaction for the blind.

Google Case: A More Usable Result Page

In summer 2008 Google put on-line a new version of the popular Web search UI, graphically equal to the previous one but optimized for navigation via screen reader. In fact, as discussed in (Leporini et al., 2008) although fully accessible, the previous version of the result page presented some difficulties for the blind since results were not appropriately structured for a screen reader user. For example in the previous version of Google UIs, no structure or navigation features were applied to the result page, so the user had to navigate sequentially line by line or jump over active

elements (via Tab key). Only experienced users were able to skip some parts by using advanced screen reader commands. Thus exploring results of a query in the previous Google version might require considerable time even if the UI was accessible via screen reader.

As proposed in (Leporini et al., 2008) each search result could be structured by assigning a heading level (to skip from one result to the next or previous) and numbered in order to facilitate user orientation. To preserve the original layout, all these features could be hidden by using CSS properties (see Table 3 and Table 4). Since screen readers with JAWS ignore elements with the "display" property set to "none", or with the "visibility" property set to "hidden" (correctly interpreting the aim of these properties) it is necessary to use absolute positioning and a second level layer. Thanks to positioning -1000, which brings the element out of the screen, (Table 3) and the second level layer, the label is not visible.

The current Google result page is easier to navigate than the previous one. The use of headings and the numbers applied to each result allow a blind person to move quickly from one result to another, and easily orientate themselves among them. In this new result page it is faster to arrive at a result or explore the next pages. Therefore, navigation is more satisfactory and efficient. It is important to remember that navigation is vital for the blind, because it is crucial for them to be aware of their current location on the webpage and be

Figure 2. Links listed by the JAWS command "Insert+F7" in the Pisa airport Home page

Table 3. Portion of CSS file: style for hidden labels

```
.hidden-label {
position: absolute;
left: -1000;
top: -1000;
z-index: -1;
}
```

able to return to the beginning, or how to reach a certain point in the material (ISO, 1998).

Wikipedia Editing Page

The editing page of Wikipedia is difficult to use via screen reader and presents three main usability issues for the blind (Buzzi et al., 2008):

1. The formatting toolbar is difficult to perceive, access and use. The widgets of the Wikipedia toolbar are graphic icons, generated by JavaScript, inaccessible via Tab key. The browser is unable to recognize these widgets as active elements (such as links, buttons, boxes, etc.) so they are skipped (never receive the focus) when the user explores the page via Tab key.
2. It is difficult to select special characters and symbols. To insert a special character or symbol, Wikipedia offers a combo-box for selecting an alphabet. After the selection, a list of links of the corresponding alphabet characters is shown. This is not suitable for navigation via Tab key; having a high number of links makes the navigation long and users become disoriented.

Furthermore, Jaws does not recognize uncommon symbols or characters, so it produces ambiguous text (for example "link e" for e, é, è, È and É). To distinguish each character, a more descriptive text should be associated (e.g. "e with acute accent").

Table 4. Fragment of result page code containing numbered result by using hidden labels

```
...
<a name="results" tabindex="1">
Results 1 - 10 of about </a>
...
<div id="result-list">
<div class="r">
<p class="hidden-label"> 1. </p>
<a href="…" tabindex="1"> First result </a> <br />
...extracted text... <br />
<a href="…"> Cached </a> -
<a href="…"> Similar pages </a>
</div>
<div class="r">
<p class="hidden-label"> 2. </p>
<a href="…" tabindex="1"> Second result </a>
...
</div>
...
```

3. Focus issue. In the Wikipedia Editing page the focus is managed via JavaScript: when one or more words in the text area are selected, all related parameters (including the focus) are stored by the script in order to apply the formatting correctly. However, when interacting via screen reader a blind user may not correctly understand how the focus is processed since the screen reader provides a "virtual focus", and this may not coincide with the system focus.

In (Buzzi et al., 2008) we discussed a modified Wikipedia Editing page using ARIA. Specifically creating a formatting toolbar with ARIA roles, properties, and attributes (i.e. 'activedescendant') makes the toolbar navigable via arrow keys (see Table 5). Once the toolbar receives the focus via TAB key, the child elements -- i.e. each formatting widget -- can be accessed by up and down arrows, and the associated formatting function (Bold, Italics, etc.) can be activated by pressing the ENTER key.

Concerning special characters and symbols, we used a second combo-box (located close to the alphabet combobox) to aggregate all characters of each alphabet. This compact solution is faster

Table 5. Fragment of the ARIA-based toolbar source code

```
...
<div role="toolbar" tabindex="1" id="toolbar1" ... aria-
activedescendant="button1"
aria-labelledby="mytoolbar" title=" Formatting toolbar">
<div id="mytoolbar" class="hide"> Formatting toolbar </div>
<span role="button" aria-pressed="false" class="selected"
id="button1" ... >
<img style="cursor: pointer;" alt="Bold" src="button_bold.
png" class="icons" />
</span>
...
</div>
...
```

since when navigating the combobox with arrow keys, the screen reader announces the character name directly while in the original interface every character read is preceded by the word 'link'. Furthermore the user skips the combobox pressing a tab key once, while in the original interface it is necessary to navigate all links.

Furthermore, to simplify selection of a special character, we also specified a clear label attribute for each <option> item of the second combo-box, so the screen reader can announce the description of the selected character.

The focus problem would be resolved by our new interface, while actually it depends on how the screen reader interpreted ARIA. For instance with Jaws English version 9, the new interface allows users to insert and edit text without having to switch to navigation modality to find active elements. Instead, with Jaws Italian version 9 the focus is in the correct position but Jaws loses the editing modality.

CONCLUSION

The aim of Universal Design is to design products that accommodate the broadest range of users regardless of age or ability. This approach calls for design that is usable for a wide range of end-users without alterations or accommodations for accessibility.

In this chapter we introduced several main principles for ensuring that applications, including the Web, are available for everyone. After introducing different types of disabilities and their corresponding assistive technologies, accessibility and usability concepts were discussed. Several practical examples were given.

The Web has changed continually over the years along with new developments in technology. Web 2.0 brings new dynamic applications and content based on AJAX, such as Google Maps (Chen & Raman, 2008), and social networks such as Facebook that integrate multimedia contents. It is crucial to make content and applications accessible and usable to all; WCAG version 2.0 and ARIA suite as well as the usability principles proposed all contribute to realizing these objectives.

Applying accessibility and usability criteria from the very beginning of the design phase is much less costly than introducing it later, so specific guidelines should be followed from the very earliest stages of the design process. In the long run, creating different ways of delivering multimedia content according to the user's ability will improve overall efficiency and effectiveness of interaction for any individual and organization, regardless of time, place and pace.

Before ARIA specification was introduced, a designer had to resort to certain tricks (e.g., applying heading levels to structure the UI areas, CSS class and properties for adding hidden labels). This requires considerable effort by designers and developers to compensate for the lack of semantics in (X)HTML languages. Today, by defining roles and communicating with the accessibility APIs, ARIA specification simplifies the designer's work, thus favoring the widespread adoption of usability and accessibility principles and furthering the creation of a more accessible society, one of the aspirations of the European Union.

In conclusion, awareness of Web barriers and the knowledge of W3C standards are essential to optimizing navigation for the differently-abled. Designers can actively contribute to closing this

digital gap and to creating a better World Wide Web within reach of all.

REFERENCES

Adobe. (n.d.). *Accessibility standards compliance*. Retrieved April 30, 2009, from http://www.adobe.com/accessibility/products/compliance/

Brewer, J. (2005). *How People with Disabilities Use the Web*. World Wide Web Consortium (W3C), from http://www.w3.org/WAI/EO/Drafts/PWD-Use-Web/

Brudvik, J. T., Bigham, J. P., Cavander, A. C., & Ladner, R. E. (2008). Hunting for headings: sighted labeling vs. automatic classification of headings. In *Proceedings of the 10th international ACM SIGACCESS conference on Computers and accessibility*, (pp. 201-208). New York: ACM Press.

Buzzi, M. C., Buzzi, M., Leporini, B., & Senette, C. (2008). Making Wikipedia Editing Easier for the Blind. In *Proceedings of ACM NordiCHI2008*, (pp. 423-426). New York: ACM Press.

Card, S. K., Moran, T. P., & Newell, A. (1983). *The Psychology of Human-computer Interaction* (pp. 29-97). London: Lawrence Erlbaum Associates.

Chen, C. L., & Raman, T. V. (2008). AxsJAX: A Talking Translation Bot Using Google IMAxsJAX. Bringing web-2.0 applications to life. In *Proceedings of the 2008 international cross-disciplinary conference on Web accessibility (W4A)*, (pp. 54-56). New York: ACM Press.

Craven, J., & Brophy, P. (2003). *Non-visual access to the digital library: the use of digital library interfaces by blind and visually impaired people*. Technical report. Manchester, UK: Centre for Research in Library and Information Management (CERLIM). Retrieved from http://www.cerlim.ac.uk/pubs/index.php

Engelhardt, M., Hildebrand, A., Lange, D., & Schmidt, T. C. (2006). Reasoning about eLearning Multimedia Objects. In J. Van Ossenbruggen, G. Stamou, R. Troncy & V. Tzouvaras (Ed.) *Proceeding of First International Workshop on Semantic Web Annotations for Multimedia (SWAMM)*.

European Union. (2008). *Communication from the Commission to the European Parliament, the Council, the European economic and social Committee and the Committee of the regions.- "Towards an accessible information society."* Retrieved from http://eur-lex.europa.eu/LexUriServ/LexUriServ.do?uri=CELEX:52008DC0804:EN:NOT

Ferres, L., Verkhogliad, P., & Boucher, L. (2007). L. Natural language interaction with graphical representations of statistical data. In *Proceeding of ACM International cross-disciplinary conference on Web accessibility (W4A)*, (pp.132-133). New York: ACM Press.

Fleming, J. (1998). *WEB navigation: designing the user experience*. Sebastapol, CA: O'Reilly.

Foraker Design. (2005). *Usability first. Accessibility: Types of Accessibility Aids*. Retrieved April 30, 2009, from http://www.usabilityfirst.com/accessibility/types.txl

Goble, C., Harper, S., & Stevens, R. (2000). The travails of visually impaired web travellers. In *Proceedings of the Eleventh ACM on Hypertext and Hypermedia* (pp. 1–10). New York: ACM Press.

International Society for Augmentative and Alternative Communication. (n.d.). Retrieved from http://www.isaac-online.org/en/home.shtml

International Standard Organization [ISO]. (1998). *ISO 9241-11: Ergonomic Requirements for Office Work with Visual Display Terminals (VDTs), Part 11: Guidance on Usability*, (1st Ed.), 1998-03-15. Geneva, Switzerland: International Organization for Standardization.

Ivory, M. Y., Yu, S., & Gronemyer, K. (2004). Search result exploration: a preliminary study of blind and sighted users' decision making and performance. In *Extended abstracts of CHI 2004* (pp. 453-1456). New York: ACM Press.

Koivunen, M., & May, M. (2002). *Exploring Usability Enhancements in W3C Process* [PowerPoint slides]. Retrieved from http://www.w3.org/2002/Talks/0104-usabilityprocess/slide3-0.html

Lazar, J., Allen, A., Kleinman, J., & Malarkey, C. (2007). What frustrates screen reader users on the web: A study of 100 blind users. *International Journal of Human-Computer Interaction, 22*(3), 247–269.

Leporini, B., Andronico, P., Buzzi, M., & Castillo, C. (2008). Evaluating a modified Google user interface via screen reader. *Universal Access in the Information Society, 7*(3), 155–175. doi:10.1007/s10209-007-0111-y

Leporini, B., Paternò, F., & Spano, L. D. (2009). *Is flash really accessible when interacting through screen readers?* Accepted by AAATE conference, 30 August - 2 September, 2009, Florence, Italy.

Leuthold, S., Bargas-Avila, J. A., & Opwis, K. (2008). Beyond web content accessibility guidelines: Design of enhanced text user interfaces for blind internet users. *International Journal of Human-Computer Studies, 66*(4), 257–270. doi:10.1016/j.ijhcs.2007.10.006

Lindgaard, G. (1989). Testing the Usability of Interactive Computer Systems, In G. Lindgaard & J. Millar (Ed.), *Testing the Usability of Interactive Computer Systems, Proceedings of Workshop at HCI Australia '89,* (pp. 1-13). Ergonomics Society of Australia, Computer-Human Interaction Special Interest Group.

Mozilla Developer Center. (n.d.). *AJAX.* Retrieved April 30, 2009, from http://developer.mozilla.org/en/docs/AJAX

Nielsen, J. (1993). *Usability engineering.* San Diego: Morgan Kaufmann.

Nielsen, J. (2001). *Designing Web Usability: The Practice of Simplicity.* San Francisco: New Riders Publishing.

Nielsen, J., & Loranger, H. (2006). *Prioritizing Web Usability.* San Francisco: New Riders Publishing.

Norman, D. (2004). *Emotional Design: Why We Love (or Hate) Everyday Things.* New York: Basic Books.

Paternò, F. (1999). *Model-Based Design and Evaluation of Interactive Application.* London: Springer-Verlag.

Pernice, K., & Nielsen, J. (2001). *Beyond ALT Text: Making the Web Easy to Use for Users with Disabilities.* Fremont, CA: Nielsen Norman Group. Retrieved from http://www.nngroup.com/reports/accessibility/beyond_ALT_text.pdf

Petrie, H., Fraser, H., & Neil, K. (2004). Tension, what tension? website accessibility and visual design. In *Proceeding of International World Wide Web Conference* (pp. 13-18). New York: ACM Press.

Scapin, D., & Vanderdonckt, J. Farenc, C.H., Bastide, R., Bastien, CH., Leulier, C., Mariage, C. & Palanque, P.H. (2000). Transferring Knowledge of User Interfaces Guidelines to the Web. In *Proceeding of International Workshop on Tools for Working with Guidelines TFWWG '2000* (pp. 293-303). London: Springer-Verlag.

Sloan, D., Heath, A., Hamilton, F., Kelly, B., Petrie, H., & Phipp, L. (2006). Contextual web accessibility - maximizing the benefit of accessibility guidelines. In *Proceedings of the 2006 international cross-disciplinary workshop on Web accessibility* (pp. 121-131). Berlin: ACM Press.

Thatcher, J. (2006). Assistive Technology: Screen Readers and Browsers. In *Web Accessibility*, (pp. 103-124). San Francisco: Apress. Wikipedia. (n.d.). *Wictionary project*. Retrieved from http://en.wikipedia.org/wiki/Wiktionary

World Health Organization. (2001). *International Classification of Functioning, Disability and Health*. Retrieved from http://www.who.int/classifications/icf/en/

World Wide Web Consortium. (W3C). (2005). *Social Factors in Developing a Web Accessibility Business Case for Your Organization*. Retrieved from http://www.w3.org/WAI/bcase/soc

World Wide Web Consortium. (W3C). (2008a). *Techniques for WCAG 2.0*. W3C Working Group Note. Retrieved December 11, 2008, from http://www.w3.org/TR/WCAG-TECHS/

World Wide Web Consortium. (W3C). (2008b). *WAI-ARIA Overview*. Retrieved from http://www.w3.org/WAI/intro/aria.php

World Wide Web Consortium. (W3C). (2008c). *Web Content Accessibility Guidelines 2.0. Recommendation*. Retrieved from December 11, 2008, from http://www.w3.org/TR/WCAG20/

World Wide Web Consortium. (W3C). (2009). *WAI-ARIA Best Practices*. W3C Working Draft. Retrieved 24 February 2009, from http://www.w3.org/TR/wai-aria-practices/.

Yesilada, Y., Harper, S., Goble, G., & Stevens, R. (2004). Screen Readers Cannot See (Ontology Based Semantic Annotation for Visually Impaired Web Travellers). In *ICWE 2004 Proceedings* (LNCS, pp. 445-458). Berlin: Springer.

KEY TERMS AND DEFINITIONS

Accessibility: The degree to which a product can be accessed by as many people as possible. A Web site or application is accessible if it can be used by everyone, including people with disabilities.

Assistive Technology: Hardware or software component that helps people with disabilities interact with the environment.

Disability: Defined by the Americans with Disabilities Act of 1990 as "a physical or mental impairment that substantially limits one or more major life activities". Impairments may be physical, sensory, or cognitive/intellectual.

JAWS: Jaws for Windows is a widely-used screen reader (http://www.freedomscientific.com/)

Screen Magnifier: A screen magnifier is a software used by the visually impaired to interact with a computer or other electronic devices, such as mobile phones. Presenting enlarged screen content, the screen magnifier is very useful for low-vision people, while totally blind persons have to use a screen reader.

Screen Reader: A screen reader is an assistive technology used by the blind person to interact with a computer or other electronic devices, such as mobile phones. The screen reader mediates between the user and the operating system (including its applications), assisting individuals by interpreting the user interface, which is read aloud sequentially by means of a voice synthesizer, or written by using a Braille display.

User Interface (UI): The means by which a person interacts with a computer or electronic device. Input devices, such as a mouse, keyboard, touch screen, remote control, joy stick or microphone, as well as output devices such as screen, speakers, or Braille display, permit interaction with the system.

Usability: The standard ISO 9241 (1998), defined usability as "the effectiveness, efficiency and satisfaction with which specified users achieve specified goals in particular environments". Web usability is determined by ease of finding desired resources, of learning and remembering website structure and functions (for future visits) as well as by user effectiveness, efficiency and satisfaction while performing a task.

World Wide Web Consortium (W3C): Develops interoperable technologies (specifications, guidelines, software, and tools) to guide the Web to its full potential. W3C is a forum for information, commerce, communication, and collective understanding.

Web Accessibility Initiative - Accessible Rich Internet Applications (WAI-ARIA): A set of documents published by the World Wide Web Consortium that specify how to increase the accessibility of dynamic content and user interface components (developed with Ajax, HTML, JavaScript and related technologies) for differently-abled persons.

Web Content Accessibility Guidelines (WCAG): The Web Accessibility Initiative (WAI) WCAG 2.0 Guidelines are high-level criteria for improving accessibility and usability of Web content and applications.

World Wide Web (Web): A system of interlinked hypertext documents accessed via the Internet. With a Web browser, one can view Web pages that may contain text, images, videos and other multimedia, and navigate between them using hyperlinks.

Widget: An element of a graphical user interface (GUI), such as a graphic button, textbox or collapsible tree, that displays information and/ or allows user input. Widgets collect and hold application data. Complex widgets may convey semantics that must be properly communicated to an assistive technology that provides interaction to the differently-abled.

Chapter 5
A Diacritical Study in Web Design:
Communicability Versus Statistical Manipulation

Francisco V. Cipolla-Ficarra
ALAIPO, & AInCI, Spain

Maria Valeria Ficarra
AInCI, & ALAIPO, Spain

ABSTRACT

In the current chapter the authors present a heuristic and diacritical analysis of the communicability in Web 1.0 and Web 2.0 carried out in the contents of the websites of Southern Europe, especially between Italy and Spain. The real examples that will be presented are related to the loss of the veracity of on-line information and the decay of credibility of the traditional information sources, such as digital newspapers, university context and the industrial or commercial sector. These results are directly related to the statistical aspect and the new phenomenon of the star enunciator and the use of statistics in the Internet, especially in websites such as university websites, social networks, digital newpapers and magazines, portals, etc., whose consequence in the short and middle term may be the total destruction of transparency in the communication process among the users of the interactive systems and the freedom of access to true online information.

INTRODUCTION

The advances of the software and the hardware in the first years of the new millenium are continuous and tend, in the multimedia or hypermedia systems, towards a merger in devices of small size, such as laptops, tablet PCs, e-books, pocket PCs, iPhones

or rather the distribution of servers in each of the homes of the users, with the purpose of boosting the intelligent home, e-learning, telework, e-commerce, virtual tourism, vidcogames, etc. In all these advances in the interactive systems there is a continuous advance in algorithms (Dileep, Yeonseung & Hyksoo, 2008), interfaces (Shneiderman, 2005), use of the new technologies (Cameron, 2009), etc.

DOI: 10.4018/978-1-61520-763-3.ch005

However, all these breakthroughs have a weak point: the veracity of the on-line contents. In the generation of the virtual communities and the lack of control in the websites it can be seen that the users are not subject to quality rules concerning the quality of the information offered in those communities. These quality rules are not respected neither at individual, nor at group or collective level. The problem gets bigger when the public institutions devoted to teaching or industrial/commercial groups foster this lack of transparency through the appearance and the implicit go-ahead of the behaviour of the "star enunciators".

The term "enunciator" derives from linguistics, semiotics and sociology, whereas the notion of "star" refers to negative behaviour and the superior position of this enunciator with regard to the remaining Internet users, that is, as if he were a Hollywood star in the movies. These enunciators have as their goal persuasion, manipulation and fascination towards the global village. The purpose is to acquire the greatest visibility in the on-line community, and in the least possible time. He will reach this goal through the last generation technological means: iPod, mobile phone multimedia, Web 2.0, etc. The costs for him or her are practically equal to zero, because he/she has a high hierarchy in the line of command of the public and/or private institutions. Consequently, we have gone in the Internet from a flat or plain structure to an irregular and steep one. That is to say, the star enunciators occupy the summits of those mountains that are generally built by rising or throwing a node inside the net. We have an evolution of this phenomenon in the following graphic.

Besides, we understand as a 'virtual community' the number of users who continuously participate in chats, videoconferences, etc. in the Internet or intranet, whether it is in long distance courses, semipresential courses, etc. or other users, with the purpose of establishing bidirectional interactive communication links among them. In the case of Internet, these users establish ad-ditional links thanks to the Web 2.0 phenomenon with applications such as LinkedIn, Facebook, Twitter, Naymz, etc.

Ferdinand de Saussure, in his work "Course in General Linguistics" maintains an interesting point of view regarding the assessment of the language that he refers to as "parochialism" (Saussure, 1990). Here it is necessary to bear in mind the orography of the territory where this discipline originated, i.e. the Alps, in whose mountains the towns, as well as their dialects develop around the churches, according to Saussure's linguistic treatise. Remarkably, in the analysis universe on-line of multimedia systems in the same geographical area, that is to say, the geographical centre of the Alps or the Pyrenees, we find that the credibility of information lessens with increasing parochialism. The origin of this problem lies in what is known in software engineering as human factors, and also in the social sciences, the capital factor for that who becomes an information source (emitter) and focuses the attention of the receptor (a kind of showman or showwoman). It is a classical phenomenon in the anchormen of news reports, for instance (Boyd-Barrett & Rantanen, 1998; Cipolla-Ficarra, 2009). If we make an intersection between both factors we have on the Internet false information about the people (training and professional experience) with a clear propaganda or publicity purpose. In the zone from which Saussure spoke there was a union, that is to say, the sale of politicians as if they were business products. A way to detect them is the momentum of the community websites of Web 2.0: Facebook or LinkedIn, for instance. In the analyzed websites we have seen that one of the instruments used by the star enunciator is statistics. That is to say, he/she needs counters and accumulators to establish scores and comparative studies inside the virtual community and/or social network sites. In this regard, the Web 2.0 uses a series of icons that boost or promote the star enunciators: hands with the thumbs up, fire flames, circuits of links or connections, score number, etc.

Figure 1. As if somebody pulled from a node turning it into a cobweb with the shape of a pyramid. At this summit node our star enunciator is to be found

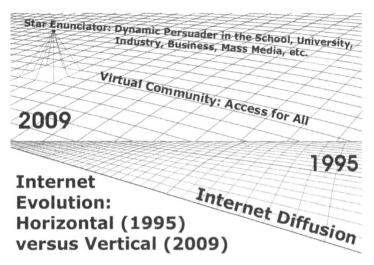

Consequently, it is a comparative work of contents, between two signs or values: the positive, the transparency of the information and the negative, the manipulation of information. That is, it is a diacritical activity, since starting from it the credibility and the veracity of the on-line information grows or falls. The diacritical term stems from linguistics. Diacritical is a adjective meaning distinctive or distinguishable. The term derives from the Greek –*diakritikós*, "distinguishing". In order for anything to function as a sign, it needs to be distinctive or disitnguishable from the other items used also as signs (Colapietro, 1993; Nöth, 1995). Because, Ferdinand de Saussure focused considerable attention on how signs are generated by their differences (by the way or ways they can be distinguished from other signs in the same system, for example, the same language).

The current work starts with a brief description of the notions of human communication and its extension to interactive design. Next, a state of the art of the evolution of software, focusing on the aspects of usability and accessibility in the web from the point of view of interactive communication. Then we analyze the main components of descriptive statistics that have been used in the elaboration of techniques and heuristic evaluation methods applied to the creation of interactive systems on-line and off-line. Some of these components with their corresponding formulas and

Figure 2. Score number for 'professional reputation evaluation' in www.naymz.com

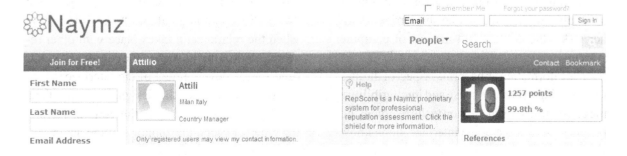

Figure 3. Icons with fire flames awards 'hot' and hands with the thumbs up or OK meaning in www. scrib.com

examples are in annex #1. Then are presented the factors of persuasion used by the star enunciator in several examples, where we find mainly an intersection between the human-computer interaction, semiotics, statistics, usability engineering, software and system engineering.

HUMAN COMMUNICATION

In the basic process of human communication man is regarded as a social and gregarious being, who needs to express and make his activities known to other people (real information is implicitly in the communication). In our case four components are analyzed: the user, how he/she carries out his/her tasks, the context and the use of computer systems.

The information is the formal aspect of the message tending to provide sense and intelligibility to the communication in relation to the recipient. For instance, in the case of the interface, upon know-

ing the profile of the potential user, the success of the communication increases. An analysis of the word "communication" shows how the verb "communicate" and the noun "communication" express the presence of two individuals who are related. Etymologically, the noun *communicatio* and the verb *communico (*both from Latin) have their origin in the word *communis f*ormed by *cum* (with) *munis* (duties or links), denoting the meaning of unite or interrelate "with" (Birwhistell, 1974).

The notion of communication implies: the dialogue between two or more people (users) and the interaction that is established with the technology (computers). It is starting from this interrelation "with" the technological and "with" the person when the relationship takes place with other research environments such as the cognitive models used for the development of the interface.

At the moment of the design of the interface, the designer must consider the cultural factors, the types of users, the supports of the databases,

the kind of interactive access to the information, etc. (Cipolla-Ficarra, 1997; Sears, 2007; Dubberly, Pangaro & Haque, 2009). These variables prompt that from the software sector since the early 90s the need has been established to incorporate sociologists, anthropologists and psychologists to improve the quality of computer systems (Basili & Musa, 1991). In Southern Europe what was enunciated by Basili and Musa was translated into involving artists, philosophers, pedagogues, etc, during the decade of the nineties and the in new millenium. Obviously, the immediate integration of these professionals with the software production teams was very complicated. The qualitative and quantitative results were scarce and increased the costs of the products and/or final services. Currently there is a growing trend towards a new profile of professionals, where there exists an intersection between the formal and the factual sciences.

In user-computer communication, the user and the interface of the computer are interdependent. The concept of interdependence in communication is complex in itself and can be depicted by defining the possible relationships between an emitter and a receptor, such as A and B (Cipolla-Ficarra, 2008a). These are independent under the condition that A does not affect B otherwise there is a dependence relationship between A and B, that is, if A affects B but B does not affect A, or vice versa. Interdependence can be defined as the reciprocal or mutual dependence. If A affects B, and B affects A, then A and B are interdependent. It is possible to establish four levels of interdependence in the process of communication:

1. Physical interdependence by definition.
2. Interdependence of action-reaction.
3. Interdependence of the expectations (inference).
4. Interaction.

1. In the physical interdependence by definition is located a greater interdependence, because in it are the dyadic concepts, that is, those relationships that cannot exist by themselves, such as is the case with the concepts: employee and employer, pupil and professor, son and father, etc. The concepts of communication between user and interface are diadic, since the one depends on the other for its existence.

2. The communication terminology comprises a term related to the interdependence of the action-reaction feedback. The feedback provides the system with information with regard to the success it had in achieving its success. By doing this the user exerts a certain control over the future messages of the system. The kind of feedback that is given determines to a large extent the next set of behaviours of the system. When the system receives a feedback that is "rewarding" it will continue to produce the same kind of message. In the negative case, it should eventually change the message.

3. Human communication entails predictions on behalf of the emitter and the receptor with regard to the way in which the others have to respond to the message. The expectations can be analyzed as a distinctive interdependence level. The designer of the system has with him/her an image of its potential user. The designer takes the user into account at the moment of interacting with the system and foresees the possible answers in the face of certain situations. This capacity for projection in the internal stages of the user is what is known as inference.

4. The word interaction designs the assumption process of a reciprocal role in the development of emphatic behaviour patterns (Preece, 1998). If at the moment of the design of the system one takes at the same time the role of the user a communication by mutual interaction takes place. The concept

of interaction is essential for an understanding of the communication process concept. The communication represents the attempt of unifying two models (the designer's mental mode and the user's mental model), of filling the gap between two individuals through the emission and reception of messages that have a meaning for both. When these two people are placed in the position of the other, they try to perceive the world in the same way in which the other does, they try to foresee in what way the other will respond. The object of the interaction is to achieve a perfect combination of oneself and the other, a total ability to know how to anticipate, predict and behave in agreement with the mutual needs of himself -designer- and the other -user-. Without any doubt, this is one of the areas of knowledge where the social sciences play a very important role, especially in the environments of Web 2.0 and Web 3.0. In view of the potential users of the interactive systems, currently it is intended to achieve the highest quality at the lowest possible cost, thanks to cognitive models that are more consistent with the current communicability era.

In the cognitive models and in a similar way to other human-based tasks, the computer user perceives, stores and retrieves information from short- and long-term memory, manipulates that information to make decisions and solve problems, and then carries out responses (Eberts, 1992). That is to say, a set of typical activities akin to those performed by a specialist in the social sciences, who resorts to certain sociology and statistics techniques to present the obtained results. Now, in these tasks for the design process in the interfaces, for example, it is necessary to remember that there is a classic triad among the conceptual model, the mental model and the interface design. Besides, there is a triadic relation with the communicability. Graphically:

Between each one of these elements there is a bidirectional relationship. Following Norman's concepts, the conceptual model is a design model maintained by the designer of the interactive system, in engineering or programming terms, so that it is accurate, consistent, and complete. In this design, if it is done carefully, the designer should consider the user's task and capabilities (Eberts, 1992). A way to know these user's tasks is through an assessment of the usability of a multimedia system, for instance. The mental model is the model that the user forms of how the interactive system, this mental model guides how the user structures the interaction tasks (Eberts, 1992). In the models aimed at the first computer aided education systems whose contents were related to the teaching of computer science (basic notions, operative systems, text processors, calculation sheets, databases, etc.), of the nineties, they were based on a unidirectional sequential communication structure in the lessons and were bidirectional at the moment of carrying out the tests to overcome the contents of each lesson (in the case that the user did not pass the test, the system automatically forced him/her to repeat the lesson). That is to say, in the technological context –hardware and software– from the example, influence in the mental and conceptual models, the design of the interface and communicability.

SEQUENTIAL COMMUNICATION: UNIDIRECTIONAL AND BIDIRECTIONAL

Regardless of the kind of support being used, the reception of the content in a lineal or unidirectional way is understood as sequential communication. The information is received by the receptor in the way of continuous segments, such as for example the reading in blocks of a tape from the backup of a server (Gray, 1996; Melis, 1996). This entails three operations inside sequential communication: (1) Recording (in digital or analogical format);

Figure 4. Communicability for cognitive model and interface design

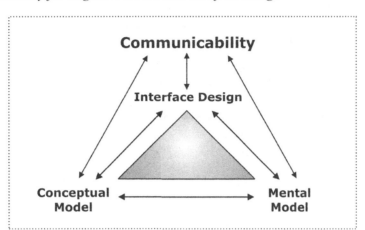

(2) Edition (modification of the stored data; (3) Execution (reproduction of the messages). These are functions that are to be found in video cameras, iPod readers, DVD readers, etc.

In the process of human communication, the interaction factor between who sends or receives the message is practically simultaneous (Marcus, 1993; Kleinberg, 2008). In this process one tends to break this unidirectionality of the message, through the interaction among the intervening agents (emitters and receptors). The relationship that is established between the emitter and the receptor gives rise to the following classification:

- Personal: the degree of interaction is high, given the possibility of mutual feedback of the participants. As a rule, the direction of the communication is bidirectional.
- Groupal: when the components of the communicational process are three or more. The communications among their members generate structures of the type: star (bidirectional in relation to the centre), lineal or sequential (typical in the transmission of data without a feedback) and circular, which can be bidirectional or monodirectional.
- Monodirectional: when it is not possible to establish a bidirectional interaction with

each one of the participants. Generally, the recipient is a crowd or a big audience.

Next an example where the several types of communication are described.

The communication between the members of the group is an important factor at the moment of the design and the evaluation of the interfaces of users, regardless of the adopted method. In the following graphic are depicted two structures of organization of the participants in the design of interfaces. The circles in grey colour depict the person of responsibility or head of the project. In the first is found a kind of unidirectional communication from the boss to the participants in the project, but the low level of communication means that the results are not good. In contrast with the structure presented in a radial bidirectional way where exists a communication among all the agents of the project, very good results can be obtained, and in short time for the development of the interfaces of users for hypermedia systems, such as was the development of several interactive systems on-line and off-line.

Some of the graphics that are generated by the previously described forms have been transferred to the design of multimedia systems for the access to the hyperbase. Hyperbase is the denomination that receives the database of a system based on

Figure 5. Outline of the main structures of the process of human communication

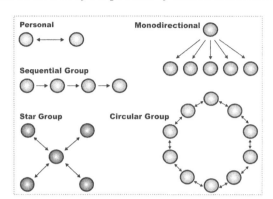

the principles of the hypertext (Tompa, 1989), whether it is for the search of stored data, or rather for the navigation among structure components. The forms of navigation are depicted in the shape of maps (Horn, 1989; Mitchell & McCullough, 1995): lineal, tree, circular, symmetrical complex, non-symmetrical complex, etc. The hyperbases change and access more and more frequently the information shown by the websites comes from data stored in databases causing usability problems derived from a lack of agreement between the information shown and the real data stored in the database. The slowness of the download, the links not updated or the download not controlled by the user are other problems related to the part of database of the web (Berners-Lee, 1996). Other problems are the synchronization among

the dynamic means, the necessity to count with algorithms for a quick understanding and decompression of the stored information, the maximum speed in the transmission of the data in the net, improving data quality, etc. (Lee & Hsu, 2005; Dileep, Yeonseung & Hyksoo, 2008). These were the reasons for which many commercial products of the nineties had design flaws, when the quality was assessed with methodologies aimed at the usability of the interactive system.

WEB EVOLUTION: DESIGN AND USABILITY

The evolution in the web has allowed us to establish different versions, starting from the democratiza-

Figure 6. Types of human organization for the development of interfaces

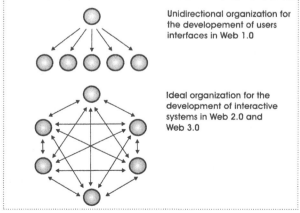

Figure 7. The different ages in software engineering. In the current era quality is an implicit component in communicability

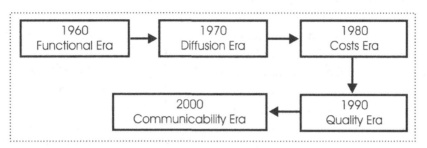

tion of on-line information. Put simply, in Web 1.0 we have the static sites, whereas in Web 2.0 there is the social or participative factor, for instance, Folsonomie –social networks: Facebook, Naymz, LinkedIn, etc. and Wiki (user created content, i.e, wikipedia.org). Finally we have what is named Web 3.0 that consists of boosting the hyperbase by allowing the access to several applications which are not the browser, for which some suggest as subjects of research and development artificial intelligence, the semantic web, 3D (to quit the idea of the website and aim at tridimensionality). From the hardware point of view, Reed Hastings established the differences in regard to the speed of data transmission, that is, "Web 1.0 was dial-up, 50k average bandwidth, Web 2.0 is an average 1 megabit of bandwidth and Web 3.0 will be 10 megabits of bandwidth all the time, which will be the full video Web, and that will feel like Web 3.0" (Hastings, 2009).

This is one of the characteristics of software engineering. That is to say, to divide the temporal periods in relation to the technological evolution. For instance, it is so that in 1960 there was talk about a functional era, characterized by the appearance of technology in the institutions. In the seventies a wide diffusion of the development of the software takes place and it is the moment in which start to spring up in literature the notion of stages or cycles of the models. It is the time of expansion. The decade of the eighties is marked by the prices factor (a fall of these takes place, both in the hardware and in the software). This

period of time can be named the costs period. In the nineties the user is the main target that must be satisfied, for which you have to give it tools and a methodology of use of easy learning and simple use. Usability engineering has played a very important role (Nielsen, 1992). Next in the Figure 8 is the scheme that marks the evolution of time in the different eras of software engineering:

However, one of the main goals of software engineering currently is to improve the quality of the products (Pfleeger, 2008). But from the point of view of design and communicability in the web, the concept of quality can be presented on more than one occasion in an ambivalent fashion. This is due to the fact that, as Fenton says, "quality, the same as the notion of beauty, is in the eyes of the people" (Felton, 1994, p. 200). Now, the 1.0 is a place where power is in the user's hands: the user, who is the person clicking the mouse, is the one who makes all the decisions. And as a result of the many opportunities offered and of the easiness of passing from one site to the other –it is so easy that all the world's competence is in a click (Nielsen, 1990). In the times of the aegis of the commercial multimedia in off-line support, in Spain and later on with the democratization of Internet there were users who showed impatience and insistence to receive quick satisfaction from the interactive system. This principle of usability engineering named subjectively pleasing was the centre of several studies with users aimed at the feedback times of user-computer interaction. If they are not able to access the information of a

website in a maximum time of one or two minutes, then they just think that it's not worth losing time and go away. Some of the main problems of that time of usability and Web 1.0 may still last in other places of the planet where they do not have fast access to the Internet or the impossibility of moving the windows on the display. Next, some examples of the usability studies and the design of interactive systems:

- **Perception:** The same stimulus can lead to really different interpretations. When, for example, some pages are designed exactly as they physically are, instead of being presented in order to be understood, this creates a kind of problem related to this perceptive stimulus. The same happens for the standard icon of the wastepaper, which is not fit for the countries where the wastepaper is more similar to a dustbin and where there are flies. In Thailand Microsoft had to

emulate the presence of flies in the dustbin icon because because the users could not find it (Russo and Boor, 1993) or the different interpretation of colours in the world (Cipolla-Ficarra, 2008b).

- **Navigation and orientation:** when the user wonders "Where am I now?", "How have I arrived here", "How can I come back?", "Where can I go?", etc. or when the users must remember a lot of items (Wilson, 2007). In the following website of Palma de Mallorca there is not only redundancy of functions, such as the impression of the contents, (homepage and in the option *més* –more) but upon opening the window for more options, the latter hides the area for video visualization, and prevents its shifting. This is an example of usability error of the Web 1.0 with contents and functions of the Web 2.0:

- **Internationalisation:** To understand the user, as we have seen, is a key factor related

Figure 8. The layout belongs to the Web 2.0, but contains classical usability mistakes

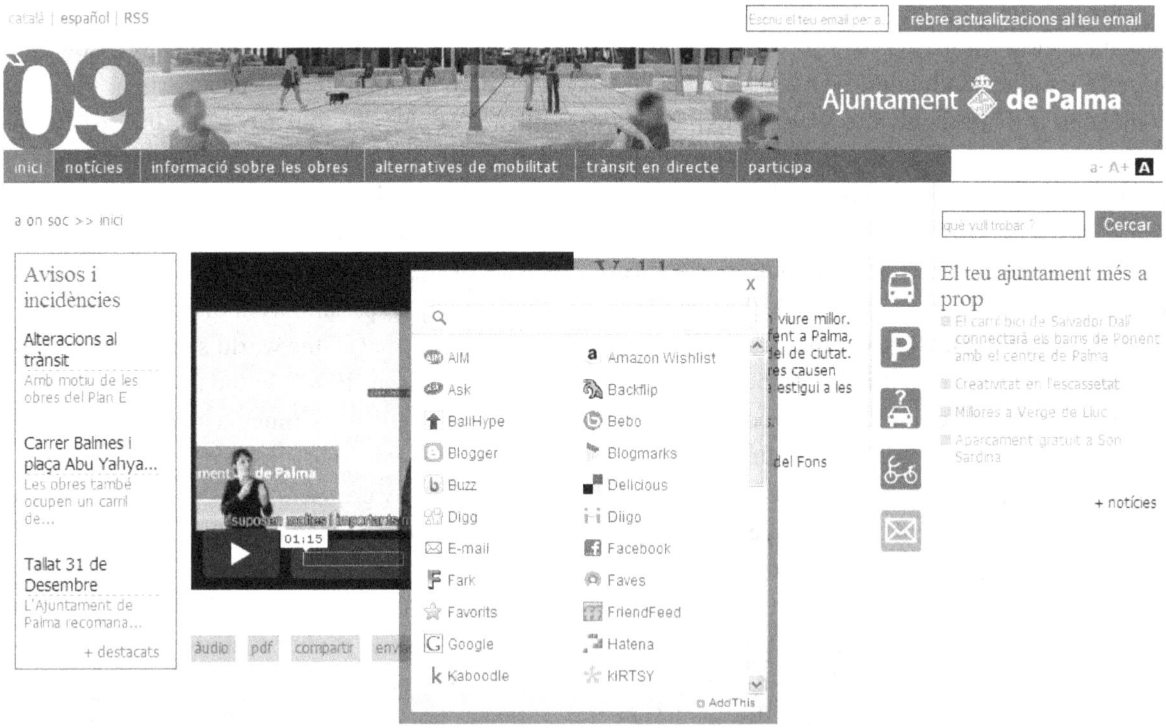

with usability that we cannot solve without considering his/her cultural background. This suggests that we need to develop cultural models that can be modelled in various ways (Fernandes, 1995; Marcus & Gould, 2000; Chavan, *et. al.* 2009). On the one hand we have the "open" factors which are tangible, obvious features, of a culture (Nielsen & del Galdo, 1996), as for example calendars, measure units or character games, and, surely, some of these factors incorporate "marks of the cultural history" (the fact that Canada, for example, shares the same calendar and date format as New Zealand gives information about its background), nevertheless, the open factors usually do not offer deep cultural penetrations (they are the daily conventions under which a society functions and must be based on in software). While on the other hand we have the "hidden" factors, which are those complex and "vaguely definite" aspects of a society, easily minsunderstood for the foreign ones, and, sometimes, so thin that can be unnoticed. The style of communication (verbal or not-verbal), the meanings of symbols. We can note that some of the problems related to perception are also strictly linked

Figure 9. Parochialism and the star enunciators prevent the accessibility to the correct on-line information

with the problems of internationalization. In the example of the Figure9, there are only two languages (Spanish and Catalan/ Majorcan) when it is an island whose main industry is tourism and in Europe an average of seven languages are necessary for the touristic websites (Cipolla-Ficarra & Cipolla-Ficarra, 2008). Besides, internationalization of each one of the design categories is essential to reach the accessibility for all and from the point of view of communicability, for instance.

ACCESSIBILITY FOR ALL

Accessibility is one of the main quality criteria that we have worked through during the quality metrics generation for over 15 years, in the multimedia/hypermedia systems in off-line support (CD-ROMs and DVDs mainly) and on-line (Internet and entrepreneurial/educative university intranets). Currently the principles that must guide the design of Web 1.0 are summed up in the shape of guidelines (Chisolm, Vanderheiden & Jacobs, 2001), for instance. However, it is easily detectable that the quality criteria are absent in some digital newspapers and/or magazines when it comes to informing the readers.

In Figure10 it can be seen how rectangular icons have been inserted in the shape of an inverted comic bubble to signal geographically where in the Google map the news has been generated, with three colours and three categories: news (light blue), recent news (green) and the most read (orange). The quality attributes of the interactive systems is equal to zero in those cases, because in the map are signalled the town of Bergamo and the municipalities of Dalmine, Terno d'Isola and Seriate, except those in which the bergamesque textile industry has decided to suspend its workers, such as: Albino and Gandino in Val Seriana. This is also a classical example of manipulation and destruction of credibility in on-line information,

due to the parochialism as defined by Saussure, and the star enunciators, such as those responsible for the newspaper and the centenary textile industry (there is not a control of the information, only institutional image). Therefore, that communication media does not ease accessibility to the correct information for the potential users.

Accessibility means proportioning the flexibility in order to adjust to the needs of each user and to their preferences and/ or limits. The possible users of an interactive system are different and in an ideal world all the user interfaces should adjust to these differences, so that everyone can use them without problems, and nobody considers himself limited while using something due to these personal differences. It is necessary to avoid designing just considering the features of specific groups of people, imposing unnecessary barriers that could be avoided simply paying more attention to their limits. Here we have other quality attributes that must exist in the interactive systems such as the empathy in the communicability for the potential users (Preece, 1998). From the point of view of navigation can be mentioned prediction and competence (Nielsen, 2001).

The abilities and attitudes of all the people are different from one another. There are groups of people that have some functional limits that prevent them from having access to facilities that they desire, or should have the right to access. In the case of access to the information through a keyboard, mouse, joystick, etc., there are people in the mentioned groups who are almost completely blind and/or deaf, with motor impairments that prevent them from moving their hands freely or with low levels of comprehension; in the vocal devices, there are those people with vocal impairments. Concerning this it is important to stress the breakthroughs that are being carried out in artificial intelligence and hypermedia, especially in the following lines of research: robotic and prothetic devices (McFarland & Wolpaw, 2008), augmented reality interfaces (Billinghurst, Grasset & Looser, 2006). kinetic interactions (Parkes,

Figure 10. A common practice in Northern Italy, where bachelors in physics, i.e., present themselves as possessors of doctorate studies, that is, PhD –red rectangle

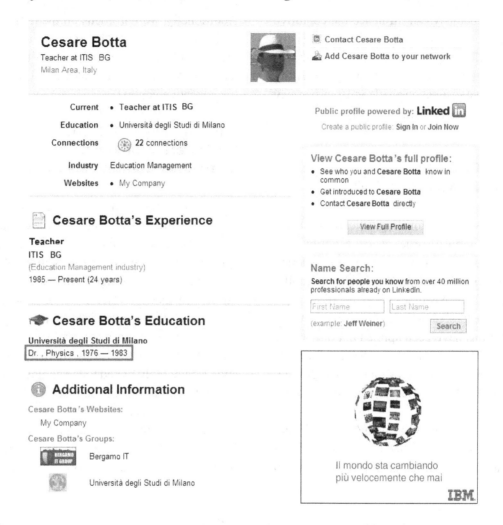

Poupyrev & Ishii, 2008), videogames (Cutumisu, 2006), etc. In our case, the examples that make up the universe of study are accessible to all those who do not have some visual or motor disability. Therefore, we do not approach the aspects related to physical accessibility, leaving it as an open line for future research, especially in the Web 2.0 and the Web 3.0

The interfaces regulate the user-application dialogue through some proceedings that include the available orders, the navigation proceedings, etc. These elements are part of a model of task to be carried out, that is usually explored as a meta-

phor of the same activity carried out without the help of the computer. In our case we have always used a quality attribute known naturaless of the metaphor (Cipolla-Ficarra, 1997b). In order to use properly, the person has to understand the metaphors, the navigation, the system structure, etc. that definitely depends on the agreement between the "world vision" of the user and of the application. That is to say, what we call emulation or simulation of reality on the screen of a traditional computer or in a computer device of small size (Cipolla-Ficarra, 1996). Besides the ageing and the cognitive impairments, aspects such as the use

of a different language from the mother tongue or the decrease of the attention to carry out another task simultaneously can influence the cognitive ability, and so it is necessary to consider this difference while designing interaction methods. In these cases, the best solution is to apply the quality criteria known as function phatic and transparency of meaning (Cipolla-Ficarra, 1999).

LINGUISTICS AND COMMUNICABILITY STUDY

The notions deriving from linguistics have made it possible to establish a series of quality attributes to avoid ambiguities at the moment of the interaction of the non-expert users with computers (Cipolla-Ficarra, 1997a). Also these notions allow us to detect the lack of transparencies in the contents. These notions have been applied not only to the texts but also to the icons in the interfaces, in order to achieve more natural metaphors (Cipolla-Ficarra, 1996). Our studies have had their origins in the Saussurian sign.

Without considering the methodological binomial form/substance applied by Hjemslev, in this investigation we focused on the transparency of concept or saussurian meaning or hjemlslevian content, in order to avoid ambiguity (Nöth, 1995). Additionally, we will focus on the notion of parochialism as indicated by Saussure to detect the presence of the star enunciator and the aegis of the loss of credibility of on-line information, in the educative context.

The Language Style for the Different Channels of Interactive Communication

Osgood Charles maintains that every language includes both mandatory and variable components at all analysis levels: phonemic, morphemic and syntactic (Reardon, 1981; Aranguren, 1986). As for Blakenship, he suggests that we leave aside the notion that the style is an ornament and a technique, and we regard it as inextricably linked to the experience, the substance (Reardon, 1981; Dillard & Pfau, 2002). He also reminds us that the style is inevitably linked to the choice among the alternatives that the language offers. Sometimes these options are conscious and sometimes they are unconscious. But in all cases they are concerned with the contexts in which they are immersed. For instance, in the messages recorded to be listened to

Figure 11. Authoritarism in this interface is boosted by the omnipresence of the star enunciator those eyes that allegedly see everything and know everything (manipulating use of statistics)

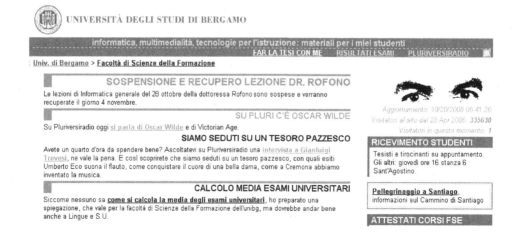

Figure 12. Excellent example of communicability where there is no persuasion or manipulation of contents

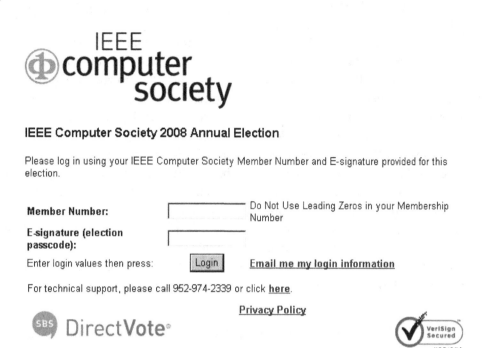

in the iPod supports, the star enunciator, following the parochialism channels enunciated by Saussure, resorts to a soft intonation. This parochialism may be strengthened if from the place where the persuasive contents are transmitted or generated, they have religious names, for instance, the case of saints or devotes. Obviously the star enunciator in his speaker role will not respect the rules of interchanging speakers in the diffusion of his messages in the audio and/or audiovisual format (he/she has to be the absolute star). We can listen and/or see only one direction: unidirectional and only one style: authoritarism.

Besides, the messages in audio format in the Web are easy to erase, and do not leave written traces as happens with a text, digital or analogical (some very valued qualities by the industrial, commercial and educative parochialism in the Alps). This great advantage from the ecological and economical point of view (reduction of produc-

tion costs) is used in a destructive way by the star enunciator in the environments of parochialism as presented by Saussure. In the university context of the Italian Alps, there are star enunciators who rail at Canadian designers for trivial usability questions such as the screen resolution of the interface. However, the star enunciator forgets that those students who have registered for his classes must attend other professors' classes or conventions in order to get valid opinions on the subject of the interfaces (see figures in annex #1). Here it is also necessary to point out that the collaborators of the star enunciators also take part in the destruction of on-line credibility of the information, such as can be the omission of the information sources or the thanks for the aid obtained.

These omissions are registered in the acknowledgments section or the bibliography of the final studies in the career, which in Italy are wrongly called 'thesis'. These are projects and not PhD

thesis, like those that are made to obtain a PhD. This is a common practice in Northern Italy, to manipulate reality in the Web 2.0, that is to say, that is, an incorrect use of the initials 'Dr'. This initials belong to a PhD, in the Anglosaxon countries, doctor or lawyer in the Iberian countries and in Latin America, for instance. In fact, the correct initials in Italian are: *dott. –dottore* for the males, and *dott.ssa –dottoressa* for females. Both initials refer to those with bachelors degrees. Nevertheless, the Lombardian bachelors present themselves by faking academic reality in the virtual community. We find examples in maps with the names of the private streets in some Bergamasque towns (incorrect us of the initials "dr or Dr") and another in the LinkedIn website (Figure10). Perhaps a solution in these cases of

academic opacity would be that some university of the area would regal them with an honoris causa PhD to these bachelors in business, with which both examples of opacity or falseness of information would no longer be valid.

In contrast with audio, the transmission of written texts in the historical base of the net (Meleis, 1996). Today, Twitter is a very positive means for sending little messages as happened in the dawn of the hypertext. Such messages can be accompanied with a video, for instance, hence the importance of knowing the styles of the word associations made by human beings. In some way there is a tendency towards the minimalism of textual style.

In 1980 Norton developed a measurement of the communicator's style to research the way in

Figure 13. The correct design of the interactive system allows a feedback by the potential users

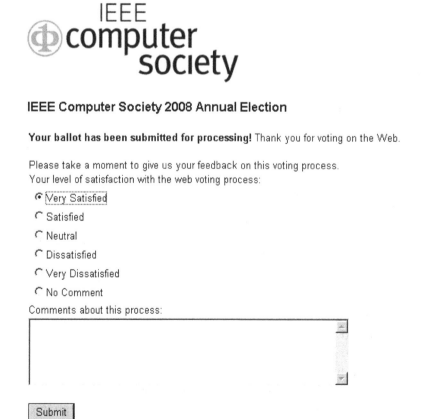

which a person interacts verbally and paraverbally to indicate to what extent the message has to be received literally, interpreted, filtered or understood (Reardon, 1981; Brown, 2008). In some way this is about setting up association patterns. According to the studies made by Sypher in 1980, these works intend to seek the mechanisms of the receptor's feelings with the eventual real world associations (Reardon, 1981; Nöth, 1995). Obviously, the contextual and cultural factor is important in the formation of these associations. For instance, the use of capital letters and the red color in the interface of texts or emails gives away anger and authoritarism (Zviran, Te'eni, & Gross, 2006; Cipolla-Ficarra, 2008b)

Now, from the persuasion contexts studied in the past millennia, the interpersonal is the one that offers the best opportunities for the autonomy of the "I" (personal autonomy) and reciprocal persuasion. Personal interactions are characterized by the predomination or rules which are intrinsic to the relationship and to which each communicator contributes systematically. As a rule, the feedback opportunities are immediate and frequent when we compare them with those that are offered by the contexts of the organizations and the social communication media, known as conventional, such as the written press, radio, television, etc. Individuals are more prone to operate in such a way that they distance themselves from the specific role prescriptions. They realize that the undesirable attributes that as a result other people may state about them can be modified or denied by the addition of consequent actions that justify or excuse the questionable behaviour. In such a way that the "I" has the opportunity of serving as a behaviour generating mechanism. However, the "I" in a virtual community may be anonymous and therefore the behaviour rules can be broken more easily (Brown, 2008). This factor is very well-known, even by the star enunciator himself, who even acquires the personality, research works, etc. from other work colleagues.

Since personal interactions offer opportunities of becoming more akin to the participants' rules, there is the possibility of using more confidently the appeals to incoherence, which are focused on personal rules. If in these contexts the "I" was not a viable mechanism generating behaviour options, the appeals to incoherence with regard to personal rules would be of very little use in the process of persuading the subject to change his behaviour. In the case of the star enunciator, the calls to attention on behalf of the virtual community and even from his peers and colleagues are to no avail, since he allegedly finds himself in a position where he is above all of them. Therefore, the appeals to the accuracy of the construct of a higher order or the adequacy of particular actions would be more effective. Since personal rules have characteristic values, they are accessible in the interpersonal interactions, and they are not immersed in the predomination of the context which characterizes the communicative acts that take place in the framework of organizations or of social communication conventional mass media, the possibility that the appeal to coherence is successful is higher. All these human factors have an

Figure 14. A total of 60 areas of diverse interests but which in fact are keywords in the websites of the star enunciator. We can see redundance and others languages –English and Spanish

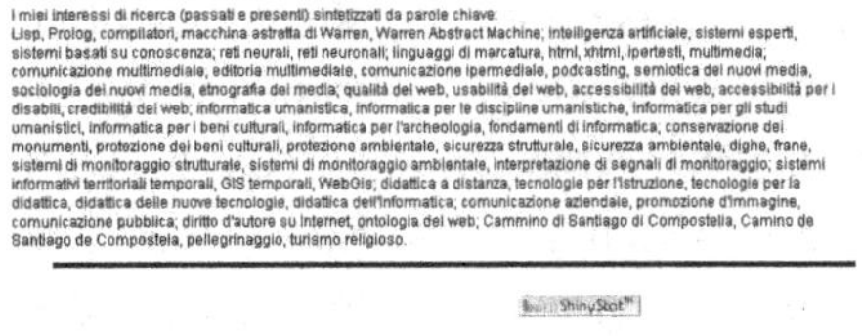
Interessi di ricerca

I miei interessi di ricerca (passati e presenti) sintetizzati da parole chiave:
Lisp, Prolog, compilatori, macchina astratta di Warren, Warren Abstract Machine; intelligenza artificiale, sistemi esperti, sistemi basati su conoscenza; reti neurali, reti neuronali; linguaggi di marcatura, html, xhtml, ipertesti, multimedia; comunicazione multimediale, editoria multimediale, comunicazione ipermediale, podcasting, semiotica dei nuovi media, sociologia dei nuovi media, etnografia dei media; qualità del web, usabilità del web, accessibilità del web, accessibilità per i disabili, credibilità del web; informatica umanistica, informatica per le discipline umanistiche, informatica per gli studi umanistici, informatica per i beni culturali, informatica per l'archeologia, fondamenti di informatica; conservazione dei monumenti, protezione dei beni culturali, protezione ambientale, sicurezza strutturale, sicurezza ambientale, dighe, frane, sistemi di monitoraggio strutturale, sistemi di monitoraggio ambientale, interpretazione di segnali di monitoraggio; sistemi informativi territoriali temporali, GIS temporali, WebGis; didattica a distanza, tecnologie per l'istruzione, tecnologie per la didattica, didattica delle nuove tecnologie, didattica dell'informatica; comunicazione aziendale, promozione d'immagine, comunicazione pubblica; diritto d'autore su Internet, ontologia del web; Cammino di Santiago di Compostella, Camino de Santiago de Compostela, pellegrinaggio, turismo religioso.

ShinyStat™

influence on the democratic process of the spread of the Internet and in the credibility on-line of its contents. Fortunately, the international organizations that foster computer science, electronics, telecommunications, etc., have adopted state of the art technological systems in the choice of their main representatives, tending to reduce the negative aspects of the described human factors.

PERSUASION AND VIRTUAL ORGANIZATIONS

One of the breakthroughs of the Net is the possibility of voting via the Internet. The computer electronic organizations such as ACM, IEEE among others have pioneered the electronic vote. This is a task that requires consistency and quality in the organizations for a worldwide electoral campaign. In these tasks several communicative strategies are used and members are persuaded to cast their votes. With this purpose emails are sent, letters with the candidate listings, the voting papers in paper format, and their corresponding envelopes to be sent through the mail, etc. thus creating a kind of model of virtual and real socialization among the participants. Now in the following examples of the IEEE we find the utmost seriousness and transparency of the enunciator since he shows an absolute neutrality in the communicability towards the virtual community of the members of those associations.

Barret introduces the socialization model. The virtual communities who follow this model operate starting from the premise that people can be persuaded to assess the activities that help the organization to achieve its goals (Weaver & Morrison, 2008). Taking some distance from Barret's approach, we can interpret that this means that it is expected that the users give up or revise the personal rules which are incompatible with rules of the virtual community (Reardon, 1981; Aranguren, 1986). The ways of persuasion which are characteristic of this model are acquiescence and

accommodation and to some extent stem from the classical structures of the working environment. The virtual community around Web 2.0 with such websites as Facebook, LinkedIn, YouTube, etc., is the persuader, the user is the persuaded individual. In some way Internet users are nowadays forced to leave their data on these websites in order to belong to the most advanced web environment. Let's not forget that the star enunciator uses these links to gain visibility on-line through a series of keywords that constantly change with regard to the modifications made by those that he intends to destroy, virtually speaking. For instance, by inserting key words related to a subject in a city in the main search engines, his name will appear in the first positions, in the same context as those of the rest of the colleagues who have been researching for decades, and developing the subjects that he is plagiarizing. Now this does not mean that the acquiescence or accommodation of some of his followers in the virtual community lack the power to persuade his superiors that he deserves to be promoted in regard to his/her interest for the organization or virtual community, since sooner or later the star enunciator will relinquish his false position. The problem lies in the fact that the destructive behaviour of on-line credibility will not only be boosted by his successors; in some corrupt university contexts it may even be boosted. The final goal is to take the first positions on the Internet, regardless of the methods and techniques used in the persuasion and manipulation of the interactive information.

The falseness of these statistic values lies in the access counters to the websites of the star enunciator, but thanks to dyacritical study it is possible to detect this credibility destruction technique. For instance, in the Figure11, it switches to an alleged daily control from the accesses of students, but funnily enough, the values are the same on two days (compare figures 05.27.2009 and 05.29.2009). However, in the system Shiny-Stat it can be seen that on the day 05.29.2009 it has had some 8, and not the 492 he shows in his

websites. Besides, these daily counters are steeled at about 23:30 hours, approximately. Obviously he/she has a computer program on-line to count fake accesses to his/her websites. Besides, in his role of manipulative and persuasive leader he fosters the destruction of credibility through the use of statistics and graphics among his public through the web. Therefore, he does not only harm the real function of statistics such as is offering accurate information of the social events in the Internet but also the graphical information. The latter is due to the fact that the graphics are also false since the data and the results of the formulas carried out in Microsoft commercial programs such as Excel or Access are not truthful. In the parochialism area this is a common situation. It is even feasible to find in the Internet graphics of yearly commercial balance sheets concerning industrial revenue which are false, and which for privacy reasons can not be inserted as example in the chapter. The parochialism described by Saussure and the lack of an international legislation find in the copyright the ideal protection to progress without interruption in the destruction of the Internet credibility. These are some of the typical examples of the destructive socialization models of veracity of on-line information.

Barret explains that the socialization model implies leadership, for instance (Reardon, 1981). The superior who lays stress on the importance of the organization's goals, and calls with conviction to their being diligently persecuted, may speed up the socialization process. To the extent in which the superiors succeed in stimulating the intimate acceptance by the users of the rules of the virtual community, it is likely that they create conditions which lead to the socialization of their peers. Nevertheless, in the environments where there are precedents of a destruction of credibility, the used cognitive models do not lack a negative and/or self-destructive persuasion of the virtual community itself. In this case the peers may also persuade each other to adopt the healthy rules of the organization, in such a way that the socializa-

tion of the users in a virtual course, for instance, becomes a vertical process (student-tutor) and horizontal (peer-peer among colleagues, whether they are professors or students). This is one of the priorities to be accomplished once serious credibility anomalies are detected in the virtual community.

The third model that Barrett introduces goes beyond the unidirectional perspective of persuasion in the former models in order to give the users some participation in the making of the rules and goals of the virtual community (Mulholland, 1994; Tscheligi & Reitberger, 2007). This is the accommodation model. A structure or virtual community which adapts this model works as follows: the needs and motivations of the members are taken into account, and the organization is structured and works in such a way that the persecution of the goals of the organization will be intrinsically gratifying and will provide the simultaneous consecution of the individual's goals, without resorting to star enunciators, for instance.

All the ways of communication expert an influence on who we are and who we want to be, and even shape it. But the ways of social communication that invade us the most are the mass-media. Today the classical systems of social communication have digitalized their messages, and they admit in most cases interactive communication. During the past century, these mass media have been the target of much criticism, both deserved and exaggerated. The most generalized complaint is that these media do not reflect our lives accurately, that they debase the taste of the fruitors/users and that they goad people into doing things that otherwise they would not even consider. In audio communication, for instance, podcasting or audiovisual such as digital interviews on the Internet, it is important to consider that each time that one opens his/her mouth to speak to other people one does not only risk a possible rejection of the enunciator's message and/or the enunciator himself. Because of this, almost all of us lend a lot of attention to the image that is broadcast and

Figure 15. Total of accesses on day 492

Figure 16. Total of accesses on day 501

we shield ourselves from undesirable attributions. On the other hand, the digital and/or analogical communication means will not demand immediate answers in some cases, that are visible to our peers. The behaviour may be postponed. For instance, in the propaganda in an electoral campaign it may not generate either needs or immediate answers, since it requires the passing of time, following the initial or continuous message in time.

INTERACTIVE COMMUNICATION MEANS: THE EFFECTS

In our case, when we speak about interactive communication media, we mean the means of social communication also known mass-media: radio, television, cinema, etc., which with the passing of time and through the advances of computer science have become 100% interactive. That is to say, the receptor, a passive person in the communication process, has acquired an active role, becoming a user. A large part of this phenomena is due to the fact that he is no longer a consumer of

Figure 17. The website ShinyStat demonstrates the falsehood of the accesses on day 05.29.2009, in the counter of the star enunciator there are indicated 492, whereas in the ShinyStat there are 8 (red rectangle)

contents, but rather an editor of contents, thanks to the Internet and the software –commercial or not– that he/she has available to generate his/her own multimedia messages. However, many of the theoretical concepts of persuasion of the classical means of social communication still apply in the interactive multimedia systems, since they were based on the persuasion exerted for the sale of products and services, that is to say, publicity in the commercial case or propaganda in the political case. Let's not forget that our star enunciator

sometimes joins these two characteristics in order to destroy on-line credibility.

In this regard, some authors claim that the contents of the messages of the classical means of social communication do not lack virtues (Mulholland, 1994; McQuail, 2005; Brown, 2008). Far from it, they have contributed to a long extent to our education. Here of course one has to differentiate very clearly which were the roles expected by the community from public means of communication as compared with the current laws in force in some

countries where their purpose now is to inform but not to train the potential audience of these means. Even in the case of the publicity whose mass and commercial persuasion have served to promote changes in the inhabitants' quality of life, such as the switch from passive communication to active communication in interactive television (Light, 2004). What is required in many cases is a greater responsibility on behalf of those persuaded in the relationships to the media. Without it, some messages from the interactive communication media inside the virtual communities will still enjoy a credibility they do not deserve. For instance, the classical model presented by Kelman suggests the use of persuasion strategies which are tantamount to the appeals to accuracy, pertinence, coherence and efficacy (Reardon, 1981; Wimmer & Dominick, 2006). Pertinence is the word more frequently used in the community, but Kelman's perspective does not exclude the use of accuracy, coherence and efficacy in the persuasive messages of the social communication media.

Another of the great experts of social communication is Denis McQuail, whose contributions still apply in the current communicability era (McQuail, 2002 and McQuail, 2005). He claims that we know enough as to explain the influence process that we observe in communication. We can access the "why" of the effects. The first step in this process consists in recognizing the difference between the effect and the influence. The latter is related to the intentional exercise of power over other people, whereas the former refers exclusively to the reaction or response of the members of the public in the social communication media, or of our virtual community in the case of university users, for instance. In relation to the main subject of persuasion, we will focus on the intentional exercise of power, something that is a main component in our star enunciator. Analyzing the triad "can-know-will" from the Greimas's semiotic prospect (Nöth, 1995), the star enunciator's "power" is annulled by the "not knowing how to do", but the "will" reaches quickly

greater power positions (visibility on-line), which leads it to destroy on-line credibility.

With regard to this, Denis McQuail describes four models of influence: information process, conditioning or association, functional and relational (McQuail, 2002; McQuail, 2005). The relational model focuses on the relationship between emitter and receptor in the classical communication media and between the designer and the user in the interactive multimedia systems. Basing ourselves on the classical television studies it can be explained what its effects are among both the "most defenceless" audience and the "most prepared" one (McQuail, 2002). McQuail stresses the role of the power in the relationship between emitter and receptor. He explains that although the concept of power has restricted applications in the mass communication media, since it is not possible to resort to material gratification, physical strength and other motivation factors which operate in the interpersonal contexts and which are not accessible here, its influence is not seriously lessened (in the case of the destruction of the on-line credibility we can see how the root links surrounding the star enunciator grow among the corrupt members of the virtual community that he is building around him). In this regard, McQuail indicates that the essential point concerning power is that "he who intends to be an influential emitter must possess certain relevant resources for the receptor's needs, and for the influence to have effect, the receptor must actively cooperate " (Brown, 2008, p. 353). In the first segment of this definition of power he mirrors the functional point of view about influence. This is the main reason why, the collaborators of the destruction of on-line credibility devote themselves to manipulate the counters, accumulators and other numerical data related to statistics, readings and downloads of on-line documents, reciprocal links between the websites of manipulators and persuaders, for instance. As we have seen, the functional theories explain the behaviour changes in regard to the personal needs. So it is that in the conventional social commu-

Figure 18. Meteoric university studies, multilayered and with scarce credibility in the obtained degree

 Cris Bus's Education

Universitat Ramon Llull

PhD , Telecommunications Engineering , 2003 — 2007

Universitat Pompeu Fabra

Master , Journalism and Audiovisual Communication , 1993 — 1995

Universitat de Barcelona

Degree in Geography & History , 1st & 2nd cycle in Anthropology & Art History , 1987 — 1992

Universitat de Barcelona

Degree in Psychology , 1st & 2nd cycle , 1986 — 1991

nication media the emitter and the receptor have to cooperate so that this power relationship may take place. The same thing happens between the persuader of the interactive means and its user. People may reject power, and in fact sometimes they do. There has got to be motivation enough to allow cooperation.

In the perspective of the social influence as defined by Herbert Kelman in 1960, he claimed that there were three basic influence processes: conformity, identification and internalization (Reardon, 1981; Dillard & Pfau, 2002). Conformity takes place when a person accepts the influence of another person or of a group because he expects to get from the other a favourable answer (for instance, in the context of the virtual community, these are stars in the websites of LinkedIn, scores in Naymz, etc). Identification takes place when an individual assumes a certain behaviour with the purpose of taking part in a relationship, that is to say, it is a means of negotiation used in interpersonal communication. The ways are four: invocation, ingratiation, the creation of shared experiences and communication as a goal (Reardon, 1981, Dillard & Pfau, 2002). He describes them as means through which the coordinated handling of meaning is

achieved. Pierce and Kelman agree that the individual participates in a role relation with another person, not necessarily because he/she believes in the contents of that role in particular, but because he/she wants to meet the other's expectations (Aranguren, 1986; Brown, 2008). This guarantees the continuity of his relation to another person or group. But in contrast to conformity, identification entails the public acceptance of the role as well as its intimate acceptance. Therefore, a pupil of the star enunciator participates in the destruction of credibility process because he identifies himself with the star enunciator and will surpass him sooner or later. Consequently, we are in the face of a process of exponential growth in the destruction of on-line credibility. Sooner or later, the virtual communities totally lack credibility, even the written texts. With regard to this there are already authors who claim that the veracity of images is dead, thanks to the commercial self-edition programs, which are internationally distributed, such as Photoshop, CorelDraw, etc. or free software: PhotoPlus, DrawPlus, Serif DrawPlus, for example. That is why there was an appeal for the return to the written text in the hypermedia/interactive systems (Debray, 1995).

Kelman's model is a relational influence model and apparently it doesn't seem to be aimed at power (Wimmer & Dominick, 2006). However, the definition of power that McQuail gives, as possessor of relevant resources for the receptor, is implicit in his model. It is the persuader's task to convince the persuaded person that a product/service or a behavior will meet the needs of social approval, the anchoring in the social relationships, or the coherence with the values (the greater is the destruction of on-line credibility by the collaborators of the star enunciator the higher will be the likelihood of profiting from it). In this sense, it may be said that there exists a power relationship between persuader and persuaded person. The virtual communities and the mass communication media create this kind of relationship with their users or public, according to the case. For instance, advertising provides the receptor with the information that facilitates social acceptance. The contents of the on-line multimedia systems may teach people how to play roles that may allow them to establish satisfactory relationships with other people. The contents of the dynamic and static means may teach people not only what to value, but also when and how to shift these values to make them coherent with the values of other significants.

Here it is necessary that the diacritical analysis considers some applications of Web 2.0 which tear apart the veracity between the significant and the signification of the contents. For instance, those who present themselves in the virtual community with a curriculum vitae or university resume, multilayered and with a meteoric speed in accumulating diplomas in Southern Europe, as can be seen in the Figure19, or also those who out of sheer working experience promote themselves as engineers or researchers inside the virtual community (Figure19).

Dorwin Cartwright introduced an outlook on mass persuasion, that like that of Kelman's focuses on the previous conditions and the effects wanted as they are perceived by the persuaded person (Reardon, 1981 and Brown, 2008). Cartwright's focus represents one of the few attempts at understanding what happens from the psychological point of view when somebody tries to influence the behavior of another person: why the effect. Obviously, a very important aspect from the point of view of the creation of the cognitive models and their perception by the users. Cartwright suggests that the influence demands a chain of processes which are at the same time complex and interrelated, but which in broad terms may be char-

Figure 19. False academic researcher (A) and degree in engineering (B) without having carried out university studies

acterized by: (1) Creating a determined cognitive structure, (2) Creating a determined motivational structure, and (3) Creating a determined cognitive structure –action– (Reardon, 1981; Brown, 2008). These processes are comparable to the previous conditions, the desired effects and the repertoire of behaviours of the model of rules studied in the persuasion context.

According to Cartwright, personal needs supply energy for behavior and contribute to the setting of goals in the person's cognitive structure. The individual achieves these goals by choosing adequately from his behavior repertoire. An instance of this are the inexpert users in the use of interactive systems when handling videogames (Cipolla-Ficarra, 2007). So that the role of the traditional mass media communication and Internet becomes that of modifying and creating needs as well as promoting the means through which it is possible to have access to these goals.

It can be taken from these general observations about the nature of human relationships that the efforts to exert influence on the behavior of another person must be aimed either at modifying the needs (and the goals) or to change a person's motivational structure as to what activities lead to what ends. This means that a person may be induced to do willingly something that otherwise he/she wouldn't have done except that it was possible to establish a need for which this deed would constitute a goal, or that the deed could be carried out to be conceived as a way to an existing goal (Reardon, 1981; Wimmer & Dominick, 2006). Oddly enough, at the time when these statements were made, little was known about the setting of needs, but it seems unlikely that a mere campaign through the mass communication media has real chances of creating new needs. Today the on-line or off-line interactive communication media and the momentum of E-commerce create in a simple way new needs among the young, especially in the case of the consumption of last generation technological goods. Obviously, the virtual communities have generated the need for a bigger visibility, and especially the websites of the kind: Google, MSN, Yahoo, etc. indicate that many people define themselves as simple commercial objects. It is not for nothing that we can find university professors in Mallorca in whose personal website you find information about their studies, interviews, seminars, lectures, publications, travels, hobbies, etc. and a shop –*tienda* dedicated to the sale of T-shirts, slippers, etc. (see Figure20).

In these websites academic credibility is equal to zero excepting the obtained diplomas. Nevertheless, if you analyze them, probably it has been a meteoric career, by resorting to all the persuasion and information manipulation resources. In this case, the star enunciator is a kind of showman of commercial and academic achievements.

Through the diacritical analysis of the analyzed websites it can be seen that the final goal of every star enunciator and his/her collaborators (or future star enunciators) is to reach the traditional means of communication, regardless of the analogical or digital support, without relinquishing their constant influence on the virtual community that follows them, through the Web 2.0 socialization systems. Once this level is overcome, he/she will also experiment in the Web 3.0, especially in the

Figure 20. The star enunciator mistakes academic reality for the commercial and self-publicity one

Hernadez Gaseosa

profesor y escritor | blog | prensa y Cv | **ilustrador** | creativo comunicador | **tienda** | © | contacto

tridimensional environments, since his behaviour is similar to the infinite semiosis as stated by Pierce. Those readers who want to go deeper into other aspects of the psychological profile and of the cognitive models in the design of interactive systems related to the star enunciator or dynamic persuasion can check the following bibliography (Cipolla-Ficarra, 2009; Cipolla-Ficarra, Vivas & Romo, 2009). The manipulation of statistics and the destruction of the credibility of the information in the virtual community are some of the keys to reach those goals.

FUTURE RESEARCH DIRECTIONS

One of the main problems we are facing nowadays in the diacritical studies is the volatility of on-line information by the star enunciators. That is to say, that the parochialism described by Saussure is not only hidden or the information in the Internet manipulated, but additionally they devote themselves constantly to change the contents in order not to be detected. Therefore, it is necessary to implement a democratic control system of the quality of information in the websites belonging to the Web 2.0 generation, Web 3.0 and all those that will be created in the future. Besides, an internationally accepted icon may serve the potential users to differentiate those websites where all the stored and accessible on-line information is transparent. This icon should be governed democratically by some institution or international association of software and/or informatics in order to avoid the umpteenth case of parochialism. Some constant control mechanism could be established and in the case of detection of falseness of the on-line information automatically the transparency icon of the information may be removed, without previous notice to the star enunciators. Simultaneously, from the legal point of view of on-line information, an international agency can be created where are listed those websites that constantly destroy the credibility and veracity of the information. Lastly

it is necessary to create international legislation which leaves without effect the copyrights of those contents in the websites which boost persuasion and manipulation of information. The final goal should be a complete listing or guidelines with examples of those public or private institutions dedicated to damaging the quality of software in the on-line and off-line interactive systems.

CONCLUSION

The parochialism, star enunciators and collaborators cannot distinguish between freedom and licentiousness. This is a serious problem for accessibility for all and free information on-line in the coming decades.

The current diacritical study in the design of on-line interactive systems has made it plain that the communicability is non-existent in those regions where parochialism is a daily practice. Moreover, 75% of the credibility problems of on-line information in Southern Europe is to be found in full swing in the mountain regions. Nowadays this phenomenon is camouflaged in the proliferation of the social networks. The users of the Internet have not only lost their bearings in those social networks –as a result of the high number that currently exist– but on top of that they are manipulated directly and indirectly by the star enunciators. The real problem is the spread of the destruction of the credibility of the information in the university environment. The members of the industrial and entrepreneurial sector also foster that decay as it has been seen in the shown examples. These examples depict an analysis carried out during the last 15 years, creating, testing and perfecting quality metrics aimed at the credibility of the software (a work that has not counted on any public or private subsidy in order to maintain the total neutrality of the obtained results). These metrics depict the intersection of software engineering and systems, usability engineering, human-computer interaction, statistics, linguistics,

semiotics, among other communication-aimed social sciences disciplines.

In the case of statistics, it has been seen how the star enunciators make excessive use of them in the websites but falsifying on-line information, in both the figures and graphics format. Descriptive statistics have been of the greatest help for the development of techniques and heuristic evaluation means in our case. It has also been verified how the essential notions of statistics are applied in the social sciences, especially those that collect and interpret the data gathered in the interaction with the users of interactive systems such as are interviews, questionnaires, remarks, etc. Many of these techniques have been adapted in usability engineering, in the early years of the nineties. Therefore, there is a continuous updating and adaptation of the knowledge among the sciences aimed at communicability. Therefore, the veracity of the information in a statistic format may not be 100% reliable in the Internet, even in the websites of public entities: universities, city councils, hospitals, schools, etc.

The traditional communication means in digital support have also been losing veracity in their contents, as compared with the analogical means of the last 25 years. However, the studies in the social sciences aimed at the mass or social communication media that have been carried out in the last decades and the main theoretical notions can be updated and adapted to the current communicability era. The goal is to have an excellent quality of the software in the on-line and off-line interactive systems in the next years. Obviously, these are tasks fitted for the communicability professionals.

REFERENCES

Aranguren, J. (1986). *La comunicación humana*. Madrid: Tecnos.

Basili, V., & Musa, J. (1991). The Future Engineering of Software: A Management Perspective. *IEEE Computer*, *24*(9), 90–96.

Berners-Lee, T. (1996). WWW: Past, Present and Future. *IEEE Computer*, *29*(10), 69–77.

Billinghurst, M., Grasset, R., & Looser, J. Designing Augmented Reality Interfaces. *Computer Graphics*, *39*(1), 17–21. doi:10.1145/1057792.1057803

Birwhistell, R. (1974). *Diccionario de las ciencias sociales*. Madrid: Aguilar.

Boyd-Barrett, O., & Rantanen, T. (1998). *The Globalization of News*. London: Sage.

Brown, G. (2008). *Social Media, Web 2.0 User-Generated Content and Virtual Communities –100 Most Asked Mass Collaboration Questions*. Brisbane, Australia: Emereo.

Brown, R. (1976). *Children and Television*. Beverly Hills, CA: Sage.

Cameron, K. (2009). The Road to Greener IT Pastures. *IEEE Computer*, *42*(5), 87–89.

Chavan, A. (2009). The Washing Machine That Ate My Sari-Mistakes in Cross Cultural Desing. *Communications of the ACM*, *16*(1), 26–31.

Chisolm, W., Vanderheiden, G., & Jacobs, I. (2001). Web Content Accessibility Guidelines. *Interaction*, *13*(4), 34–53.

Cipolla-Ficarra, F. (1997a). Evaluation of Multimedia Components. In *Proceedings IEEE* [Washington, DC: IEEE Computer Society.]. *Multimedia Systems*, *97*, 557–564.

Cipolla-Ficarra, F. (1997b). Method and Techniques for the Evaluation of Multimedia Applications. In *Proceedings HCI International '97*, (pp. 635-638). San Francisco: Elsevier.

Cipolla-Ficarra, F. (1999). MEHEM: A Methodology for Heuristic Evaluation in Multimedia. In *Proceedings Sixth International Conference on Distributed Multimedia Systems - DMS'99 (KSI), IFIP* (pp. 89-96). Aizu, Japan: Elsevier.

Cipolla-Ficarra, F. (2007). A Study of Acteme on Users Unexpert of Videogames. []. Berlin: Springer-Verlag.]. *Lecture Notes in Computer Science, 4553*, 215–224. doi:10.1007/978-3-540-73111-5_25

Cipolla-Ficarra, F. (2008a). Dyadic for Quality in Hypermedia Systems. In *DVD Proceedings Applied Human Factors and Ergonomics*. Las Vegas: AEI.

Cipolla-Ficarra, F. (2008b). HECHE: Heuristic Evaluation of Colours in HomepagE. In *DVD Proceedings Applied Human Factors and Ergonomics*. Las Vegas: AEI.

Cipolla-Ficarra, F. (2009). Persuasion On-Line and Communicability: The Destruction of Credibility in the Virtual Community and Cognitive Models. *Psychology of Persuasion*. New York: NovaPublishers.

Cipolla-Ficarra, F., & Cipolla-Ficarra, M. (2008). Multimedia, User-Centered Design and Tourism: Simplicity, Originality and Universality. *New Directions in Intelligent Interactive Multimedia* (pp. 461-470). Berlin: Springer-Verlag.

Cipolla-Ficarra, F., Vivas, E., & Romo, J. (2009). Credibility On-line: Quality Metrics for Evaluation. Online Communities. []. Berlin: Springer-Verlag.]. *Lecture Notes in Computer Science, 5621*, 172–181. doi:10.1007/978-3-642-02774-1_19

Colapietro, V. (1993). *Glossary of Semiotics*. New York: Paragon House.

Cutumisu, M. (2006). Generating Ambient Behaviors in Computer RolePlaying Games. *IEEE Intelligent Systems, 21*(5), 19–27. doi:10.1109/MIS.2006.92

Debray, R. (1995). *Vie et mort de l'image*. Paris: Gallimard.

Dileep, K., Yeonseung, R., & Hyksoo, J. (2008). Quality of Service (QoS) of Voice over MAC Protocol 802.11 using NS-2. In *Proc. MSCommunicability '08* (pp. 39-44). New York: ACM Press.

Dillard, J., & Pfau, M. (2002). *Persuasion Handbook*. Thousand Oaks: Sage.

Dubberly, H., Pangaro, P., & Haque, U. (2009). What is Interaction? Are There Different Types? *Interaction, 16*(1), 69–75. doi:10.1145/1456202.1456220

Eberts, R. (1992). *User Interface Design*. London: Pretince-Hall.

Fenton, N. (1994). Software Measurement: A Necessary Scientific Basis. *IEEE Transactions on Software Engineering, 20*(3), 199–206. doi:10.1109/32.268921

Fernandes, T. (1995). *Global Interface Design: A Guide to Designing International User Interfaces*. San Diego: Academic Press Professional.

Gray, J. (1996). Evolution of Data Management. *IEEE Computer, 29*(10), 47–58.

Hastings, R. (2009). *Web 1.0*. Retrieved July 19, 2009 from http://en.wikipedia.org/wiki/Web_1.0

Horn, R. (1989). *Mapping Hypertext*. Waltham: Lexington Press.

Kleinberg, J. (2008). The Convergence of Social and Technological Networks. *Communications of the ACM, 51*(11), 66–72. doi:10.1145/1400214.1400232

Kleinberg, J. (2008). The Convergence of Social and Technological Networks. *Communications of the ACM, 51*(11), 66–72. doi:10.1145/1400214.1400232

Lee, M., & Hsu, W. (2005). Improving data quality: eliminating dupes & I-D-ing those spurious links. *IEEE Potential*, *24*(2), 35–38. doi:10.1109/MP.2005.1462465

Light, A. (2004). Audience Design: Interacting with Networked Media. *Interaction*, *11*(2), 60–62. doi:10.1145/971258.971279

Marcus, A. (1993). Human Comunications Issues in Advanced UIs. *Communications of the ACM*, *36*(4), 101–109. doi:10.1145/255950.153670

Marcus, A., Gould. (2000). Crosscurrents –Cultural Dimensions and Global Web User-Interface Design. *Interaction*, *12*(4), 32–46. doi:10.1145/345190.345238

McFarland, D., & Wolpaw, J. (2008). Brain-Computer Interface Operation of Robotic and Prothetic Devices. *IEEE Computer*, *10*(4), 52–56.

McQuail, D. (2002). *Reader in Mass Communication Theory*. London: Sage.

McQuail, D. (2005). *Mass Communication Theory*. London: Sage.

Meleis, H. (1996). Toward the Information Network. *IEEE Computer*, *29*(10), 59–67.

Mitchell, W., & McCullough, M. (1995). *Digital Design Media*. New York: ITP.

Mulholland, J. (1994). *Handbook of Persuasive Tactics: A Handbook of Strategies for Influencing Others Through Communication*. London: Routledge.

Nielsen, J. (1990). *Hypertext and Hypermedia*. San Diego: Academic Press.

Nielsen, J. (1992). The Usability Engineering Life Cycle. *IEEE Computer*, *25*(3), 12–22.

Nielsen, J. (2001) *Coordinating User Interfaces for Consistency*. San Francisco: Morgan Kaufmann Publishers.

Nielsen, J., & del Galdo, E. (1996). *International User Interfaces*. New York: John Wiley & Sons.

Nöth, W. (1995). *Handbook of Semiotics*. Indianapolis: Indiana University Press.

Parkes, A., Poupyrev, I., & Ishii, H. (2008). Designing Kinetic Interactions for Organic User Interfaces. *Communications of the ACM*, *51*(6), 58–65. doi:10.1145/1349026.1349039

Pfleeger, S. (2008). Software Metrics: Progress after 25 Years. *IEEE Software*, *25*(6), 32–34. doi:10.1109/MS.2008.160

Preece, J. (1998). Empathic Communities: Reaching Out Across the Web. *Interaction*, *5*, 32–43. doi:10.1145/274430.274435

Reardon, K. (1981). *Persuasion. Theory and Context*. London: Sage.

Russo, P., & Boor, S. (1993). How Fluent is Your Interface? Designing for International Users. In *Proceedings INTERCHI '93*, (pp. 342-347). Amsterdam: ACM Press.

Saussure, F. (1990). *Course in General Linguistics*. New York: McGraw-Hill.

Sears, A. (2007). *The Human-Computer Interaction Handbook: Fundamentals, Envolving Technologies and Emerging Applications*. New York: LEA.

Shneiderman, B. (2005). *Designing the User Interface*. Reading, MA: Addision Wesley.

Tscheligi, M., & Reitberger, W. (2007). Persuasion as an Ingredient of Societal Interfaces. *Interaction*, *14*(5), 41–43. doi:10.1145/1288515.1288538

Weaver, A., & Morrison, B. (2008). Social Networking. *IEEE Computer*, *41*(2), 97–100.

Wilson, C. (2007). The Problem with Usability Problems: Context is Critical. *Interaction*, *14*(5), 46–47. doi:10.1145/1288515.1288542

Wimmer, R., & Dominick, J. (2006). *Mass Media Research: An Introduction*. Belmont, CA: Thompson-Wadsworth.

Zviran, M., Te'eni, D., & Gross, Y. (2006). Does Color in Email make a Difference? *Communications of the ACM, 49*(4), 94–99. doi:10.1145/1121949.1121954

KEY TERMS AND DEFINITIONS

Credibility: Are the objective and subjective components which define the ability to be believed of a source or a message. In the design of interactive systems it is basically related to the categories of the content and presentation, that is to say, the way of presenting the information in the user's interface.

Descriptive Statistics: These are part of mathematical statistics and serve for the numerical description of sets, being particularly useful when these possess many elements, evaluating mathematically and analyzing the collective depicted by the set without trying to obtain more generalized conclusions, which is the goal of statistical inference. That is to say, in each case some given characters of one or different collectives are going to be described and the relationships existing among them.

Diacritical: This is an adjective that refers to a diacritic sign, that is, a graphical sign that confers the written signs (not necessarily letters) a special value. It is a term that derives from the Greek *–diakritikós*, distinguishing.

Manipulation: From the psychological perspective and in the context of the interactive systems it is the behavior which goes against certain principles and ethical rules which lead the users of interactive systems to perform deeds which go against their will. In transparent communication this should be either absent or in its minimum levels.

Parochialism: This is a term stemming from the Alpine saussirian linguistics and serves to indicate those pressure groups which are made up by star enunciators and their collaborators. Today they have as a priority the destruction of credibility in the hypermedia and interactive information in the Internet, with the purpose of their personal and/or institutional image to the detriment of the rest of the virtual community.

Persuasion: It is an activity of demonstrating and trying to modify the behavior of at least one person through symbolic interaction. It entails an active means of influence which tries to lead the potential users towards the adoption of an attitude, an idea or a behavior through rational or emotive measures.

Virtual Community: Users who continuously participate in chats, videoconferences, etc. in the Internet or the Intranet with the purpose of establishing bidirectional interactive communication links among them.

Chapter 6
How to Develop Intelligent Agents in an Easy Way with FAIA

Jorge Roa
CIDISI-UTN-FRSF-CONICET, Argentina

Milton Pividori
CIDISI-UTN-FRSF-CONICET, Argentina

Ma. De los Milagros Gutiérrez
CIDISI-UTN-FRSF-CONICET, Argentina

Georgina Stegmayer
CIDISI-UTN-FRSF-CONICET, Argentina

ABSTRACT

In Artificial Intelligence courses, the development of intelligent agents is a common practical work. However, it is a programming extensive and consumed time practice that much of the time the student cannot solve in full and in time. In this work the authors present FAIA, a framework to develop intelligent agents giving a partially design solution. With FAIA the teacher and student will have benefits. On the one hand, it helps to guide in the correct design and learning process. On the other hand, it helps in the teaching and evaluation process.

MOTIVATIONS

After several years of teaching an Artificial Intelligence (AI) course, we have detected some problems in the teaching/learning methodology used. First of all, students know how to do programming in different languages and have different programming skills. Second, there is a short period of time to solve the practical work to pass the course and pitfalls in it can result in a low score, sometimes even in the student re-doing it. Third, the practical work needed for course approval, in order to be useful, must involve the development of an agent, its strategy to solve problems and the environment where the agent acts. Finally, evaluation of this practical work takes a lot of time, and at the same time it is difficult to qualify the student because of the variety of presented designs, the need to inspect the code and the different programming levels.

The most common mistakes committed by students are: (i) not separated responsibilities between

DOI: 10.4018/978-1-61520-763-3.ch006

agents and the environment, (ii) incorrect object-oriented design, (iii) lack of graphical representation for the results (i.e the solution of a search tree when the agent uses a search algorithm as a decision mechanism) and (iv) delay in the due date. Some of those mistakes are hard to eliminate, such as (i) and (ii), while (iii) takes lot of time, resulting in more delay in the work delivery.

In order to solve the mentioned problem we have designed a framework for AI agents (FAIA) that can be used by students for the practical work development, which pursues the following objectives:

- to provide a framework that can be instantiated in order to develop, in a easy and quickly way, an agent and its environment;
- to provide well defined agent and environment (or simulator) interfaces, where each interface properly describes the respective responsibilities;
- to provide well-defined interactions between an agent and its environment;
- to provide a well-designed and easy-to-understand architecture for intelligent agents development, such as a problem solving agent or a knowledge based agent;
- to allow modular agent development;
- to provide a guide in the agent knowledge base development;
- to provide the basic strategies for search, such as depth search, breadth search, best-first search, among others;
- to provide a simple graphical representation of a search tree;
- to provide teachers with a useful tool for fair evaluation of several possible solutions to a given practical problem.

CONTRIBUTIONS

During the last two years we have been working on the development of FAIA, with the objective in mind to offer a tool that could help students in the development of agents as well as professors in the evaluation of these agents.

FAIA was developed as a practical framework (Fayad & Johnson, 1999)(Johnson & Foote, 1988) that encloses the most important concepts of intelligent agents according to the traditional AI book of Russell & Norvig (2003). On the one hand, the provided partial design of an agent avoids pitfalls in the development of the practical work, and at the same time it is a kind of guide to students that directs the agent development in the correct way. On the other hand, the framework helps professors in the evaluation process, due to the fact that the object-oriented design is identical in all the solutions and they have to inspect if the interfaces are well implemented.

FAIA has been used during the first semester of 2008 in the AI course developed at Universidad Tecnológica Nacional - Regional Santa Fe - Argentina (UTN-FRSF)1, with successful results. While learning the framework requires extra time in the development of the practical work, its use reduces mistakes and necessary revisions, at the same time helping students: (i) to design the software solution, (ii) to select the strategy to be used, (iii) to understand the modular composition of an agent, (iv) to understand the interaction between agents and environment, (v) to finish the practical work on due time and in full, and finally (vi) to show the results in a suitable graphical way.

FAIA also helps professors: (a) to evaluate the results, (b) to base the evaluation on homogenous solution-design, (c) to evaluate the students in more complex problem cases and (d) to correct the practical work quickly. This framework is an important tool in the learning/teaching process for novice students who are learning about agents. It is a bridge from theoretical concepts to implementation design that makes it easier to pass from theory to the implementation in a programming language.

ORGANIZATION

This chapter is organized as follows. First, background and the relation between AI and games are presented, showing a review of the state-of-the-art and a comparison of FAIA with existing approaches. After that, the framework architecture is shown in detail, its components and the concepts involved in its design. Then, examples of FAIA instantiation with an agent that solves a search problem and an agent that uses situation calculus to decide its movements are explained and exemplified with real problems in detail. Finally, the conclusions and future work can be found.

BACKGROUND

Nowadays, teaching artificial intelligence in system engineering programs is a required subject. Undergraduate courses of AI cover a wide diversity of topics such as solving problems, knowledge representation, inference systems, agents, and others. The goals are analyzing the concept of intelligence in computer and studying the available techniques to implement intelligent behavior in machines. In order to reach these goals, the instructors propose problems that must be solved using intelligent agents that apply different problem-solving techniques, such as search, planning or situational calculus in order to decide what action to take.

The problems are presented to the students as programming projects, with the objective of evaluating the different course topics (the AI techniques). In order to develop the agents, students not only need knowledge about agents and their strategies but also good programming abilities are required. It is very common, however, that students know how to program in different languages and have different levels of programming skills. This is a problem when it is necessary to evaluate them. The instructor's and student's tasks can be simplified if all of the agents are developed using

a framework that provides a basic object-oriented design for agent development and the environment where it has to act. In this work we present FAIA, a framework that, on the one hand, helps students to develop an agent and its environment in an easy way, and on the other hand, it helps the teachers to evaluate student's results using a homogeneous design.

The AI course at UTN-FRSF is dictated in the senior year of an engineering degree in computer science. Different authors propose different definitions regarding what is an agent (Maes, 1995; Wooldridge, 2002). In this course, an agent is defined based on the main concepts of intelligent agents proposed by Russell & Norvig (2003) in their traditional AI book, where an agent is everything that can be considered perceiving its environment through sensors and responding or acting upon the environment through actuators.

An agent perceives its environment through sensors that let it know the universe or environment where it works, to decide what action to take, which will be executed by the actuators, changing the environment. The world in which the agent operates is an important element in its design, since it represents the problematic situation the agent must solve. The sensors are implemented in hardware when it is embedded in a physical environment (for example a video camera or temperature sensors) or it is simulated by software. The sensors output is a perception (for example an image or a temperature map), that is to say, information that the agent is interested in for carrying out its mission. On the other hand, the agent executes its actions on the environment, changing it. The agent designer has to define what those actions are and which effects they must have.

The work of the AI is to design the agent program. This is a function that implements the relationship between the agent's internal state and the perceptions and actions. It is assumed that this program will run on any computing device. Possible architectures for the agent program are really software architectures for decision-making

systems that are embedded in an environment. Not all agents are equal and the designer must select the most suitable architecture according to their design goals. The different agent architectures seen in class are: (i) simple reactive agent, (ii) reactive model-based agent, (iii) objective-based agent (iv) utility-based agent, and finally (v) agent that learns (Russell & Norvig, 2003).

According to this definition, the class instructors propose a programming project that consists in developing a software agent that must act (interact) in a certain environment (receiving perceptions and executing actions) in order to achieve its design goal. The agent must implement different problem-solving strategies according to the problems to be solved, or even for solutions comparison among several strategies. This way, it is necessary to develop an agent that can use search for action selection, while another agent may use situation calculus to solve the same problem. It should also be possible for the search-agent to change the search strategy dynamically according to the problem characteristics, in order to compare among different search strategies.

Moreover, it is desirable to be able to compare the performance of the two agents. This project requires time and high programming skills, because it consists not only in designing and implementing the agent with different decision-making strategies, but also in developing the environment simulator. The problem that arises in this context is that students do not have enough time to meet the goal. One of the causes is that they are learning what an agent is at the same time that they must implement it and, sometimes, poor understanding of the concepts requires the students to constantly re-build their solutions.

The framework that we propose in this work, FAIA, provides the necessary tools to solve the programming project with the desired characteristics. It has been developed using software development techniques. It guides the students in the design of an agent because it proposes a basic object-oriented structure that defines different types of agents, their decision-making strategies and the environment simulator. Students must instantiate the proposed abstract classes according to the problem-solving technique they want to implement. In this way, mistakes in the design can be reduced and revisions are diminished. As a consequence, students can develop in time and in full the project proposed by instructors.

Artificial Intelligence and Games

There is an important relationship between AI and games. Historically, games such as chess, backgammon, checkers, poker, and more recently Go, have provided challenge problems for AI researchers. It seems especially fitting then, to use games to teach students about aspects of intelligence and how it may be artificially simulated. The use of AI in games presents an opportunity for AI educators to motivate students to learn about AI technologies. They also introduce students to an important application area by designing learning experiences around the use of AI in these kinds of games (Hingston et al., 2006).

There have been reported in literature several examples of AI teaching with games. In (Chiang, 2007) a traditional maze game has been adapted to provide student learning motivation for case-based reasoning AI technique learning. In (Kim, 2006) a virtual agent platform is presented for teaching agent systems design through a tournament game. This work aims at teaching agents in the first year of a computer science career and, similarly to this approach (Pantic et al., 2005), the authors use this tool as part of a formal course and for students' evaluation.

This chapter describes a flexible method for teaching introductory artificial intelligence techniques using a novel, Java -implemented, simple agent framework developed specifically for the purposes of this course (Roa et al., 2008). Although numerous agent frameworks have been proposed in the vast body of literature, none of these available frameworks proved to be simple enough and

specifically oriented to teaching, and most of them are for multi-agents simulation. Hence, the authors set out to create a novel framework that would be suitable for the aims of the course, for the level of computing skills of the intended group of students, and for the size of this group of students. The content of the mentioned introductory AI course is a set of assignments that require the students to use intelligent agents and other AI techniques to play some toy-problems based on popular games (see application examples section)

In the case of the proposed framework FAIA, students develop programs for their controllers, implement the AI program and simultaneously view a result. Thus students can see and experience the results of their program on two levels: the programming in action and operationally as a finished product in the game. Students can then make changes to their original program based on observations of the result. They are engaged with the learning materials and in charge of the learning process. This learning-by-doing reflects real-world situations where products are created, tested, evaluated and improved (Hingston et al., 2006).

There are similar projects that offer strategies and data structures coded in Java, but they are not intended to be a guide to assist the student in the design of the agent but to facilitate implementation, offering reusable code. Instead, FAIA offers an integrated object-oriented design in Java. There are free-use available frameworks that allow the development of agents, such as Jade (Bellefemine et al., 2006), IBM Aglets (Aridor, 1998) and Zeus (Collis et al., 2000), but they are not oriented to students who are learning how to develop agents, instead, their target are experienced developers. Moreover, Jade is oriented to develop multiagent systems, Aglets is oriented to develop mobile-agents and Zeus is oriented to develop reactive-agents that use rules and messages. All of these specific characteristics add complexity at the moment of a single agent definition. Other examples that can be named are2: Agent Factory, AMETAS, Bee-

gent, Cougaar, DECAF, Grasshopper, Hive, Jack, JAFMAS, Kaariboga, LIME, Madkit, NOMADS, OpenCybele, SeMoA, Tryllian, Voyager, CIAgent (Bigus & Bigus, 2001), FIPA-OS3, Pathwalker4, Tagent5 and SAF (Pantic et al., 2006).

However, none of the available Java -based agent frameworks is simple enough to be used by undergraduate students and almost all of them have the following drawbacks: they are not oriented towards teaching, they lack readable documentation and good examples, if provided, they demand a time-consuming consultation of the documentation and finally they are not flexible enough to provide tools for different kinds of agents definition, that may move in different kinds of environments or worlds.

FAIA: FRAMEWORK FOR INTELLIGENT AI AGENTS

The FAIA framework realizes an agent general abstraction. The basic concept that has been represented in the proposed framework is the fact that an *agent* interacts with an *environment* through two relations: *perception*, which the environment gives to the agent in order to show some of its aspects; and *action*, which the agent executes on the environment in order to change it. Then, as it is well known, an agent has an *internal state* that typifies its knowledge about the environment, a *decision engine* that allows the agent to take an action in a given situation, and a *set of actions* that represents the procedures that the agent can perform. The environment is a model of a real world, which has a *state* that represents relevant information about the world and the behavior that represents the environment simulator able of interpreting the agent actions. Based on these definitions, the FAIA architecture shown in figure 1 has been proposed.

This architecture has to be useful in order to develop the different type of agents taught in the AI course. The state representation and the

Figure 1. FAIA architecture

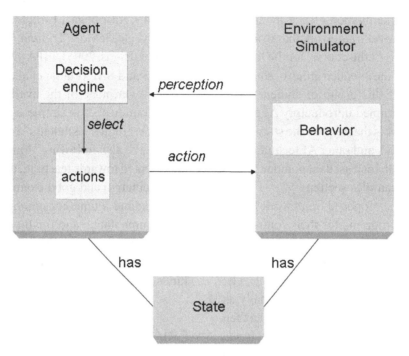

mechanism to take the decision must be flexible enough to change the decision engine and the state representation without altering the interaction with the environment. Consequently, for a given example, it is possible to reuse the simulation environment with different agent definitions, thanks to the properly defined interface between environment and agent.

As regards agent state, it has been considered that it can be represented through different data structures such as lists, arrays, a matrix, vectors, a stack, graphs, pairs and queues, among others. In this first release of the framework, the decision engine can use one of two strategies: search and situation calculus inference (other strategies would be added to the framework as future work). The use of the first strategy for decision making gives as a result a **search-based** Agent, a type of agents known as **Problem-solving** agents because the search strategy uses the **Problem** concept. The use of the second strategy for deciding gives as a result a **knowledge-based** Agent. Both kinds of agents are in the category of **goal-based** Agents.

The FAIA architecture has three main components: *Environment simulator*, *Agent* and *State*. The first component, *Environment simulator*, represents the model of the real world and its behavior, that is to say, the world model and the simulator that mimics it. Then, the *Agent* component represents the agent with its decision engine and its actions. The relations between these components are: *perception* that the environment gives to the agent representing the things that the agent can see in the environment; and *action* that the agent performs on the environment to alter its state. Both components have a *state*. The state component contains the different possible data structures needed to represent an internal version of the real world and the agent internal state too. This architecture has been implemented with the class diagram shown in figure 2. The clear separation between *agent* and *environment simulator* avoids one of the most common mistakes that students make: to mix agent state with environment state, giving as a result a decision making process based on the environment information

Figure 2. Class diagram of the FAIA framework

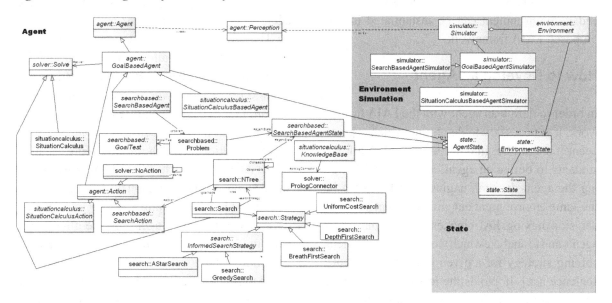

instead of the internal agent knowledge about the environment. FAIA is a guide for students, who are implementing their first agent. FAIA provides an agent object-oriented design that students have to understand and extend according to give a solution for the proposed problem.

On the one hand, in order to solve a problem using a *goal-based agent*, students must define: (i) *state* as a data structure, (ii) *actions* as methods that the agent can execute on its state and the environment can interpret in the correct way; (iii) *goal*, as a set of desired states; and (iv) *strategy*: representing one of the search strategies taught in class (breadth-first, depth-first, greedy search, A*, among others). In this case, the agent decision process implies the development of a *search tree* that represents the reasoning mechanism. FAIA provides a tree object-oriented design and its representation in *pdf* format. Students only need to define the search operators, the search goal, the search state and the search initial state properly. FAIA provides the general search algorithm and some basic implementations of uninformed strategies (such as depth-first). Other algorithms should be programmed by the students (for example for

informed strategies or more efficient algorithm for uninformed search).

On the other hand, to solve a problem using a *knowledge-based agent*, students must define: (i) a *knowledge base (KB)* as a set of logical sentences that represent the agent state; (ii) *diagnostic rules* to infer knowledge about the environment according to perceptions; (iii) *causal rules* represented by logical rules to infer knowledge about future perceptions or hidden world properties based on the actual state; (iv) *actions*, as logical sentences that modify the agent state; (v) *successor state axioms* that define the next state given that an action has occurred; and finally an (vi) *action ranking*, representing which actions are better than others to be performed in a given situation.

In other words, FAIA allows students to define an agent, and permits changing the agent decision engine in order to act in the same environment but with different strategy decision making. FAIA makes it easy to play with agents and to analyze which would be the best problem solving strategy for a given problem. It avoids the loss of information, and time-consuming revisions, minimizing the effort needed to build intelligent agents.

The next two sections describe how an agent and its environment can be instantiated in the proposed FAIA framework.

How to Develop an Agent

In order to define an agent with the FAIA framework, it is necessary to determine which type of agent it should be. In other words, FAIA allows students to define an agent, and permits changing the agent decision engine in order to act in the same environment but with different strategy decision making. FAIA makes it easy to play with agents and to analyze which would be best problem solving strategy for a given problem [duplicate sentence s.a.]. It avoids the loss of information, and time-consuming revisions, minimizing the effort needed to build intelligent agents. [duplicate sentence, s.a.]. Based on this decision, an instance of *SearchBasedAgent* or *SituationCalculusBasedAgent* should be created, both subclasses of the *GoalBasedAgent* class. After that, the state, actions, perceptions and the decision engine must be defined according to the selected agent type. Figure 3 shows a partial view of the FAIA class diagram, with the focus on the agent definition. The hierarchy on the left shows the type of agent. *Agent* is specialized in *GoalBasedAgent* representing an agent that defines a goal to guide its actions. This type of agent is specialized in two subtypes: *SearchBasedAgent* and *SituationCalculusBasedAgent*. On the right of the figure the classes related with the agent definition are associated with *Agent* and *GoalBasedAgent* classes. Then, *Perception*, *Action*, *Solve* and *AgentState* represent the perception, the action, the decision engine and the state of the agent that are necessary in order to create an Agent.

The *Solve* class represents the decision engine, that it to say, the method used to select the action in a given situation. As we have previously mentioned, it is possible to use search or situation calculus as decision strategy. The *State* and *Action* definitions involve the representation of the agent world and the possible actions that the agent can perform on it.

The proposed approach to generate an agent using the framework allows students to identify each part of an agent and represent it in a different module. For instance, when students have to define *Action*, they must concentrate their attention on which actions the agent can execute and in which way these actions affect the internal representation of the agent world. The agent appears split into smaller units, giving as a result two important facts: on the one hand, each unit is easier to solve and define than the whole agent; on the other hand, each unit is related to one another and students can understand how each part works together in order to realize the desired agent behavior. The proposed class design allows students to understand the different possible ways of representing the state, the action, the perception and the engine according to the agent type. Students can abstract the agent representation without taking into account the environment implementation, the only thing that they must consider, is the perception, which represents the part of the environment that the agent can see.

When a **search-based** agent is selected to instantiate, it is necessary to: (i) define the search problem, (ii) define the goal and (iii) select the search strategy. As defined in Russell & Norvig (2003): a search problem consists of a goal-test, a state and a set of operation which can be executed on the state. Therefore, in FAIA, it is possible to represent a problem following the definition given above. FAIA provides a set of algorithms implementing the most popular search strategies: Depth first search, Breadth first search, Uniform cost search, greedy search and A*. Figure 4 shows the class diagram that involves the search-based agent definition. In the figure, the class *Search* has a *Strategy* associated, which is in term specialized in different strategies. This design realizes the Strategy design pattern (Gamma & Vlissides, 1995; Pree, 1996) that defines a family of algorithms. Its design lets the algorithm vary

Figure 3. Class diagram of the Agent point of view

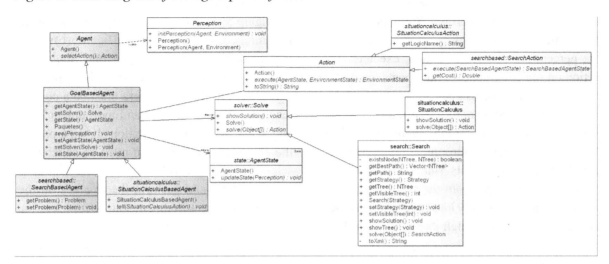

independently from the client that uses it. Consequently, it makes it easy to change the strategy with which to perform a search.

The *NTree* class depicts the tree search and shows the steps followed by the agent in order to decide which action to perform. This tree has a graphical representation in a .PDF file that can be used by students to control the proper functioning of their solution and by teachers in order to check the practical work and detect possible implementation mistakes.

How to Develop the Environment

Once the agent has been defined, the environment and its simulation must be also defined. The *Environment* has a state associated that represents the model of the real world. The *Simulator* represents

Figure 4. Class diagram of search strategies

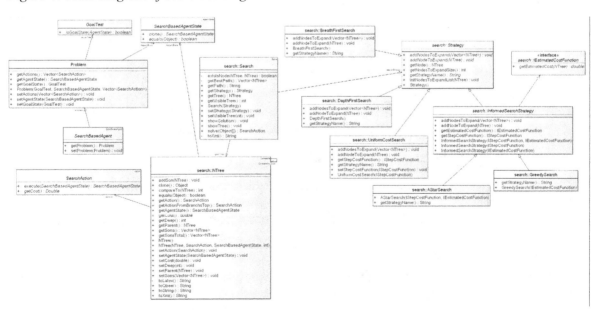

the behaviour of the environment and emulates the way that an agent acts on it. Simulator implements the simulation cycle where the agent gets the perception, decides an action, executes the action on the environment and repeats the cycle until the agent meets its goal.

The representation of the environment and its simulator is separated from the agent representation. The state of the environment represents the world where the agent acts. But it is important to differentiate this state from the agent state. The agent does not necessarily know the whole world, but only a part of it through its perceptions. The

FAIA framework highlights this difference.

Figure 5(a) shows the class diagram focus on Environment representation, and figure 5(b) shows the interaction between *Agent* and *Simulator*. The *Simulator* class is in charge of creating the perception. In this case, there must be a consistence representation between Environment State and agent State. The perception shows a part of the environment. The agent must be capable of selecting an action within it, which the simulator must interpret and perform the changes on the corresponding environment state.

Figure 5. (a) Environment class diagram (b) Environment- Agent interaction

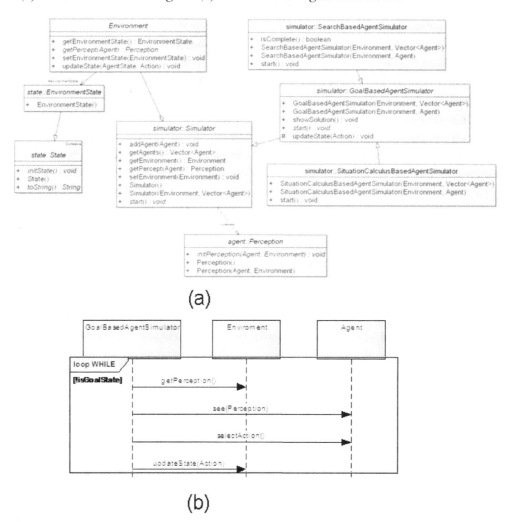

FAIA APPLICATION EXAMPLES

This section presents two application examples of the proposed framework FAIA to typical AI problems. The first part of the section presents a problem that must be solved using some search strategy. The second part of the section presents a problem that can be modeled using first order logics and situation calculus.

Using FAIA for a Search Problem: the Pac-Man World

The original *Pac-Man* game6 consists in a maze game where the player should guide a yellow PacMan through the maze, eating the dots and prizes while avoiding to be eaten by some enemies. A simplified version of the original game is proposed to the students, where a PacMan-agent must survive in a 4 by 4 cell-world, eating food and avoiding or eliminating its enemies.

The agent has initially some energy, which can be increased by eating fruits (randomly distributed over the world), can be diminished by fighting against the enemy ghosts. There are four different possible directions to move the PacMan (up-down-left-right).

The agent does not initially know its world, but is provided with sensors that give it the following information: an energy counter, which indicates its actual energy level (if equal to zero, the agent has died); and neighbourhood cells sensors that indicate whether each of the nearby cells has fruit or enemy or is empty. At each simulation cycle, the environment (the Pacman world) provides the agent with perceptions regarding the information for the sensors, and the agent replies with a selected action. The action selection or decision mechanism must be implemented by using informed or uninformed search strategies. The possible actions for the agent are: moving towards a nearby cell, fighting or eating.

The next subsections will show how this problem can be modelled according to the AI concepts presented in the first part of the chapter and solved with a search strategy, by using FAIA.

Defining the Agent State

Figure 6(a) shows the framework classes that must be extended for the representation of the agent and environment state. *SearchBasedAgentState* class is an abstract class defined in the framework. This class has methods to update the agent's internal state according to the perceptions received from the environment. To accomplish this, the *PacmanState* class is defined by extending from this class, which is used by the agent to represent its state. This class is defined with data structures already proposed by the framework and has two attributes: the first one is a matrix that represents the maze where each cell has a value to indicate whether the cell is empty, has an enemy or food. The second attribute is a pair that represents the agent position into the board. This position is identified with coordinates (x,y) (file,column).

Besides these attributes the abstract method *updateState(Perception p)* inherited from the *AgentState* class must be implemented. With this method the agent updates its internal state when new perceptions are received from the environment. The correct implementation of this method is a critical issue in order to obtain a correctly performing agent.

In order to allow the simulator updating the environment state according to the actions executed by the agent, it is necessary to define the environment state. To accomplish this, the *PacmanEnvironmentState* class is defined as subclass of *EnvironmentState*, which is used by the environment to represent its state. This class has been defined with a data structure proposed in the framework in this case only one attribute is necessary, the matrix that represents the maze.

Figure 6. Framework classes

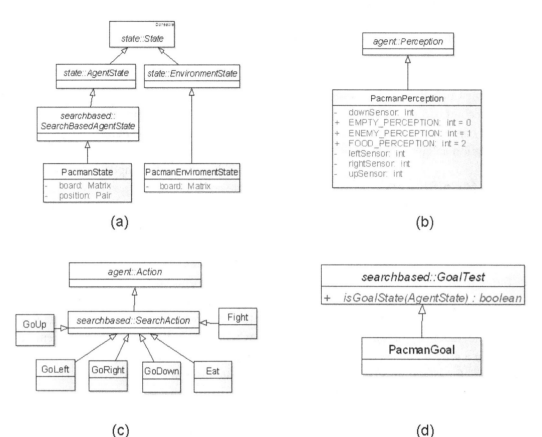

Defining the Agent Perceptions

Figure 6(b) shows the framework classes that must be extended to define the perceptions that the environment sends to the agent. Through these perceptions the agent knows how to update its internal state.

The *PacmanPerception* is a subclass of *Perception*. It has a set of attributes and constants to represent the agent sensors and their possible values. In order to represent the states that a sensor can comprise, three constants are set: FOOD_PERCEPTION to represent that a cell might have food, ENEMY_PERCEPTION to represent that a cell might have an enemy and EMPTY_PERCEPTION to represent an empty cell. All of this information is stored in the sen-

sor attributes. For this purpose four sensors are defined, one for each cell adjacent to the actual Pac-Man position (up, left, right and down). Each sensor can have one of the values defined in the constants mentioned before.

In order to allow the initialization of the perception, the implementation of the *initPerception(Agent, Environment)* abstract method, inherited from the *Perception* class, is needed. This method must set the four sensors defined in the *PacmanPerception* class with the correct information obtained from the environment. With this method the simulator uses the agent and the environment to initialize a new perception for the agent.

Defining the Agent Operators

Figure 6(c) shows the framework class that must be extended to define the agent operators (the possible actions is may execute). *SearchAction* is an abstract class that must be extended to define the operations or actions that the agent might execute on the environment.

The possible actions for the PacMan agent are six: *GoUp, GoLeft, GoRight, GoDown, Eat* and *Fight*. For each action, a new class must be defined. This way, it is easier to add a new action to the agent without worrying about modifying the simulator. In order to update the agent state after its effective execution, each of these classes must implement the abstract method *execute(AgentState, EnvironmentState)*, where the state change produced by the execution of the actions must be coded.

Defining the Goal

Figure 6(d) shows the framework class that must be extended to define the agent goal. *Pacman-Goal* extends the abstract class *GoalTest* and it represents the goal test used by the Pac-Man agent to know whether it has reached its design objective or not.

In order to determine if the agent has reached the goal state, the abstract method *isGoalState()* must be implemented on this class. For the given example, it is considered that the agent goal is to eat all of the food in the environment. This implies that the agent shall know (perceive or visit) the entire environment to determine if the objective has been reached or not.

Defining the Agent and Selecting its Strategy

In order to define the agent, the *PacmanAgent* class must be extended from the abstract class *SearchBasedAgent*. To let the Pac-Man agent reach its goal, the problem to be solved must be set. To achieve this, a new *Problem* is associated to the *PacmanAgent* in the constructor. This problem must be composed by the goal, agent state, and agent operators defined in previous sections. Next there is a Java code extract from the Pac-Man example that shows how to set a new problem to an agent:

```
// Pac-Man goal instantiation.
PacmanGoal goal = new Pacman-
Goal();
// Pac-Man initial agent state.
PacmanState state = new Pacman-
State();
this.setAgentState(state);
// Pac-Man operators instantia-
tion.
Vector<SearchAction> operators =
new Vector<SearchAction>();
operators.addElement(new Eat());
operators.addElement(new
Fight());
operators.addElement(new
GoLeft());
operators.addElement(new
GoUp());
operators.addElement(new
GoRight());
operators.addElement(new
GoDown());
// Problem initialization.
PacmanState agentState = (Pacm-
anState) this.getAgentState();
Problem problem = new
Problem(goal, agentState, opera-
tors);
agent.setProblem(problem);
```

$$(1)$$

However, in order to solve this problem, the agent needs a strategy. An instance of the *Search* class indicating the strategy must be generated to make use of the strategies provided by the frame-

work. Uniform cost is the strategy selected for the Pac-Man agent where *g* is equal to the *number of visited cells*. In this way, the strategy allows the agent to save energy by executing the lower amount of possible movements.

For the agent to work properly, the *PacmanAgent* class must implement the abstract method *selectAction()*. This method is invoked by the simulator and uses the problem and the strategy defined before to select the proper action to be taken by the agent. After that, this action is returned to the simulator so that it can continue with its execution. Also, *see(Perception p)* method needs to be implemented. It is responsible of updating the agent's internal state with new perceptions received from the environment.

Obtaining the Search Tree

FAIA allows the generation of search trees that the agent uses in the decision process. *NTree* class has defined a method to store the search tree in a XML[7] file. In this way, the XML standard is used to generate search tree views. With this tree in XML format students can make the depuration process in an easy way and also teachers may have a painless correction process. As an example, the following code has been extracted from a XML search tree file:

```
<NTree>
<Node
id="0"
execution_order="1"
action="null"
position="(3,3)"
visited_cells="1">
order:1 pos:1,1 act:null visit-
ed_cells=1
<Node>
...
    <Node>
    ...
```

```
  </Node>
  </Node>
</Node>
</NTree>
```

The tree shows the root node. The action attribute determines the action that originated the node. In this case this action is null because it is the root node. Initial position is on coordinates (3,3) and the amount of visited cells is one (the initial). Suspension points indicate the presence of more nodes inside the tree that are not shown due to space restrictions.

The other option to generate the search tree is to use a .PDF file. FAIA provides a graphical representation of the tree. Nodes are represented by rectangles with information regarding the node state. Nodes are related to their parents by rectilinear lines. With the help of this simple graphical representation students can make the depuration process in an easy way and also teachers may have a painless correction process.

Using FAIA with Situation Calculus: the Wumpus World Problem

The Wumpus world problem[8] is a very simple game devised to help teaching the concept of intelligent agents in artificial intelligence. This is the world description from Russell & Norvig, 2003:

The wumpus world is a cave consisting of rooms connected by passageways. Lurking somewhere in the cave is the wumpus, a beast that eats anyone who enters its room. The wumpus can be shot by an agent, but the agent has only one arrow. Some rooms contain bottomless pits that will trap anyone who wanders into these rooms (except for the wumpus, which is too big to fall in). The only mitigating feature of living in this environment is the possibility of finding a heap of gold.

The agent has five sensors, each of which gives a single bit of information:

- *In the square containing the wumpus and in the directly (not diagonally) adjacent squares the agent will perceive a stench.*
- *In the squares directly adjacent to a pit, the agent will perceive a breeze.*
- *In the square where the gold is, the agent will perceive a glitter.*
- *When an agent walks into a wall, it will perceive a bump.*
- *When the wumpus is killed, it emits a woeful scream that can be perceived anywhere in the cave.*

In the classic Wumpus world, the "player" is an artificially intelligent computer program which must make some very important decisions. It must travel through a darkened cave, try to find the hidden gold, and escape back outside without falling into a bottomless pit or being devoured by the repulsive Wumpus, a hungry monster that eats any living thing it comes across. The wumpus world has been considered a good example to show FAIA capabilities on situation calculus.

Approach

The procedure to implement a situation calculus based agent with FAIA is similar to the one described in the previous section, the Pac-Man example. The main difference here is that SWI-Prolog must be used for the agent design and implementation. Some Java code is necessary to implement a simulator and to connect it with the logic agent written in Prolog. This connection is possible thanks to the JPL library[9], which provides an interface between Java and Prolog that can be used to embed a Prolog program within a Java one.

FAIA is independent of the agent design. The user has only a few rules to follow. In the Java program, some abstract classes must be implemented, which will give the simulator information about the main predicates, for example the ones to get the next best action chosen by the agent.

Agent Design and Implementation in Prolog

A file called *wumpus_world.pl* is created to write the agent logic in Prolog, which will contain the diagnostic rules, causal rules, successor-state axioms, actions evaluation and other important definitions necessary for choosing the best action given the current information about the world.

Perceptions

The agent receives from the environment a perception vector which is represented by the logic sentence *Percept*, with five elements, depending on the current state of the square at which the agent is. For example, the following sentence shows the perception vector:

```
Percept ([Stench, Breeze, Glit-
ter, Bump, Scream],5)        (2)
```

This data implies certain facts about the current state. For example, the sentence 2 indicates a breezy square (among other facts), which is represented with the following logic sentence:

```
breeze(P,S):-
 percept([_,breeze,_,_,_],S),
 position(P,S).            (3)
```

The S variable indicates the situation at which the perception has occurred.

Diagnostic Rules

Diagnostic rules lead from observed effects to hidden causes. For example, if a square is breezy, some adjacent square must contain a pit. Prolog code below can be used to infer this knowledge:

```
belief(pit,Pa,S):-
 breeze(P,S),
```

```
adjacent(P,Pa).              (4)
```

If the agent perceives nothing in the square, then this and the adjacent ones are safe places to go to as shown in the following sentences:

```
safe(P,S):-
 at(nothing,P,S).           (5)
safe(Pa,S):-
 at(nothing,P,S),
 adjacent(P,Pa,S).          (6)
```

Successor-State Axioms

Successor-state axioms have the following form (Russell & Norvig, 2003):

Action is possible ⇒
(Fluent is true in result state ⇔
Action effect made it true ∨ It was true before and action left it alone)

$$(7)$$

For example, the following successor-state axiom for the agent position says that the agent is at P after executing the *go* action—either if the action is possible and consists of moving from X to P—or if the agent was already at P and the action is not to *go* to somewhere else.

$$position(P,result(action,S)) \Leftrightarrow$$
$$action = go(X,P)$$
$$\lor(position(P,S),action \neq go(P,Z)) \quad (8)$$

For the example in (sentence 8) the successor-state axioms should be written in Prolog as is shown in the following sentences:

```
ssa(S1):-
 S is S1-1,
 action(go(X,Y),S),
 asserta(position(Y,S1)).   (9)
ssa(S1):-
```

```
 S is S1-1,
 position(X,S),
 action(A,S),
 A=\=go(X,Y),
 asserta(position(X,S1)).   (10)
```

The *KnowledgeBase* class from the framework is responsible for finding all solutions for the "ssa" predicate. In this way, knowledge is copied from the situation S to the new situation S1 *if and only if* the last action effect made it true *or* if it was true before and action left it alone. In the example above, the only action capable of changing the position of the agent is *go*. Without this "copying operation" Prolog execution might be very slow.

Actions Evaluation

The agent needs to know how to choose the best action in the known current state. If it is holding the gold (sentence 11), then it has reached its goal—note that the action returned in this case is "noAction". If not, there are "excellent" and "very good" actions (sentences 12 and 13), but others can be "risky" (sentence 14). The agent will always try to perform the former ones, but if this is not possible, it will be willing to risk his life to find the gold:

```
bestAction(noAction,S):-
holding(gold,S).            (11)
```

```
bestAction(A,S):- excelent(A,S).
                            (12)
```

```
bestAction(A,S):- veryGood(A,S).
                            (13)
```

```
bestAction(A,S):- risky(A,S).
                            (14)
```

As said before, the agent always wants to perform, if possible, those actions evaluated as "excellent". For example, if a glitter is perceived, *grabbing* the gold is an excellent action (sentence 15).

```
excelent(grab,S):-
 position(P,S),
 glitter(P,S).          (15)
```

If there are no excellent actions, it will choose a "very good" one. For example, if some adjacent square is safe for the agent to move into and this is an unknown place, then a very good action is to *go* there (sentence 16).

```
veryGood(go(X,Y),S):-
position(X,S),
adjacent(X,Y),
unknown(Y,S),
safe(Y,S).             (16)
```

If the agent cannot find an excellent or very good action, it will take a risk choosing a "risky" action, like going to an unsafe place, where the wumpus may live (sentence 17).

```
risky(go(X,Y),S):-
position(X,S),
adjacent(X,Y),
belief(wumpus,Y,S).    (17)
```

Connecting the Simulator and the Agent

Once the logic agent is ready, it is necessary to write some Java code in order to connect the simulator with it. Some abstract classes provided by the framework must be implemented.

WumpusAgentState class

The WumpusAgentState class inherits from the abstract *KnowledgeBase* class. It is important to notice that all the agent knowledge is stored in the Prolog program. The only purpose of this class is enabling communication between the real state of the agent depicted in the Prolog program and the Java environment where the simulation is running. In this way, this class makes it possible to add new information to the knowledge base and make queries against it.

As said before, the simulator needs to know some things about the logic agent, for example, the name of the predicate to ask for the best action. So the method *getBestActionPredicate()* will return the string "bestAction".

As explained for the Pac-Man example, the simulator will send perceptions to the agent. The agent will add this new information to its knowledge base. To achieve this, the method *updateState(Perception perception)* must be implemented:

```
public void
updateState(Perception
perception) { this.
tell(perception); }      (18)
```

The source code shown above is very simple. This abstract method has the purpose of showing the student that here we are adding new information to the knowledge base. *tell(Perception perception)* method resides on the *KnowledgeBase* class. It adds to the agent knowledge base a new perception sent by the simulator.

The *tell(Perception perception)* method resides on the *KnowledgeBase* class. It adds to the agent knowledge base a new *Percept* predicate sent by the simulator.

The *WumpusAgentState* class can have other useful methods, for example:

```
public int[] getPosition() {
 String positionQuery =
"position([X,Y]," +
this.getSituation() + ")";
 Hashtable[] pos = this.
query(positionQuery);
 int x = Integer.
parseInt(pos[0].get("X").to-
String());
 int y = Integer.
parseInt(pos[0].get("Y").to-
String());
 return new int[]{x, y};
}                              (19)
```

getPosition() asks the knowledge base for the current position. It creates a string with the query to send to the knowledge base by the method *query(String query),* which is defined in the parent class *KnowledgeBase.* It hides the underlying complexity of communicating a Java program with a Prolog one, providing several other methods as useful as *query(String query).*

WumpusAgent Class

The *WumpusAgent* class inherits from the abstract *SituationCalculusBasedAgent* class. Methods that need to be implemented are almost the same that were shown in the Pac-Man example. Some are specific to this new strategy: *tell(SituationCalculusAction action)* is called by the simulator with an action the agent must add to its knowledge base, as a previously executed action. On the *selectAction()* function it is only necessary to change the solver by a *Situation-Calculus* one.

SituationCalculusAction Class

SituationCalculusAction inherits from the *Action* class. Both are provided by the framework. It is necessary to create one class per action defined in Prolog, for example *Grab, Shoot, Forward*

among others. Each one of them must implement two methods: (i) *execute(AgentState ast, EnvironmentState est)* is used by the simulator to modify the real world, (ii) *toString()* must return the action name exactly as it was defined in Prolog.

WumpusWorldEnvironment, WumpusWorldState and WumpusPerception Classes

The *WumpusPerception* class inherits from the abstract *Perception* class. It must override the *toString()* method, returning a string representation of the perception, such as it is shown on sentence 2.

Both classes, *WumpusWorldEnvironment* and *WumpusWorldState,* inherit from *Environment* and *EnvironmentState* respectively, and must implement the same methods explained in the Pac-Man example. This means it is possible to use other types of agents for the wumpus world—a Planning based one for example—and reuse all the written environment code. They are independent of the agent implementation.

WumpusActionFactory Class

The *WumpusActionFactory* class inherits from the abstract *ActionFactory* class. When the simulator asks the agent for the best action, it receives a string representation, but it needs a *SituationCalculusAction* object. The purpose of this class is to translate from string representation of actions to *SituationCalculusAction* objects.

The abstract *KnowledgeBase* class needs the *getActionFactory()* method to be implemented, returning an *ActionFactory* object. This implementation is defined in the previously mentioned *WumpusAgentState* class.

The *WumpusActionFactory* has two methods: *endActionString()* and *stringToAction(String),* which are shown in the following lines.

```
protected String endAction-
String() {
 return "noAction";
}                               (20)
```

```
protected Action
stringToAction(String stringAc-
tion) {
 Action actionObject = null;
 if (stringAction.
equals("climb")) {
 actionObject = new Climb();
 } else if (stringAction.
equals("forward")) {
 actionObject = new Forward();
 } else if (stringAction.
equals("grab")) {
 actionObject = new Grab();
 } else if (stringAction.
equals("shoot")) {
 actionObject = new Shoot();
 } else if (stringAction.
equals("turnleft")) {
 actionObject = new TurnLeft();
 } else if (stringAction.
equals("turnright")) {
 actionObject = new TurnRight();
 }
 return actionObject;
}                               (21)
```

As explained in (20) and (21), the *stringToAction(String stringAction)* method creates a *SituationCalculusAction* object from the string that represents the action. The *endActionString()* must return the name of the constant that indicates the agent reached the goal. In this case, the return action is "noAction" (see sentence 11).

CONCLUSION AND FUTURE WORK

This chapter has presented the FAIA framework, aimed at helping students in the resolution of academic problems related to Artificial Intelligence techniques teaching in an Engineering career. Two examples have been explained for the resolution of two practical problems to illustrate the framework use.

The main advantages of the proposal are the following:

- It is a theoretical and practical guide that directs students to create, without error, the elements that form an AI agent;
- The clear separation between *agent* and *environment simulator* provided by FAIA helps students avoiding one of the most common mistakes: mixing agent state with environment state, giving as a result a wrong decision making process;
- The application of the strategy design pattern allows changing a strategy dynamically, which may help understanding and comparison among them;
- It is possible to visualize the different search trees generated during the process of reaching the agent objective, in a standard XML format, which allows the student to better understand that process;
- It is also possible to produce a graphical representation of the search trees in a .PDF file that is used by students to control the proper functioning of their solution and by teachers in order to check the practical work and detect possible implementation mistakes;
- The framework hides the underlying complexity for defining a situation calculus based agent in Prolog.
- Finally, FAIA may be a useful tool for teachers-work in class, because it is possible to generate search trees dynamically

and show how they are being generated according to the different strategies.

As future work, we plan to incorporate more features to FAIA that will enable a goal-based agent to solve problems with other AI techniques, such as planning.

REFERENCES

Aridor, Y., & Lange, D. (1998). Agent Design Patterns: Elements of Agent Applications Design. In *Proc. Second Int. Conf. Autonomous Agents,* (pp. 108-115).

Bellifemine, F., Caire, G., & Greenwood, D. (2006). *Developing Multi-Agent Systems with JADE,* (Ed.). New York: Wiley & sons.

Bigus, J. P., & Bigus, J. (2001) *Constructing Intelligent Agents Using Java.* New York: Wiley.

Chiang, A. (2007). Motivate AI class with interactive computer game. In *Proc. of IEEE Int. Workshop on Digital Game and Intelligent Toy Enhanced Learning, 1*(1).

Collis, J. Ndumu, D. & van Buskirk, C. (2000) The Zeus. *Agent Building Toolkit – ZEUS Methodology Documentation.* Retrieved from http://labs.bt.com/projects/agents/zeus

Fayad, M. E., & Johnson, R. E. (1999). Domain-Specific application Frameworks. *Frameworks experience by Industry.* New York: John Wiley & Sons, Inc.

Gamma, R., & Vlissides, J. (1995). *Design Patterns: Elements of Reusable Object-Oriented Software,* (Ed.). Boston: Addison-Wesley Professional Computing Series.

Hingston, P., Combes, B. & Masek, M. (2006). Teaching an undergraduate AI course with games and simulation. *LNCS 3942,* (vol. 1, pp. 494-506).

Johnson, R., & Foote, B. (1988). Designing Reusable Classes. *Journal of Object-Oriented Programming, 1*(2), 22–35.

Kim, I.C. (2006). 3D interactive computer games as a pedagogical tool. *LNCS 4270,* (Vol. 1, pp. 536-544)

Maes, P. (1995). Intelligent Software. *Scientific American, 273*(3), 84–86.

Pantic, M., Zwitserloot, R., & Grootjans, R. J. (2005). Teaching introductory artificial intelligence using a simple agent framework. *IEEE Transactions on Education, 48*(3), 382–390. doi:10.1109/TE.2004.842906

Pree, W. (1996) *Patterns.* Sigs books and multimedia, New Cork.

Roa, J., Gutierrez, M., & Stegmayer, G. (2008). FAIA: Framework para la enseñanza de agentes en IA. *IE Comunicaciones: Revista Iberoamericana de Informática Educativa, 1*(7), 1–10.

Russell, S., & Norvig, P. (2003). *Artficial Intelligence: A Modern Approach,* (2nd Ed.). New York: Prentice-Hall.

Wooldridge, M. (2002). *Introduction to Multiagent Systems.* New York: John Wiley & Sons.

KEY TERMS AND DEFINITIONS

Decision-Making System: It is a process that allows leading to the selection of a course of action among several alternatives. Every decision-making process produces a final choice, which can be an action or an opinion of choice.

Design Pattern: A general reusable solution to a commonly occurring problem in software design. It is not a finished design but also it is a template for how to solve a problem that can be used in many different situations.

FAIA: Framework for Artificial Intelligent Agents

Framework: A set of classes that embodies an abstract design for solutions to a family of related problems.

Planning: A problem-solving technique which task is to find some composition of operatiors that transforms a given initial world model into one that satisfied some state goal condition.

Search: A problem-solving technique that systematically explores a space of problem states in order to find a solution to a given problem. Search is a process of formulating and examining alternatives.

Situation Calculus: A formalism for representing and reasoning about dynamical domains. In this context, a *situation* is a finite sequence of action, in other words, it is a history.

Software Architecture: The structure of a system, which comprise a set of computational *components* and the description of the relationship between them, know as *connectors*.

ENDNOTES

[1]   http://www.frsf.utn.edu.ar/matero/visitante/index.php?id catedra=142

[2]   AgentLink. Agent Software: http://www.agentlink.org/resources/agent-software.php

[3]   FIPA–OS Agent Toolkit: http://www.emorphia.com/research/about.htm

[4]   Fujitsu Laboratories, Agent-oriented programming library: http://www.labs.fujitsu.com/en/freesoft/paw/

[5]   IEEE Distributed Systems Online- Distributed Agents Projects: http://dsonline.computer.org/agents/projects.htm

[6]   http://www.pacmangame.net/

[7]   www.w3.org/XML/

[8]   http://aima.cs.berkeley.edu/

[9]   http://www.swi-prolog.org/packages/jpl/

Chapter 7
E–Governance Survey on Municipalities Web Sites

Rocío Andrea Rodríguez
National University of La Matanza, Argentina

Daniel Alberto Giulianelli
National University of La Matanza, Argentina

Pablo Martín Vera
National University of La Matanza, Argentina

Artemisa Trigueros
National University of La Matanza, Argentina

Isabel Beatriz Marko
National University of La Matanza, Argentina

ABSTRACT

E-Governance aims to provide high quality of government for citizens. It covers services, information delivery and interactive community / government communication. This goal can be achieved by adopting the ICT (Information and Communication Technologies) tools in the government web site's design and contents. This communication channel allows a redefinition of the traditional role played by each one of the actors of the relation. The government as provider of: services, information, transparency and interactive communication. The citizens acting as active subjects with their government, using services, receiving information, controlling the government's decisions and returning feedback to them. This feedback includes opinions, complaints and suggestions delivered by the web sites' interactive tools. This research surveyed if the implementation of ICT tools regarding national and international norms and regulations for web sites development and content, increases the fulfillment of the key concepts of e-governance: e-democracy, e-services, e-transparency and active and passive communication. 30 local government web sites of Argentine were analyzed by checking if they implemented the ICT tools expressed by the seven basic concepts of design and contents: Navigability, Veracity, Friendliness, Functionality, Accessibility, Usability and Information through 152 weighed aspects that fulfill these seven concepts. The analysis of the score obtained by the web sites showed their e-governance development level and what aspects they have to implement to improve e-governance quality.

DOI: 10.4018/978-1-61520-763-3.ch007

DESIGN AND CONTENTS

Environment

Assuming that one of the aims of the municipality's web sites is to increase the development and comfort of their citizens, this paper analyzes the aspects that will allow those sites to get a more effective approach to their citizens, increasing the delivery of services, information and participation.

Taking as a premise the intuition (the possibility to use new or unknown software by making an analogy with the applications that are frequently used), this analysis wants to establish similarities and differences on web sites' design and functionality. National and international norms, regulations and publications are taken as a basis, in order to determine the most important aspects to perform the analysis. Finally, some aspects that have not been found in the quoted sources were included, according to the needs, capabilities and restrictions of the studied communities.

There are a high percentage of citizens that uses internet only to check email and other percentage doesn't have enough resources (economical and/or technological) to access a computer. Within this environment Argentina begins to consider e-Governance as a tool to simplify citizen's life.

Technological ignorance of a big percentage of citizens creates a very difficult barrier to avoid when terms like connectivity, Internet, Broad Band, and so on, are mentioned. Lots of communities choose a technological isolation and continue to do a lot of administrative procedures personally.

Administrative procedures generally mean long queues. A lot of people that tries to access web sites by curiosity or motivation of changing, finds a lot of interfaces, different types of connectivity, very despair pages and generally loosely design, turning this motivation in confusion.

It would be much easier for people that are no familiar with web site browsing, to find menus at the same position, have a site map to quickly find wanted information, and so on. If web sites would follow standards it would be easier to find required information in less time.

Design's standards allow relating previously acquired concepts on using software tools, with others that are being used for the first time, allowing the user to count with basic knowledge for using the new software. Government's web sites should have the same appearance and fulfill the same standards. These standards will be essential when using Internet to realize e-governance.

eGovernance

Following UNESCO (Castro & Mlikota, 2002), "e-governance regards adopting ICT (Information and Communication Technologies) normative by the public government with the aim of improving the delivery of information and services to their citizens. Therefore, it promotes the community participation in the decision making process in order to increase the government's responsibility, transparency and effectiveness".

Research Central Axis

The research focuses in testing the degree of fulfillment of municipalities' web sites of Buenos Aires Urban Cone with several aspects groups by levels of basic topics that interacts each other to reach quality.

The 30 communities that surround Buenos Aires City have approximately 9.000.000 inhabitants, more or less 25% of Argentina's total population according to 2001 Census (INDEC - Statistics and Census National Institute, 2001). National University of La Matanza (UNLAM), is placed in one of the Buenos Aires Urban Cone districts. A high percentage of the students of this University are citizens of these communities, so this research wants to be a contribution to the place where it belongs.

Figure 1 shows the geographical placement for the 30 municipalities that conform the Buenos Aires Urban Cone.

Figure 1. Map of Buenos Aires urban cone

1. San Fernando
2. San Isidro
3. Vicente Lopez
4. General San Martín
5. Tres de Febrero
6. Móron
7. Ituzaingó
8. Hurlinghan
9. San Miguel
10. Malvinas Argentina
11. Tigre
12. Pilar
13. Lujan
14. General Rodríguez
15. Moreno
16. José C. Paz
17. Merlo
18. Marcos Paz
19. La Matanza
20. Ezeiza
21. Esteban Echeverría
22. Lomas de Zamora
23. Lanus
24. Avellaneda
25. Quilmes
26. Almirante Brown
27. Presidente Perón
28. San Vicente
29. Florencio Varela
30. Berazategui

The following list shows the analyzed municipalities, including their names and the websites URLs. List numbering allows identifying each municipality on the map of Figure 1.

It can be notice that two of the municipalities' don't have a website (municipalities numbered on the map as 9 and 20). Most of domain names are quite representative, showing community name, but some of them are acronyms causing possible confusion to the citizens.

1. San Fernando: http://www.sanfernando.gov.ar
2. San Isidro: http://www.sanisidro.gov.ar
3. Vicente López: http://www.vicentelopez.gov.ar
4. General San Martín: http://www.sanmartin.gov.ar
5. Tres de Febrero: http://www.tresdefebrero.gov.ar
6. Morón: http://www.moron.gov.ar
7. Ituzaingó: http://www.miituzaingo.gov.ar
8. Hurlingham: http://www.munhurli.gov.ar
9. San Miguel: Hasn't got website
10. Malvinas Argentinas: http://www.malvinasargentinas.gov.ar
11. Tigre: http://www.tigre.gov.ar
12. Pilar: http://www.pilar.gov.ar
13. Lujan: http://www.lujan.gov.ar
14. General Rodríguez: http://www.generalrodriguez.gov.ar
15. Moreno: http://www.moreno.gov.ar
16. José C. Paz: http://www.josecpaz.mun.gba.gov.ar
17. Merlo: http://www.merlo.gov.ar
18. Marcos Paz: http://www.municipiomarcospaz.gov.ar
19. La Matanza: http://www.lamatanza.gov.ar
20. Ezeiza: Hasn't got website
21. Esteban Echeverría: http://www.estebanecheverria.gov.ar
22. Lomas de Zamora: http://www.lomasdezamora.gov.ar
23. Lanús: http://www.lanusweb.com
24. Avellaneda: http://www.avellaneda-ba.gov.ar
25. Quilmes: http://www.quilmes.gov.ar
26. Almirante Brown: http://www.almirantebrown.gov.ar
27. Presidente Perón: http://www.peron.mun.gba.gov.ar
28. San Vicente: http://www.msv.gov.ar
29. Florencio Varela: http://www.florenciovarela.gov.ar
30. Berazategui: http://www.berazategui.gov.ar

There is no standard defined for websites domain names. If domain names would have a relation between them, it wouldn't be necessary to use a search engine to find municipality web sites.

The 65% of tested web sites has municipality name as domain name. In the other 35% domain names of type "MunicipalityName.gov.ar" are not used. Only it's used in the case of Lujan where the domain "lujan.gov.ar" is used for tourism information but the municipality web site is placed at a secondary page inside it. So those domains could have been chosen for the rest of municipalities sites. So the question is: why some municipalities have chosen a domain name like "msm.gov.ar" instead of sanmiguel.gov.ar or "miituzaingo.gov.ar" instead of "ituzaingo.gov.ar"?

The Seven Design and Contents Concepts

The following concepts, that contribute to create quality web sites, were taken to analyze Buenos Aires Urban Cone web sites:

1. Functionality (FU): We define functionality as the possibility to allow citizens' access to services like: information, administrative procedures, payments, state of debts, etc, without the need of personally going to City Hall, saving time, money and effort for both the citizen and de council. That's why our vision of web sites is oriented to "User Centered Design". Example aspects are: Printing of forms, tracking administrative procedures.
2. Friendliness (FR): User must be able to browse web sites no matter his skills level. Communication language should be simple allowing to access main contents in a clear way. Example aspects are: Categorized Information, Color contrast

3. Usability (US): Quality of User experience when interacting with a product or system. ISO 9241-11 standard defines usability like: The ability of a product of being used by a user to reach specifics goals with effectiveness, efficiency and satisfaction, inside a particular user context. ISO 13407 defines user centered design like:
    ◦   User active participation and clear knowledge of user requirements and tasks
    ◦   Correct function localization between user and technology
    ◦   Interaction of solutions design
    ◦   Interdisciplinary design

    Usability can be measure by several aspects like:

    •   Effectiveness
    •   Efficiency
    •   Satisfaction
    •   Easy to learn
    •   Easy to remember
    •   Errors rate and severity

    Web site standard unification will be designed to allow any user that has already use a government web site, to apply all previously learned procedures to the new upcoming site. Example aspects are: Show on every page the path to reach it from the home page, Banner with organization name.

4. Accessibility (AC): Is the chance of a product or a web service of being accessed and used by the greatest possible number of people, regardless individual limitations or limitations of context of use. Example aspects are: Cross browsing, Weight of pages.
5. Veracity (VE): Government web site cannot have disclaimers of its own information. Published information must be of informative character (updated, real, and relevant for

the one that is accessing the site). Example aspects are: Updated News, Contradictory information

6. Information (IN): Information regarding municipal government and its activities is one of the basic services that a municipal web site must provide.

The citizen logs to a municipal web site basically to get information on schedules, time tables, news, addresses, taxes, and so on, because it is generally quicker, easier and cheaper to query a web site instead of phoning or going to the town hall.

From the government point of view, information delivered on the web site, becomes an advantage because the citizens can get to it at any time, without long queues, and clerks to attend those people.

The information provided by the web site must be true, opportune, up to date and relevant.

7. Navigability (NA): Navigability is the way with which the user, actually the municipality's citizen, is able to move through a web site in order to access all the web pages that belong to it.

This movement (navigation) through a web site is performed by the use of buttons, icons, hypertext, hyperlinks, menus, etc., that allows the user to move from one page to another, or from one site to another, depending on the user's will.

All this site-user's interaction must be performed in the simplest and clearest way.

Aspects

Based on all this concepts, aspects of official standards (national or international), that are useful for testing municipality web sites, are taken. Afterwards, internationals publications will be taken to fill uncovered aspects of standards. Once finished this analysis and with the experience

provided by the research team, some relevant aspects are incorporated to cover all aspects of studied web sites.

Sources of the Aspects

- The W3C (World Wide Web Consortium), is an international consortium which objective is to take internet to its maximum potential developing protocols and guidelines that assure the growing at long term of the web.(W3C, 2008)
- ONTI (Information Technology National Office) is the main reference on the use of information technology on government in Argentina. It depends on Sub Secretary of Public Management of the Headquarters of Minister's Cabinet. It is formed by a group of multidisciplinary specialized professionals. It aims to create politics for the implementation of development process of technology innovation for the updating and transformation of the government, and also allows the use of new technology in the public sector and its compatibility, interoperability and promotions of technological standardization.(ONTI - National Bureau for Information Technologies, 2005)
- Considering internationals publications (see (Department of the Premier and Cabinet - Office of e-Government, 2006), (Pontifical Catholic University of Chile, 2006), (State Services Commission, 2007), (Web Managers; Requirements and Best Practices Checklist for Government, 2005), (Marcos Mora M., & Rovira Fontanals C, 2005) new aspects are taken especially those that can be applied to municipality web sites. These aspects are not mentioned in ONTI and W3C regulations.
- Research Team's proposed aspects: To finalize, aspects designed by members of the research team, are taken for testing municipalities of Buenos Aires Urban Cone.

Aspects' Source and Quantity

Taking in account international and national organizations such as W3C and ONTI, described above, international publications (called PUB), that are relevant to the design and contents concepts of the web sites, and adding aspects proposed by the research team (called RT), this work shows 152 aspects (see Annex #2).

Quantity of aspects by each source is shown below, with their related percentage:

- W3C + ONTI: 102 (67%)
- PUB: 11 (7%)
- RT: 39 (26%)

Aspects Hierarchy

For each of the 152 selected aspects, a relevance level was assigned, according to the aspect's contribution to the seven design and contents concepts.

The following aspects allow evaluating local government web sites. Each aspect is assigned a relevance level according a scale defined by the research team:

- Essential = Score 5
- Very Significant = Score 4
- Significant = Score 3
- Desirable = Score 2
- Optional = Score 1

The level "Essential" (score 5) is assigned to those aspects that are indispensable for the fulfillment of one or some of the seven concepts. The relevance level decreases as the aspect becomes less important. One aspect can contribute to different concepts at the same time and also can get different score according to different design and contents concepts. Some examples are: The presentation page could be skipped before the site is loaded, contributes to Friendliness, Usability and Accessibility. The aspect: The web site offers content's readers for deaf users contributes to Friendliness and Accessibility, while the aspect: The web site includes semantic search contributes to Friendliness with a score of 3 also to Navigability with the same score, Usability with a score of 1 and Functionality with 4 points.

The score is calculated based in the fulfillment of aspects weighed by relevance. The weigh used in the work is based in the following relevance scale (set of values): 5 Highest relevance, 3 Medium relevance, 1 Lowest relevance (values 4 and 2 are considered to get more accuracy).

This scale was built to match with the hierarchy suggested above. According to this, one aspect that belongs to the highest level will get a score of 5 and it is place in level 5. Therefore if one aspect belongs to the lowest level it will get a score of 1 and the highest hierarchy level gets 5 points, consequently, an aspect which belongs to the lowest hierarchy level gets only 1 point.

Table 1 shows the quantity of aspects organized by hierarchy and concept.

Aspects Categorization

The 152 selected aspects to evaluate government web sites were sorted in 23 categories, according to the implementation of each one in the design and contents of a government web site.

1. Technical aspects: they allow analyzing design problems or very poor web site content understanding due to technical problems such as bad coding practices, no crossbrosing, etc.
2. Banner: It is called "banner" the main rectangular section placed generally on top of each page of a site. It is usually an image and the first site element seen by a user when he or she enters a web site, therefore there are several aspects that it must achieve to be clear, useful and efficient.
3. Browsers: The user seldom remembers the web site' address, therefore it is mandatory

Table 1. Quantity of aspects organized by concept and hierarchy

Assigned Points	Hierarchy	FR	NA	US	AC	IN	VE	FU
5	Essential	28	20	13	23	5	5	3
4	Very Significant	17	8	14	25	3	3	4
3	Significant	30	12	18	16	7	4	8
2	Desirable	4	1	4	1	6	5	6
1	Optional	3	1	2	0	1	0	1
Quantity of Aspects		**82**	**42**	**51**	**65**	**22**	**17**	**22**

that after searching it in internet he or she will be able to reach the web site that is looking for. So this work analyzed if the studied municipal web sites are registered in the most popular browsers specifying "official site", country, state, etc. without any doubt.

4. General Characteristics: it is a set of aspects that contributes to good web site's navigation.

5. Main menu categories: It is very important for a web site's main menu to be very well organized, allowing the user to understand each option's function and also allowing him to reach each page and content into the web site.

6. Colors/Design: The colors and design of a web site are very important when a user is navigating it. The information and contents shown in it can be very useful for a citizen but sometimes the color contrast doesn't allow the user to see or understand it. The different aspects that belong to this category cover background color, contrast, text color, etc.

7. Multimedia contents: Multimedia resources add value to a web site, but if they are not well organized can be worse than the lack of it. If the web site includes a video it must also show the same information by text mode. A deaf user will not be able to reach that information if there is only a video showing it. It is desirable for all the information of the web site to be shown as text mode in order

to be reached by blind users using content's reader.

8. Legal stuff: Sometimes, web sites include sentences saying that the government is not responsible for the published information of the site. These facts and others are covered by the aspects that belong to this category.

9. Downloads: These aspects shows the details to be considered when a web site includes files to download such as to inform the file's weigh, the file's content, etc.

10. Published documents: the published documents must include information about themselves such as date.

11. Forms: the forms to be filled by a user are very important to grant the web site quality. They must cover the following ítems:
    ◦ To allow the user to fill them in a clear way with clear labels such as mandatory fields.
    ◦ To show clear error messages, etc.

These are some of the aspects included in this category.

12. Administrative procedures: this category includes information about administrative procedures and services offered by the local government, such as appointments to get driver license, information about taxes, etc.

13. Icons: This category reinforces the importance of adding icons to the web site such

as send a mail, print, more information, etc. It is very important to include the large text icon to increase the accessibility.

14. Images and Sizes: this category includes all the facts about images (image's format, weigh, label, etc.). It is very important for an image to be light, so the page can be loaded and seen very quickly.

15. Web site's information: this category includes local government information such as: Contact information (telephone numbers, town hall and other addresses, electronic addresses, maps and how to reach the Town Hall, buses, etc.). Government laws and regulations, Goals, Programs, Projects, Budget, Contracts, etc.

16. Links: this category includes different characteristics about links such as: link's format, links that allow linking the web site with national or international organizations, etc.

17. Lists: if the web site includes lists, they must be clearly labeled.

18. Main menu: it is the most important of all the web site's menu, so this category shows different characteristics about it.

19. Menus: this category shows all the characteristics that must have "any" menu in a web site (main menu included).

20. Navigators: It is very important for the web site to be crossbrowsing, which means that can be seen in a proper way no matter what navigator is used by the citizen.

21. Resources: A municipal web site must count with some resources that add functionality to it. These resources have the following goals:
    ◦ To increase communication: chat, newsletters, complaints, newsgroups, etc.
    ◦ On line Help: search, help options, site map, FAQ (Frequently Asked Questions), etc.
    ◦ To allow citizen's participation: citizen's suggestions, web site's surveys, government's surveys.

22. Technology: This category covers some resources like: semantic search, RSS (Really Simple Syndication) and mobile sites.

23. Text: this last category covers all the aspects that must have a text when included inside a web site. If a web site doesn't add them, the user will have understanding difficulties such as abbreviations, acronyms and symbols without explanation, etc.

Annex #2 shows all the aspects considered during the research. They are organized by the categories explained previously.

Each category shows:

- The aspect's number used all over the research.
- The source from which the aspect was taken.
- The score that was given to each aspect according to its contribution to the implementation of the concepts of friendliness, navigability, usability, accessibility, information, veracity and functionality and also to its contribution to the implementation of the e-governance mainstays (will be explained in item 2).

Perfect Total Score

Adding scores of each of the 152 aspects, a site that fulfills all of them would have an ideal score of 1138 points, obtained from:

- Friendliness: Score 309
- Accessibility: Score 268
- Usability: Score 192
- Navigability: Score 171
- Information: Score 71
- Functionality: Score 68
- Veracity: Score 59

Figure 2. Percentage of fulfillment of each municipality

The list shown above has been organized by concept's score in descending score's order. It can be watched that the highest score belongs to the Friendliness concept (309 points), followed by Accessibility concept (268 points), and Usability concept (192 points), as a consequence of the "User Centered Design" which is the research's approach.

The perfect score of 1138 points, could be achieved by a web site that had implemented the 152 aspects proposed by the authors in its design and contents.

Web Sites' Evaluation

The 30 municipality web sites were observed and analyzed by the research team to check if they fulfill each one of the 152 aspects shown in Annex #2. The results of this survey were marked in a spreadsheet, assigning the web site the corresponding score of every aspect only in the positive cases. Afterward each score was added, and that sum is the total score of each web site.

Figure 2 shows the percentage obtained by each municipal web site. The municipality web site's percentage is obtained dividing the web site score by the perfect (1138) score and multiplying

Table 2. Percentage of fulfillment of the 7 highest total scores municipalities.

Concept	Municipality						
	Lujan	Morón	Vicente Lopez	San Fernando	Pilar	San Isidro	Ituzaingo
Friendliness	78%	77%	81%	73%	73%	75%	65%
Navigability	82%	72%	77%	71%	71%	68%	80%
Usability	82%	80%	75%	71%	74%	68%	68%
Accessibility	69%	74%	69%	68%	62%	71%	74%
Information	62%	75%	63%	75%	79%	69%	58%
Veracity	54%	69%	54%	73%	66%	61%	69%
Functionality	56%	40%	32%	60%	56%	49%	40%
TOTAL	74%	73%	71%	71%	69%	69%	68%

Table 3. Quantity of municipality web sites that fulfill the concepts of design and contents

Concept	Less than 40%	Between 40% y 70%	Greater than 70%
Friendliness	5	13	10
Navigability	5	14	9
Usability	5	17	6
Accessibility	4	20	4
Information	9	16	3
Veracity	6	21	1
Functionality	22	6	0

its result by 100: Percentage = (Municipality Score / Perfect Score) x 100

The "Municipality Score" will always be less or equal to the "Perfect Score". As an example it can be mentioned Lujan Municipality, which got a score of 837 points, so the calculation is:

(837 / 1138) x 100 = 73.55% (rounded 74%)

It can be watch that no municipality web site exceeds 75% of the perfect score. The highest score belongs to Lujan Municipality which got a percentage of 74%.

It is noticeable that most of the municipality web sites (23 municipalities from 30 municipalities) exceed the 50% of the perfect score.

There were 2 municipalities that didn´t have a government web site when the surveys was done.

Table 2 shows the percentages of fulfillment of each concept obtained by the 7 municipality web sites that achieved the 7 best total score and therefore the best percentages. The gray cells belong to the best percentage by concept (highest percentage by row).

According to the survey, the highest percentage (82%) belongs to the navigability and usability's concepts, followed by friendliness's concept (81%), information's concept (79%), accessibility's concept (74%) and veracity's concept (73%). The lowest percentage (60%) belongs to the functionality concept.

Figure 2 shows the total score obtained by each municipal web site in descending order by total score.

It can be watch in Figure 2 that Ituzaingó Municipality, that was 7th in overall ranking, got the first place in Accessibility which is one of the main concepts that allow accessing the web site to handicapped users.

It can be watch too, that Moron Municipality, that was 2nd in the overall ranking, didn´t get the first place in any concept.

Table 3 shows the quantity of municipality web sites that fullfil the 7 concepts of design and contents with the ranks of: less than 40%, between 40% and 70%, and greater than 70%.

Analyzing Table 3 it can be notice that:

- More than 33% of the web sites got more than 70% of the perfect score for friendliness and only 18% of the web sites got less than 40% of friendliness.
- 50% (14) of the municipality's web sites fulfil between 40% and 70% of the perfect score. Again, only 5 web sites got less than 40%.
- There are very few municipality web sites that fulfil more than 70% of the perfect score for usability. 60% of the web sites achieved a percentage between 40% and 70% and only 5 web sites got less than 40%.
- Most of the municipality web sites (72%) fulfil accessibility perfect score in a

percentage between 40% and 70%. Only 4 web sites got more than 70%.

- There are 9 web sites that have a poor implementation of the information concept. In addition, it can be seen that only 3 web sites got more than 70% in this concept.
- Only one municipality web site fulfils the concept of veracity with a percentage greater than 70%. The rank between 40% and 70%, got 75% of the web sites, and 6 web sites got less than 40%.
- Functionality is the less fulfilled concept, because 79% of the web sites implement it in percentage lower than 40%. In addition there is not any web site that got more than 70%.
- It is important to highlight that the most municipalities in 6 of the 7 concepts belongs to the rank between 40% and 70%. Only the functionality concept has the most municipalities (22) in its lowest percentage (less than 40%). It can be watch in this concept too, that no municipality web site exceeds 70%, and only 6 web sites belong to the 40% and 70% rank.
- As it was quoted above the most fulfilled concept was friendliness and the less one functionality.
- Accessibility, information and veracity are the concepts that fulfil the most of the web sites in this rank.

Founded Deficiencies

A list of main deficiencies founded on analyzed web sites is shown here:

Technical Characteristic

1. Main page is not centered (21%): When maximizing main page all content stays on left side of the window
2. Opposing design of secondary web pages and main page (21%): Different colors, menus, fonts, etc

3. Links to external sites are not opened on a separated window (25%): When opening a link of an external site the content of current explorer window is replace by the new location
4. Intro can only be skipped when it's fully loaded (4%): There is no external link to skip intro. User must wait the full loading of the intro to be able to skip it.

Content - Based

5. Versions in other languages (8%): Municipality web sites are not tourist or general information sites, they are oriented to offer services to citizens, and it's no relevant having contents in different languages
6. Doesn't have links to external sites (29%): It's important to show relevant links of other useful government web sites for example: Taxes, Tourism, etc
7. Basic Municipality information is missing (46%): Some relevant information is missing like addresses, telephone numbers, schedules for services, etc
8. Doesn't have a geographical map (75%): Web site has no geographical map to allow citizens to know the physical place where the city hall is placed and how to reach it
9. Missing contact form (38%): There is not a contact form to allow citizens to fill personal data in order to ask for help or give suggestions
10. Missing contact form and e-mail address (4%): There is no way to electronically contact Municipality

Functional

11. No search engine is present (50%): None simple or advance search are present to allow to find data inside web site
12. Site Map is missing (50%): Sitemap is not present to allow to see web site contents at a glance

13. Site Map and Search Engine missing (21%): There is no a quick way to see if some determined information is present at the web site, the only solution is to open all pages browsing from menus and links to find what is wanted. This can discourage users for using the site

14. Only simple search is present (39%): No advance search is present to allow experienced users to find data in a quicker way

15. Showing an Intro page (29%): Intro pages are useful for example for tourisms pages to show pictures, of the place but for municipality web sites that are oriented to bring services this only can slow down to user experience

16. Web site has sound (13%): In an service oriented web site sound can be nuisance after a while and doesn't bring any advantage to the user experience

17. Doesn't have on-line help (88%): No help is offered explaining procedures about using the web site

18. No Menu on Main Page (4%): No organized menu is present, only some isolated links or buttons are present inside the body of the main page

19. Menus are not present on secondary pages (19%): Menus of the main page are lost when entering on a secondary page.

E-GOVERNANCE MAINSTAINS

E-governance can be represented as the intersection of two nowadays social phenomenons: global communication, created from ICTs (Information and Communication Technologies) and a new scope of governance, where the citizen takes an active role, instead of the traditional passive receiver of the government's decisions and actions. E-governance idea has evolved in time and with the experience based in different countries and communities' implementation. One of the mainstays

that have evolved is the communication between citizen and government. This communication can be active or passive, where the role that the government plays is to provide news, information and services. While the citizens play the passive receiver role of the issues that the government decides to deliver. This point of view is old and primitive.

Starting from the ICTs possibilities, it is considered that better e-governance implementation entails interactive communication between government and citizen, where both of them plays the sender-receiver role.

The government as:

• Services, information and news deliverer. Besides the government can show its actions, decisions, purchases, budget, laws, contracts, decrees and every other information that contribute to transparency.

• Suggestions, opinions, complaints, congratulations and control receiver, sent by the citizens.

The citizen as:

• Suggestions, opinions, complaints and congratulations sender and control performer.

• News, information and services receiver.

The citizen becomes an active individual and increases his participation in the government using the tools provided by e-governance, instead of being a passive individual who receives, and lots of times "suffers" government's actions and decisions.

This interactive communication allows improving the real democracy concept. This can be found in the communication between local government and its community where government's decisions and actions have positive or negative influence in each one of the citizens and their families.

Interactive communication brings both parties a lot of advantages. It allows the citizen to exercise his rights, to control the government's actions and decisions and to participate in the government process. It allows the citizen to look up information, to perform online pays, transactions, and questions. Interactive communication allows the government to gain transparency, and to provide citizens with more efficient services, saving time and money.

Transparency becomes a key concept and mainstay in e-governance improving. This mainstay allows reducing corruption, increasing the government's credibility and responsibility, to favor citizen's participation and to know their opinions. So the government has to inform on taken decisions and their enforcement following rules and regulations. This information must be available to all the citizens in an easy to understand and to find, format with free, friendly, true and accessible contents.

The following classification, based in the UNESCO (UNESCO, n.d.) specification, shows e-governance's basic mainstays and also fields of application.

1. Electronic administration (e-administration): It refers to improve the internal working of the public sector and its agents' administration, with new ICT information process.
2. Electronic services (e-services): It refers to provide information and delivering services to citizens. It also includes information on events, shows, public transportation, district's maps, job vacancies, employment's policy, budget, purchases and contracts. Some examples of interactive services are: request for public or legal documents, certificates, appointments, on line tax and services payment.
3. Electronic democracy (e-democracy): It refers to increase the engagement of citizens in public decisions and actions by using the ICTs. Some examples are: opinion polls,

forums, panels, blogs, chat rooms, referendums, mailing lists, e-mail, bulletin boards, direct contact with government agents and representatives, opinions, suggestions, complaints, frequently asked questions and their answers.

The authors navigated each one of the 30 municipality's web sites checking if the web sites fulfills or not each one of the 152 aspects shown above.

The municipality's total score was obtained adding the score of each aspect if the web site implements it and 0 if it doesn´t.

According to "good governance" characteristics, explained in (Castro & Mlikota, 2002), the following basic mainstays were added to the previous ones by the research team.

4. Electronic transparency (e-transparency): "means that decisions taken and their enforcement are done in a manner that follows the rules and regulations. It also means that information is freely available and directly accessible to those who will be affected by such decision and their enforcement. It also means that enough information is provided and that it is provided in easily understandable way and media". It crosses through the last two concepts (e-services and e-democracy). It can be seen as e-services when delivering information on the government's actions and decisions for the citizens to know why the government takes them. It also can be seen as e-democracy, because the government provides the citizens with information and communication channels that allow them to participate in decisions and to control the government.
5. Active and passive communication: As it was previously explained, active communication can be thought as a two way communication, where both actors send and receive at the same time and passive communication

Table 4. Aspect's quantity and perfect score by each mainstay.

Score	Hierarchy	SER		DEM		TRA		ACC		PAC	
5	Essential	10	50	17	85	13	65	12	60	15	75
4	Very Significant	1	4	1	4	0	0	1	4	1	4
3	Significant	21	63	11	33	10	30	8	24	23	69
2	Desirable	11	22	0	0	5	10	2	4	10	20
1	Optional	9	9	0	0	2	2	1	1	8	8
	Perfect Total Score	52	148	29	122	30	107	24	93	57	176

as one way communication where one actor always send and the other always receive.

The research is focused in the following mainstays: e-services, e-democracy, e-transparency, active communication and passive communication. The concept of e-administration is considered an internal government function, and it is not measurable from the web sites.

Aspects Selection

Using a subset of 80 aspects from the 152 defined previously it is possible to analyzed data from the point of view of e-governance mainstays.

Therefore the sources of the aspects are the same as those explained above in 1.5.1. Each one of the selected aspects contributes to one or more of the 5 e-governance mainstays: e-services, e-democracy, e-transparency, Active Communication and Passive Communication. The following list shows the source of the 80 selected aspects organized by quantity and the percentage.

- W3C + ONTI: 60 (75%)
- PUB: 7 (9%)
- RT: 13 (16%)

The scale, the relevance level and hierarchy used to evaluate each aspect are the same explained in item 1.5.1

The level "Essential" (score 5) is assigned to those aspects that are indispensable for the fulfilment of one or some of the mainstays of e-governance. The relevance level decreases as the aspect becomes less important. One aspect can contribute to different mainstays at the same time and also can get different score according to different mainstays. Some examples are: "The web site has e-mail or contact form" contributes to the e-democracy, active communication and e-transparency. The aspect "The web site shows government's purchases and contracts", contributes to e-services, passive communication and e-transparency. The aspect "The web site includes the curriculum vitae of the government's agents", gets a score 3 for e-services (information), it also gets score 3 in passive communication, but it gets score 5 for e-transparency.

Table 4 show the aspects selected by the research team. Each aspect is shown with its score on the five mainstays of e-governance: e-services (SER), e-democracy (DEM), e-transparency (TRA), active communication (ACC), and passive communication (PAC). For each mainstay there are two columns. The first column represents aspects quantity and the second the ideal score if they all were fulfilled.

Annex #2 shows the design and contents aspects that were selected by the authors because they contribute to the five e-governance mainstays' implementation. The aspects are organized by the same categories used previously.

Table 5. Mainstays' percentage and total percentage

Municipality	SER	DEM	TRA	ACC	PAC	Total Percentage
San Fernando	73.33	72.13	70.09	61.29	78.77	72.35
Pilar	78.67	67.21	65.42	60.22	80.45	72.20
Morón	72.00	63.93	68.22	45.16	80.45	68.36
San Martín	63.33	65.57	57.01	51.61	70.95	63.13
San Isidro	67.33	54.92	60.75	49.46	68.16	61.60
Malvinas Argentinas	64.00	57.38	52.34	58.06	62.57	59.60
Ituzaingo	50.00	63.93	58.88	40.86	64.25	56.68
Lujan	68.67	48.36	36.45	52.69	63.13	55.76
Moreno	49.33	60.66	62.62	40.86	61.45	55.76
Lomas de Zamora	58.67	43.44	42.99	39.78	58.10	50.38
Vicente Lopez	65.33	33.61	37.38	36.56	58.66	48.85
Lanús	47.33	48.36	51.40	26.88	58.66	48.39
Tigre	49.33	49.18	42.06	36.56	55.87	48.08
Florencio Varela	54.00	43.44	42.06	31.18	58.66	48.08
Marcos Paz	50.00	43.44	45.79	45.16	48.04	46.85
Almirante Brown	41.33	48.36	42.06	26.88	53.63	49.09
La Matanza	52.00	39.34	30.84	30.11	54.75	43.78
Quilmes	56.67	31.15	32.71	21.51	57.54	43.16
Tres de Febrero	54.67	19.67	28.97	16.13	50.84	37.33
Avellaneda	34.67	40.16	32.71	19.35	46.37	36.41
Presidente Perón	43.33	29.51	22.43	25.81	43.02	34.72
Esteban Echeverría	34.67	33.61	18.69	29.03	36.87	31.64
Hurlingham	36.00	25.41	22.43	13.98	40.22	29.80
José C. Paz	20.67	17.21	18.69	8.60	20.58	19.05
General Rodríguez	6.67	0.00	0.00	0.00	5.59	3.07
San Vicente	3.33	0.00	0.00	0.00	2.79	1.54
Berazategui	2.67	0.00	0.00	0.00	2.23	1.23
Merlo	1.33	0.00	0.00	0.00	1.12	0.61

Perfect Score

The following list shows the perfect score organized by each one of the five e-Governance mainstays, and the total perfect score:

- Active Communication: 93
- E-services: 148
- E-democracy: 122
- E-transparency: 107
- Passive Communication: 176

A municipality's web site that would have implemented the 80 aspects would have reached the perfect score of 646 points.

Mainstays Evaluation

Taking the 28 municipalities websites of Buenos Aires Urban Cone (see Figure 1) the score for each site is analyzed from the point of view of e-governance mainstays: e-services (SER), e-democracy (DEM), e-transparency (TRA), active

Figure 3. Percentage of total score by municipality's web site

communication (ACC), and passive communication (PAC).

From table 5 it can be notice that:

- Only 5 (16%) of the municipality's web sites reach more than 60% overall percentage. 17 (57% of the evaluated web sites) reached a percentage between 30% and 60%, and there are 8 (27% of the evaluated web sites) that are below 30%.
- Only 4 web sites exceed the 60% of the total score assigned to e-transparency, 16 of them achieved a percentage between 30% and 60%, and 10 web sites don't reach 30%.
- It is important to remark that there's none municipality web site where active communication exceeds passive communication.

Total Score

Adding the score obtained by each web site in the 5 mainstays, the total score for each website is shown and the fulfillment percentage was calculated as is show in Figure 3

CONCLUSIONS

Through the present chapter it can be watched that municipality web sites from the Buenos Aires Urban Cone don't satisfy all the rules established by the ONTI nor W3C consortium. The research checked that there is no pattern for the site's design. The icons for common action are different (Contact, Site Map, Search...) also the place of the same content in different sites is different, etc. This and other differences can be seen not only in different web site but in different pages of the same web site (21% of the analyzed web sites, changes: colors, font type, place of menus, etc.).

The research team could often watch web sites hosted in different servers, developed with different technology. A very high number of these sites doesn't have site map and some of them doesn't provide search box so it is very difficult for the user to navigate the entire site to see if he can find the information he is looking for.

After checking and testing in each one of the municipality web sites the aspects regarding design and contents established in this work, differences, problems and lack of some aspects of the web sites were analyzed, and afterwards it

was possible to determine a score that shows the actual position of each web site regarding some aspects of e-governance properly documented. 43% of the web sites don't reach the 50% of the aspects that we consider are very useful to bring the citizens closer to e-governance.

- From the overall evaluated mainstays, only 36% of the municipalities fulfill more than 50% of the perfect score.
- 46% of the municipality's web sites got a score between 50% and 30% of the perfect score.
- 18% of the municipality's web sites got a score less than 30% of the perfect score.
- Friendliness and Accessibility were the most fulfilled concepts.
- Functionality was the less fulfilled concept.

Regarding the five e-governance mainstays, this work reveals that only 5 municipalities over 30 (17%), have developed web sites with an actualized focus on electronic governance, giving citizens not only the opportunity of getting electronic services, but also the possibility of participation with government with critics, opinions and suggestions.

- About 57% (17 municipalities) got a score between 30% and 60% for e-governance, another 26% (8 municipalities) implement e-governance in a primitive way, and there are another two municipalities with no web site at all.
- From the overall evaluated mainstays, only about 30% of the municipalities fulfill more than 50% of them.
- The municipalities with the higher scores in e-services and e-democracy, also have the higher scores in active and passive communication.
- In most of the cases, e-services scores were greater than e-democracy ones and passive

communication is always greater than active communication.

According to each municipality web site place in the overall ranking it can be said that:

- 6 of the 28 municipality web sites keep the same place in the overall ranking.
- 4 got a place with a difference of 2 from one ranking to another.
- There were 2 municipalities that got the greatest difference (8 places). Both of them got better place in e-governance 5 mainstays than in design and contents 7 concepts.
- Only one municipality web site got a difference of 7 points more in design than in e-governance.

REFERENCES

W3C - World Wide Web Consortium. (2008). *Web Accessibility Brief guide*. Retrieved from http://www.w3c.es/divulgacion/guiasbreves/Accesibilidad

Castro, S., & Mlikota, K. (2002). *Overview On E-Governance. ICTs as Tools for Improving Local Governance*. UNESCO (United Nations Educational, Scientific and Cultural Organization). Retrieved from http://portal.unesco.org/ci/en/files/6532/10391876090Overview_on_e-governance_working_paper.doc/Overview%2Bon%2Be-governance%2Bworking%2Bpaper.doc

Department of the Premier and Cabinet - Office of e-Government. (2006). *Guidelines for State Government Websites Version 2.1*, Australia. Retrieved from http://www.egov.dpc.wa.gov.au/documents/WebGuidelinesVersion2.1_final.doc

INDEC - Statistics and Census National Institute. (2001). *Censo Poblacional.* Argentine. Retrieved from http://www.indec.mecon.ar/

Marcos Mora, M., & Rovira Fontanals, C. (2005). *Usability Evaluación de la Usabilidad en Sistemas de Información Web Municipales: Metodología de análisis y desarrollo.* Barcelona, Spain: Pompeu Fabra University. Retrieved from http://www.semanticaweb.net/archives/2005_evaluacion-municipales-isko.pdf

ONTI - National Bureau for Information Technologies. (2005). E-Governance Plan Decree 378/2005; Argentine. http://www.sgp.gov.ar/contenidos/onti/productos/pnge/docs/pnge_decreto_378_2005.pdf

Pontifical Catholic University of Chile. (2006). *Estudio Sitios Web Municipales: e-Government en Chile.* Retrieved from http://www.cetiuc.cl/wp-content/uploads/2007/01/presentacion-estudio-municipalidades.pdf

State Services Commission. (2007). *NZ Government Web Standards and Recommendations; Version 1.0; New Zealand.* Retrieved from http://www.e.govt.nz/standards/web-guidelines/web-standards-v1.0/web-standards-v1.0.rtf

UNESCO - United Nations Educational, Scientific and Cultural Organization. (n.d.). *E-Governance: Engaging E-Governance Capabilities.* Retrieved from http://portal.unesco.org/ci/en/files/14896/11412266495e-governance.pdf/e-governance.pdf

Web Managers, & the Requirements and Best Practices Checklist for Government. (2005). Retrieved from http://www.usa.gov/webcontent/reqs_bestpractices/checklist/long.pdf

KEY TERMS AND DEFINITIONS

Accessibility: It is the chance of a product or a web service of being accessed and used by the greatest possible number of people, regardless individual limitations or limitations of context of use.

Active and Passive Communication: Active communication can be thought as a two way communication, where both actors send and receive at the same time and passive communication as one way communication where one actor always send and the other always receive.

E-Governance: "It regards adopting ICT (Information and Communication Technologies) normative by the public government with the aim of improving the delivery of information and services to their citizens. Therefore, it promotes the community participation in the decision making process in order to increase the government's responsibility, transparency and effectiveness" (Following UNESCO).

Electronic Democracy (E-Democracy): It refers to increase the engagement of citizens in public decisions and actions by using the ICTs. Some examples are: opinion polls, forums, panels, blogs, chat rooms, referendums, mailing lists, e-mail, bulletin boards, direct contact with government agents and representatives, opinions, suggestions, complaints, frequently asked questions and their answers.

Electronic Services (E-Services): It refers to provide information and delivering services to citizens. It also includes information on events, shows, public transportation, district's maps, job vacancies, employment's policy, budget, purchases and contracts. Some examples of interactive services are: request for public or legal documents, certificates, appointments, on line tax and services payment.

Electronic Transparency (E-Transparency): It means that decisions taken and their enforcement are done in a manner that follows the rules and regulations. It also means that information is freely available and directly accessible to those who will be affected by such decision and their enforcement. It also means that enough information is provided and that it is provided in

easily understandable way and media". It crosses through the last two concepts (e-services and e-democracy). It can be seen as e-services when delivering information on the government's actions and decisions for the citizens to know why the government takes them. It also can be seen as e-democracy, because the government provides the citizens with information and communication channels that allow them to participate in decisions and to control the government.

Friendliness: User must be able to browse web sites no matter his skills level. Communication language should be simple allowing to access main contents in a clear way. Example aspects are: Categorized Information, Color contrast

Functionality: It is defined as the possibility to allow citizens' access to services like: information, administrative procedures, payments, state of debts, etc, without the need of personally going to City Hall, saving time, money and effort for both the citizen and de council. That's why our vision of web sites is oriented to "User Centered Design". Example aspects are: Printing of forms, tracking administrative procedures.

Information: Information regarding municipal government and its activities is one of the basic services that a municipal web site must provide. The citizen logs to a municipal web site basically to get information on schedules, time tables, news, addresses, taxes, and so on, because it is generally quicker, easier and cheaper to query a web site instead of phoning or going to the town hall. From the government point of view, information delivered on the web site, becomes an advantage because the citizens can get to it at any time, without long queues, and clerks to attend those people. The information provided by the web site must be true, opportune, up to date and relevant.

Navigability: Navigability is the way with which the user, actually the municipality's citizen, is able to move through a web site in order to access all the web pages that belong to it. This movement (navigation) through a web site is performed by the use of buttons, icons, hypertext, hyperlinks, menus, etc., that allows the user to move from one page to another, or from one site to another, depending on the user's will. All this site-user's interaction must be performed in the simplest and clearest way.

Usability: It is defined as the quality of user experience when interacting with a product or system. ISO 9241-11 standard defines usability like: The ability of a product of being used by a user to reach specifics goals with effectiveness, efficiency and satisfaction, inside a particular user context. ISO 13407 defines user centered design like: User active participation and clear knowledge of user requirements and tasks; Correct function localization between user and technology; Interaction of solutions design; Interdisciplinary design. Usability can be measure by several aspects like: Effectiveness; Efficiency; Satisfaction; Easy to learn; Easy to remember; Errors rate and severity

Veracity: Government web site cannot have disclaimers of its own information. Published information must be of informative character (updated, real, and relevant for the one that is accessing the site). Example aspects are: Updated News, Contradictory information, Web site standard unification will be designed to allow any user that has already use a government web site, to apply all previously learned procedures to the new upcoming site. Example aspects are: Show on every page the path to reach it from the home page, Banner with organization name.

Chapter 8
Changing the Rules:
Injecting Content into Computer Games

André Koscianski
UTFPR – Federal University of Technology, Brazil

ABSTRACT

The increasing availability of information and communication technology makes it possible to explore new concepts and strategies in teaching and learning processes. The reduction of cost and the amelioration of processing power of computers allow bringing to the classroom software of greater complexity. This way, the use of simple computer presentations is gradually replaced by hypermedia systems capable of combining different kinds of information. Interactive simulators represent a next step, allowing students to participate in an active process of experimentation. These tools make use of numeric models to represent the dynamics of systems with high accuracy. Video games can blend the numeric and media capabilities of computers with a presentation format that provides a pleasant experience and promotes a deep engagement in activities. These characteristics have a positive impact on learning results, explaining the interest on such software. The construction of educational games requires knowledge from very diverse fields, like pedagogy, cognitive psychology, computer graphics, simulation and software engineering. Each area of expertise has its own view from the issues involved; bringing together different professionals in a coherent manner can be a challenging task. This work describes tools to help organize the design and decisions during the implementation of an educational game. They facilitate the communication between project members, by documenting design options in different stages.

INTRODUCTION

Many subjects studied in science, engineering and technology present a procedural character, represented by sequences of events and interactions involving elements inside a system. For instance, protein synthesis, water cycle and current flow in galvanic cells are a few examples of contents studied in secondary and undergraduate curricula that present such characteristics. Modern systems exhibit increasing structural complexity and intricate

DOI: 10.4018/978-1-61520-763-3.ch008

behaviours; this can be observed in electronic devices, software and industrial processes. Several abstract and conceptual problems have an algorithmic nature with similar aspects. Numerical calculus, system control and signal filtering are examples involving sequence of operations. These processes are, indeed, frequently described with the help of flowcharts.

Mechanisms that cannot be concretely observed and that contain dynamic features are particularly hard to study and understand. In this case, students are required to figure out the functioning of a system from models and descriptions, most of the time using static diagrams and texts. Systems where several activities occur simultaneously are even more complicated to deal with.

Information Technologies can be used to address many issues in this context. Hypermedia software enables the combination of texts, sounds and animated images, contributing to clarify explanations and to enhance the cognitive experience of the students. Simulation programs go one step further and provide interaction, allowing students to formulate and test hypothesis, independently or under teacher guidance. This creates a space of experimentation and can be identified with a learn-by-doing paradigm, generally recognized as more effective than passive learning to absorb information.

Computer games share with simulators the capability to handle user interaction. This functionality is carefully projected to obtain an engaging, enjoyable environment. The user acceptance is a central objective to developers, who must create compelling activities inside a pleasing scenery; the success of a video game can be measured by its capability to keep users focused on the action. In essence, this is similar to what teachers strive to do in class and is one of the factors that explain the interest in edutainment.

Video games have a strong potential in pedagogical applications, but their construction with this objective still lacks well established methodologies. Computer interfaces are unusual

blackboards and teachers are not acquainted with all the ergonomic issues that permeate their design. On the other side, computer developers do not have the necessary background to deal with pedagogical requirements. Finding the correct balance between playfulness and information transmission remains an open issue. Besides this, the translation of contents from biology, chemistry and other areas into the video game vocabulary of symbols, images and characters still relies primarily on the creativity of teachers and programmers. These problems stand on an interdisciplinary boundary, not fully explored in the current literature. It relates teaching-learning methodologies with the development of computer applications targeted at education.

THE ROLE OF GAMES IN EDUCATION

Facilitating the transfer of information is a central issue in the teaching-learning process. Teachers combine texts, diagrams and oral expositions in order to explain subjects under different perspectives, creating several opportunities for the students to review, analyse and retain information. Nonetheless, the traditional tools used in classroom, like slides and books, are not completely adapted to describe dynamic processes. Representing this kind of phenomena on a blackboard can be a daunting task. The wrong choice for the diagrams or the sequence of events can make it difficult for the students to follow the explanations, or give a false and frustrating impression of complexity. Systems where processes can occur in parallel add another complication for both teachers and students.

Complex mechanisms that involve large amounts of information represent another barrier, forcing teachers to fragment the presentation of material. The result is often an abstract, highly theorized view that requires the students to construct mental representations:

Figure 1. Different media used in education

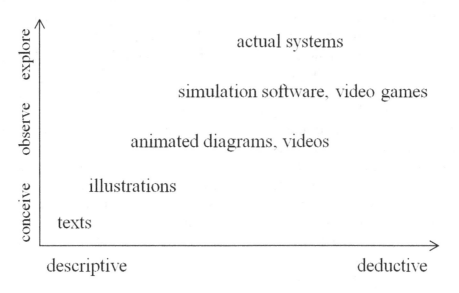

"*If the student does not bring a preconceived model to class, then we must ensure that a viable hierarchy of models is constructed and refined as learning progresses*" (Ben-Ari, 1998).

Videos and multimedia may circumvent many representation and communication difficulties, providing direct, immediate explanations. They help students make sense of texts and oral expositions, giving rise to better analysis (Newhouse et al. 2007). Graphical animations can be as effective as traditional lessons (Baker 1988; Davies, Goel, & Nersessian, 2005) and, in some cases, can help students learn faster (Dharaskar, Bajpayee, Chube, & Thakre, 2005).

Interactive multimedia introduce additional capabilities: simulators and virtual worlds allow controlling equipment and modifying parameters in virtual experiments. These tools contribute to a shift from passive to active learning (Shaffer 2006) and provide means for students who need to experience things in order to assimilate knowledge (Felder & Breng, 2004). The Figure 1 depicts a of these different instructional means.

The terms listed along the axes of Figure 1 make a loose classification of media, according to their usage in a pedagogical context. Texts are likely to require the greater effort to be constructed and interpreted, owing to the requirement that information is accessed in a linear manner. Diagrams improve on this aspect and are more suited to represent chunks of data (Gobet et. al, 2001), but as it happens with texts, their meaning can not be correctly understood if a certain background is lacking, like a lexicon established in class. Films and animations are closer to the reality and, in this sense, require little or no translation effort; the dynamic operation of a system can be observed, instead of conceived by the student. There are indications that the dynamic character of these media increases retention (Mayer & Anderson, 1992, Champoux, 1999). The same characteristic applies to simulations, with the addition that the object of study can be manipulated (Tan, Biswas, 2007). Users can deduce the operation of the system from causal relations, or by examining the internal mechanisms if they were made accessible through the simulator.

Given the appropriate conditions, texts, videos or software can be used in class to implement a specific instructional design, like problem-based learning. However, static representations are mainly used to transfer information; in fact, the

students do not perceive them as a space where the learning occurs. Interactive tools, on the other hand, may have this connotation. The interaction with software allows a user to follow different paths of experimentation and require the planning of actions. During these processes, information is gathered, hypothesis tested and knowledge may be constructed. The sensation of having control over the outcome of an experiment, even simulated, is essentially different from a tacit assumption that a given mechanism will function as described.

Video games are a particular case of interactive multimedia software, conceived with the primary objective of entertaining. As a consequence, the use of games to teach seems at first paradoxical: playing is a leisure activity that should relief stress and fatigue, while studying is generally viewed as an imposed task. The key to bridge this gap is the fact that an educational video game will still be perceived as fun, as long as the action is centred around the idea of playing (Fisch, 2005).

Enjoyment is a key ingredient for motivation, contributing for awareness and information retention. Moreover, it is not bound to any particular activity such as playing. This fact received special attention from the researcher Miháli Csikszentmihályi, who describes this psychic state as "optimal experience" or Flow (Csikszentmihályi, 1990). His studies pointed to a set of characteristics that are present in flow episodes:

- People feel apt to conclude the activity;
- The goals of the task and the progress of the users are clearly identified;
- People experience a loss of self-consciousness and are highly focused on the task at hand;
- People disconnect from the surrounding reality; there is a distorted sense of time;
- Flow experiences are naturally rewarding, dismissing any additional recompenses external to the activity itself.

Video games are associated with most of the cited characteristics, sometimes occupying users for hours. The positive relations between motivation, flow state and games have been established from an educational perspective (Facer, 2003; Hildmann, Hainey, & Livingstone, 2007) and constitute an important argument in favour of the use of games as learning tools (see also Egenfeldt-Nielsen, 2005).

Besides their fun character, games provide a rich cognitive environment. Sounds, colours and images may be used to group and to classify information. These elements function as sensory clues, helping students to make associations and create mnemonics.

GAME BUILDING BLOCKS

The first game consoles were released in the seventies; only thirty years later, the costs of development of a single title reached millions of dollars. Game programming became a serious business, requiring the careful application of engineering methods.

The implementation of games relies extensively on the software engineering principle of reuse and on component-based and modular designs. They constitute solutions for quality control and to handle architectural complexity. There are specialized code libraries for every subsystem in a game, like artificial intelligence, geometry and physics simulation. Besides software artefacts, developers maintain catalogues of elements like geometric models, characters and sets of rules. These components are essential to accelerate the implementation and also form the basis to several genre classifications (Bethke, 2003; Dondlinger, 2007; Owen, 2004; Rollings & Morris, 2000).

The construction of a new title begins with the creation of a concept and proceeds by choosing and shaping the elements that will implement it. Artefacts such as sound tracks, scenery and mul-

timedia can be treated simply as non-functional requirements; the whole software life cycle can be handled with classic engineering methodologies.

Educational objectives bring an additional, unusual dimension: pedagogical quality (Amory & Seagram, 2003). As it happens with interface design, pedagogical requirements may be addressed with the help of heuristics (Chalmers 2000; Desurvire, Caplan, & Toth, 2004; Mallone, 1980). Checklists of qualitative criteria are common tools used to guide the development. Some examples of heuristics applicable to educational games are:

- match class and game activities (Howard, 2006);
- match learning styles and contents presentation (Carver, Howard, & Lane, 1999);
- add 'gameability' to an existing teaching tool, like a simulator (Galvão, 2000);
- follow guidelines about assessment and language (Johnson & Schleiyer, 2003).

Each game genre is, in principle, more closely related to a given instructional design. For instance, hit-miss titles can give an immediate feedback which may correspond to a behaviourist approach. Examples of application are activities to practice a skill as musical perception, or to memorize information like multiplication tables. Certain construction puzzles seem less interesting for repetitive tasks, but allow students to explore different paths of action to solve a problem. Finally, role-playing games and virtual worlds give much flexibility to dispose contents along a storyline, but require a careful planning to present information in an adequate way.

Most educational titles fall in the category of quizzes and questionnaires, which are easy to conceive but are extremely limited vis-à-vis the diversity of instructional designs and games that exist. This is indeed an indication of the difficulty to integrate these two universes.

MODELLING DYNAMIC PHENOMENA IN GAMES

The basis of most video games is to conduct the user through intense, non-stop interactions, providing a certain level of challenge but avoiding frustration. Action titles put the player in control of objects in a simulated world obeying Newtonian mechanics, where properties like speed, friction or weight help mimic reality to make a credible experience. Humans seem highly sensitive to these kinetic clues, despite the limitation of interfaces to only visual and auditory stimuli. Players tend to follow the motion of objects on screen with their bodies, may get motion sickness (Bos, Bles, & Groen, 2008) and show physiological stress responses like increase of blood pressure (Hébert, Béland, Dionne-Fournelle, Crête, Lupien, 2005). These effects may occur even with modest graphic resources.

Genres like sports and action are very popular; the high acceptance of these games among the public (Berk, 2008) make them an interesting choice for educational purposes. However, the success of this objective requires the learning contents to be interwoven into the interface in an authentic manner, preserving the original character of the software. This is not easy to achieve; the translation of educational contents into video games is frequently based on the creativity of developers, a factor that can lead to erratic results.

In order to improve the predictability of this process, a systematic approach is described in the following sections. It provides guidelines to conduct the developer through the conceptual creation of the software, making more evident the possible design alternatives. The method aims to help teachers and programmers to reduce the strict dependency on creativity, by providing means to reveal a range of applicable game designs. It does not place limits nor preclude any modifications along the way.

Describe the System Under Study

The first step in order to conceive an educational game is to accurately describe the mechanisms of the system being studied. This description will delimit the scope to be treated, the possible prerequisites and allow identifying the core concept of the game. Indeed, all these aspects are essential during the conception of any learning materials, from text and slides to multimedia.

Diagrams are very adequate for this task; they are universally used in science and technology to make descriptions and blueprints. They can convey dense information using simple construction rules. In many cases, there is a unique one-to-one correspondence between a mechanism and its representation, avoiding possible ambiguities.

UML – Unified Modelling Language (Booch, Rumbaugh, & Jacobson, 2005) encompasses a series of different diagrams. It was originally devised for software engineering, but has enough generality to describe a variety of systems exhibiting complex semantics. The activity diagram is one of the most intuitive UML representations. It does not require a technical background to be used and is particularly adequate to deal with sequences of actions.

An activity diagram resembles a flowchart, with support for decisions, iterations, parallelism and synchronization. To clarify its use in the project of a game, a simple biochemical process has been chosen: the photosynthesis, outlined in Figure 2.

The round-corner boxes represent actions and the rectangles represent physical objects or informations. Each part of a system may be treated with a different level of detail, revealing minor features or hiding entire mechanisms in single boxes. The system may also be decomposed into several diagrams that can be directly used in the game project, for example to define different levels and puzzles. During this early stage of the game conception, the teacher will decide which aspects of the phenomenon are more relevant to be presented.

The diagram in Figure 2 is partitioned into two chemical reactions: the first is activated by solar light to produce ATP, while the second converts CO_2 into a more complex organic compound (G3P or Glyceraldehyde 3-phosphate), used in the synthesis of sugar. The proposed diagram emphasizes the identification of the principal chemicals in the photosynthesis, but simplifies the Calvin-Benson Cycle. A possible instructional

Figure 2. UML activity diagram for the photosynthesis process

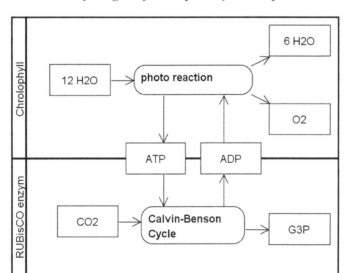
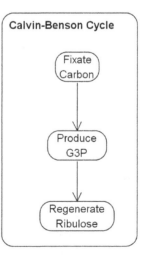

objective here would be to lead the students to describe and explain this system.

List Possible Game Actions

Creating a representation of physical processes, suitable for a video game, has a parallel with making a translation. Elements from the real world are replaced with game building blocks, like sprites, actions and rules. This change must preserve causal relations, synchronization and other relevant characteristics, in order to ensure the coherence between the system being studied and the model constructed for the software.

The UML activity diagram clearly shows sequences of events, mechanisms and elements that compose a system. The actions contained in the diagram are central to the definition of a game. The dynamic aspects of a phenomenon can be captured by numerous game metaphors,

like moving projectiles, sprites and obstacles, or changes in colour, size and speed.

The terms listed in Table 1 provide examples of game actions and different meanings that can be associated with them. The list was obtained from an analysis of different titles and genres and provides an initial reference.

The first column of the table contains keywords with the general meaning of a group of verbs. The second column lists the corresponding actions, which can be found in actual games. The last column of the table brings examples that can take place in real systems.

In the case of the Figure 2, the molecules are a natural choice for the sprites that will perform visible actions on the screen. They can be represented by icons, bubbles, insects or any object or character, two or three dimensional, that can give rise to a set of rules and a storyline. The adequacy of the theme to a given public and age range can

Table 1. A list of game actions

Meaning	Game actions	Examples of use
movement	walk, run, jump, swim, dive, fly, drag, push, pull, climb, descend, fall, bounce, guide, enter, exit, tele-transport	transport, remove organize, classify
selection, deselection	hit, touch, drop, place, paint, mark, aim, click, catch, clear away, enter or exit an area	select object, property or action start or stop a process or mechanism
throw	cause another action to happen, hit, harm, drop	trigger event, start process
avoid	deviate, hide, disable, disengage	avoid wrong choice of element or avoid an operation
build, assemble	glue, cover, paint, attach, create an instance	construct or complete an object assemble a molecule, a machine
disassemble	detach, destroy an instance, dig, remove	step back during assemble, detach an element
connect, turn on	trace, draw, drag, create a path, open a door	link, bind, compose, start flow relate concepts, properties or objects identify right/wrong relations construct or complete an object
disconnect, turn off	break, unlink, split, close a door or barrier	halt a process stop or pause an action
fill	accumulate, paint, store	accumulate material or property increase quantity
empty	spend, use, dig, clear, burn	spend, destroy decrease, reduce

be postponed while the ideas are enumerated. The adaptations can be done later by modifying the decor and the characters, generally with little or no repercussion on the rules and objectives.

The choice of the molecules as sprites opens several possibilities:

- movement: the molecules are thrown and must be directed to the correct reaction; or, the right chemicals must be selected as products exiting a reaction;

- selection or connection: the correct substances must be associated with specific reactions;

- fill and use: the player chooses and consumes the right number of molecules for each reaction.

Besides objects, sprites can also represent actions. This is particularly useful when the object of an action is implicit or is not represented at all, as it happens with the Calvin-Benson Cycle in the right part of the Figure 2. Each phase of the cycle may be represented by a game object, controlled by commands like move, select or sort.

Derive Possible Game Designs

Once the dynamic objects and actions have been identified, the alternatives for implementation become more evident and can be refined in one or more design options. At this point a catalogue of game genres would be useful to seed a brainstorm or discussion and storyboards can be drawn to communicate ideas. The initial rules and game objectives can also be derived during this phase.

Table 2. A summary of possible designs for the photosynthesis game

Overall idea	Rules and objectives	Distracters
Molecules are ballistic projectiles. The player controls the angle and the force of the shots using the position of the mouse (no values are typed).	The molecules are **thrown** towards moving targets and the resulting chemicals fall from them. The player must **catch** or **select** molecules in the lower part of the screen. Changes between night and day may be used to switch between reactions. A cannon consumes ATP; low reserves must be administered.	Additional, unwanted molecules and other obstacles, move on screen; they block and remove targets.
Molecules are represented by moving bubbles and reactions by rectangular regions.	The bubbles move freely and must be **dragged** to the correct areas. Resulting chemicals are new bubbles that **exit** the reactions.	Bubbles that touch each other blow. An object – a bird or a plane – moves on the screen and also blows or consumes bubbles.
Coloured dots represent molecules that must be joined. The screen switches between two modes: day and night.	The player must **connect** molecules of the right type, using lines drawn with the mouse. The whole game field scrolls continuously. When a pair ADP-H2O is obtained, it is transformed into one ATP and one O2.	The lines drawn by the player must not cross any obstacle. The speed of the game increases with time. Wrong substances appear on the screen to confound the player.
Space Invaders	The player must **aim** and **hit** the correct substances (enemy spaceships). They are **accumulated** and when the right amount is obtained, the game shifts between the two reactions of Figure 2.	Power-ups and different weapons are available along the game. They may be distributed, or must be bought using credits or points.
Reactions and molecules are moveable objects. The reactions are controlled by the user. Substances are represented by icons or by name.	The player **guides** a spaceship or a boat that represents a reaction, towards the correct molecules that must be **hit**. The resulting chemicals are expelled behind the vehicle. When sufficient molecules of one type are obtained, the spaceship switches between the light reaction and the Calvin-Benson Cycle, requiring the pilot to target different substances.	The inertia of the vehicle requires skill to be controlled. The player must deviate from wrong molecules, like pollutant substances. Enemy ships may attack the player.

Another feature to consider is the inclusion of distracters. They are genuine game elements that temporarily take the user's attention away from the contents being studied. They improve the software making it more fun and help to balance the design between enjoyment and instructional objectives. An example of distracter is an intermediate game phase, containing a puzzle, a pinball or an arcade, that the player must win in order to advance to new levels. Hidden passages, extra points, enemies and bonuses can also be used. The inclusion of these items distributed along the storyline makes the game more fun and motivates the users to continue playing in order to discover new surprises.

The Table 2 develops the ideas listed for the photosynthesis game. Each line describes different game objects, rules and the corresponding objectives; the highlighted verbs correspond to actions from the repertory listed in Table 1. Different distracters are also suggested.

Refine the Game Design

When the theme has been chosen, the developers can start to detail the game contents and refine architectural requirements for the implementation.

The use of prototypes is very convenient to help artists, teachers and programmers have a better perception of the software. Each person can form a picture from the storyboard that does not match the way objects move and look on the screen. A prototype allows evaluating these aspects and may also be used to make the first adjustments to the parameters that control the game difficulty.

The Figure 3 depicts two prototype screens, corresponding to the ideas described in the last line of the Table 2: a classic arcade shooting game. The genre is well known and the general principle of playing – shooting and deviating – makes it simple for users to understand the software. The theme is generally well accepted among players of different ages and is easy to modify without adding complicate rules.

The Figure 3 shows two possible screens. The player controls a spaceship and collects or shoots the substances as it moves. The computer pilots the enemies and fires projectiles against the player. In the right view of Figure 3, the sprites have been hidden; this is an effect that can be used in certain moments of the game, in order to ensure that the students will memorize the name of the substances and not only the corresponding icons.

Figure 3. Two prototype screens for the photosynthesis game

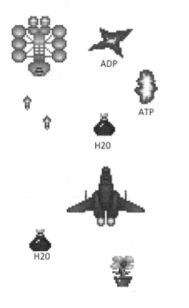
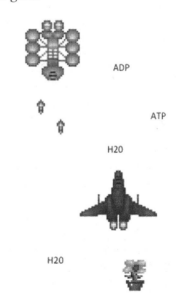

The game opens the way for the inclusion of additional concepts. For instance, the balance of substances can be indicated by 'energy' bars. Different spaceships can be used to represent the photo reaction and the Calvin-Benson cycle. Other molecules and reactions can be included, as the glycolysis that uses G3P, or the production of carbon monoxide by combustion at high temperatures. The whole game scenery can be shown as a mini-universe that is part of a plant leaf, opening the way to study other phenomena, like the physics involved in the transport of liquids in vascular plants.

While the game details are elaborated, the parameters that control the difficulty must also be identified. Certain methods to implement this function, like limitations of time, may have an impact on the internal architecture of the software. Other strategies, like adding lives or power-ups, may involve changes in the rules and should be discussed early during the project. The definition of variables and parameters that have a technical character should be avoided, in favour of values that can be easily understood and modified by everyone involved in the project. For instance, the maximum depth of a search algorithm can be replaced by an estimate of the success rate of the computer.

Finding the ideal level of difficulty requires tests with groups of different users. A method to directly select any level or phase of the game, like a hidden menu, can be very helpful. To facilitate the calibration of the parameters, they should be easily accessed and modified by testers, for example by means of scripts and configuration files. The Table 3 enumerates some parameters that can be implemented this way.

In the case of an educational game, it may be necessary to adjust parameters that are directly related to the subject being taught. Some examples are values in equations and number of items that compose a problem. Generally these values can be randomly chosen by the software, but this process must be carefully controlled. Teachers should provide limits and constrains, like combination of values that must be avoided by the game, because they may lead to irregular or invalid results. In some cases the formulation of an inverse problem is possible, so that given a range of correct answers, the software can calculate the initial values of the question that will be shown to the player.

The automatic control of difficulty is an interesting feature to envisage, but it is hard to implement and still constitutes a research subject. This function would allow a game to automatically adjust the level of challenge, avoiding the frustration of users who can not finish a level and, inversely, increasing the difficulty when a skilled player quickly solves puzzles and problems. Generally the use of predefined sets of parameters give good results, allowing to provide levels of increasing difficulty or different modes of operation, like 'easy', 'medium' and 'hard'.

The Figure 4 summarize the steps presented in this section. They were arranged according to a sequence for clarity purposes. During the actual project, the workflow does not necessar-

Table 3. Examples of parameters used to control game difficulty

Game parameter	Notes
time limits	Can be used to challenge the user and to simulate the duration of physical phenomena. Easy to adjust.
accuracy of computer controlled adversaries	Can be implemented with simple probabilistic rules to determine hit or miss.
number, size and speed of obstacles	Require extensive testing but the effects of changes are immediately perceived.
number of lives and power-ups, number of recharges of fuel and ammunition	Adjusting the quantity and distribution of these items is more difficult than other parameters and should be based on the average user progression.

ily follows a strict linear ordering. Tasks may be performed in parallel and cycles of evaluation-adjustment are likely to occur as well.

A division between "game space" and "pedagogic space" is sketched in Figure 4. The square boxes in the left list general information and elements employed in the design and implementation of games, while the right part of the figure lists information more specific to the project of educational software. The "instructional design" in the figure is meant to contain several topics, like instruction goals, strategies for exposition, evaluation and revision.

To improve the clarity of the diagram, software artefacts, artwork and other elements appear associated only with the activities more closely related to them. As an example, the choice of a definitive soundtrack would be expected to take place as the team approaches a final design. In fact, especially composed scores may require the visualization of complete sceneries and graphical artwork. However, the inverse is also possible, with a music background serving to inspire the scenery, the rhythm of playing activities or even the plot of the game. Similarly, a rendering engine is part of the final product, but functional characteristics like availability or not of special graphical effects must be considered early as restrictions to the software conception.

The first two steps, "Draw activity diagram" and "Identify objects and actions" are essentially descriptive and objective. Relations between the subject to be studied and other phenomena or disciplines should be clearly stated during this phase. This can be helpful during the development of the project, for example providing hints for sceneries that show the application of concepts.

Figure 4. Overview of steps in pedagogical game construction

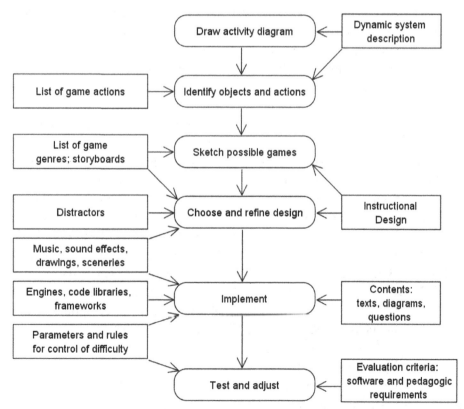

Storyboards and brainstorm sections are essential tools to perform the next steps, where the initial game possibilities are refined. If the development team does not have worked together, some points will require special attention. An instructor who never got involved with software development may find it difficult to foresee the implementation effort associated with a given scenery or object behaviour. At the same time, programmers and systems analysts may show a tendency to conduct the project in the benefit of software architecture or efficiency of implementation. This posture is frequently unconscious and may be the result of lack of experience. The project leader must balance the views from teachers and game developers in order to find the best compromise solution.

Prototypes and executables with limited functionality help to evaluate the game design and to spot problems and inaccuracies. The cost of developing prototypes is largely compensated by the reduction of risks, specially in large projects. By running a prototype, teachers and students acting as test users can have a first impression of the game and evaluate its interface and functionality. Not rarely, their conceptions with regard to aspects as layout, ergonomy or clarity of interface differ from those of the development team. Eventually, a prototype may help to make the first adjustments in the game difficulty.

Tests and inspections of the software should be performed by teams distinct from those in charge of the implementation. This principle maximizes the objectivity and effectiveness of the reviews and can be applied to every phase of the project.

INTEGRATING A GAME IN THE CLASSROOM

The project and implementation of educational video games follow the same general criteria used with other digital learning objects. For instance, a characteristic like self-contained information is a basic requisite for materials that can integrate a repository and that will be reused under different contexts. Portability is another important attribute, breaking the dependence on specific platforms; games implemented with technologies like Java can be executed practically on any computer. The cost of using technologies in the classroom is a concern to administrators that must be addressed by developers.

An educational video game can be used by teachers in several different ways. If the students are allowed to install their own copies at home, the software becomes an instrument to review a subject, or at least a reminder that invites to study in an agreeable manner. In this sense, the recreational character of games contributes to create a positive atmosphere in the class; students tend to be very sensitive to the efforts made on this sense. A simple pause to play an educational game in a computer laboratory can help to make students more comfortable and more willing to participate.

Games are generally used as a means to review subjects that have been taught in formal classes, but in some cases it is also possible to invert this process: the software can be used to introduce new contents that will be discussed and detailed later. The game scenery can help the teacher and students, by functioning as a reference to explain dynamic aspects of the phenomenon being studied.

Finally, in certain cases a game can also have a role as an assessment tool. Business simulation games are already used with this purpose. The evaluation process is not automatic: it is continuously performed by the teacher, who follows the progress of the participants as they explore and solve problems inside a virtual world. The software may assist teachers by providing quantitative data, like statistics of success, time spent and number of tasks accomplished.

CONCLUSION AND REMARKS

The human capability to automate tasks and the need to communicate with each other are strong driving forces, which have transformed our society through all its history. The transmission of culture and the teaching of science are intrinsically part of this process, at the same time using the available technology and helping its progress. The transformations are fast: in a matter of few decades, we jumped from vacuum tubes restricted to research laboratories, to computers embedded in cell phones affordable to adolescents at school.

This speed of change seems to outpace the means used for the transmission of knowledge. Textbooks at school are constantly updated to reflect the changes in the society and work; however, objects and technologies of everyday use take longer to make their way to our classes. The use of computers in education is still considered a recent or new idea and, in a significant part of schools, it is restricted to office software and simple internet tasks.

Teachers and programmers can not bridge this gap uniquely from their own perspectives. The task of projecting educational software is not different from other contemporary professions, requiring a combination of specialized knowledge and cross competencies. Fortunately, most issues involved in the question can be treated by applying the correct methodologies to each different aspect of the problem.

The present chapter approaches the problem in a methodical manner to facilitate a crucial point of interdisciplinary projects: the communication among teams with different expertises. The interaction between teachers, artists and developers must be managed so that it evolves into straight collaboration, to obtain a coherent and efficient product. The text shows when and how common tools, like storyboards, diagrams and checklists, can be used to organize the software project and, at the same time, help to improve the exchange of information.

REFERENCES

Amory, A., & Seagram, R. (2003). Educational game models: conceptualization and evaluation. *South African Journal of Higher Education, 17*(2), 206–217.

Ben-Ari, M. (1998). *Constructivism in computer science education*. Paper presented at the SIGSCE - Technical Symposium on Computer Science Education, Atlanta, GA.

Berk, K. (2008). *Greystripe consumer insights report*. San Francisco: Greystripe Inc.

Bethke, E. (2003). *Game development and production*. Plano, TX: Wordware Publishing Inc.

Booch, G., Rumbaugh, J., & Jacobson, I. (2005). *The unified modeling language user guide*. Reading, MA: Addison Wesley.

Bos, J. E., Bles, W., & Groen, E. L. (2008). A theory on visually induced motion sickness. *Health and Safety Aspects of Visual Displays, 29*(2), 47–57.

Carver, C. A., Howard, R. A., & Lane, W. D. (1999). Enhancing student learning through hypermedia courseware and incorporation of student learning styles. *IEEE Transactions on Education, 42*(1), 33–38. doi:10.1109/13.746332

Chalmers, P. A. (2000). User interface improvements in computer-assisted instruction, the challenge. *Computers in Human Behavior, 16*, 507–517. doi:10.1016/S0747-5632(00)00022-4

Champoux, J. E. (1999). Film as a teaching resource. *Journal of Management Inquiry, 8*(2), 240–251. doi:10.1177/105649269982016

Csikszentmihályi, M. (1990). *Flow: the psychology of optimal experience* (1 ed.). New York: Harper Perennial.

Davies, J., Goel, A. K., & Nersessian, N. J. (2005). *A cognitive model of visual analogical problem-solving transfer*. Paper presented at the Nineteenth Annual International Joint Conference on Artificial Intelligence, Denver, CO.

Desurvire, H., Caplan, M., & Toth, J. A. (2004). *Using heuristics to evaluate the playability of games*. Paper presented at the Conference for human-computer interaction, Vienna, Austria.

Dharaskar, R., Bajpayee, V., Chube, N., & Thakre, V. (2005). E-learning software for mathematical concepts and algorithms of computer graphics. *Information Technology Journal, 5*(1), 172–176.

Dondlinger, M. J. (2007). Educational video game design: a review of the literature. *Journal of Applied Educational Technology, 4*(1), 21–31.

Egenfeldt-Nielsen, S. (2005). *Beyond edutainment: exploring the educational potential of computer games*. University of Copenhagen.

Facer, K. (2003). *Computer Games and Learning* (Report). Bristol, UK: FutureLab.

Felder, R. M., & Breng, R. (2004). *The ABC's of engineering education: Abet, Bloom's taxonomy, cooperative learning, and so on*. Paper presented at the American Society for Engineering Education Annual Conference & Exposition.

Fisch, S. M. (2005). *Making educational computer games 'educational'*. Paper presented at the 4th International Conference for Interaction Design and Children, Boulder, CO.

Galvão, J. R. (2000). *Modeling reality with simulation games for a cooperative learning*. Paper presented at the Winter Simulation Conference.

Gobet, F., Lane, P. C. R., Croker, S., Cheng, P. C.-H., Jones, G., Oliver, I., & Pine, J. (2001). Chunking mechanisms in human learning. *Trends in Cognitive Sciences, 5*(6), 236–243. doi:10.1016/S1364-6613(00)01662-4

Hébert, S., Béland, R., Dionne-Fournelle, O., Crête, M., & Lupien, S. J. (2005). Physiological stress response to video-game playing: the contribution of built-in music. *Life Sciences, 76*, 2371–2380. doi:10.1016/j.lfs.2004.11.011

Hildmann, H., Hainey, T., & Livingstone, D. (2007). *Psychology and logic: design considerations for a customisable educational resource management game*. Paper presented at the Fifth Annual International Conference in Computer Game Design and Technology, Liverpool, UK.

Howard, C. (2006). *Learning, study and review methods: a fun way to learn and study complex theoretical content*. Paper presented at the Annual ASCILITE Conference: Who's learning? Whose technology? Sidney, Australia.

Johnson, L. A., & Schleiyer, T. K. L. (2003). Developing high-quality educational software. *Journal of Dental Education, 67*(11), 1209–1220.

Mallone, T. W. (1980). *What makes things fun to learn? Heuristics for designing instructional computer games*. Paper presented at the Symposium on Small Systems, Palo Alto, CA.

Mayer, R. E., & Anderson, R. B. (1992). The instructive animation: helping students build connections between words and pictures in multimedia learning. *Journal of Educational Psychology, 84*(4), 444–452. doi:10.1037/0022-0663.84.4.444

Owen, M. (2004). *An anatomy of Games, a discussion paper*. Bristol, UK: Futurelab.

Rollings, A., & Morris, D. (2000). *Game architecture and design*. The Coriolis Group.

Shaffer, D. W. (2006). *How computer games help children learn*. New York: Palgrave.

Tan, J., & Biswas, G. (2007). *Simulation-based game learning environments: building and sustaining a fish tank*. Paper presented at the IEEE International Workshop on Digital Game and Intelligent Toy Enhanced Learning, Taiwan.

KEY TERMS AND DEFINITIONS

Code Library: A piece of software that implements a function, calculation or other data processing and that can be reused to build another software.

Content Translation: A given study subject must be represented in a appropriate way, in order to be perceived as an authentic element composing a videogame.

Educational Game Design: This is a specialized branch of software development, requiring the blending of software engineering techniques, videogame technology and expertise in instructional design.

Educational Videogame: This term encompasses a broad range of software and entertainment devices like portable games, which can be targeted at educational purposes.

Game Vocabulary: Every videogame is composed of a set of characters, actions and storyline. These elements must form a coherent, harmonious group in order to provide an agreeable, convincing experience to the players.

Geometric Model: A numeric representation of a two-dimensional or three-dimensional object, suited for computer processing

Non-Functional Requirements: A set of constrains, qualities or criteria that describes the operation of a computer software, without specifying functions or specific behaviours

Representation of Dynamic Systems: Studying complex, dynamic mechanisms can be very difficult with traditional methods. Replacing abstraction with metaphors and static descriptions with dynamic images are efficient pedagogic means.

Software Ergonomics: Field of study concerned with the easy of use, efficiency, understandability and other aspects of interaction between humans and software.

UML: Unified modelling language, a pictorial language used to specify software architecture.

Chapter 9
An Integrated Process for Aspect Mining and Refactoring

Esteban S. Abait
UNICEN University, Argentina

Santiago A. Vidal
UNICEN University, Argentina

Claudia A. Marcos
UNICEN University, Argentina

Sandra I. Casas
UARG - Universidad Nacional de la Patagonia Austral, Argentina

Albert A. Osiris Sofia
UARG - Universidad Nacional de la Patagonia Austral, Argentina

ABSTRACT

Aspect-Oriented Software Development (AOSD) aims at solving the problem of encapsulating cross-cutting concerns, which orthogonally crosscut the components of a system, in units called aspects. This encapsulation improves the modularization of a system and in consequence its maintenance and evolution. In this work, the authors propose a systematic process for the migration of object-oriented systems to aspect-oriented ones. This migration is achieved in two main phases: crosscutting concern identification (aspect mining) and code transformation (aspect refactoring). The aspect mining phase is based on dynamic analysis and association rules to identify potential crosscutting concerns. The aspect refactoring phase, on the other hand, uses inference rules to identify the refactoring that can be applied. The whole process is described and its application on a real system is assessed.

INTRODUCTION

One of the main problems that software developers have to deal with is the unexpected and continuous evolution inherent to all software systems. This evolution implies that successful software systems must change or become less satisfactory (Lehman & Belady, 1974). Improving the separation of concerns (Parnas, 1972) in those software systems is likely to ameliorate their adaptability for changing

DOI: 10.4018/978-1-61520-763-3.ch009

environments. This separation of concerns is of vital importance in order to avoid many of the problems that complicate software engineering: degradation of software comprehensibility, invasive modifications due to maintenance and evolution tasks, reduced reusability of the developed artifacts and limited traceability (Tarr, Ossher, Harrison, & Sutton, 1999).

Aspect-Oriented Programming (AOP) (Kiczales et al., 1997) is a programming paradigm that promotes the separation of concerns in software systems. Particularly, AOP provides mechanism for the correct encapsulation of crosscutting concerns. Such concerns crosscut the dominant decomposition of the application restricting the separation of concerns on software. For instance, tracing, persistence or synchronization are common examples of crosscutting concerns. Code related to these crosscutting concerns can show two symptoms of bad modularization: it can be scattered over the whole project or it can be tangled with other code (Hannemann & Kiczales, 2001). AOP introduces a new modularization unit, called aspect, whose goal is the encapsulation of these crosscutting concerns.

The migration of an object-oriented software system into an aspect-oriented one is far from being a trivial task. Due to the large size of the implementation and the lack of sound documentation there is a need for tools that automate the identification, quantification and refactorization of crosscutting concern into aspects of the new systems. A first step towards achieving this goal is to discover the different crosscutting concerns present in the code, in order to decide whether they are aspect candidates for a future system. The task of identifying the crosscutting concerns that are amenable for an aspectoriented implementation is called aspect mining (Kellens, Mens & Tonella, 2007). Transforming those crosscutting concerns to aspects of the new systems is regarded as aspect refactoring (Kellens, Mens & Tonella, 2007).

This work presents a comprehensive approach to perform the gradual evolution of an object-

oriented system to an aspect-oriented one. The proposed approach aims at assisting the developer in: performing the evolution process, automating most tasks involved in this process, taking advantage of precise aspect mining techniques, and applying different types of aspect refactorings. We argue that the migration from an OO system to an AO one improves the structure and quality of the software, and thus eases software evolution. Besides, we believe that the provision of semi-automated support to help the developer to discover crosscutting concerns and to encapsulate them into aspects is beneficial. A novelty of the proposed approach is the use of dynamic analysis together with data mining techniques for identifying candidate aspects. In addition, an aspect refactoring process based on existing types of refactorings is presented, which automates the major steps of the migration.

The chapter is organized as follows. Firstly, the whole process is presented and its different steps are detailed. Next, the aspect mining and refactoring techniques are introduced and explained through a toy example. The following section presents the results of applying the full migration process on real software system. Afterwards, the related work is presented and the conclusion and future works are drawn.

THE APPROACH

The proposed approach consists of two main phases (Figure 1): (i) aspect mining, and (ii) aspect refactoring. The first phase receives an object-oriented system (to be evolved) as input, and produces a number of candidate aspects as output. These aspects are identified by making a dynamic analysis of the system and applying association rules. The information of candidate aspects and the initial system's source code are then passed to the aspect refactoring phase. In this phase, different refactorings are evaluated and eventually applied to the code. As output,

Figure 1. Integration of aspect mining with aspect refactoring

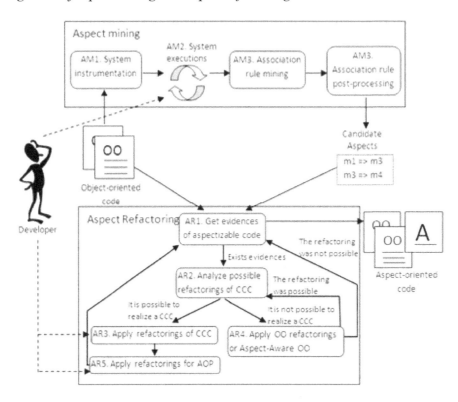

this second phase generates a new version of the system that contains aspect-oriented final code.

The whole approach is supported by an Eclipse-based prototype tool called AspectRT (Aspect Refactoring Tool). This tool helps developers to carry out the evolution process by automating parts of the tasks involved in each phase. The tool asks the developer for information that cannot be inferred like the name of the aspects, methods or attributes. The developer also needs to confirm real candidate aspects to be migrated.

A DYNAMIC APPROACH TO ASPECT MINING

In this section the basic concepts for dynamic analysis (Ball, 1999) and association rules (Agrawal & Srikant, 1998) are presented, then

the proposed aspect mining process is introduced and finally an example of its application on a toy example is explained.

Dynamic Analysis Basics

As Ball (1999) put forth, dynamic analysis is the analysis of the properties of a running program. While this definition is quite vague, it encompass a wide range of techniques which base their function on the analysis of data gathered during the execution of programs. For instance, software testing, profiling or some program comprehension techniques are based on dynamic analysis.

Dynamic analysis techniques have as a precondition for their utilization the definition of one or more execution scenarios, where an execution scenario is an instance of one or several use cases (Jacobson, 1995). Generally, those scenarios are

Figure 2. Simplified view of the tracing mechanism

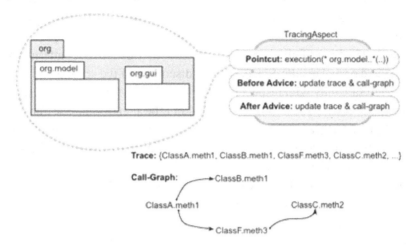

used to exercise the system and obtain execution traces. Execution traces register the methods that are called while the system is running.

Methods for Collecting Data

According to Salah and Mancoridis (2004) there are three methods for collecting runtime data: source code instrumentation, compiled code instrumentation and profiling-based data collection. The first one entails inserting additional sentences to the entire or parts of the source code of an application. The second one involves the instrumentation of compiled code, which is widely used to instrument Java bytecode. Lastly, the third method is based on debugging and profiling, this method does not require code instrumentation.

The proposed approach employs an aspect-based tracing mechanism developed using AspectJ (Kiczales et al., 2001), an aspect-oriented language, in order to instrument the target application (Figure 2). Depending on the kind of weaving used, static or load-time, the instrumentation can be over the source code or over the compiled application.

As depicted in Figure 2, when a given application is exercised through an execution scenario, the tracing mechanism creates an execution trace containing all the invoked methods and a dynamic call-graph consisting of call-relations between pairs of methods. For example, the call-graph of Figure 2 has an arc from ClassA.meth1 to ClassB. meth1 since during a system execution meth1 of ClassA invoked meth1 of ClassB.

Dynamic Analysis Benefits and Limitations

The use of dynamic analysis for program comprehension or reverse engineering has several benefits and limitations with respect to static analysis based approaches.

As being noted by some authors (Cornelissen, Zaidman, van Deursen, Moonen, & Koschke, 2009; Ernst, 2003), dynamic analysis techniques share a number of benefits. First, these techniques enable a goal-oriented strategy, so the user can concentrate on the parts of the system she is interested. Second, they are precise regarding the use of polymorphism in object-oriented systems. Moreover, Stroulia (2002) claims that in order to understand today software systems, i.e. object-oriented systems with components distributed in multi-tier architectures, developers need runtime analysis tools to complement the traditional view of the reverse engineering static tools.

On the other hand, several drawbacks on the use of dynamic analysis have been previously described (Cornelissen et al., 2009; Ernst, 2003; Koschke & Quante, 2005). First of all, dynamic analysis techniques yield partial results. Since all dynamic techniques are safe only with respect to the input that was actually considered during runtime to gather the information, generalizing from these data may not be safe. For instance, software testing only demonstrates the presence of errors yet not their absence. Secondly, sometimes is difficult to determine which scenarios executions are needed in order to trigger the program elements of interest. A further problem is the scalability issue due to large amounts of data that may affect the cognitive load the human can deal with. Finally, the observer effect, i.e. the phenomenon in which software acts differently when under observation, might pose a problem for multi-threading or multi-process software.

In general, both static and dynamic based approaches can be applied to a single problem, producing results that are useful in different contexts (Ernst, 2003). Concerning the aspect mining problem, previous experiences have shown that static and dynamic aspect mining techniques yield complementary set of results when applied on the same case study (Ceccato et al., 2006).

Association Rules Concepts

Association rule mining extract interesting correlations, frequent patterns, associations or casual structures among sets of items in the transaction databases or other data repositories (Kotsiantis & Kanellopoulos, 2006).

Two types of patterns can be found in association rule mining (Hegland, 2003). A first type is "if-then-rules" and are of the form: "If a customer buys milk then she also buys bread". That kind of pattern is regarded as an association rule. A second type relates to co-occurrence of items in a database transaction: "A customer buys bread and milk together". That kind of pattern is

regarded as a frequent itemset. The discovery of frequent itemsets is simpler than the discovery of association rules; moreover, one can see that the discovery of the first pattern can be based on the discovery of the second one.

Formally, let $I = \{i_1, i_2, ..., i_m\}$ be a set of items. Let D be a set of database transactions where each transaction T is a set of items such that $T \subseteq I$. An association rule is an implication in the form $X \Rightarrow Y$, where $X, Y \subset I$ are sets of items called itemsets, and $X \cap Y = \varnothing$ (Agrawal & Srikant, 1998). Moreover, X is called antecedent while Y is called consequent, the rule means X implies Y.

There are two important basic measures for association rules, support (s) and confidence (c) (Kotsiantis & Kanellopoulos, 2006). The support s for a rule $X \Rightarrow Y$ is the number of transactions T that contain X and Y. The confidence c for a rule $X \Rightarrow Y$ is the number of transactions T that contains X and Y regarding the overall number of transactions that contains X (Agrawal & Srikant, 1998).

A set of items is referred to as an itemset. The support count of an itemset is the number of transactions that contain the itemset. An itemset satisfies minimum support if the support count of the itemset is greater than or equal to s. If an itemset satisfies minimum support, then it is a frequent itemset (Han & Kamber, 2006).

Association rule mining is a two step process (Han & Kamber, 2006):

1. Find all frequent itemsets. Those itemsets will occur at least as frequently as a minimum support count threshold.
2. Generate association rules from the frequent itemsets. The resulting rules must satisfy a minimum confidence threshold.

Applying Association Rules to Discover Crosscutting Concerns

The proposed aspect mining technique consists in the generation of execution traces and its analysis

Figure 3. Aspect mining phases

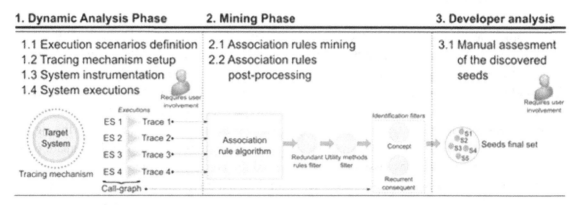

with association rules algorithms. The outputs of the technique are seeds that indicate the presence of scattering symptoms on the subject application. Particularly, those seeds pinpoint two well known kind of crosscutting concerns: role superimposition and consistent behavior concerns (Ceccato et al., 2006; Marin, Van Deursen, & Moonen, 2007).

Figure 3 depicts the process used to discover crosscutting concerns in object-oriented systems.

This process is divided in three phases. The first one encompasses all the activities concerning dynamic analysis: definition of execution scenarios (step 1.1), setup of the tracing mechanism (step 1.2), instrumentation of the subject system (step 1.3) and executions of the system according the scenarios defined in the first activity (step 1.4). The output of this phase is a set of execution traces and a call-graph. The second phase takes as input each execution trace and the call-graph and uses an association rule mining algorithm to extract the patterns (step 2.1). Then, the obtained rules are analyzed according to a set of post-processing filters (2.2). The 'Redundant rules' and 'Utility methods' filters discard association rules that are considered spurious for the developer analyzing an application; alternatively, the 'Identification filters' tag those rules that could represent an aspect candidate. The rest of the rules are discarded. Finally, the developer has to browse the resulting

set of rules and confirm which candidates are seeds and which ones are false positives.

Association Rule Mining from Execution Traces

Applying data mining techniques (Han & Kamber, 2006) on a set of execution traces yield patterns consisting of methods and classes executed during runtime. An execution trace is made of method calls obtained during the execution of a given scenario; consequently, executing different scenarios on the same program should yield different execution traces. Even though, sometimes the same class could collaborate in the realization of multiple use cases, so a method belonging to a class can be in several use case traces. Thus, classes and methods that are present in more than one execution trace are good candidates of crosscutting concerns, since their behavior is orthogonal to the executed functionality. The proposed approach employs association rule algorithms (Agrawal & Srikant, 1998) to find those methods and classes that are present in more than one execution trace.

In order to generate association rules from a set of execution traces, each execution trace is considered as a transaction T and the methods contained in all the traces as the set of items I. Therefore, the transactional database D consists of several execution traces, which is the input for the association rule algorithm. Particularly,

the Apriori (Agrawal & Srikant, 1998) algorithm was used to find the association rules.

The resulting association rules are then post-processed by several association rules filters. The next section introduces and gives examples on each kind of post-processing filter.

Post-Processing Filters

The proposed approach defines two kinds of post-processing filters for association rules. The first kind, discards rules that are considered to be spurious since they do not provide any knowledge. Examples of such spurious association rules are rules that include utility methods in their antecedent or consequent (e.g. Main.main $\Rightarrow$ JWindows. show) and redundant association rules. The second kind identifies association rules that may uncover the presence of potential crosscutting concern, and hence are regarded as 'Identification filters'.

Redundant Rules Filter

This filter removes association rules that capture the same semantic information. For example, given rules A $\Rightarrow$ B and B $\Rightarrow$ A those two rules present the same information although the rules are different. If both rules have similar support and confidence values, then one of them can be discarded.

Utility Methods Filter

Association rules that include utility methods, like 'main', 'toString', 'hashCode', 'hasNext', among others, must be removed because these methods are not evidence of crosscutting concerns.

Identification Filters

In order to identify potential aspect candidates from the set of generated association rules to filters were defined. The first one target methods that could correspond to superimposed roles on the classes. While the second one, target methods that implements crosscutting behavior and could correspond to a consistent behavior concern.

Concept Filter

The concept filter looks for methods that belong to a concern implemented using naming conventions or aspectizable interfaces (Tonella & Ceccato, 2005), and which behavior is present in several execution traces. A rule A.$m \Rightarrow$ B.m' will be tagged as an aspect candidate if the signature of m is equal (or similar) to the signature of m' and the confidence value c of the rule exceed a minimum confidence threshold. As a result, this filter target methods of classes that are called together to fulfill some responsibility that is apparently orthogonal to the executed scenarios. The confidence value ensures that the methods in the consequent are activated together with the methods of the antecedent during the execution of the scenarios, enforcing the assumption that those methods collaborate in the realization of the same responsibility.

Recurrent Consequent Filter

When two or more rules share the same consequent (A.$m1 \Rightarrow$ B.$m2$ and D.$m3 \Rightarrow$ B.$m2$), the immediate assumption is that the method of the consequent is consistently invoked from the methods included in the antecedents of the rules. The method of the consequent could be implementing functionality that is required from various places of the system (like a 'log' method). Therefore, the existence of such method is a possible indicator of consistent behavior concern. The recurrent consequent filter is defined as follow: given an association rule A $\Rightarrow$ B, where A and B are methods, the following conditions must hold,

- An arc from A to B exists in the call-graph. This means that A call B during the execution of the scenarios.
- B must be included as a consequent in another association rule C $\Rightarrow$ B that also holds the previous condition.

Figure 4. Class diagram for the example (left) and final set of seeds (right)

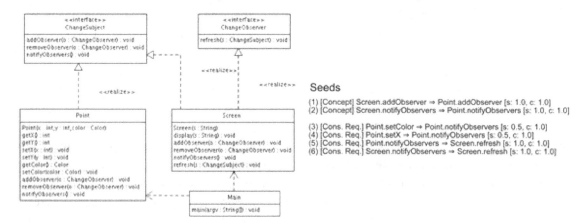

Example: Observer Pattern

This section explains the aspect mining technique through its application on an implementation of the Observer design pattern (Gamma, Helm, Johnson, & Vlissides, 1995). The same example was used by Hannemann and Kiczales (2002) to demonstrate the benefits of using AspectJ (Kiczales et al., 2001) to implement design patterns.

The example, as depicted in Figure 4, is a figure package where the Point class plays the Subject role and the Screen class plays the roles of both Subject and Observer (of Point and itself). The crosscutting concerns that this pattern superimposes on both classes are: functionality for mapping between subjects and observers, the notification mechanism and the update logic (Hannemann & Kiczales, 2002).

In order to use the proposed approach, the first phase consist in the definition of two execution scenarios, the instrumentation of the source code through the tracing mechanism previously presented, and the execution of the system to obtain the execution traces and the call-graph.

Afterwards, the execution traces provide the input for the Apriori algorithm. The simply execution of this algorithm yields 70 association rules with support and confidence value set to 0.1. The support and confidence values were chosen in order to get the largest set of association rules.

The post-processing step removes 91% of the association rules, yielding only six association rules as the final set of seeds. For instance, the utility method filter discarded rules like Main.main ⇒ Point.setColor or Main.main ⇒ Point.addObserver. The redundant rules filter removed, for example, the rule Screen.addObserver ⇒ Point.addObserver, because another rule exists with the same information: Point.addObserver ⇒ Screen.addObserver. Both, the utility method filter and the redundant rules filter remove 56 from the 70 generated association rules. From the remainder 14 association rules the identification filters tagged 6 rules as candidate aspects and discarded the rest. Those six association rules are the final output of the proposed aspect mining process. Indeed, all of them correspond to crosscutting concerns (Figure 4): rule 1 correspond to the mapping subject-observer concern, rules 2, 3 y 4 correspond to the notification mechanism concern and, lastly, rules 5 y 6 corresponds to the update logic concern.

To sum up, the proposed aspect mining approach was able to discover all the crosscutting concerns present in the analyzed source code and, what is more, it only generated six seeds reducing the user involvement during the aspect mining process.

A RULE-BASED APPROACH TO ASPECT REFACTORING

The purpose of aspect refactoring is to achieve a process applicable to aspect orientation similar to the object-oriented refactoring process. The Fowler refactoring catalog (Fowler, 1999) describes how to reorganize object-oriented systems. Although, those OO refactorings are not applicable in an aspect-oriented system, since their application breaks the links between aspects and the base code (Iwamoto & Zhao, 2003).

A variety of aspect refactorings have been proposed over the last years (Gamma et al., 1995). In this context, and in order to facilitate the evolution process, it is desirable to have tools to support current and future refactorings. The proposed aspect refactoring approach is based on different kinds of aspect refactorings. Particularly, the approach uses the following classification (Hannemann, 2006):

- *Aspect-Aware OO Refactorings*: This includes those object-oriented refactorings which were extended and adapted to be used in the aspect-oriented paradigm. That is, this type of refactoring ensures that the OO refactorings correctly update the references to the AOP constructions. The Aspect-Aware OO refactorings have been discussed in (Hanenberg, Oberschulte, & Unland, 2003) (Iwamoto & Zhao, 2003).
- *Refactorings for AOP constructs*: The refactorings grouped under this type have the property of being specifically oriented to elements of the aspect-oriented programming. Its objective is basically to improve the internal structure of aspects so that they are more legible and modifiable (Iwamoto & Zhao, 2003; Monteiro, 2004; Monteiro & Fernandes, 2005).
- *Refactorings of CCCs (CrossCutting Concerns)*: The objective of this third group is to transform the crosscutting concerns

into aspects. Regarding the basic idea of the aspect-oriented paradigm, these refactorings group the different concerns that are dispersed throughout the code while modularizing them into an aspect (Marin, Moonen, & van Deursen, 2005; Monteiro, 2004).

The proposed approach follows an iterative process that starts with an object-oriented code and evidences of "aspectizable" code. This evidence is actually provided by the candidate aspects resulting from the aspect mining approach previously presented. Each cycle of the process produces a code refactoring by adding aspect-oriented code in AspectJ. For each piece of evidence that suggests aspectizable code in the system, the developer has to evaluate the application of one or more aspect refactorings that transform parts of the code into an aspect.

The main steps of the refactoring approach, as shown at the bottom of the Figure 1, are the following:

1. *Get evidences of aspectizable code*: This step recovers the code that has been identified as aspectizable by the aspect mining phase. That is, there is a description of OO code attributes, methods, classes, etc. that should be transformed to encapsulate the crosscutting concerns into aspects. The connection with the aspect mining process is achieved through a XML file, which contains a list of candidate aspects with relevant data about those aspects.

2. *Analyze possible refactorings of CCCs*: This step examines the possibility of applying one or more CCCs refactorings to the target code. The reason for using CCC refactorings in this step is that the fragments of aspectizable code identified in the previous step may contain crosscutting concerns that must be encapsulated into an aspect.

3. *Apply refactoring of CCCs*: The refactorings previously selected are applied, so that every crosscutting concern is extracted from the object-oriented code and inserted in an aspect. The code refactorings are applied automatically by the AspectRT tool. Eventually, the developer has to take some decisions, such as: choice in which aspect a code fragment will be encapsulated, the name of a new pointcut, among others.

4. *Apply OO refactorings or Aspect-Aware OO*: If it is not possible to apply any refactoring of CCCs, this step seeks to apply object-oriented refactorings and/or aspect-aware OO ones on the target code in order to restructure it and retry step 2. Sometimes, the identified code cannot be encapsulated directly into an aspect, and a previous OO refactoring is needed for the OO code to be adapted to the aspect refactoring pattern. For example, if the aspect refactoring Move Method from Class to Inter-type (Monteiro, 2004) is needed and the selected method contains logic that should stay in the class, the refactoring Extract Method (Fowler, 1999) must be applied to the fragment of code that contains that logic.

5. *Apply refactoring for AOP constructs*: Finally, this step tries to apply refactorings for AOP constructs to the aspects that has been recently created through the application of CCCs refactorings. Sometimes, when extracting a crosscutting concern, multiples refactorings are applied. Even though, the internal structure of the aspect that encapsulates the aspectizable code may need to be refactored so as to improve its legibility and modularity, remove duplicate code, etc. For instance, this situation may happen after repeatedly applying the aspect refactoring Extract Fragment into Advice (Monteiro, 2004). The goal of Extract Fragment into Advice is to encapsulate a fragment of objective code into an aspect creating a new advice

and a pointcut. Because of this refactoring, repeated points may appear in the new aspect. If so, the duplicate pointcuts are removed and the advice references are updated accordingly. This way, the approach ensures that not only the crosscutting concerns selected by the developer are encapsulated into an aspect, but also the internal structure of aspects is improved.

In the following section the refactoring process is described in detail.

Analysis of Possible Refactorings

In order to identify the refactorings that can be applied to a given aspectizable code (AR1), a rule-based paradigm (Casas & Marcos, 2008) is used. The inference engine can identify code smells (Monteiro & Fernandes, 2005) from a class or from structural patterns, and then infer a set of possible refactorings for the current context. When a set of aspect refactorings is identified, the process informs the developer about it. The developer is responsible for accepting or refusing the refactoring of this code smell. The code smells supported by the approach have been grouped in three categories: tangling and scattering code, abstract class and inner class.

The structural patterns serve to delimit a subset of refactorings to be applied in an aspectizable code. These patterns use the information of the aspectizable code of the iteration, that is, they look whether the code is a method, a field, code inside a method, an inner class, etc. Based on this information, the engine can infer possible aspect refactorings to apply on the code.

The code smell and structural patterns are implemented in terms of simple rules like:

```
If (the aspectizable code is a
method)
then (try these possible refac-
```

Table 1. Structural patterns

Structural attribute	Applicable aspect refactorings
Method	Move Method from Class to Inter-type, Extract Feature into Aspect
Abstract class	Change Abstract Class to Interface, Split Abstract Class between Aspect and Interface
Class	Inline Class within Aspect
Inner class	Extract Inner Class to Standalone
Field	Move Field from Class to Inter-type
Implements declaration	Encapsulate Implements with Declare Parents
Code inside a method	Extract Feature into Aspect, Extract Fragment into Advice
Interface	Inline Interface within Aspect,
Inner interface	Extend Marker Interface with Signature
Aspect	Generalise Target Type with Marker Interface, Tidy Up Internal Aspect Structure, Extract Superaspect
Inter-Type method	Replace Inter-type Method with Aspect Method, Pull Up Inter-type Declaration, Push Down Inter-type Declaration
Inter-Type Field	Replace Inter-type Field with Aspect Map, Pull Up Inter-type Declaration, Push Down Inter-type Declaration
Advice	Pull Up Advice, Push Down Advice
Declare Parents declaration	Pull Up Declare Parents, Push Down Declare Parents
Pointcut	Pull Up Pointcut, Push Down Pointcut

```
torings: Move Method from Class
to Inter-type  Extract Feature
into Aspect)
```

This rule means that if the aspectizable code is code inside a method the applicable aspect refactorings are Extract Feature into Aspect and Extract Fragment into Advice. In the Table 1 a distribution of the possible aspect refactorings according to its structure is shown. This information is represented by means of structural patterns for its automatic identification. As is shown for the most of the attributes exist a limited set of aspect refactoring that can be applied. This situation promotes a more precise identification in the technique.

The three kinds of refactorings (CCC, AOP y Aspect-Aware OO), have been represented with structural patterns. Each one of these patterns indicates the necessary data for the identification of the refactorings and the activities needed in order to migrate the code. AspectRT, using the data provided by the aspect mining process, identifies automatically which refactorings to apply.

In this work a subset of the refactorings presented by Monteiro (2004) was utilized, however, the process is able to easily add new refactorings. In AspectRT, the mechanism for applying a refactoring is to select the code to be reestructured and then choose the corresponding refactoring. Basically, the aspect refactoring interface is based on the same approach that Eclipse uses for the object-oriented refactorings.

Refactoring for the Observer Example

In order to understand how the aspect refactoring phase works, the Observer example is used to describe the approach.

The first association rule in Figure 4 point out the method addObserver as part of the subject-observer mapping concern. During the iterations, the process can identify a set of aspect refactorings

to be applied. In this case, since the aspectizable code is a method, it is possible to apply aspect refactorings like Move Method from Class to Inter-type and Extract Feature into Aspect (Monteiro, 2004). The developer is responsible for selecting which refactoring to apply. The Extract Feature into Aspect refactoring is more appropriate, because a complete crosscutting concern needs to be encapsulated. When the developer chooses the aspect refactoring, the tool executes the changes on the source code. For this example, a new aspect called ObserverPointAspect is created, which contains the list of observers and the method addObserver. Later, the process tries to execute the step 5. As the code related to this step is the target code, no automatic AOP refactoring is provided. The process assists the developer indicating which AOP refactorings are applicable to the selected fragment of code, and applying it automatically. In the example, such a refactoring is not necessary because the structure of the aspect is very simple. Next, the process goes back to step 1, so as to analyze the next candidate aspect. The following aspect candidates to be analyzed are the methods notifyObservers and removeObservers. Both are encapsulated into the ObserverPointAspect using the aspect refactoring Extract Feature into Aspect, this way all the methods implemented from the interface ChangeSubject are moved to a new aspect. When the last method of the interface (removeObservers) is refactored, the aspect refactoring Encapsulated Implements with Declare Parents is applied in order to encapsulate the role that plays the interface ChangeSubject in the class Point.

STUDY CASE: JHOTDRAW

This section presents the results of applying our approach to version 5.4b1 of JHotDraw (JHotDraw), a Java objectoriented framework, with approximately 18,000 noncommented lines of code and around 2800 methods. JHotDraw is a framework for drawing structured 2D graphics and was originally developed as an exercise to illustrate good use of objectoriented design patterns (Gamma et al., 1995). Since its original adoption, JHotDraw has been the target for many aspect mining (Ceccato et al., 2006; Marin et al., 2007) and refactoring (Marin, 2004; van Deursen, Marin, & Moonen, 2005) studies.

The goal of this study case is to show how the proposed approach can be used to evolve an object-oriented application into an aspect-oriented one. Particularly, this section presents the results of applying the proposed process to encapsulate the persistence concern into aspects. The persistence concern in JHotDraw spans 36 classes all of them realizing the Storable interface. Interfaces like Storable are regarded by Ceccatto and Tonella (2005) as aspectizable interfaces. Such interfaces crosscut the principal decomposition of a system, and are amenable for aspect refactoring.

The following sections provide further details on how this evolution was accomplished.

Aspect Mining Phase

In order to identify which interfaces, classes and methods belong to the persistence crosscutting concern, a goal-oriented strategy was used to conduct the aspect mining phase. This goal-oriented strategy involves defining execution scenarios that are supposed to exercise the persistence functionality. As a consequence, eight execution scenarios were defined, including save a drawing with one figure, save a drawing with multiple figures, load a drawing with one figure, load a drawing with multiple figures, etc.

After applying the association rule algorithm and the post-processing filters the approach yielded 115 association rules. The support value was set to 0.25 with the purpose of obtaining association rules that were valid in at least 2 execution traces. The confidence, on the other hand, was

Table 2. Some association rules for the persistence concern

Identif. Filter	Association Rule	Supp.	Conf.
Rec. Consq.	AnimationDecorator.write ⇒ StorableOutput.writeInt FigureAttributes.writeColor ⇒ StorableOutput.writeInt	0.25	1.0
Concept	AnimationDecorator.read ⇒ AbstractFigure.read	0.25	1.0
Concept	AttributeFigure.write ⇒ AbstractFigure.write	0.25	1.0
Concept	DecoratorFigure.write ⇒ AttributeFigure.write	0.25	1.0

set to 1.0 so that the generated association rules correspond to the strongest correlations between method invocations.

Analyzing the resulting association rules (Table 2), from the set of 115 association rules 44 of them correspond to the persistence concern. As a result, the precision of the technique to identify the persistence concern was 38%, that is, only 44 out of 115 association rules are confirmed seeds for the target concern.

Although, a further examination of the final set of association rules shows that all the association rules considered as confirmed seeds for the persistence concern have a support value of 0.25. Consequently, if only the association rules with support value of 0.25 are considered the precision of the approach raise up to 61%, this is 44 over 71 association rules. According to Hegland (2003), the interesting rules are often found in an area of intermediate support size, in between the noise which has low support value, and the trivial and well-known rules with very high support. In particular for this study case, the interesting rules, those corresponding to the persistence concern, are in the lower area of support size and the rules with higher support value are the false positives. Most of them represent delegation relations between classes, like DiamondFigure.getPolygon ⇒ RectangleFigure.displayBox, or accessor methods such as DiamondFigure.getPolygon ⇒ RectangleFigure.displayBox.

Besides analyzing JHotDraw following a goal-oriented strategy, a full analysis of the application was performed.

In this regard, 21 execution scenarios were defined based on the available documentation. Those scenarios span most of the application functionality including opening and saving a draw, creating a figure, changing the color of a figure, undoing and redoing an action, among others. The support and confidence values for the analysis were set to 0.2 for support and 0.8 for confidence. The selected thresholds were chosen in order to obtain rules valid in at least two execution traces, since support count was 2. The confidence value was set so as to obtain rules with a strong correlation between the antecedent and the consequents.

The application of the association rules algorithm yielded 482 association rules, from which 283 corresponds to crosscutting concerns and 199 to false positives. As a consequence, the approach precision was 59%. All the previously crosscutting concerns reported by other authors (Ceccato et al., 2006; Marin et al., 2007) were also discovered by the proposed aspect mining technique.

Aspect Refactoring Phase

This phase takes as input 44 association rules corresponding to the persistence concern of JHotDraw. As a consequence, the refactoring phase will consist in at most 44 iterations, although some iteration can be skipped if the aspect candidate is not important for the migration task. Table 3 shows for each aspect refactoring applied, its name, to which group the refactoring belong and the number of times that refactoring was used.

As can be seen from the above table, the refactoring process is somewhat repetitive and tedious;

Table 3. Aspect refactoring phase results

Aspect Refactoring	Type	N° of times
Extract Fragment Into Advice	CCC	14
Move method from class to inter-type	CCC	6
Encapsulate Implements with Declare Parents	CCC	5
Extract method	OO	3
Tidy Up Internal Aspect Structure	AOP	5

more than 30 refactorings have been applied. The result of this refactoring phase was the creation of seven aspects that cleanly encapsulates the persistence concerns.

RELATED WORK

Several approaches have been proposed in order to identify crosscutting concerns and transforming their code into aspects. However, just a few works address the whole process.

Regarding the aspect mining techniques, all of them employ static or dynamic program analysis techniques to search for typical symptoms of crosscutting concerns, such as code scattering and code tangling (Kellens, Mens, & Tonella, 2007).

Static aspect mining techniques analyze the source code looking for differents concepts indicating the presence of crosscutting concerns. (Marin et al., 2007) proposed the use of fan-in metric as an indicator of methods implementing behavior required from many different places, which can be seen as symptom of crosscutting concerns. Other authors have developed different techniques to exploit the naming conventions commonly used to implement crosscutting concerns (Baldi, Lopes, Linstead, & Bajracharya, 2008; Shepherd, Pollock, & Tourwé, 2005; Tourwé & Mens, 2004). The use of clone detection techniques for aspect mining purposes have been studied by (Shepherd, Gibson, & Pollock, 2004) and (Bruntink, van Deursen, van Engelen, & Tourwe, 2005). Zhang and Jacobsen (2007) proposed an approach

that adapt the page-rank algorithm for locating program elements with high levels of fan-in or fan-out. Tonella and Ceccato (2004) developed a technique which identifies interfaces that are most likely to represent crosscutting concerns.

On the other hand, dynamic techniques analyze the runtime behavior of an application in order to identify scattering or tangling symptoms. Similar to our work, (Breu & Krinke, 2004) analyze the program traces for recurring patterns of methods executions, such patterns are considered aspect candidates if they occur more than once in a uniform way. To ensure that the recurring relations are sufficient crosscutting they should appear in different 'calling context'. Those patterns are very similar to the recurrent consequent filter of the proposed approach. Our technique also allows the application of other filter (such as the concept filter) facilitating the implementation of better heuristics for aspect identification. Another dynamic approach (Tonella & Ceccato, 2004), analyze the execution traces through formal concept analysis. The aspect candidates are extracted from the resulting lattice and correspond to tangling and scattering symptoms.

Some drawbacks on those techniques has been described by (Mens, Kellens, & Krinke, 2008), like low precision (fraction of correct aspects among those retrieved), low recall (fraction of aspects actually mined among those to be identified), scalability, and difficult for correct empirical validation.

Concerning the aspect refactoring approaches, the first works were related to manual refactorings

of existing code (Marin, 2004), and then, more automatic processes were proposed. AJaTS (Arcoverde, Lustosa, Sousa, Soares, & Borba, 2007) migrates code to a template oriented one, similar to AspectJ. Refactorings and transformations can be defined, stored and reused. The approach defines an automatic process and provides a plug-in for Eclipse. Classes are mapped to syntactic trees and the transformations are applied using pattern-matching and the Visitor pattern. (Kessler Piveta, Hecht, Soares Pimenta, & Price, 2006) define an algorithmic approach to automatic identify a set of bad smell in AspectJ code. The approach presents a prototype as a plug-in for Eclipse. (Tourwé, Kellens, Vanderperren, & Vannieuwenhuyse, 2004) use inductive logic programming to generalize an extensional definition of a pointcuts into an intentional one. (Binkley, Ceccato, Harman, Ricca, & Tonella, 2005) considered a set of automated refactorings from OOP to AOP aimed at intercepting the original execution at the point where aspect behavior must be added. The process has four main steps, finding, transforming, selecting and refactoring, and assume aspect mining has been applied earlier. (Hannemann, Murphy, & Kiczales, 2005) propose an approach to the aspect refactoring of design patterns based on a library of abstract roles. The role-based refactoring requires the developer to map the implementation of pattern onto the predefined roles describing the pattern and then applies a set of instructions to refactor the implementation into aspects. An important issue to take into account when selecting or defining a refactoring technique is its level of automation the refactorings supported. The refactoring approach described in this work, supports three different refactorings, Aspect-Aware OO refactorings, refactorings for AOP construct, and Refactorings of CCCs. Those refactorings solve not only the problem of migrating object-oriented systems to aspect-oriented ones, but also the maintenance and evolution of the aspect-oriented target system. As a drawback, in spite of having several automatic tasks, the aspect refactoring process needs user

intervention for some activities that cannot be automated.

An integrated strategy for the whole migration process has been addressed by (Marin, van Deursen, Moonen, & van der Rijst, 2009). They present a method to semi-automatically perform the migration of crosscutting concerns to aspects, consisting of four steps: (1) idiom-driven identification of crosscutting concerns, i.e. aspect mining; (2) exploration of the concerns identified and their context; (3) query-based modeling and documentation of crosscutting concerns in the system; (4) template refactoring of the object-oriented idioms into aspect-oriented programming solutions. An important concept introduced by them is crosscutting concerns sorts. A sort describes a typical implementation idiom and relation of crosscutting concerns. For aspect refactoring the authors use idiom-driven approach and define template aspect solutions for each concern sorts. Our approach uses dynamic analysis for aspect mining and following several automatic steps it is possible to obtain the final aspect-oriented code with little developer interaction.

CONCLUSION

In this work, an integrated migration process from object-oriented systems to aspect-oriented ones is proposed. This process consist of an aspect mining technique based on dynamic analysis and association rules, and an aspect refactoring technique which uses a rule engine in order to infer a set of applicable refactorings.

The dynamic aspect mining technique employs association rules to analyze execution traces and identify potential crosscutting concerns. Since the aspect mining technique is based on dynamic analysis, the proposed approach was able to detect crosscutting behavior by applying association rules algorithms. The generated association rules can pin point two kinds of crosscutting concern: role superimposition and consistent behavior (Cec-

cato et al., 2006). The proposed aspect refactoring technique employs a rule engine in conjunction with structural patterns to identify which refactorings must be applied to the aspect candidates obtained during the previous phase. Indeed, this refactoring approach works in an iterative fashion by taking each generated aspect candidate and the object-oriented code and assisting the developer on the application of three kinds of aspect refactoring. As a result, the object-oriented application is semi-automatically evolved into an aspect-oriented one.

As has been shown through the Observer design pattern example and the JHotDraw study case, the proposed process has been validated and its results prove the feasibility of the approach. In this regard, the precision of the aspect mining technique was in most cases above the 50%, similar to the precision reported by Marin, van Deursen and Moonen (2007) for the same application. A further advantage of using dynamic analysis is performing a goal-oriented refactoring process, where the aspect mining phase yields only aspect candidates concerning the feature to migrate. In this way, the refactoring phase is able to encapsulate the target crosscutting concern.

As a future work, we pretend to reduce the user intervention during the whole process by developing mechanism and heuristics for the dynamic identification of which aspect refactoring apply.

REFERENCES

Agrawal, R., & Srikant, R. (1998). Fast Algorithms for Mining Association Rules. In *Readings in Database Systems,* (3rd Ed.), (pp. pages 580-592). San Francisco, CA: Morgan Kaufmann Series In Data Management Systems.

Arcoverde, R., Lustosa, P., Sousa, A., Soares, S., & Borba, P. (2007). AJaTS – AspectJ Transformation System: Tool Support for Aspect-Oriented Development and Refactoring. In *SBES – TOOLS 2007 Brasil.*

Baldi, P. F., Lopes, C. V., Linstead, E. J., & Bajracharya, S. K. (2008). A theory of aspects as latent topics. *SIGPLAN Not., 43*(10), 543–562. doi:10.1145/1449955.1449807

Ball, T. (1999). The concept of dynamic analysis. In *ESEC/FSE-7: Proceedings of the 7th European software engineering conference held jointly with the 7th ACM SIGSOFT international symposium on Foundations of software engineering,* (pp. 216-234). London: Springer-Verlag.

Binkley, D., Ceccato, M., Harman, M., Ricca, F., & Tonella, P. (2005). Automated refactoring of object oriented code into aspects. In *21st IEEE International Conference on Software Maintenance (ICSM).*

Breu, S., & Krinke, J. (2004). Aspect Mining Using Event Traces. In *Proceedings of the 19th IEEE international Conference on Automated Software Engineering: Automated Software Engineering.* Washington, DC: IEEE Computer Society.

Bruntink, M., van Deursen, A., van Engelen, R., & Tourwe, T. (2005). On the use of clone detection for identifying crosscutting concern code. *IEEE Transactions on Software Engineering, 31*(10), 804–818. doi:10.1109/TSE.2005.114

Casas, S., & Marcos, C. A. (2008). Exploración de Reglas de Inferencia para Automatizar la Refactorización Aspectual. *II Latin American Workshop on Aspect-Oriented Software Development (LA-WASP 2008)*, Campinas, Brasil.

Ceccato, M., Marin, M., Mens, K., Moonen, L., Tonella, P., & Tourwé, T. (2006). Applying and combining three different aspect mining techniques. *Software Quality Control, 14*(3), 209–231.

Cornelissen, B., Zaidman, A., van Deursen, A., Moonen, L., & Koschke, R. (2009). A systematic survey of program comprehension through dynamic analysis. *IEEE Transactions on Software Engineering, 20*(6), 476–493.

Ernst, M. D. (2003). Static and dynamic analysis: Synergy and duality. In *WODA 2003: ICSE Workshop on Dynamic Analysis* (pp. 24-27), Portland, OR.

Fowler, M. (1999). *Refactoring: Improving the Design of Existing Code*. Reading, MA: Addison Wesley.

Gamma, E., Helm, R., Johnson, R., & Vlissides, J. (1995). *Design patterns - Elements of reusable object-oriented software*. Reading, MA: Addison Wesley.

Han, J., & Kamber, M. (2006). *Data Mining, Second Edition: Concepts and Techniques*. San Francisco: The Morgan Kaufmann Series in Data Management Systems.

Hanenberg, S., Oberschulte, C., & Unland, R. (2003). Refactoring of aspect-oriented software. In *4th International Conf. on Object-Oriented and Internet-based Technologies, Concepts, and Applications for a Networked World*, (pp. 19-35), Erfurt, Germany.

Hannemann, J. (2006). Aspect-Oriented Refactoring: Classification and Challenges. In *Workshop on Linking Aspect Technology and Evolution (LATE'06), 5th International Conference on Aspect-Oriented Software Development (AOSD'06)*, Bonn, Germany.

Hannemann, J., & Kiczales, G. (2002). Design Pattern Implementation in Java and AspectJ. In *Proceedings of the 17th ACM conference on Object-oriented programming, systems, languages, and applications*, (pp. 161-173). New York: ACM Press.

Hannemann, J., Murphy, G. C., & Kiczales, G. (2005). Role-based refactoring of crosscutting concerns. In *Proceedings of the 4th international conference on Aspect-oriented software development*, (pp. 135–146). Chicago: ACM Press.

Hegland, M. (2003). *Algorithms for association rules*, (LNAI, pp. 226-234). New York: Springer-Verlag.

Iwamoto, M., & Zhao, J. (2003). Refactoring aspect-oriented programs. In *Proc. of 4th AOSD Modeling With UML Workshop, UML'2003*, San Francisco.

Jacobson, I. (1995). *The use-case construct in object-oriented software engineering*, (pp. 309-336).

Kellens, A., Mens, K., & Tonella, P. (2007). A Survey of Automated Code-Level Aspect Mining Techniques. In *Transactions on Aspect-Oriented Software Development IV*, (LNCS Vol. 4640 pp. 143-162). Berlin: Springer Verlag.

Kessler Piveta, E., Hecht, M., Soares Pimenta, M., & Price, R. T. (2006)... *Detecting Bad Smells in AspectJ. JUCS*, *12*(7), 811–827.

Kiczales, G., Hilsdale, E., Hugunin, J., Kersten, M., Palm, J., & Griswold, W. G. (2001). An overview of aspectj. In J.L. Knudsen, & J.L. Knudsen, (Eds.), *ECOOP*, (LNCS Vol. 2072, pp. 327-353). Berlin: Springer.

Koschke, R., & Quante, J. (2005). On dynamic feature location. In *ASE '05: Proceedings of the 20th IEEE/ACM international Conference on Automated software engineering*, (pp. 86-95). New York: ACM Press.

Kotsiantis, S., & Kanellopoulos, D. (2006). Association rules mining: A recent overview. In *International Transactions on Computer Science and Engineering*, (pp. 71-82).

Marin, M. (2004). Refatoring Jhotdraw's Undo Concerns to AspectJ. In *Proceedings For Workshop Aspect Reverse Engineering (WARE2004)*.

Marin, M., Moonen, L., & van Deursen, A. (2005). An approach to aspect refactoring based on crosscutting concern types. In *Proceedings of the 2005 workshop on Modeling and analysis of concerns in software,* (pp. 1-5). St. Louis, MO: ACM Press.

Marin, M., Van Deursen, A., & Moonen, L. (2007). Identifying crosscutting concerns using fan-in analysis. *ACM Transactions on Software Engineering and Methodology, 17*(1), 1–37. doi:10.1145/1314493.1314496

Marin, M., van Deursen, A., Moonen, L., & van der Rijst, R. (2009). An integrated Crosscutting Concern Migratin Strategy and ts Semi-Automated Application to JHotDraw. *Automatic Software Engieneering, 16,* 323–356. doi:10.1007/s10515-009-0051-2

Mens, K., Kellens, A., & Krinke, J. (2008). Pitfalls in aspect mining. In *WCRE '08: Proceedings of the 2008 15th Working Conference on Reverse Engineering,* (pp. 113–122). Washington, DC: IEEE Computer Society.

Monteiro, M. P. (2004). *Catalogue of refactorings for AspectJ.* Universidade do Minho.

Monteiro, M. P., & Fernandes, J. M. (2005). Towards a catalog of aspect-oriented refactorings. In *Proceedings of the 4th international conference on Aspect-oriented software development,* (pp. 111–122). Chicago: ACM Press.

Salah, M., & Mancoridis, S. (2004). A hierarchy of dynamic software views: from object-interactions to feature-interactions. In *Software Maintenance, 2004, Proceedings 20th IEEE International Conference,* (pp. 72-81).

Shepherd, D., Gibson, E., & Pollock, L. L. (2004). Design and evaluation of an automated aspect mining tool. In *Arabnia, H. R., Reza, Software Engineering Research and Practice,* (pp. 601-607).

Shepherd, D., Pollock, L. L., & Tourwé, T. (2005). Using language clues to discover crosscutting concerns. *ACM SIGSOFT Software Engineering Notes, 30*(4), 1–6. doi:10.1145/1082983.1083129

Stroulia, E., & Systä, T. (2002). Dynamic analysis for reverse engineering and program understanding. *SIGAPP Appl. Comput. Rev., 10*(1), 8–17. doi:10.1145/568235.568237

Tonella, P., & Ceccato, M. (2004). Aspect mining through the formal concept analysis of execution traces. In *WCRE '04: Proceedings of the 11th Working Conference on Reverse Engineering (WCRE'04),* (pp. 112-121). Washington, DC: IEEE Computer Society.

Tonella, P., & Ceccato, M. (2004). Migrating interface implementation to aspects. *Software Maintenance, IEEE International Conference,* (pp. 220-229).

Tonella, P., & Ceccato, M. (2005). Refactoring the Aspectizable Interfaces: An Empirical Assessment. *IEEE Transactions on Software Engineering, 31*(10), 819–832. doi:10.1109/TSE.2005.115

Tourwé, T., Kellens, A., Vanderperren, W., & Vannieuwenhuyse, F. (2004). Inductively Generated Pointcuts to Support Refactoring to Aspects. In *Proceeding Software Engineering Properties of language for Aspect Technology (SPLAT) Workshop at AOSD'04.*

Tourwé, T., & Mens, K. (2004). Mining aspectual views using formal concept analysis. In *Proc. Of the Fourth IEEE International Workshop on Source Code Analysis and Manipulation (SCAM 2004)* (pp. 97-106).

van Deursen, A., Marin, M., & Moonen, L. (2005). *A Systematic Aspect-Oriented Refactoring and Testing Strategy and its Application to JHotDraw.* Amsterdam: CWI.

Zhang, C., & Jacobsen, H. A. (2007). Efficiently mining crosscutting concerns through random walks. In *AOSD '07: Proceedings of the 6th international conference on Aspect-Oriented Software Development,* (pp. 226-238). New York: ACM Press.

Chapter 10
The Imaginary 20th Century:
Re-Constructing Imagination

Andreas Kratky
USC School of Cinematic Arts, USA

ABSTRACT

To understand historic developments of the past the authors normally turn to facts: Archival records, testimonies or remains from the past – they are looking for tangible evidence to reconstruct the past. In particular in respect to the technological development that originated at the turn from the 19th to the 20th century the role of deterministic interpretations has been very strong. The focus is on technologies and how they improved along an inevitable time line towards technical perfection (Marvin, 1988). Another historic perspective that takes the social aspects into account mainly traces how people negotiated the old and the new and how technologies changed the social fabric. What stays out of the focus of most research is what people in the past felt and thought and how their imagination of what is possible and desirable influenced the development of technologies and the society. The following will use the example of the interactive media art piece The Imaginary 20th Century to discuss an approach to turn the attention to the re-construction of historical imagination with a particular focus on the imaginative processes and their communication to a current audience.

INTRODUCTION

The Imaginary 20th Century explores how the twentieth century was imagined at the end of the 19th. It is a collaboration of the writer Norman M. Klein, the historian and curator Margo Bistis, and the media artist Andreas Kratky.

DOI: 10.4018/978-1-61520-763-3.ch010

The Imaginary 20th Century is an interactive experience that can be navigated by the viewer. The piece is a hybrid of a novel and a research database containing a vast archive of items of the popular culture from the time between 1895 and 1926. In the attempt to reconstruct the contemporary imagination our piece in part leaves the realm of historically warranted factual "evidence" and crosses over to fiction. Drawing from information

circulating in contemporary magazines, news-papers, books, films etc. we try to reconstruct how people imagined the future inspired by these sources. Accompanied by a fictional story told by its author Norman M. Klein, the viewer sorts through a database of items that potentially fueled the imagination of the people at the turn of the century. The objects are presented in loose association with the story according to a poetic keyword-system that connects each item on one hand to its historical context and on the other hand to the story.

The turn of the century was a period of fundamental transformations in all areas of life. Growing cities, dense traffic, new technologies of communication, production, consumption, and warfare, new scientific inventions, a wealth of new utopian ideas – as a sum effect the futuristic vision of the coming century was dazzling and a strong challenge for the traditional experiential background.

The project raises multiple questions about how we can communicate the particular mood of the time that framed those visions. How can we address aspects of historic imagination with a focus on the transient every-day phenomena rather than on the elaborate formulations that are transmitted to us in utopian texts? How can we voice our assumptions, which inevitably contain elements of both fiction as well as factual information in a responsible and informative way?

CHALLENGES OF THE PROJECT

The project aims at reconstructing what people living around the turn from the 19th century to the 20th expected from the future. An attempt to trace these expectations cannot only work with existing historical materials but rather has to address the imaginary formulations that circulated during that time. There is no shortage of literature ranging from science fiction to social utopia. But the questions we are raising in our project are targeted at the everyday culture and how signs of the future are woven into the fabric of the normal day-to-day life. In this sense the project is trying to locate the material that informed both the literary creations as well as the average people's expectations and fears: The raw material for the construction of the imagination of the future before it is shaped into literature.

WHAT IS IMAGINATION?

For this purpose it is necessary to develop a method to describe the process of how imagination takes form, how it weaves the bits of information into a coherent fabric that has the predictive power to picture what the coming century will be like. In most definitions of imagination the consensus is that it creates and operates with mental images of scenes and objects that are not currently present to the eye. David Hume and several other philosophers see imagination as a mental activity that can bridge gaps in the sense-experience and fill them with 'imagery' that does not come directly from experience. One example of Hume's description of imagination is how we imagine that a rock has remained all the time in the same place when we passed by a first time in the morning and again in the afternoon, even though we did not witness what happened in the meantime. Similarly we imagine that a building continues even though part of it may be obscured and we do not have actual sense-data for how the building continues (Furlong 1961). In this assumption we build on previous experiences with other situations and use those in combination with the sensory data in order to 'synthesize' the missing information.

In order to reconstruct how people might have extrapolated from the data and experiences that existed in their environment we ourselves need to employ a certain amount of imagination. Different from the predictive imagination of the contemporaries of the 19th century our perspective is oriented toward historic reconstruction. In

Figure 1. Depictions of urban life: "Snapshots from our airship" from Life Magazine, March 8, 1906 (© 2007 by the author)

a useful distinction between these two kinds of imagination E.J. Furlong introduces the concept of "directed imagination". This is the imagination that a historian employs in order to piece together individual pieces of evidence to reconstruct in imagination a series of events in the past (Furlong 1961). This dual concept reflects the imaginative connections and inferences that the contemporaries made in their attempt to fathom the future and the presumptive imagination that we apply to reconstruct their thought processes. At the same time it points to another quality that the choice of material for our project has to support: Since the imagination is based on preexisting experience and generally the viewers of the project do not have firsthand experience of the late 19th and early 20th century our project needs to deliver this material in a form that allows its use as the source for the imaginary construction.

CHOICE OF MATERIAL

In our choice of material we focused on items from every day culture, in particular the imagery that circulated in printed media. Newspapers and magazines were the prominent source of information and imagery at the turn of the century. As states 19th century philosopher Walter Benjamin, these media are paradigmatic for the time and

contributed significantly to the transformation and erosion of the coherent fabric of experience. In his essay "On some motifs in Baudelaire", Benjamin describes the difficulties people had at the turn of the century to negotiate the challenges of modern life with their past experience. He sees the coherent fabric of experience consisting of accumulated and often subconscious data as being destroyed by the chock events of the modern life (Benjamin 2002). In particular the focus on newness, shortness, and the disconnectedness of the different pieces of information as presented in newspapers are sign as well as support of a fragmented perception of the environment.

The fragmented and self-contained quality of these materials of every-day-culture is close to the combinatorial approach described in Furlong's concept of directed imagination. Moreover the transient and unpretentious aspect of these materials has very close parallels with a concept that emerges at the end of the 19th century, which the Italian historian Carlo Ginzburg calls the "presumptive paradigm". With three prototypical examples, the method of art historian Giovanni Morelli, Arthur Conan Doyle's novels, and Sigmund Freud's interpretation of dreams, Ginzburg points to a research paradigm for a combinatorial reconstruction of the past that focuses on small details, the subconscious act and on the elements that normally are overlooked by the attention of investigators (Ginzburg 1992).

A DATABASE NOVEL

At the core of our project is a large database containing more than 3000 objects including newspaper clippings, illustrations, photos, texts, film sequences, music and sound pieces. The discreet elements of the database are displayed in arrangements of several items, which are navigated by the viewer along with the voiceover narrative. Through the act of navigating and interpreting

the viewer connects the individual items to their interpretational context.

The experience comprises four tiers each of which is subdivided into several chapters. A table of contents allows the user to quickly access the different chapters and get an overview over the different sections of the experience. The centerpiece of the novel is the third tier, where four different fictional characters formulate their versions of the future. Each character is introduced in the earlier tiers with some of his back-story where the viewer gets to know something about the person and his preferences. Each of the characters focuses on a different aspect that informs his version of the future corresponding to a particular subset of the database. The co-existence of different characters foregrounds the subjective choice and the role of personal inclinations raising awareness for the dependence on preferences, ideologies, and philosophical concepts in the process of the historic imagination.

The Imaginary 20th Century does not present itself as a piece of consumable and readily formulated historiography, it is in the status of its making, it brings the database as a research tool into the foreground and makes the viewer participate in the production of the interpretational flow. The way the viewer experiences the piece is like a simulation of the process of piecing together elements of historic evidence to formulate an interpretation.

THE AESTHETIC CONCEPT

The aesthetic concept for the interface is determined by the combinatory approach of the project. The inspiration comes from the contemporary visual culture, which is dominated by a tableau-like composition style. In particular in the imagery representing the urban environment we see many images that show interweaving perspectives of complicated dense structures. The composition of

Figure 2. Screenshot of the table of contents showing the overview of the first tier

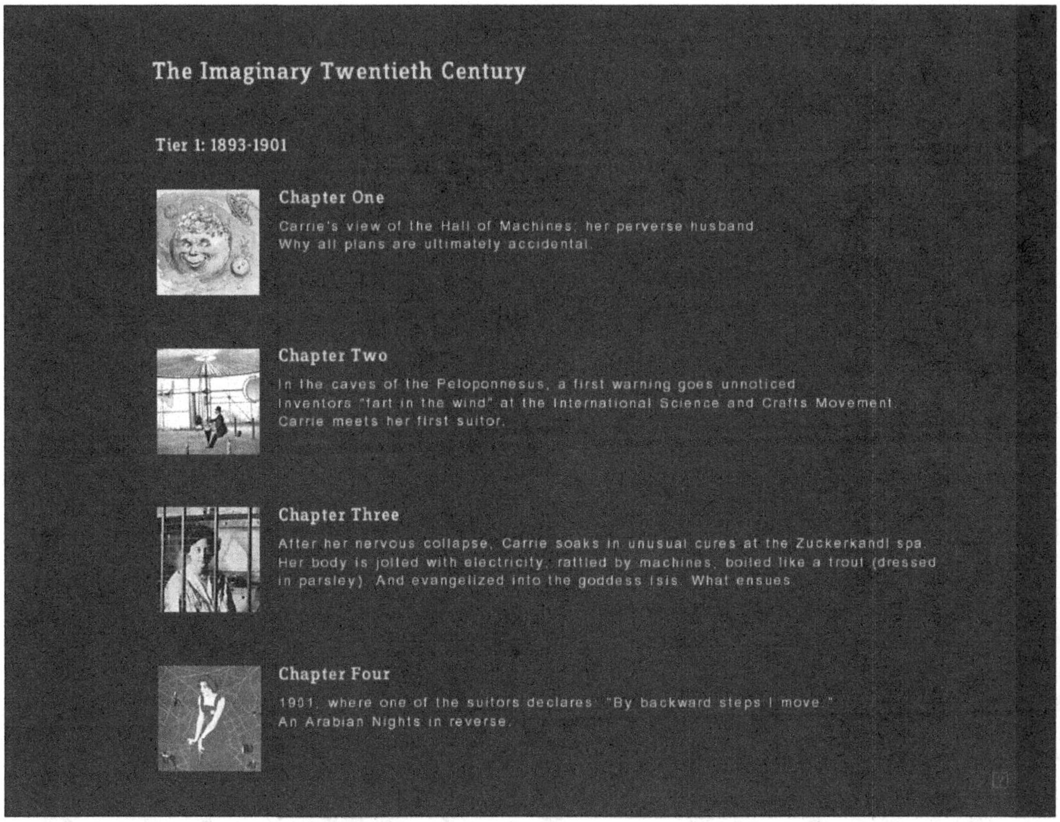

larger newspaper spreads is complex and combines many elements that have to be read successively by the viewer. The entire image is shown at once, and the viewer's eye then dives into the image and explores it in detail. This paradigm is quite different from the streaming image of film that becomes prevalent from the 1920s on for the rest of the twentieth century, which shows normally one image of reduced complexity unfolding over time. Our piece is situated right at the intersection of these two visual modes: The complex tableau of synchronous visual information and the streaming image of film. The interface of the project integrates elements from both paradigms using panels composed of multiple individual elements that move in a swinging motion reminiscent of the streaming film image.

The combination of the individual elements follows a montage principle, which is again situated between the filmic montage and the idea of collage and assemblage as it develops at the beginning of the twentieth century. This montage approach allows us to implement a flow of recombinant elements that proceed along with the story.

The overall design of the interface is rather simple and goes in the opposite direction of the rich interfaces dominating the landscape of current interactive experiences that mostly strive for verisimilitude and immersion. The majority of these interfaces try to deliver a smooth and seamless experience that immerses the user into an imaginary world delivered in a "hyper-real" quality. These seamless experiences have no gaps or ruptures – every gap is filled. In our project we did the opposite of this: Our interface that accentuates the space between the individual elements. The space in-between – in a metaphorical sense – is the space where the imagination resides. In

Figure 3. Screenshot of an assembly of several items in tier 1, chapter 1

a similar way as some graphic novels integrate the space between the panels as the universe of what is not said, what is not represented or what is not representable (Gerbier 2001), we are using the negative space in our compositions as a space imbued with meaning. By activating this space and developing a layout engine that is able to include it into the composition we try to direct the viewer's attention to include this space into his reading of the piece. The implied absence of information becomes a metaphor for the gaps in our historic reconstruction and foreground the process of selective inclusion and exclusion of data in the historic reconstruction.

CONCLUSION

It is particularly worthwhile to engage into a project like *The Imaginary 20th Century* at our current time – one century later at the turn from the twentieth to the twenty-first century. After the end of the cold war situation we witnessed the downturn of the main proponent of the idea of communism, the Soviet Union and now with several decades of delay we are in the midst of a crisis that suggests a deep transformation of the main proponent of the capitalist system, the USA. The waning of the main powers of the world order throughout most of the twentieth century questions regarding the future world order and the coming political systems pose challenges to our imaginative forces.

Figure 4. Screenshot of the interface with one individual item enlarged for detailed exploration

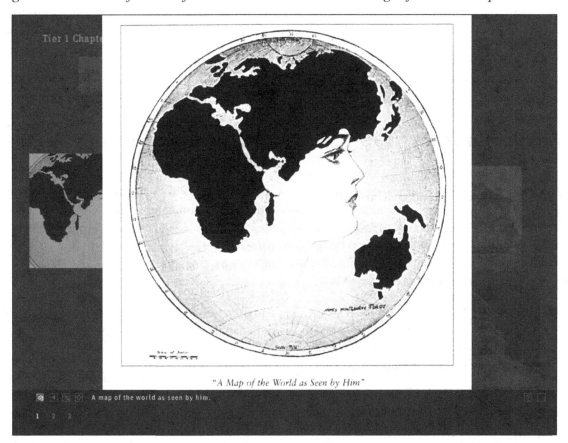

"A Map of the World as Seen by Him"

As a 'mental exercise' it is valuable to turn to an earlier instance of this kind of situation to see how people conceived of their future and what was realized of these expectations. In retrospect many developments seem much clearer and as if they were following an inevitable logic. Therefore it is very important to conceive of methods that allow an analytical approach including also aspects that often escape the focus of scientific analysis. *The Imaginary 20th Century* tries to make a contribution in creating a form that addresses these questions in an effective and responsible way to a current audience. The particular combination of techniques, the hybrid approach between factual and fictional combined with a carefully researched database and viewer involvement through interactive techniques offers several unique features that allow us to address these questions in a creative way.

REFERENCES

Benjamin, W. (2002). *Medienaesthetische Schriften*. Frankfurt am Main, Germany: Suhrkamp.

Furlong, E. J. (1961). *Imagination*. London: George Allen & Unwin.

Gerbier, L. (2001). Découpage fantastique et continuité graphique dans la bande dessinée. *Image and Narrative, 2*. Retrieved Sept. 12, 2008 from http://www.imageandnarrative.be/

Ginzburg, C. (1989). *Clues, Myths, and the Historic Method.* Baltimore: Johns Hopkins University Press.

Marvin, C. (1988). *When Old Technologies Were New.* New York: Oxford University Press.

ADDITIONAL READING

Anderson, S. (2008). *Technologies of History.* Berkeley, Los Angeles, London: University of California Press (forthcoming).

Baetens, J. (2000). *The Burden of Coherence.* Image and Narrative, Issue 1. Retrieved Sept. 12, 2008 (http://www.imageandnarrative.be/)

Bremond, C., & Cancalon, E. D. (1980). *The Logic of Narrative Possibilities.* In *New Literary History,* Vol. 11 (3), *On Narrative and Narratives II,* p. 387-411. Baltimore: Johns Hopkins University Press.

Buchloh, B., & Coles, A. (1999). *The Optic of Walter Benjamin.* London: Black Dog Publishing.

Carlin, J., Karasik, P., & Walker, B. (2005). *Masters of American Comic.* New Haven, and London: Yale University Press.

Crary, J. (1992). *Techniques of the Observer.* Cambridge, Massachusetts: MIT Press.

Crary, J. (2001). *Suspensions of Perception: Attention, Spectacle, and Modern Culture.* Cambridge, Massachusetts: MIT Press.

Domike, S., Mateas, M., & Vanouse, P. (2003). *The Recombinant History Apparatus Presents Terminal Time.* In *Narrative Intelligence: Advances in Consciousness Research* (46), p. 155-173. Amsterdam: John Benjamins Publishing.

Gunning, T. (1995). *Tracing the Individual Body Photography, Detectives, and Early Cinema.* In Charney, L. (Ed.) and Schwartz, V. (Ed.), *Cinema and the Invention of Modern Life.* Berkeley, Los Angeles, London: University of California Press.

Laermans, R., & Gielen, P. (2007). *The Archive of the Digital An-Archive.* Image and Narrative, Issue 17. Retrieved Sept. 27, 2008 (http://www.imageandnarrative.be/)

Mahne, N. (2007). *Transmediale Erzähltheorie.* Göttingen: Vandenhoek & Ruprecht.

McCloud, S. (1994). *Understanding Comics: The Invisible Art.* New York: Harper Perennial Publishers.

Nichols, B. (1987). History, Myth, and Narrative in Documentary. [Berkeley, Los Angeles, London: University of California Press.]. *Film Quarterly, 41*(1), 9–20. doi:10.1525/fq.1987.41.1.04a00030

Nichols, B. (1991). *Representing Reality – Issues and Concepts in Documentary.* Bloomington and Indianapolis: Indiana University Press.

Nichols, B. (1995). *Blurred Boundaries.* Bloomington and Indianapolis: Indiana University Press.

Ryan, M. L. (2001). *Beyond Myth and Metaphor – The Case of Narrative in Digital Media.* In *Game Studies,* Vol. 1, (1), July 2001. Retrieved Sept. 12, 2008 (http://www.gamestudies.org/0101/ryan)

Ryan, M. L. (2001). *Narrative as Virtual Reality: Immersion and Interactivity in Literature and Electronic Media.* Baltimore: Johns Hopkins University Press.

Sadowski, M. (1992). *Imagination, Cognition, and Persona. In Rhetoric Review,* Vol. 10 (2), p. 266-278. London: Taylor & Francis.

Sartre, J. P. (2004). *The Imaginary: A Phenomenological Psychology of the Imagination.* London: Routledge.

Singer, B. (1995). *Modernity, Hyperstimulus, and the Rise of Popular Sensationalism.* In Charney, L. (Ed.) and Schwartz, V. (Ed.), *Cinema and the Invention of Modern Life.* Berkeley, Los Angeles, London: University of California Press.

KEY TERMS AND DEFINITIONS

Archive: A collection of historical records consisting of original documents that witness a certain event or historical period.

Database: A computer-based collections of digital records that generally have a logical relationship among each other.

Documentary: The term documentary is generally used to describe films that depict a certain aspect of reality in a truthful and factual way. In the context of this paper the term is extended to include digital works and their capability to represent aspects of reality.

Hyperstimulus: A heightened stimulation of the human sensory apparatus. The human senses receive to external stimuli and a corresponding response to the stimuli is generated. When the stimuli or their intensity exceed the amount that can be process by the human it becomes unable to generate appropriate responses. The increasing dynamic of everyday life around the turn of the 19th to the 20th century was perceived to exceed what people of the period could deal with, therefore they felt hyperstimulated.

Imagination: The process of formulating mental representations of events or sites that are not present to the perception at the time they are imagined.

Interactive Media Art: An art form presented on a computer that involves the viewer/user in an active way. Interactive media art pieces are constituted by a multitude of different media such as images, moving images, text and sound.

Reconstruction: In architecture this terms is used to describe how the ruins or remains of an old building are restored to a complete building. In the context of this paper reconstruction refers to the attempt to restore a coherent understanding of how people imagined the future by piecing together the fragmentary remains from the past.

Chapter 11
Communicability Era:
New Professionals for Interactive Systems

Francisco V. Cipolla-Ficarra
ALAIPO, & AInCI, Spain

Emma Nicol
University of Strathclyde, UK

Miguel Cipolla Ficarra
HCI Lab. – F&F Multimedia Communic@tions Corp. & AInCI, Spain

ABSTRACT

In the current chapter are analyzed the main reasons for which it is necessary to count with a new pro-file in design, realization and assessment of the interactive systems. The whole of the observations and proposals is the result of theoretical research, experiences in projects of interactive multimedia systems in the public and private Spanish and Italian university context in the last two decades. Through all this time it has been seen how the lack of training among the professionals in the interactive systems, especially in some university environments, not only has increased the production costs but the detection of a low quality of design and communicability has discouraged the interaction of the novel users with these systems. One of the goals that we set ourselves is to determine the set of necessary knowledge and/ or experiences that these professionals must possess to carry out satisfactorily the interactive systems of the present and the future, in the least possible production time, with reduced costs and a high final quality. Obviously, the key factor of these shortcomings lies in the university educational systems and in the organization of the contents in the study plans, leaving behind the business factor of university teaching. Therefore, we have structured the current work in the following way: study of the evolution of the multimedia systems, anchoring of the notions related to communication, determination of the main areas of knowledge of the future professional, analysis of the software quality, signalling of the business-oriented factors in the structuring of the university study plans, especially related to degrees, engineering titles and masters.

DOI: 10.4018/978-1-61520-763-3.ch011

INTRODUCTION

Human communication takes place when a person or persons transmit something to others through signs that depict, express or substitute what is intended to be communicated. This use of signs is intentional in order to cause a more or less predictable effect and to prompt a congruent answer, but its meaning has to be convened upon and shared. A message has ambiguity and redundancy: the first is generated by using concepts which denote more than one meaning: in such situations and in relation to the used language (in a text, but not only in these), another term must be sought which avoids confusions, so that the linguistic bi-univocal relationship of signifier and significant is as straightforward as possible and avoids confusing connotations (Cipolla-Ficarra, 1994).

This problem multiplies itself when several languages are used in an interactive multimedia system. A method followed by some designers is to be redundant in the messages, that is, to repeat the same thing in several possible ways so as to avoid ambiguities. This entails explaining twice or more times what one is trying to present with the different communicational resources, what may be positive in educational processes, but counterproductive in processing time and in the space occupied in the off-line information supports, for instance (Cipolla-Ficarra, 2005). Cutting down the ambiguity of the message as well as its redundancy is a basic formula of gaining speed and space: a good strategy is to use images of universal meaning which serve as anchor to what is being shown. It is necessary to count with good designers not only from the aesthetic or artistic point of view, but also of the software. Nevertheless, both ambiguity and redundancy are issues pending of resolution inside the elaboration processes of contents for the interactive systems.

The information of a multimedia interactive system reaches the user in three basic ways: text, images (static or animated) and sound. These are combined among themselves, but some of them prevails over the others at specific moments and according to the part of the content that is interacting, for instance, in a e-learning system. However, it has been seen that the visual component prevails over the sound part, whether it is in the shape of text and/or images. The images bring about a bigger effect on the user (Balakrishan, Fitzmaurice & Kurtenbach, 2001). Cinema, television and personal computers have generated a whole visual culture throughout the 20th century (Reves & Nass, 1998). Among the images, the animated ones are those that have a greater acceptance by the user and the virtual community and/or social network.

The computer animations that follow the rules of cinema productions and digital films have a peculiar realism strength for the communicational process. That's why, with the exception of hypertexts, most of the current interactive systems incorporate 2D animations and/or 3D, (in spite of the room they take up in storage and the quality problems of the algorithms that regulate compression and decompression). All of this has its origins in the classical audiovisual media: cinema and television. The human being of the second half of the 20th century is audiovisual par excellence (Reeves & Nass, 1998). In the nineties with the computer in the classroom (Piaget, 1993), the bidirectional interaction in the communicative process has been boosted (Kraemer, Dedrick & Sharma, 2009). It is important to know some details of that evolution because it allows one to establish a before and an after in the needs of the information societies, especially when we talk about professionals of interactive qualitative communication.

EDUCATION, COMMUNICATION AND NEW TECHNOLOGIES

Education is one of the cornerstones of the growth of societies (Shih *et al.*, 2008). The technology in the classrooms in many institutes of the eighties

were the classical audiovisual systems, through the projection of slides, in some cases the voice of the teacher was accompanied by the real sounds in order to increase realism. It was the time of the sequential multimedia, that is to say, the classical technology of multimedia stemming from print and television, characterized by the lack of informatics. The sector of printing and graphic arts is one of the main contexts when you talk about the contributions to visual communicability. Then we go into a short period of the partially interactive multimedia. That is to say, the emulations of the manual operations controlled from the computer, such as can be the advance of a video in a CD-Rom support. Until arriving at the totally interactive multimedia, where each source of information is in a digital format and allows a high degree of user-computer interaction (Cipolla-Ficarra & Cipolla-Ficarra, 2008). The first to show a great interest in digitalizing the information in Europe, for instance, was the sector of the graphic arts in the nineties, aimed at the sector of distance education or virtual campus.

However, there is not yet a unique interactive multimedia technology inside the digital environment. Obviously, remarkable breakthroughs have been made in the basic technology (hardware), nonetheless, such questions persist as: the tools of the software do not use yet the whole potentiality of the hardware (it is enough to see the statistic data which show that the users ignore 100% of the functions of the mobile phones in Europe, for instance, and yet they keep on demanding more functions), the hypermedia systems are based on partial design models, with primitives not unanimously accepted in the computer context, of the human-computer interaction, usability, user-centered design, etc. Consequently, the lack of a unique model causes in many cases time loss and human resources (Scott, 2009). The only way to solve these problems is by resorting to the standards and basic notions of the historic concepts with international circulation. Fortunately, the technical English used in computer science,

telecommunications and electronics mainly has allowed the creation of a common vocabulary when we refer to software (Furnas *et al.*, 1987) and hardware (Robinson & Cargill, 1996). However, in the context of design there are plenty of notions which may seem ambiguous to the users, designers and programmers of interactive systems (Cipolla-Ficarra, 2005).

It is important to carry out in some cases the anchoring operations of the relationship of signification and significant of the terms, as it is the way in the framework of semiotics and/or linguistics. For instance, in the later stage of the evolution of the interactive multimedia systems, we have the notion of hypermedia, which is an acronym between hypertext and multimedia. Here are assembled the advantages of both technologies inside the multimedia communication process. As it has been observed in the origins of the hypertext, where the textual aspects of the first systems prevails (including the static graphics, in a wide sense), where it is established the associative character in the structure of information (this aspects generates a less frequent denomination in the hypermedia systems, such as is the case of the electronic book). Whereas in multimedia and through the intersection of the media there is a dynamic content of the information: video, audio and computer animations. This dynamic aspect entails the time or synchronization factor among the diverse means, which in our case we call panchronism –from Greek *pan* and *chronos*, time (Cipolla-Ficarra, 1998). This synchronization must be constant along the time that the emission of the dynamic means lasts. This is a very important category of design when we analyze communicability in the on-line and off-line contents of interactive systems.

Many failures of the quality of the system stem from it and seriously damage the motivation and the attention of the users at the moment of interacting with the hypermedia contents (Cipolla-Ficarra & Cipolla-Ficarra, 2009). In contrast, when there is panchronism, a good design of the contents boosts

the navigation through the system, for instance. Consequently, the hypermedia in a classical sense of the notion allows: the selected access to those parts determined beforehand by the user, a greater degree of detail in the structure of information, that is to say, it is possible to resort to the richness of the content, in regard to the several means used in the transmission of the messages and reinforcing the communication process.

Along the evolution of hypermedia, it can be said that it is an interactive extension of the multimedia (Cipolla-Ficarra & Cipolla-Ficarra, 2008). In other words, this is the reason why the notion of multimedia is used indistinctly with that of hypermedia in many research works (Grimes & Potel, 1991; Botto, 1992; Muller, 1996), although the relationship between the signification and the significant may be not strictly symmetrical according to Ferdinand de Saussure (Saussure, 1990). In the hypermedia the synchronism of the active and static and dynamic means is essential. Besides, the amount of interaction required by the system and the control of the fruition of the user over the system are two quality criteria and assess in the current hypermedia systems (Cipolla-Ficarra, 1999).

Now in the evolution of the communication means as in the hypertextual, multimedia and hypermedia systems there has also been an interrelation between the professionals of the factual and formal sciences –to quote Mario Bunge's division of the sciences (Bunge, 1981). Making a brief analysis of the term communication in the last five decades in the social sciences may serve us to better to understand that this bidirectional relationship that has existed since then.

In the current chapter are analyzed the main reasons for which it is necessary to count with a new profile in design, realization and assessment of the interactive systems. The whole of the observations and proposals is the result of theoretical research, experiences in projects of interactive multimedia systems in the public and private Spanish and Italian university context in the last

two decades. Through all this time it has been seen how the lack of training among the professionals in the interactive systems, especially in some university environments, not only has increased the production costs but the detection of a low quality of design and communicability has discouraged the interaction of the novel users with these systems. One of the goals that we set ourselves is to determine the set of necessary knowledge and/or experiences that these professionals must possess to carry out satisfactorily the interactive systems of the present and the future, in the least possible production time, with reduced costs and a high final quality. Obviously, the key factor of these shortcomings lies in the university educational systems and in the organization of the contents in the study plans, leaving behind the business factor of university teaching. Therefore, we have structured the current work in the following way: study of the evolution of the multimedia systems, anchoring of the notions related to communication, determination of the main areas of knowledge of the future professional, analysis of the software quality, signalling of the business-oriented factors in the structuring of the university study plans, especially related to degrees, engineering titles and masters.

Communication vs. Information: A Terminological Study

In the context of the factual and formal sciences there are plenty of theoretic and practical works which talk about communication. In these researches it is easy to observe several definitions, where there are common elements among them (Hemmendinger, 2007). However, the momentum of the word communication in the daily and colloquial environment has generated a sort of deficiencies in its scientific sense, that is to say, a terminological status is missing. This deficiency becomes even more obvious when we talk about communicability in the interactive systems. Therefore, we will try to rank the dif-

ferent points of view with both notions. In the case of communication, inside the context of the social sciences and more specifically in the social communication, some experts traditionally made a study of the differences between communication and information: Abraham Moles, David Berlo, Frank Dance, Luka Brajnovic, Rau Birdwhistell, Wilbur Schramm, etc. (Aranguren, 1986), others, in contrast, exclude the notion of information (Birdwhistell, 1974). Currently in the design of the interactive systems the word communication is linked to contents, that is to say, communication of contents.

In the specific case of the studies made by Moles, Berlo, Dance, Shramm, etc. (Dance, 1974) we can see that many are developed in a simultaneous way between the evolution of informatics and the massive communication means of the time: radio, television, etc. (Macdonald, 2004). That is to say, on the one hand there is the formal aspect through the information mathematic models and on the other hand we have the models stemming from the social sciences. Many of these studies made a clear-cut difference between what was understood as data, information, communication, etc. (Dahlbom & Mathiassen, 1997). However, the study plans between Europe and America were going to bring about a strong division of meanings around the term "information". For instance, "information sciences" in Italy is related to computer science. On top of that, an Italian bachelor degree in sciences of the information in Italy in the 20th century is someone who has knowledge of programming, mathematics, physics, databases, etc. In contrast, in Spain, "information sciences" is related to social sciences, that is to say, journalism, publicity, public relations, marketing, audiovisual, radio, cinema, etc. Therefore, a bachelor degree in information sciences of the 20th century is usually a journalist, with newsroom knowledge, that is, for the circulation of news. Therefore, "information sciences" needs always the anchoring of the notion of agreement in accordance with the context where it is used.

The intersection of both study plans, one oriented at factual sciences and the other at formal sciences took place in many universities of the American continent in the 1980s. There we find that a bachelor in communication has knowledge of both sciences. That is to say, an ideal figure for the development of the interactive systems with a high quality. Nevertheless, to the theoretical knowledge and/or acquired experiences in the university classrooms of many American universities, with the momentum of the Internet the vision of the formal sciences rather than the factual sciences has prevailed. The latter have been put on the back burner, even in professions clearly belonging to the social sciences such as the task of giving textual contents to the Web. This conceptual deviation or mistake is one of the causes why there is a slowing down of the expansion of the Internet phenomenon in Europe. The financial costs have been high, for instance, in the framework of E-commerce or E-learning. Since 1995 the labor market of the Old Continent persists mistakenly in demanding Internet professionals hailing from computer science faculties, in design tasks, content management, publicity on-line, etc., when in fact it is feasible to acquire in a short time the necessary knowledge to work with commercial programs aimed at the editing of images, generation of websites, creation of databases, etc. That is to say, any professional of the social sciences can be turned into an editor of Web 1.0 or Web 2.0 websites, for instance, with scarce economical resources.

The origin of all these ambiguities, conceptual mistakes and university educative policies lies in the term "communication". Besides, in the human-computer interaction there is an implicit dynamic process. For instance, through the relationship with the stored information in the multimedia on-line and/or off-line system, the human being widens his knowledge. Regarding this, Schramm considers communication as a real established relationship which consists in the discovery of the "I", the "other" and "others", and a donation of a

content which entails a duality of terms between emitter and receptor, who coexist in a contained environment and which is the foundation to its corresponding process (Aranguren, 1986; Dance, 1973). In the notion of emitter in our case we understand the designer of the multimedia system, whereas the receptors are the potential users of that interactive system. Schramm shows the need of a cultural understanding between both to obtain optimal results in the communication process (Aranguren, 1986). On his side Luka Brajnovic tells us about and communication and information differentiating each one in the following way: "communication consists in getting in touch two or more people, things or bodies, in their different combination possibilities and its meaning can be manifold, and have diverse procedures and effects" (Brajnovic, 1979, p. 13). It is a sort of direct channel or creative encounter that ties presences and distances, sometimes, without the information goal, although it can be a vehicle of information. Therefore, information can be included in communication. When the information is incorrect there is no feedback, in the interactive communication process, for instance, because human communication is a psychosocial process. Moreover, if we consider that communication is a psychosocial phenomena, we must admit that this phenomena is given in the human being with all his rational and creative possibilities to organize the message and interpret its reception. That is to say, that from the point of view of social communication, it is not a simple direct channel of relationships, but rather a socialization process (Ellison, Lampe & Steinfield, 2009).

Therefore, communication is a social fact, updated by the human being, through a process among the integrants who make it up, where the interchange of experiences entail the enrichment of the participants, through the internalization of the messages that have been expressed in a given space and time (Edmundson, 2008). Among the human beings there is a will of encounter in the communication and a desire of putting something in common, spontaneous binding achieves the integration of man with nature, cultural heritage, education, health, work, social media, etc. and the community he inhabits. We not only communicate the data, the fact but besides that we can communicate our ideas, experiences, feelings, real or imaginary events, the objective and the subjective, the presence of two or more people in their different combinatory possibilities. Once we have quality in communication we are in front of the notion of communicability. That is to say, that communicability includes automatically quality. In our case, we sometimes use both notions simultaneously and redundantly to strengthen the idea of quality in the process of interactive communication.

In the design of the interactive systems it is easy to detect the presence of communicability, although as it happens with the notion of beauty, it requires time to describe each one of the elements that make it up. In short, it is starting from this interrelation "cum" technological and "cum" the individual when the relationship in other research environments take place such as are the cognitive models used for the development of the interface. At the moment of the design of the interactive system, the designer must consider the cultural factors (Edmundson, 2008), the types of users (Cipolla-Ficarra, 2008), the geographical location of the system (Shih *et al.*, 2008), accesibility for all (Chisolm, Vanderheiden & Jacobs, 2001), information surrogates (Ruthven *et al.*, 2008), etc. These variables make that since the software sector at the start of the nineties the need of incorporating sociologists, anthropologists and sociologists has been affirmed to improve the quality of the interactive systems (Basili & Musa, 1991). However, in the new millennium it is necessary to talk of experts in communicability (Cipolla-Ficarra, 2008).

Figure 1. Analyst in communicability has knowledge and/or experiences in the intersection area of the factual and formal sciences

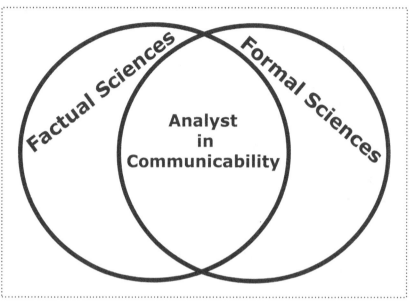

COMMUNICABILITY ANALYST

Software engineering has provided the human-computer interaction community with tools and techniques for the design and implementation of interactive systems (Buie, 1999). The evaluative analysis of multimedia systems requires, as well as method, a professional trained in both computer science and social sciences. New technologies are a constant intersection of several areas of human knowledge. The acceptance of the software products by the end users rapidly and with a minimum error –ideally none at all – is one of the main objectives regarding quality in software, for example (Broy, 2006). Increasing or maintaining the quality of software with a minimum cost ad minimum production time requires professionals with training and/or experience factual sciences and formal sciences (Cipolla-Ficarra, 1997). These concepts are illustrated in Figure1.

We propose a profile of an ideal professional for analyzing and evaluating communicability in interactive systems, applicable to other sectors of new technologies. For instance, computer science

has the systems analyst (whether functional of managerial), who does not need other analyst to carry out his work. It would be advantageous to introduce the figure of the communicability analyst, whose knowledge and/or experience come from a background of social sciences and formal sciences. Such an analyst would be able to carry out the analysis of these systems and reach reliable results unaided, without the need for a test group. Group evaluation at a later stage might be useful to reinforce the technique employed. Such an interactive systems analyst would have to combine experience and/or knowledge in both the factual and the formal sciences. In order to illustrate this, a list including the communicability analyst's experience and/or knowledge. Each of the components has a one-to-one relationship with the others:

- Communication social
- Communication and information theory
- Computer science
- Computer graphics and computer animation

- Cultural system
- Digital design
- Ergonomics
- Information technology
- Linguistics and literature theory
- Mass media theory
- Metaphor theory
- Methods and techniques for communicability testing methodology of scientific research
- Pedagogy
- Planning and administration of control
- Publishing communication
- Semiology or semiotics
- Social psychology
- Sociology
- Statistics
- Telecommunications
- Theory of science
- Usability engineering

This set is not a curriculum or specific course modules. Here we see an intersection of the fields of computer science and social sciences with is oriented in the direction of communication and takes us a little further towards defining the concept of human factors, which in the multimedia context tends to be ambiguous and vague. The essential difference lies in the emphasis placed on the need for integration of knowledge as consequence of a qualitatively new situation –the emergence of new communication technologies.

It is obvious that the listing of these domains of knowledge is to be found in a diametrically opposed position from the commercial or business-like picaresque used by private or public institutions focused on education, through their summer courses, masters courses, courses of continuous training, etc. where we can read a continuous redundancy of notions, ambiguity of terms or null originality of the educational proposals. Some examples from Spain:

- Transdisciplinary masters degree in cognitive systems, virtual reality and interactive media.
- Interdisciplinary masters degree in digital photography, digital video, animation, computer games and arts.
- Multidisciplinary masters degree in creativity, digital creation, global software engineering and dynamics and statics media.
- Pluridisciplinary master in design, illustration, journalism and multimedia technologies.

In this list we observe how a very poor use of the intersection and inter-disciplinarity of the factual and formal sciences is made. That is to say, that the professionals who attend these courses cannot be regarded as experts in communicability. It is necessary to go back to the classical, unambiguous and to get rid of notions of business aims.

Intersection of the Sciences

In social communication science it is not simple to establish limits in a precise way because it is necessary to establish a monosemic scientific vocabulary, which allows the univocal use of the word communication when it is applied to very different fields such as interpersonal communication, communication between machines, communication between PC and person, etc. Inter-disciplinary studies that involve comparison, exchange of methods and exchange of opinions can be positive when they go beyond the sum or juxtaposition of discoveries, for example. The prime degree of cooperation lies in transdisciplinary studies.

For example, trans-disciplinary studies would propose concepts and theories common to different social sciences. Nevertheless, it is in dual-disciplinary studies that we can reach the best results in the field of communication. That is, it would consist of sharing methods, and interpreting

aspects and historical experiences of two different disciplines. Consequently, the intersection between computer science and communicability can be very positive to increase the quality of communication between a user and a PC.

Another phenomenon stemming from the misinterpretation of the trans-disciplinary or interdisciplinary notions is the presence of professionals who are alien to the interactive systems, especial those related to the hypermedia contents. Currently it is usual in Italy to find graduates in physics, nuclear engineers, mathematics, engineers in chemistry, bachelors in foreign literature, etc. devoted to the design of cognitive models for children, for instance. Obviously, to avoid the resounding failure of the product continuous collaborations of the social sciences professionals are required. Something similar happens in Spain, where we have bachelors in fine arts for the design of architecture in the databases or hyperbases (Tompa, 1989); bachelors in chemistry for the design of interfaces, bachelors in computer science for the interviews to users, bachelors in history or anthropologists to solve the connectability problems in the touristic telecommunication systems, etc. This is the reason why it is not surprising at all when academic barbarism is proposed in the context of the interactive systems in semiotics engineering (de Souza, 2004). In short, we are dealing with some kind of orchestra-man or orchestra-woman in the design, programming and evaluation of the interactive systems who seriously damage their quality. It is as if they had to generate just by themselves the interactive systems since the design stage. Correcting this deviation or mistake entails time and additionally incurs high economic costs when it comes to software.

Media Era: Mythology

Another of the problems that derive from the lack of communicability professionals is presenting as novel something that has existed for decades: interactive and micro-multimedia (iPhone, iPod, PDA, laptop, etc.) for many hailing from the telecommunications context, electronic engineering or architecture means the era of the media (this is a mythology vision of the communication and information sciences). In reality it is just hypermedia in small computer supports. The era of media, mass or social media refers to the social sciences. In this sense the contributions made by numerous experts are very important since they have become general goals for the computer scientific community, such as the global village through the Internet (Dias & Brewer, 2009).

In the same way, the historical contribution of McLuhan was to talk about media types as isolated entities, because he believed that these technical tools constitute, together with man, an anthropological unit, destroying the traditional separation between channel and receiver as in Lasswell's paradigm: sender, receiver, channel and message (McLuhan & Power, 1992). When McLuhan says that the medium is the message, he means that the technical features of the medium substitute the content (McLuhan & Power, 1992). On the contrary, it is sure that the technical structure of media affects and determines the content, while the messages are entities of semiotic nature, and so they have two structurally linked areas: the area of expression and the area of content.

From the semiotic point of view, it is evident that all the material elements intervening not only in the message configuration, but also in its circulation, have incidence and influence in the content area. The use of semiotics as a basis to create a methodology of analysis of content quality, access to information and presentation in multimedia/hypermedia systems independently from digital support, i.e., CD-ROM, DVD, Internet, multimedia mobiles phones, PDA's, iPod's, lectors of MP3, E-books, etc. has given excellent theoretical and practical results. The success of the results is due to the bi-directional relation between computer science and interactive multimedia communication, and to the creation of a new kind of professional figure in the field of formal sciences

and factual sciences: the heuristic evaluator of multimedia/hypermedia systems The origin of this professional aimed in principle at usability in 1995 has evolved towards communicability in the new millennia.

However, its presence is not yet detected in the maps that refer to the different design areas from a theoretical or practical point of view, for instance; user-centered design, participatory design, design+ emotion, critical design, dialogue design, graphic facilitation, etc. (Sanders, 2008; Valenza & Adkins, 2009). By inserting communicability within it, it is feasible to solve most of the problems mentioned by Liz Sanders (Sanders, 2008), for instance. Obviously, the communicability is involved in each one of them. Graphically, the communicability thus is represented:

Communicability does not mean eradicating usability studies. It is rather a complement that updates the current demand for new methods and technologies to meet the requirements of the users in the face of the new multimedia interactive devices which do not work with the classical desk personal computers (Scott, 2009). The methods and techniques used in usability, many of them hailing from the social sciences in the study of the communication media, must be updated and adapted for communicability. In this regard, the use of semiotics has been positive in the design of interactive systems during the last 15 years.

The advantage of using semiotics in the design of the interactive systems is that it has made it possible to break down in a coherent way each one of the components of the interactive systems in two great sectors: structural and systematic. The former are those which are more difficult and more costly to modify once implemented, for instance, the order of the areas in a database. The latter can be modified more easily and may even appear as an active component of the interactive system: colour change in the interface background, increase or decrease of the typography size, etc. In regard to breaking down, the division of the design categories is essential to establish a language without ambiguities among the participants in the creation of the interactive system.

In Figure3 the first heuristic table is to be found –the interested reader can refer to the bibliography in (Cipolla-Ficarra, 1996; Cipolla-Ficarra, 2003) for a complete description. It is made thanks to the notions of semiotics. It was used to analyze in detail the design categories in off-line multimedia systems. Next it was adapted for the on-line systems and several contents, such as: E-learning, E-commerce, E-Tourism, for instance (Cipolla-Ficarra, 2009). The ease of use and the adaptation speed in the face of several users and interactive contents has been achieved thanks to semiotics.

However, the advances in information technology and communication in the last decade have brought about mergers and not intersections of scientific knowledge. Regrettably, many of these mergers do not have previous studies among the disciplines and respond rather to marketing factors.

Figure 2. In the graphic we can see how communicability is present in each one of the interactive design areas, occupying the central zone of the intersections

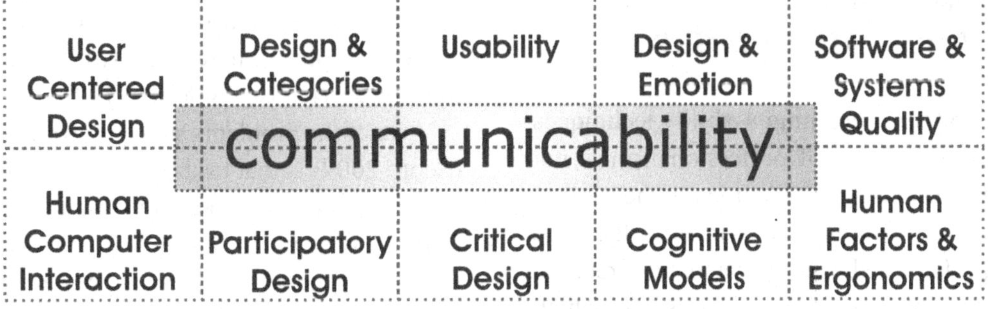

User Centered Design	Design & Categories	Usability	Design & Emotion	Software & Systems Quality
communicability				
Human Computer Interaction	Participatory Design	Critical Design	Cognitive Models	Human Factors & Ergonomics

Figure 3. First heuristic table for evaluation of the multimedia systems

1	Static (passive) media:
	a) Formatted date. b) Text strings. c) Images. d) Graphics. e) Maps.
2	Active (dynamic) media:
	a) Animation. b) Video. c) Sound
3	There is a predominance of:
	a) Animation. b) Sound. c) Video.
4	Synchronisation between: audio, text and images (complex slot).
	a) 0/1 sec. b) 2/5 sec. c) 5/10 sec. d) More.
5	Active (dynamic) media: Possibilities of Rew (rewind). FF (fast forward). Stop. Pause. Play. Slow-in. Slow-out.
6	Expert system: Intelligence Artificial. Geographic Information System (GIS)
7	Different languages and/or dialects.
8	Interaction direction: a) By queries or filter. b) Explorative.
9	Input and output interaction time: a) 0/1 sec. b) 2/5 sec. c) 5/10 sec. d) More.
10	Input recognition (cursor and symbolic for recognising the input):
	a) Sandglass or wristwatch icons: Static. Dynamic. b) Special: Static. Dynamic. c) None.
11	The user and navigation:
	1. Feed-back levels: a) Only visual. b) Visual and sound. c) Nothing.
	2. Constant possibilities for:
	a) Escape. b) Option changes. c) Content printing. d) Message writing. e) Message recording. f) Message listening. e) Connection to multimedia system on-line or off-line.
	3. Content levels: a) Only one. b) Several.
	4. Advance motivational effects through the multimedia environment:
	a) Phrases. b) Sound. c) Images: Static. d) Animation.
12	Error treatment: a) Feed-backs in order to avoid them. b) Various levels of helps.
13	Explanation of the functions of the navigation icons:
	a) In the presentation. b) In the help. c) When the arrow pointer is placed on them. d) None.
14	Organisation of textual: a) Normal pyramid. b) Inverted pyramid.
15	Focal point of the narration (the narrator/locutor):
	a) The narrator/locutor says more than the characters/user know.
	b) The narrator/locutor says the same as a particular character/user knows or sees.
	c) The narrator/locutor says less the main character/user knows.
16	Narration/locution is indicated in the text by: a) A cursor or a arrow. b) Underling the words.
	c) Illumination by means of a kind of highlighting as in karaoke. c) A cursor or a arrow. d) None.
17	Semiotics:
	1. Isotopy:
	a) Homogeneity between the main topic and secondary topics.
	b) Correlation between images and texts.
	2. Topology: a) The same position for the navigation keys. b) Shared text and image screen position.
	3. Coherence of graphic aspects:
	a) Base colour: Primary. Secondary. Primary & Secondary combination.
	b) Base texture: Text, colours and images. Only text and images. Only images.
	c) Transparencies: All screen. Frame.
	d) Illumination and effects: Global. Gouraud or Lambert shading. Ambient. Multi-directional.
	e) Effects of 3D: Borders with shades. Reflection of light. Diffuse of the image.
	f) Video: Colour. Black & white.
	g) Camera effects: Zoom in. Zoom out. Horizontal or vertical or angular movement. Dolly.
	h) Plane: General. Medium. First. Possibility of changes between two or more perspective.
	i) Emission movement: Constant. Stop or break.
	j) Animation classes: Morphing. Only 2D. Only 3D. 2D and 3D.
	k) Typographies: Classical. Special.
	k) Typographies: Classical. Special.
	l) Object or image presentation: With rendering. Without rendering. Wire.
	m) Possibility of changes between wire frame and full rendering.
	n) Photographies: White & Black. Colours. Wire.
	o) Drawings: White & Black. Colours. Wire.
	p) Key of navigation: 2D. 3D. Static. Animation. Arrows. Special Icons. Draws.
	4. Analysis of the content :
	a) Manifest content or latent content.
	b) Synchronic or diachronic content.
	c) Literal or metaphorical content.
1	Effects of images motions: Zoom in. Zoom out.
2	Printer: All screen. Part of screen.
3	Plays: a) Classical: Chess. Checkers. Puzzle. Others. b) Special development.
4	Sounds:
	a) Possibility of changing the volume. b) Possibility of eliminating the volume only.
	c) Noises at the instant of recording and/or emission of the sound.
5	Screen aspects:
	1. Transition types: Cut. Dissolve. Random Bars Horizontal. Split Vertical Out. Split Vertical In. Wipe Up. Blinds central. Diagonal. Spiral. Uncover. Strips. Cover. Box in/out. Fade. Through. Black
	2. Screen content attention elements:
	a) Special symbols: Circle or ellipse. Squared or rectangle. Arrows. Icons.
	b) Sounds. c) Words.
	3) Space occupied by animation and videos on the screen: a) Full screen. b) A frame on the screen.
	4) The open screens overcome (they do not close).
6	Map of the structure (tree and roots).
7	The content of the text is on lines.
8	The content of the text is on numbered pages.
9	Part of a document is shown in a windows with:
	a) Horizontal scroll bar. b) Vertical scroll bar. c) Combination of horizontal and vertical scroll bar
10	Available browsing methods:
	a) Single word or phrase (text, etymology, definition, quotation) search.
	b) Alphabetical index of node names.
11	Command line search:
	a) Standard search. b) Detailed search (levels of detail in the search).
12	Number of quantity nodes displayed at one time: a) Only one. b) 2/3. c) More.
13	The frame are presented: a) Automatic. b) By query (manual).
14	Do similar nodes have similar frames?
15	Nodes: a) Go home. B) Go back one node. c) Go back several nodes.
16	Index links: connect the collection-node to each member of the collection, and vice versa.
17	Index links: traversing from an index (collection-node) to a member, or vice versa.
18	Structural links: a) Unidirectional. b) Bi-directional.
19	Link: traversing the link, presenting and activating the destination.
20	Collection: a) 1/5. b) 6/15. c) More.
21	The collection-node have a preview.
22	Guided tour: Linear or Circular. Automatic or Manual.
23	Guided tour (total of frames): a) 1/5. b) 6/15. c) More.
24	Web index: a) Active. b) Passive.
25	Components have two or more perspectives.
26	Basic types of access structures:
	a) Graphic: Circle. Arbitrary. b) Linear. c) Circular. d) Indexed. e) Tree. f) Free-form network.
27	Links action: History list. Trails. Bookmarks.

These factors should be avoided in the academic environment, especially in the state or public universities. In the case of cooperations with the private sector, such as industry or commerce, for instance, it is always advisable to carry out a previous study. The main goal of it is to find the common points among theoretical and practical knowledge. The secondary goals are: discovering and boosting the intersections.

COMMUNICABILITY EVALUATION: ADVANTAGES

In the literature concerning usability techniques the assessors' degree of professionalism is not determined (Nielsen, 1993). It is not the same if the evaluation of the interface is made by the users or by a professional. Here is where the first split of the research takes place and works arise which back up the possibility of carrying out analysis without experience and/or previous knowledge on the side of the users, but with little success in the search for mistakes without a guide. On his side Virzi maintains the necessity of carrying out a heuristic assessment conducted by specialists (Virzi, 1997). The reason for the disagreement is that the requisites in knowledge and/or experiences of the heuristic assessment specialist are not defined, as we have established. Moreover, in the case of Nielsen and Molich they obviously required interdisciplinary teams, because they did not foresee other study plans where there was an intersection of sciences (Nielsen & Mack, 1994).

One of the problems stated by Katie M. Scott (Scott, 2009) is that usability currently lacks the methods and techniques to assess the new multimedia systems in small-size supports: video consoles, iPhone, Palm, etc. In regard to this, it

is necessary to establish a time or diachronic anchoring (Cipolla-Ficarra; Cipolla-Ficarra 2008). When Nielsen enunciated usability engineering in the early nineties Nielsen, 1993), the initials PC 'Professional Computer' switched to 'Personal Computer'. That is to say, in the eighties the users had access to computers with occupational purposes up to then, and the few personal programmable computers – Commodore, Atari, Spectrum, Amstrad, etc. – could be used for interactive games. With the reduction in costs and the spread of the computer to millions of homes, the analysts and programmers of the interactive systems needed to follow the premises enunciated by Nielsen. The goal was to make the use of the computers by novel users easier. With the democratization of the Internet, millions of users came little by little into the era of communicability. Evidently, usability is not the same as communicability.

However, there have been many works made from usability towards areas clearly belonging to the social sciences, and specifically in areas studied for decades by these sciences: publicity, marketing, education, etc. Obviously, the costs in these cases are high, whether it is from the point of view of the training of the professional to carry out these assessments on design, for instance, such as organization and maintenance in the time of a usability laboratory. Although Katie M. Scott rightly states that in many cases the usability laboratories are mobile (Scott, 2009). The main problem remains the same: the need of counting with new heuristic assessors.

This heuristic evaluator does not need a usability laboratory to carry out a study of communicability of a multimedia system. Academic education allows him to know the problems of the system, divided into the following areas of design: presentation or layout, content, navigation, structure, compatibility or conectibility and panchronic. Nevertheless, the first results obtained can then be compared with techniques and methods carried out in the laboratory, for example to evaluate the usability. Our primary set of techniques is based mainly on direct observation, the compilation of tables of binary presence of the main components of the design categories and the use of statistics. There is a second set of techniques such as user interviews, indirect observations, etc., and instruments such as a disk of heuristic evaluation, interactive programs of evaluation of the interface, etc. which can also be used in the case of verifying the obtained results. It is also feasible to translate the obtained results in the evaluation of communicability in the classical usability labs to test them. Therefore, our method and techniques are a triadic relation between observation, data summary and interpretation of results obtained.

The main advantage of this methodology is to be able to find the design and communicability mistakes of the system analysed before proceeding to the massive production of a CD-ROM, DVD or to activate a website without needing special laboratories or sophisticated instruments. As for the work instrument, the evaluator counts on a series of quality metrics of interactive communication, a table, and a disk for heuristic analysis (Cipolla Ficarra, 2005). Other advantages are:

- It eliminates the use of the laboratory, and consequently, the costs are lower with respect to techniques and methods to measure usability. Consequently, the assessment of the communicability is either mobile or dynamic. Besides, the communicability may lend its services in the different environments where either services or products are projected, whether it is in situ or through e-work or telework.
- It analyses the home page or home menu of an interactive system, detecting weak and strong points of the interface, content, structure, navigation, etc., according to the potential user of the system (Cipolla-Ficarra, 2002).
- There is a greater flexibility towards the understanding and resolution of the eventual problems stemming from the new

technological devices because communicability is implicit in their design stage.

- It divides the effectiveness of communication between on-line and/or off-line hypermedia supports, bearing in mind the connectibility and compatibility of the devices for the continuity of the interaction along time.
- It allows for partial evaluation of the quality of the interactive system, reducing time and costs. The partial results may serve as a basis for later usability tests, for instance.
- It establishes a list of tasks to be developed by the potential evaluators of the system in the usability laboratory, in order to detect mistakes and/or certify the mistakes detected by the communicability expert, if some user or client so wishes.
- It allows an inference of possible success or failure of communication through the use of the evaluation media. The inference of a communicability expert allows one to know beforehand the potential user, the context where the interactive system will be used and the possible drawbacks that user may have at the moment of interacting with the system.
- It creates statistical information through metrics for possible corrections to the design and draws an international map of the main characteristics of communicability in keeping with the different peoples and cultures in the context of information and communication technologies.
- It determines a common vocabulary in order to facilitate communications between persons who intervene in the design stage of the interactive system.

Each one of these advantages stems from the main areas which make up the theoretical framework of communicability in the interactive systems, such as software engineering, the different models of design used in the interactive

systems, human-computer interaction, usability engineering and communication. In software engineering are to be found the basis of the motivation of why it is necessary to measure the quality and the necessary instruments such as are the different kinds of metrics, which from the formal and factual sciences can be used by our communicability evaluator.

SOFTWARE QUALITY AND DESIGN

In software engineering we find a constant and growing interest towards quality and design, for example, ISO–norms international standard for the evaluation of software quality. Besides, the works by Basili and Musa (Basili & Musa, 1991), have coincided with usability engineering as stated by Nielsen in the dawn of the nineties (Nielsen, 1993). They already detected the need of counting with other professionals at the moment of developing systems aimed at either services or products. Besides, it was a time where the high financial budgets available for research and developments allowed one to incorporate additional professionals into software development projects, under the label of temporary collaborations and/or outsourcing in the cases of services that were performed.

Initially, sociology, psychology and cultural anthropology are often mentioned as examples, but these are only a small section of the huge range of areas of human knowledge that come into play in the design of multimedia systems. Furthermore, it should be borne in mind that university training varies from country to country, and consequently the range of knowledge and/or experience in the creation of multimedia systems of potential professionals should be more precise so as to avoid confusion. The concepts of social sciences should be defined previously, with exactness and avoiding generalization.

One of these deviations is to be found in many Spanish universities or other universities in the Mediterranean region since for their research and

development projects they started to hire temporarily or under the outsourcing formula (Hardaway, Hogan & Mathieu, 2005), with philosophers, anthropologists, psychologists, artists, etc. That is to say, no previous study was made of the local academic reality. It was proposed in the early nineties to work with another kind of professional for the nascent multimedia interactive industry, which was aimed at education or entertainment. That is to say, not even in the academic university framework were those adjustments made. Consequently, both theory and practice hailed from software engineering in the American universities, whose contexts in the syllabuses was not identical to the European.

Mistakes are made not only in the context of software engineering or in the formal sciences; sometimes, the new departments or European faculties aimed at the new technologies but which are included in the context of the social sciences, for instance, philosophy, education, literature, foreign languages, etc. think that the ideal solution for the "humanistic + informatics" aspects is the classical computer expert with a masters degree in marketing or public relations. However, this is not the best solution because that individual lacks the classical knowledge of communication. That is to say, that university and its students will miss a decade until they reach the required formation level, and another decade in reaching the quality and originality in the contents of the study plans.

In the beginning, that individual will simply devote himself to cut and paste contents from the subjects of university colleagues. An analysis of the programs of the subjects and their bibliography through direct objective observation allows one to see the constant changes that are introduced in each academic year (obviously, that individual can not belong to the group of the communicability professionals). Besides, this equation "humanism + informatics" where interfaces, cognitive models, museums, ecology, electronics, artificial intelligence, multimedia, philosophy, pedagogy,

anthropology are joined, etc. gives away a lack of epistemological orientation in software engineering and the social sciences.

The reality that has been described prevents the training of professionals with the necessary tools to reach quickly the quality of the current and future interactive systems. The main reason is the lack of an adequate theoretical framework in those teaching environments of continuous hybrid experimentation. Some of them, in the context of the interactive systems, go as far as to establish a parallelism with the time of the Renaissance and in a special way with the works of Leonardo Da Vinci. However, they make the mistake of joining different knowledge and diverse experiences, without finding the common denominators among them. Consequently, and following Umberto Eco's dichotomic view, we have the integrated and the apocalyptic (Eco, 2001).

In the first group, are those technicians for whom everything is a patching-up of several different branches of knowledge and/or experiences, without previous studies, for instance. In the second are those scientists who demand analysis and verifications of the obtained results before going on to the union of the different disciplines. This dichotomy is important, because for instance, in usability engineering Nielsen claimed in the beginning that it was not easy to establish measures or metrics to the quality of design (Nielsen, 1996). However, the existing instruments in the social sciences and very especially in communication and software engineering have demonstrated with the passing of time that it is possible to quantify or detect the quality of an interactive system.

SOFTWARE METRICS

Measurement is one of the main tasks of our expert in communicability. He will count for that purpose with instruments stemming from software engineering, human-computer interaction, semiotics, social communication, statistics among others.

With this purpose, he will apply the instruments of evaluation, his knowledge and experiences to reach the highest quality of the systems.

In general terms there are different types to measure with regard to the goals to be achieved, that is to say, focused on the object or in the effects on the object (Fenton, 1997). For instance, the purpose of a measurement in the software engineering can be: the process, the product, the language, the methods and the tools. It can also be considered the intention of that who carries out the measurement which can be: passive (one simply seeks the understanding of the object) or active (when one wants to predict, control and improve the object). Making a summary of the different kinds of measurements with regard to the goals to be achieved the following classification is obtained; Direct and indirect; Process and Product: Objective and subjective.

The objective measurements are those in which two people can reach the same result considering the object in an independent way, for instance to count the lines of the code of a program. Subjective measurements are recorded on the basis of subjective assessments. For instance, the experience of a person for the management of projects. The objective measurements turn out to be easier to automate then the subjective ones (Carey, 1996). Besides, these measurements of the physical world make up two types of categories of the measures to be used:

- Direct measures. For instance, those measures that in order to determine the dimension of a program it the space that occupies the feasible program in megabytes can be seen.
- Indirect measurements. Through these measures the quality of a programmer's work can be assessed by the percentage of failures detected in the summing-up.

The direct measure of an attribute is that measure that does not depend on the measurement of any other attribute. Whereas the indirect measurement of an attribute is that measure which includes the of one or more other attributes.

In regard to the process of measurement in the engineering of the software, Fenton states the following formal definition: measurement is a process in which numbers or symbols are assigned to the attributes of the entities of the real world, to describe them accurately, in accordance with rules that have been clearly defined (Fenton, 1997). Measurement assigns numbers or symbols of those attributes of the entities with the purpose of describing them. Starting from such entities, a first classification for measurement can be made -also called generically metrics in software engineering (Pressman, 2005). Pressman presents the following classification:

- Quality metrics: they respond to how to satisfy the needs expressed by the customer/user, and it is usability (Nielsen, 1993) and communicability that occupies itself the most with these aspects, whether it is from the point of view of the interaction of the formal and factual sciences (Bunge, 1981).
- Size-oriented metrics: through them direct measures of the result can be watched as well as the quality of software engineering. Currently the reliability of its reach is reason for discussion, since in the literature regarding it, it is usual to resort to the guidelines (code lines) as a unity of measure.
- Function-aimed metrics: Such metrics focus on the functionality or usefulness of the program. They are based on the method presented by Albrecht in 1979, called point of function, and designed in its origins for the management information systems (Pressman, 2005). In 1986 Jones put forward the characteristic features, to be used in software engineering applications and systems. In both cases one resort to heuristic tables, with a value scale (Pressman,

2005).

- Person-aimed metrics: they give information about the human point of view of effectiveness of the tools and of the used methods. They are the first target of study in usability engineering, for instance. Implicitly therein lies communicability.

The set of metrics that has been used in the current chapter regards the quality metrics within the intersection between those aimed at the person (Ghezzi, Mandrioli & Jazayeri, 2003). For instance, the application of this set of metrics aimed at communicability in the human factors and on-line hypermedia systems allows one to detect quickly those websites that damage the credibility of on-line information, such as website www.gens.labo.net:

In this website the surnames are illuminated on the map in the shape of a dot, and with a total of city and town councils where they are to be found. However, this is not trustworthy information, because these surnames have been extracted from the phone guides in the whole state, that is, it is not an information source like the population census (which would be the logical source for veracity in this case). The mistake becomes more apparent as soon as the Italian surnames are visualized in the USA map (see Figure5). It is usual that the staff employees or those responsible in public and/or private bodies look up that website before hiring an employee. In this case the lack of credibility enhances in some way an unfair exclusion or marginalization of human beings. A classical way to see this is to insert the executive board of a university or multinational enterprise and see where appear the surnames (the further to the north and in fewer locations they appear, the higher working chances they will have in those bodies that avail themselves of this website to hire staff). We invite the reader to try with the following names in the Italian maps: Agazzi, Barcella, Bondensan, Colleoni, Corna, Crippa, Faliva, Giavazzi, Meani, Meda, Nembrini, Paraboschi, Pesenti and Valotti (other examples related to the current website in the Annex #1). Finding websites whose credibility

Figure 4. The surname Gavazzeni is concentrated in the provinces of Lombardy (a northern region in Italy)

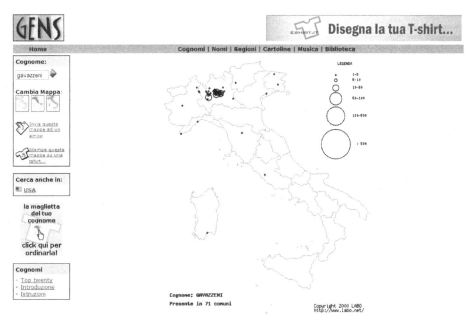

is equal to zero but with serious consequences inside the whole of the human factors, because it affects some of the elementary principles of the Universal Declaration of Human Rights – i.e., article #1, http://www.un.org/en/documents/udhr –, as in this case. It is a task that requires special software metrics. Besides, they represent a continuous and qualitative process in the evaluation and improvement of the metrics.

As with other products, the software also has implicitly an elaboration process. The communicability analysis (methods and techniques) developed for heuristic assessment can be applied in different stages; the production, with the purpose of maintaining and raising the quality of the interactive system. Among the internal and external attributes there is a bi-directional relationship that affects the quality of the software (Kit, 1995). However, it is necessary to eradicate certain axioms that relate to the internal and external attributes but are false in the interactive systems environment, such as: the external qualities are

those that have a greater importance in relation to the internal concerning the final product; a good internal structure yields as a result a good external quality (Fenton, 1997); the bigger the financial resources, the better the final quality and vice versa (Cipolla-Ficarra, 1997).

Finally, another area of knowledge that will be used by our communicability expert in his measurement process is statistics. The goal of its use is to sum up the conclusions reached in the measurements and to turn the data into easily interpretable information, for instance through the use of graphics, tables, etc. Many of these measurement activities have been made in usability laboratories in the nineties and more especially in human-computer interaction labs. Although communicability is implicit in usability, we consider that the most natural environment for its study remains in the interaction between users and computers (human-computer interaction), regardless of the names that the different labs working on the issue take.

Figure 5. The surname Colleoni is allegedly not wide spread in the USA

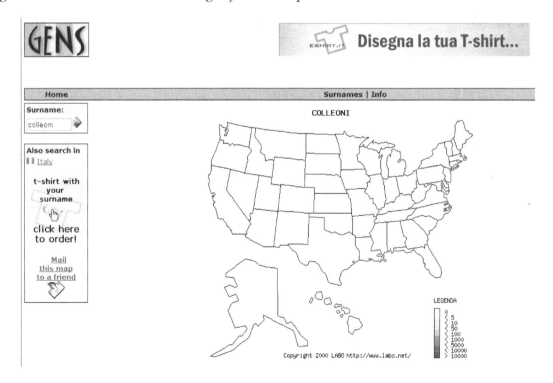

SCIENCES, SEMIOTICS AND EDUCATIONAL COMMERCE

Theoretically, the sciences should have the same financial resources available to carry out their research. However, in the history of the sciences, those disciplines belonging to the social environment and which allegedly can serve to boost the quality of life of all the citizens in the global village have always counted with fewer financial resources than the disciplines belonging to the formal sciences: physics, chemistry, mechanics, electronics, etc. This is the main reason why the training of new professionals in the social sciences is slowed down, from several points of view, such as: epistemological, the university academic, the demands for professional profiles in the labour market, etc. Within that reality it has been made for many decades the following premise: "In North America they do, and in Europe they explain what was done". That is to say, there is a greater training of theoreticians in Europe than in North America, where the praxis and the experiments prevail. The new European universities have tried to insert this model, forgetting about the centuries of theories in which they are immersed. The solution lies in finding a point of balance between practice and theories.

At present, professionals in the formal sciences are making incorrect analysis of the evolution and scientific content in multimedia/hypermedia, for example. They maintain that in the evolution of multimedia systems, at first there was multimedia in the commercial sense of the word, then the audio-visual sense, and at last in virtual reality. That is, the development of multimedia, audio-visual has resulted in virtual reality (Brunet, 2002). Obviously there's great confusion between the real history of multimedia and its derivations, or different meanings of technical definitions from different technical points of view. The confusion is easily detectable in the new orientations that are attempted in semiotics from the point of view of the formal sciences.

Present research uses concepts deriving from linguistics and semiotics (the European notion) or semiology (the American notion). The source of confusion is not coming from semiotics engineering (De Souza, 2004) because we understand that the semiotic context belongs to the field of social sciences and we cannot talk about engineering in the same way. The aim of promoting this hypothetical new area "semiotic engineering" (De Souza, Barbosa & Silva, 2001), in regards to usability engineering (Nielsen, 1993), implies explicitly the eternal trend of the sector of formal sciences to quantify human communication, be it among people or between user and computer. This flawed vision of science theory makes clear various remarks that have been considered in the present work of investigation.

New professional people inside the field of communication sciences (in an Italian context) or information sciences (in a Spanish context), for example are necessary for the correct development of interactive systems. The education and experience of these professional people must be at the intersection between factual sciences and formal sciences, the sector of development of this new profile in order to improve the interaction between person and computer (human-computer interaction). Talking about semiotics engineering is the same as creating a holistic whole belonging to formal sciences and including semiotics in it. It is clearly a large error, as semiotics has had its own autonomy for decades.

The correct direction of those interested in going deeper into the application of semiotics in interactive design –this is to be understood in a broad sense; interfaces, cognitive models, user-centered design, etc. – must start from the social sciences towards the main disciplines that make up the technological universe of informatics: programmers, systems analysts, software engineers, etc. The inverse sense generates endless disruptions in the scientific and academic environment. An environment that should stay neutral to the ups an downs of educative profiteering (mercantilism).

The aim of the terminology "semiotic engineering" is to draw attention for commercial purposes or to create false new areas that have existed for decades, such as in the academic Latin field belonging to social sciences.

The era of usability had its aegis in the nineties. Now users are living in the era of communication, and semiotics can help this process, but it does not mean creating an engineering medium for this purpose, as expected by semiotics engineering, especially when we talk about interface design, contents of interactive systems or communications between user and computer. The study of the media must begin in the social sciences, not with the interactive media. It is there where the first studies of their interaction with society are to be found. The interactive media underlie a big part of the theories, experiments and results that have been developed in the last decades in the social sciences until reaching the current global village and web accessiblity for all. At the same time, it is very important that from computer science the differences are established among hypertext, interactive multimedia (totally or partially) and hypermedia. Talking about the media era, as if it were something new, among the classical and interactive media is mistaken. Nonetheless, these errors are to be found in the modern theoretical framework concerning semiotics and new technologies.

The hypothetical new area of semiotics engineering does not separate from the previous era because it goes on mixing the concepts coming from social sciences with computer science. Some models for the design of interfaces use concepts from object-oriented programming, thus creating confusion inside the same field of computer science because you do not know whether they're speaking about programming or design.

It is necessary to endow with bigger financial resources and decision power to the social sciences professionals and very especially those who have training and experience in the intersection of the formal and factual sciences. This error usually brings about high costs in the R+D products aimed at the interactive systems. In the area of the European Mediterranean, usually those in charge do not know how to carry out quality evaluations in an autonomous way, whether it is about usability or communicability of a hypermedia system, for instance.

According to Ezequiel Ander-egg and Mario Bunge, it is important to keep in mind the following fundamental aspects of science philosophy, before creating new scientific disciplines (Ander-egg, 1986; Bunge, 1981). In our case, we are in front of a methodology of analysis and evaluation applied to communication and design of an interactive system. All methodology overflows with methodological problems, as it implies investigations of gnoseological, metaphysical and world-conception kind. In order to place a methodological problem into a wider context of comprehension, we have to consider, at least, five classes of implications (Ander-egg, 1986):

- Firstly, there are ontological implications. We are referring to the nature of the social object, i.e., to the class of reality that is the social reality; these implications influence all the others. If it is a method, it is in fact a way to approach reality. Before deciding which is the most suitable method for the study of the social facts and their derivations, we can establish the class of reality of a social fact.

- There are also gnoseological or knowledge-theory implications. They refer to the opportunities of knowledge, its way of production, and its forms of validation, that establish or determine the relationships between reality and thought, or, more precisely, between subject and object. For example, the empathy of communication for the designer's part is important during the planning of a new system that will be used by potential users.

- Logical implications refer to the methods in the truest sense of the word, that is, to the paths and procedures of the human

spirit which, from a general point of view, derive from scientific knowledge.

- As for the epistemological implications, they refer to the formal structure of sciences, including that of man and obviously the social sciences; these implications concern the principles of methodology, the scientific truth, etc.

- Finally there is the paradigm or disciplinary matrix, basically constituted by questions in terms of the principles of social science, as such: the whole of postulates and assumptions, methods, fields of work, limits, problems, etc. that separate the researchers of a certain scientific community. A lot of the techniques presented in the heuristic evaluation: observation, enquiries, interviews, etc. belong to the field of social sciences and more specifically to sociology.

Now, in every science, the basic questions mentioned before are of great importance if there is real scientific activity. The answer given to these questions depends on the structure of science, its limits, its problems, the connection among them, the method and of course progress and scientific results.

The development and advance of the scientific community according to the precepts stated by Mario Bunge and Ezequiel Ander-egg goes into endless practical difficulties which spring from the mercantilistic environment, even in the context of public education (Cipolla-Ficarra, 2009). Interactive communication or new technologies, whether it is from the theoretical or the practical point of view has always drawn the attention of those who intend to get economical profits in the short term. The consequence of this is that the terms are emptied of their academical or scientific meanings to obtain the highest benefit in the least possible time. A clear example has been the fierce Spanish marketing campaign in front of the notion of multimedia in the mid nineties. Multimedia was presented as

synonymous with computers with CD-ROM/DVD readers and loudspeakers. Consequently, until now, in the collective imagination of the Spanish population, multimedia is tantamount to interactive communication in off-line supports.

FUTURE RESEARCH DIRECTIONS

Our main goal in the short term is to start to analyze the syllabuses of the faculties in the universities of America and Europe, especially those which have studies aimed at the human-computer interaction and the disciplines that comprise it. Through these results it is intended to establish a map of those universities where is detected the possibility of obtaining communicability experts with the least possible changes in the current study programs. Also a curriculum or study module will be established in computer science, telecommunications and social sciences studies. Besides, three levels will be set for the analysis and evaluation of the interactive systems; user, professional/productive, and scientific. In a parallel way the set of communicability principles of the interactive systems will be definitively organized, bearing in mind the new mobile technological devices of small size. Finally, to aim the research towards the tridimensional interfaces, Web 3.0 and the immersive interactive systems.

CONCLUSION

Interactive communication is a reality that has changed communication between human beings. It is an interactive communication that constantly adapts the latest technological novelties in the daily life of millions of inhabitants in our planet. However, inside this daily coexistence it is necessary to improve the conditions of quality and the horizontality of the digital or binary information. That is to say, to go on with the process of free access to the information for everybody but eradicating the factors that damage the credibility

of on-line information. The latest technologies that are being incorporated in classrooms and in syllabuses should serve to reach these goals in the least possible time. The generation of a new professional who is an expert in communicability is not an easy task within the current university context –when we refer to an expert, we do not do it with a mercantilistic purpose, but rather scientific. In some private or public universities but which actually work as if they were a private firm with lucrative purposes, we find study plans aimed at the new technologies under the notion of interdisciplinary. In computer science faculties, the pressure exerted by the formal sciences professionals is such that they prevent the insertion in the study plans of subjects which are typical of the social sciences. Some exceptions to this reality exist in the study plans of public universities in the south of the American continent for thirty years. There it is feasible to find professionals in whom the theoretical and practical knowledge of the factual and formal sciences converge. That is to say, they are ideal professionals for the era of communicability. However, it is always necessary to differentiate between those professionals who from the formal sciences have gone the whole way (through 5 or 6 years –long university studies) towards computer science. (the logical direction in the context of the interactive systems) from those belonging to the sector of the formal sciences who usually seek the academic shortcuts of one or two years to reach the social sciences (through specialization courses and masters, for instance). The professional that we need in this time must escape from the mere notion of humanism or other similar. That is to say, their formation must be aimed at each one of the aspects of social communication and the information in the interactive systems. Without any doubt, the constant studies that are being made from the software in defining the curricular profile for the next years are very positive. In these studies the term "quality" has always been present.

REFERENCES

Ander-egg, E. (1986). *Techniques of Social Investigation*. Buenos Aires, Argentina: Hvmanitas.

Aranguren, J. (1986). *La comunicación humana*. Madrid: Tecnos.

Balakrishnan, R., Fizmaurice, G., & Kurtenbach, G. (2001). User-Interfaces for Volumetric Displays. *IEEE Software*, *34*(3), 37–45.

Basili, V., & Musa, J. (1991). The Future Engineering of Software: A Management Perspective. *IEEE Computer*, *24*(9), 90–96.

Birwhistell, R. (1974). *Diccionario de las ciencias sociales*. Madrid: Aguilar.

Botto, F. (1992). *Multimedia, CD-ROM and Compact Disc*. Wilmslow, UK: Sigma Press.

Brajnovic, L. (1979). *El ámbito científico de la información*. Navarra, Spain: EUNSA.

Broy, M. (2006). The 'Grand Challenge' in Informatics: Engineering Software-Intensive Systems. *IEEE Computer*, *39*(10), 72–80.

Brunet, P. (2002). Virtual Reality. *Infovis*. Retrieved April 2002, from http://www.infovis.net/printMag.php?num=82&lang=2

Buie, E. (1999). HCI Standards: A Mixed Blessing. *Interaction*, *6*(2), 36–42. doi:10.1145/296165.296177

Bunge, M. (1981). *The science: your method and your philosophy*. Buenos Aires, Argentina: Siglo XXI.

Carey, D. (1996). Is Software Quality Intrinsic, Subjective, or Relational? *Software Engineering Notes*, *21*, 74–75. doi:10.1145/381790.565678

Chisolm, W., Vanderheiden, G., & Jacobs, I. (2001). Web Content Accessibility Guidelines. *Interaction*, *13*(4), 34–53.

Cipolla-Ficarra, F. (1994). Sistemas Multimediales Interactivos: Aproximación a la Perspectiva Comunicacional. *Novática, 112-113*, 4–6.

Cipolla-Ficarra, F. (1996). A User Evaluation of Hypermedia Iconography. In *Proceedings Computergraphics* (pp. 182-191). Paris: GRASP.

Cipolla-Ficarra, F. (1997). Evaluation of Multimedia Components. In *Proceedings International Conference on Multimedia Computing and Systems,* (pp. 557-564). Washington, DC: IEEE Computer Society.

Cipolla-Ficarra, F. (1998). Method for evaluation of hypermedia usability. In *Proc. 7th IFAC/ IFIP/IFORS/IEA Symposium on Analysis, Design and Evaluation of Man Machine Systems and Human Interface,* (pp. 173-178). Kyoto, Japan: Elsevier.

Cipolla-Ficarra, F. (2001). Panchronics: An Attribute of the Quality for Hypermedia Systems. In *Proceedings International Conference on Information Systems Analysis and Synthesis,* (pp. 289-294). Orlando, GA: ISAS.

Cipolla-Ficarra, F. (2002). Homepage and Communications: Quality Metrics. In *Proceedings Eight International Conference on Distributed Multimedia Systems,* (pp. 202-209). San Francisco: DMS.

Cipolla-Ficarra, F. (2003). Table of Heuristic Evaluation for Communication of the Multimedia Systems. In *Proceedings HCI International '03,* (pp. 940-944). Crete: LEA.

Cipolla-Ficarra, F. (2005). An Evaluation of Meaning and Content Quality in Hypermedia. In *CD-ROM Proceedings.* Las Vegas: HCI International.

Cipolla-Ficarra, F. (2008). Communicability design and evaluation in cultural and ecological multimedia systems. In *Proceedings MSCommunicability '08,* (pp. 1-8). New York: ACM Press.

Cipolla-Ficarra, F. (2009). Virtual Classroom and Communicability: Empathy and Interaction for All. *New Directions in Intelligent Interactive Multimedia Systems and Services,* (LNCS, pp. 117-127). Berlin: Springer-Verlag.

Cipolla-Ficarra, F., & Cipolla-Ficarra, M. (2008). Interactive Systems, Design and Heuristic Evaluation: The Importance of the Diachronic Vision. In *Proceedings International Symposium on Intelligent Interactive Multimedia Systems and Services, KES IIMSS,* (pp. 625-634). Berlin: Springer-Verlag.

Cipolla-Ficarra, F., & Cipolla-Ficarra, M. (2009). Attention and Motivation in Hypermedia Systems. In *Proceedings HCI International 2009,* (LNCS, pp. 78-87). Berlin: Springer-Verlag.

Dahlbom, B., & Mathiassen, L. (1997). The Future of Our Profession. *Communications of the ACM, 40*(6), 80–89. doi:10.1145/255656.255706

Dance, F. (1973). *Teoría de la comunicación humana.* Buenos Aires: Troquel.

De Souza, C. (2004). The *semiotic engineering on human-computer interaction.* Cambridge, UK: The MIT Press.

De Souza, C., Barbosa, S., & Silva, S. (2001). Semiotic Engineering Principles for Evaluating End-User Programming Environments. *Interacting with Computers, 13*, 467–495. doi:10.1016/ S0953-5438(00)00051-5

Dias, B., & Brewer, E. (2009). How Computer Science Serves the Developing World. *Communications of the ACM, 52*(6), 74–80. doi:10.1145/1516046.1516064

Eco, U. (2001). *Apocalitici e integrati.* Milano: Bompiani.

Edmundson, A. (2008). *Globalized E-learning –Cross Cultural Dimension.* Saarbrücken, Germany: VDM Verlarg.

Ellison, N., Lampe, C., & Steinfield, C. (2009). Social Network Sites and Society: Current Trends and Future Possibilities. *Interaction, 16*(1), 6–9. doi:10.1145/1456202.1456204

Fenton, N. (1997). *Software Metrics: A Rigorous Approach.* Cambridge, UK: Chapman & Hall.

Furnas, G. (1987). The Vocabulary Problem in Human–System Communication. *Communications of the ACM, 30*(11), 964–971. doi:10.1145/32206.32212

Ghezzi, C., Mandrioli, D., & Jazayeri, M. (2003). *Fundamentals of Software Engineering.* Upper Saddle River, NJ: Prentice Hall.

Grimes, J., & Potel, M. (1991). What is Multimedia? *IEEE Computer Graphics, 11*(1), 49–52. doi:10.1109/38.67700

Hardaway, D., Hogan, M., & Mathieu, R. (2005). Outsourcing the University Computer Lab. *IEEE Computer, 38*(9), 100–102.

Hemmeninger, D. (2007). The ACM and IEEE-CS Guidelines for Undegraduate CS Education. *Communications of the ACM, 50*(5), 46–53. doi:10.1145/1230819.1230838

Kit, E. (1995). *Software Testing in the Real World –Improving the Process.* New York: Addision Wesley.

Kraemer, K., Dedrick, J., & Sharma, P. (2009). One Laptop Per Child: Vision vs. Reality. *Communications of the ACM, 52*(6), 66–73. doi:10.1145/1516046.1516063

Macdonald, N. (2004). Can HCI Shape the Future of Mass Communications? *Interaction, 11*(2), 42–47. doi:10.1145/971258.971272

McLuhan, M., & Power, B. (1992). *The Global Village: Transformations in World Life and Media in the 21st Century.* Oxford, UK: Oxford University Press.

Muller, N. (1996). Multimedia over the Network. *Byte, 31*(3), 73–83.

Nielsen, J. (1993). *Usability Engineering.* London: Academic Press.

Nielsen, J. (1996). Usability Metrics: Tracking Interface Improvements. *IEEE Software, 13*(6), 12–13.

Nielsen, J., & Mack, R. (1994). *Usability Inspection Methods.* New York: Wiley.

Piaget, J. (1993). *The Children Machine.* New York: Basic Books.

Pressman, R. (2005). *Software Engineering –A Practitioner's Approach.* New York: McGraw-Hill.

Reeves, B., & Nass, C. (1998). *The Media Equation –How People Treat Computers, Television, and New Media Like Real People and Places.* Cambridge, UK: Cambridge University Press.

Robinson, G., & Cargill, C. (1996). History and Impact of Computer Standards. *IEEE Computer, 29*(10), 79–85.

Ruthven, I. (2008). Contextual factors affecting the utility of surrogates within exploratory search. *Information Processing & Management, 40*(2), 437–462. doi:10.1016/j.ipm.2007.08.002

Sanders, L. (2008). An Evolving Map of Deing Practice and Design Research. *Interaction, 15*(6), 13–17. doi:10.1145/1409040.1409043

Saussure, F. (1990). *Course in General Linguistics.* New York: McGraw-Hill.

Scott, K. (2009). Is Usability Obsolete? *Interaction, 16*(3), 6–11. doi:10.1145/1516016.1516018

Shih, E. (2008). IT Diffusion in Developing Countries. *Communications of the ACM, 51*(2), 43–48. doi:10.1145/1314215.1340913

Tompa, F. (1989). A Data Model for Flexible Hypertext Database System. *ACM Transactions on Information Systems, 1*, 85–100. doi:10.1145/64789.64993

Valenza, C., Adkins, J. (2009). Understanding Visual Thiking: The History and Future of Graphic Facilitation. *Interactions, 16* 4), 38-43.

Virzi, R. (1997). Usability Inspection Methods. In *Handbook of Human-Computer Interaction,* (p. 705-716). Amsterdam: Elsevier.

KEY TERMS AND DEFINITIONS

Analyst in Communicability: An expert professional who has knowledge and/or experiences in the intersection zone of the factual and formal sciences. Its main goal is to increase at the maximum the communicability of the on-line and off-line interactive systems.

Communicability Metrics: A set metrics from software engineering, human-computer interaction, social sciences (including semiotics) and usability.

Communicability: A qualitative communication between the user and the interactive system, such as hypermedia, mobile phones, virtual reality, immersion multimedia, among others. The extent to which an interactive system successfully conveys its functionality to the user.

Interactive System: It is a computer device made up by a CPU and peripherals, whose functioning requires a constant interaction with the user. Currently these systems tend to their miniaturization, the mobility and wireless connectability among them.

Quality Metrics: A set of attributes to assess an interactive system (product or service), for instance, an E-commerce website or a geographic information system software on a pocket PC.

Semiotics: The study or doctrine of signs, sometimes supposed to be a science of signs but not an engineering, for instance.

Final Remarks

Lastly we are transiting through the era of communicability and this quality must be translated to the whole global village quickly without wasting time for the welfare of the whole of humanity.

Also that it is necessary an opening towards new professionals in the context of the multimedia in order to increase quality and cut down production costs. Therefore, the new philosophy and team work required in the context of the software industry to obtain products and high quality services, particularly in the multimedia framework, is the intersection of the fact and formal sciences. We have also seen what the new generation of the web might eventually be like. Without any doubt it is a real challenge towards the future.

I would like to close this book with two authors, Plato[1]: *"Some day, in the distant future, our grandchildren's grandchildren will develop a new equivalent of our classrooms. They will spend many hours in front of boxes with fires glowing within. May they have the wisdom to know the difference between light and knowledge"*, and Kevin Kelly[2]: *"It is communication that makes the world move, not computers. Communication is the base of our civilization, culture, memory and of our identity as human beings"*, who have laid the stress on education and communication.

ENDNOTES

[1]   Gruwell, F. (2007). *The Gigantic Book of Teachers' Wisdom*, New York: Skyhorse, p. 651.
[2]   http://archiviostorico.corriere.it/1998/novembre/15/Kelly_hippy_alla_conquista_Internet_co_0_9811155378.shtml

Annex 1:
Descriptive Statistics for the Communicability Studies

Francisco V. Cipolla-Ficarra
ALAIPO, & AInCI, Spain

Maria Valeria Ficarra
AInCI, & ALAIPO, Spain

INTRODUCTION

In the present section are described the most relevant components of descriptive statistics which are used in communicability and usability research mainly. We have been using these components through the years in the recompilation of results through the use of methods and techniques of heuristic assessment aimed at the quality of on-line and off-line interactive systems, regardless of both their contents and their potential users. As can be seen, it is not necessary to be an expert in mathematics for their application. Many of them are constantly used in the social sciences environment, especially those that are related to publicity communication in the face of the appearance of new services and/or products, the voters' opinion prior to the elections, etc. Therefore, the components of descriptive statistics belong to the following measures: frequency (relative and absolute), measurements of central tendencies (average,

median, mode), dispersion measurements (average deviation, standard deviation, the variance and range, minimum and maximum measures. Each one of these concepts, examples and the deductions of the presented formulas belong to the following authors: Murat (1974); Chatfield (1983); Tomeo-Perucha & Uña-Juarez (1989); Johnson & Bhattacharyya (1992); Moore (1995); Berenson, Levine, & Rindskopf (1998); Canavos (1998); Lea & Brooke (2004); and Hand (2008). The symbols of the equations of the statistics are represented with letters or abbreviations in Spanish or English, although regardless of them, the results are identical. The purpose has been to create a kind of bridge towards all those interested in communicability and who do not have knowledge or previous experiences in descriptive statistics. These concepts are accompanied by a set of real examples on-line with regard to the incorrect use of statistics, at the end of the annex. Their purpose is to make apparent the human factors that have a

negative influence on the quality of the software and human-computer interaction.

DEFINITIONS AND GOALS

"Statistics is the key disciplines for predicting the future or for making inferences about the unknown, or for producing convenient summaries of data" (Hand, 2008, p. 3). Tomeo-Perucha and Uña-Juárez define mathematical statistics as the science that studies random phenomena and which in a second stage generalizes and predicts or infers results (Tomeo-Perucha & Uña-Juárez, 1989). As a part of mathematical statistics, descriptive statistics deals with the numerical description of sets, and it is particularly useful when these have many elements, mathematically evaluating and analyzing the collective represented by the whole without trying to reach more general conclusions, which is the purpose of statistic inference. Canavos establishes that the purpose of descriptive statistics is the study of high-numbered collectives, which means that in each case certain characters of use are going to be described and analyzed in each case, or different collectives and the relationships existing among them (Canavos, 1998). To carry out the statistical process are several stages are necessary, which can be summed up in four bullet points:

1. The design or outline, through which is determined the goal to be pursued, the population or sample that is going to be studied., the features that are of interest, and the presentation that will be made with the gathered data.
2. The gathering of data may be direct or indirect. Direct when it is the individual himself who delivers the data, generally through a questionnaire. Indirect when one resorts to a file, database, etc.
3. The obtainment of results through the data treatment: these are the arithmetic opera-

tions, boxes, tables, graphics, etc. foreseen in the heuristic evaluation procedure of communicability that has to be carried out to obtain the results.
4. The interpretation of results. The evaluator with the obtained results must advise those who must make the decisions, who, logically, will act bearing in mind the received information. In the case of not having sufficient knowledge and/or experiences in statistics it is necessary to request the expert's help to avoid unforeseen costs in the future before making decisions.

FREQUENCY MEASUREMENTS

Most of the results of the heuristic assessments are a set of observations and "values" which refer to the studied attributes or variables. For instance, if in the research one started by counting the total of navigation keys which make up an interface, the initial or primary data consist in a numeric value associated to each examined screen. These initial data are usually grouped in frequency tables with the purpose of processing them in an efficient and fast way. The frequencies can be either absolute or relative.

Absolute Frequency and Relative Frequency

Absolute frequency is the number of times that a given value is observed, whereas relative frequency is the proportion of times that a given value is registered in the analyzed sample or population. Next there is an example of absolute frequency and relative frequency. If the total of nodes that make up the guided links range between 10 and 25, and once a systematic reading of a sample of Web 2.0 has been made, it is observed that the values in the variable nodes oscillate from 10 to 25, that is to say, they encompass a 15 unit range, where each one of the possible values of the guided

link variable can be represented by 0, 1, 2, ... *n* sometimes in the data recompilation. Supposing that the value 22 has been registered 30 times then the absolute frequency of 22 is 30. This means that in the sample of evaluated cases there were 39 guided links with 22 nodes. If the number of studied cases was 60, the relative frequency is calculated in the following way:

$$\frac{\text{Total of the reading of a given value}}{\text{Studied cases}} = \frac{30}{60} = 0.5$$

From the example, it is deduced that a way of summing-up in an efficient and conventional manner what precedes is via the formula:

$$f' = \frac{f}{N}$$

In which f= absolute frequency of a given value; f= relative frequency of a same value; N= number of values of the study cases.

Grouping of Data

There is the possibility of grouping the original data in a distribution of frequencies. This grouping can be made with two different "methods" which are presented next:

1. Indicating the frequency of the values into groups or class intervals of measurement scale
2. Indicating the frequency of the noted values in the groups or categories intervals formed by two or more units of the primitive measurement scale

If the first method is used, for instance in the case of the total of nodes of a guided link, it would be necessary to indicate the frequencies with which were registered the total figures of the nodes that make up these guided links: 10, 11, 12, ...25. It is possible that in a randomly chosen sample a determined amount of total

figures. of nodes in the guided links was not registered, consequently its frequency will be null. By using the second method, it is established that the total run of the values of the studied variable be divided into intervals of 2, 3 or more units each.

- **First category:** Includes the values of 10, 11, 12
- **Second category:** Made up by the values 13, 14, 15
- **Third category:** Has the values 16, 17 18 and so on until value 25

In this second method one can find guided links in the same category with 3 different amounts of nodes. For instance, in the first category there are 5 guided links with a total of 10 nodes, another three guided links with a total of 11 nodes, 2 guided links with a total of 12 nodes. However, at the moment of the recount of the data grouped in such a way, it is considered that all the cases that belong to the same category present the same value, regardless of their original value. The value that is attributed to the cases included in a same category is the central point thereof. That is to say, the guided links grouped in the category 10-12 are regarded as if they all had 11, since this is the central point of the category. It is obvious that the reduction of the original data in this second method introduces an error, which will have to be taken into account at the moment of carrying out the recount of the examined sample.

As Murat (1974), Bulmer (1979), Chatfield (1983), Johnson & Bhattacharyya (1992), Moore (1995), Canavos (1998), Lea & Brooke (2004), Hand (2008), Ross (2009) maintain in order to cut down the original data to a distribution of frequencies it is necessary:

1. Establishing the range of the values of the variables
2. Registering the number of times that was recorded each one of the values that make up the range

3. Selecting preferably the first method, or rather the second method by grouping two or more original categories to make up new categories: which will be so formed by two or more units of the original scale

Next an example of distribution of frequencies, where the grouping of original data (total of nodes of the guided links) is in categories of a unit each, whose purpose is to determine the absolute frequency.

MEASURES OF CENTRAL TENDENCIES

The measures of the central tendencies (also known as centralization tendencies or averages) are the indexes that characterize the focus of a distribution of frequencies. These are:

- Average or Mean
- Median
- Mode

The Average

The average is the addition of the different values (N) that make up the field of study (it can also be a sample) and dividing then this result by N. The average or arithmetic average is the most important index to characterize a distribution of frequencies. For instance, if the values registered in a sample are:

$$X_1 \ X_2 \ X_3 \ X_4 \ X_5 \ X_6 \ .... \ X_N$$

Table 1. Distribution of frequencies

The arithmetic average is:

$$M = \frac{1}{N} \sum_i X_i$$

i = 1, 2, 3, 4, 5, 6, ... N

Where:

M = Population arithmetic measurement.
N = Number of objects that make up the population.
X_i = value of the object i-umpteenth in the X variable.

The Median

The median is that value in measurement scale which divides the whole of the objects that make up the sample in two equal parts. The median can be calculated both in non-grouped as in grouped data.

The median of a non-grouped set of data is obtained by ordering from major to minor or from minor to major the data and determining by a simple recounting the value of the element that divides the total set in two numerically equal subsets. However, here it is possible that two situations arise:

1. If the total number of registered values is odd, then the median is given by the value of the element that occupies the centre of the groups. For instance, given the following set

Distribution of the frequencies		
Values taken by variable X (X = total of the nodes in guided tours)	Number of times with which was written each value of X	Absolute frequency
12	√ √	2
11	√ √ √	3
10	√	1

of nodes that represent the active medians (tridimensional animations in 11 analyzed videogames), that is, the following set:

$$E = \{20, 25, 27, 30, 32, 34, 21, 33, 24, 22, 29\}$$

Making an ordination from major to minor (it is possible from minor to major) we have: 20, 21, 22, 24, 25, <u>27</u>, 29, 30, 32, 33, 34. Since there are 11 elements, the sixth (27) is the central value, that is, it represents the median.

2. The total number of registered values is even, the median is given by the centre of the interval which is among the two central objects. Referring to the previous example but eliminating the last encyclopedia whose total of active nodes is 29, we have the following set:

$$E = \{20, 25, 27, 30, 32, 34, 21, 33, 24, 22\}$$

Making an ordination from major to minor we have: 34, 33, 32, 30, <u>27</u>, <u>25</u>, 24, 22, 21, 20. Consequently, the total of the data is an even number (10), the median in the current data set is given by the centre of interval, that is to say, between the two central values: the fifth and the sixth (27 and 25). Median = 26. Assuming that the central values are equal, therefore they have a centre of interval equal to zero, it is considered that the median is equal to the common value to the central elements.

The Mode

The mode is a n index of the central tendencies of a distribution of frequencies. The mode is a distribution of non-uniform frequencies (that is, the values in the measurement scale that was written down more times. Now, if the distribution presents two maximum frequencies in two adjoining categories, the mode is given by the limit that separates both categories. Whereas if the distribution has two maximum frequencies in non-adjoining categories, that is, that the distribution is bimodal and besides it possesses two modes. In the case that the work is done with random samples of a universe, the frequency distributions are unimodal. In the supposition that two groups of elements belonging to different universes are working in a single one, the distribution of frequencies may be bimodal. Next an example with which it is seen how the mode is calculated. In a set of 30 analyzed home pages, in which have been registered the total of icons (whose values vary from 0 to 10) for different operations, navigation, edition, searches, etc, on the first screen of a selection, we can depict it in Table 2.

The highest frequencies were registered in two adjoining categories, the fifth and the sixth. Therefore, the mode of the aforementioned distribution is the limit that divides them, that is 6.5

DISPERSION MEASURES

The dispersion measures represent the basic descriptive indexes of a frequency distribution. The degree of dispersion is the measure in which a set of values concentrate around a central index. Hence dispersion is understood to mean diversity or heterogeneity of the observed values.

If in the face of two sets of random samples formed by an identical number of elements the

Table 2. Mode: example

Number of icons	0	1	2	3	4	5	6	7	8	9	10
Total of icons in the first screen of the collection	0	0	1	4	1	<u>6</u>	<u>6</u>	1	2	4	5

Table 3. Example of the calculation of the medium deviation.

X_i	f_i	$f_i X_i$	$X_i - M$	$f_i \, X_i - M$
1	4	4	3.83	15.32
2	3	6	2.83	8.49
3	2	6	1.83	3.66
4	7	28	0.83	5.81
5	1	5	0.17	0.17
6	3	18	1.17	3.51
7	6	42	2.17	13.02
8	1	8	3.17	3.17
9	2	18	4.17	8.34
10	1	10	5.17	5.17
	N = 30	145		66.66

range of the first sample is bigger than the range of the second, consequently the values that make up the first prove to be more dispersed or heterogeneous than the second. The dispersion is lesser the smaller the range. It may happen that all the analyzed elements have the same value, therefore dispersion is equal to zero. The most used dispersion indexes according to Murat (1971), Bulmer (1979), Chatfield (1983), Johnson & Bhattacharyya (1992), Moore (1995), Berenson, Levine & Rindskopf (1998), Canavos (1998) and Ross (2009) are:

- The range (also called total range or rank)
- The median deviation
- The standard deviation (its square is called variance)

The Range

The range of a distribution is given by the number of units in the scale of measure that lies between the lower and the higher value, including both. That is to say:

- P_{max} = Maximum registered value
- P_{min} = Minimum registered value

So the formula to register the range is:

- $Range = P_{max} - P_{min} + 1$

The Medium Deviation

The medium deviation is the arithmetic average of the absolute values of the deviations with regard to the arithmetic average. In order to calculate the average deviation in non-grouped data the following formula is used:

$$DM = \frac{1}{N}\sum_i |X_i - M|$$

$$i = 1, 2, 3, 4, ... N$$

Next an example of calculation of the medium deviation, applied to the evolution of exact synchronism between audio and image in a movement (dynamical means) for which 30 video files were considered. The calculations require the following operations:

- The calculation of the arithmetic average.
- The determination of the deviation of the value of each category in regard to the average.

- Calculation of the products.
- Addition of all the products obtained in the third operation.
- Division of the addition obtained in the fourth operation by the total number of observations that were made.

In the following table are all the data to carry out the different operations to reach the medium deviation:

1. The arithmetic average of the example is:

$$M = f\frac{1}{N}\sum_i {}_i X_i = \frac{145}{30} = 4.83$$

The deviations of each one of the X_i (once the average is known) are in the fourth column. The negative sign of some results is omitted because they are absolute deviations. The products $f_i \mid X_i - M \mid$ are in the fifth column. The addition of them is 66.66 Applying the average to the total of the products of the fifth column, the result by approximation is: 2.22 Therefore, the average of the deviations (whether it is with a positive or negative sign) of the values of each one of the considered elements and in regard to the arithmetic average is approximately 2.2 units in each measurement scale.

The Variance and Standard Deviation

The variance is the arithmetic average of the squares of the deviations with regard to the average. The variance is the measure of dispersion of greatest use in the description and analysis of statistic data. The positive square root of the variance receives the name of standard deviation. There are two analogous symbols to depict it: V o δ^2

If one works with not grouped data the formula is:

$$s = \frac{1}{N}\sqrt{N\sum X^2_i - \left(\sum X_i\right)^2}$$

Table 4. The following is an example applied to a set of 10 DVDs in which the total figures of the guided link with the highest number of screens was

DVD #	Total
1	13
2	10
3	14
4	16
5	8
6	10
7	12
8	11
9	14
10	16

Table 5. A way of presenting the operations of $\sum X^2_i$ and $(\sum X)^2$

X_i	X^2_i
13	169
12	144
14	196
16	256
8	64
10	100
12	144
11	121
14	196
16	256
$\Sigma = 126$	$\Sigma = 1646$

In contrast, if one works with grouped data, the formula is:

$$s = \frac{1}{N}\sqrt{N\sum fX^2_i - \left(\sum fX_i\right)^2}$$

$$s = \frac{1}{10}\sqrt{16460 - 15876} = \frac{\sqrt{584}}{10} = 2.41$$

For the calculation of the variance of the same example of the totals of the guided links, the average has to be calculated previously:

Table 6. Example of the calculation of the variance

X_i	$x = (X_i - M)$	$X^2 = (X_i - M)^2$
13	0.4	0.16
12	- 0.6	0.36
14	1.4	1.96
16	3.4	11.56
8	- 4.6	21.16
10	- 2.6	6.76
12	- 0.6	0.36
11	- 1.6	2.56
14	1.4	1.96
16	3.4	11.56
$\Sigma = 126$	$\Sigma = 0$	$\Sigma = 58.4$

$$M = \frac{1}{N}\sum_i X_i = 12.6$$

Applying the formula of the variance:

$$V = \frac{1}{N}\sum_i X_i^2$$

Replacing the obtained values in the table the following fraction is reached:

$$V = \frac{58.4}{10}$$

Consequently, the result is:

$$s = \sqrt{5.84} = 2.41$$

CATEGORY

Next we find the definitions of category or class, interval, exact limits of category and focal point of category:

1. The classes or categories are the categorization criteria of the original values and may be formed by one or more units of measure of the original scale. For instance, if the original measurement scale has a range of 60 units, it is possible to make new categories to speed up the recompilation process of the data. The interval or width of the category is the number of units that make up a class.

2. The total range is divided into k (k = k-umpteenth) categories, in such a way that their number is no fewer than 10 nor higher than 20. The criteria to determine the width of the categories and consequently their number is arbitrary. However, one tends to make categories with an odd map of units that make up a category which is generally indicated with the letter "i". A continuous scale is formed by units of measure which are in theory divisible in infinitely small subunits. If they are not, the scale is poor.

3. The exact limits of the category serve the purpose of obtaining a higher accuracy in the calculation of statistical data, It is convenient to specify which are the exact limits of a category. The measuring instrument specifically applied, in all the cases, allows only a limited subdivision of the basic units, (for instance the 100 centimetres that make up a metre) in such a way that

the value of an object whatsoever can only be expressed in an approximate way to the nearest mark in the scale of the used instrument. For instance, if the units of the scale are centimetres, an object whose real length is 15.8 centimetres will be approximated to 16, whereas if another object has a length of 15.4 centimetres, it will be close to 15. A class made up by the values 10, 11, and 12 that is to say, with an interval of three units, has its apparent limits in 10 and 12, but its exact limits in 9.5 and 12.5, since all the objects bigger than 9.5 and smaller than 12.5 belong to this category.

4.   The central point of the category is the point that is to be found at an equal distance of its own exact limits. It is obtained by dividing by two the number of units that make up the interval of the category, and later on by adding the result to its exact lower limit. For instance, if we have a category made up by 2 units, whose exact limits are between 9.5 and 11.5 its central point is:

$$9.5 + \frac{2}{2} = 10.5$$

Note: The letter or symbol used for the central point is X'_i (the apostrophe means that the X_i value is arbitrary)

THE ROUNDING OF THE FIGURES

The following criteria have been used to round the figures of the research. If the first figure to be eliminated is 0, 1, 2, 3 or 4, then it is simply eliminated. If it is a 9, 8, 7, 6 or a 5 followed by other figures then the figure is increased in a unit. For instance, the result of rounding 65.4 is 65, of 231.27 is 231, of 0.27503 is 0.28.

If the figure to be eliminated is a 5 which is not followed by other significant figures, the same mistake is made if we wipe out the 5 than if we increase in one the preceding figure. In this case it is rounded so that the previous figure is even; in this way, when one operates with many numbers, the excesses of some can make up for the defects of others, and the final mistake will be lesser. For instance, 273.5 is rounded to a whole in 273, and 39.35 is rounded to decimals in 30.2.

THE SAMPLING

As Canavos to understand the nature of statistics it is necessary to understand the population notions –also called universe or collective (Canavos, 1988). A population is the collection of all the possible information that characterizes a phenomenon.

In statistics, population is a much more general concept that the one held by the general definition of this word. In this sense, a population is any collection, whether it is of a finite number of measurements or a big collection, virtually infinite, of data about something of interest. On the other hand, the sample is a selected representative subset of a population (Lea & Brooke, 2004; Ross, 2009). A good sample is that which reflects the essential characteristics of the population from which it was obtained. In statistics one resorts to random methods to guarantee these essential characteristics.

The probabilistic random samples or randomly chosen are those that are reached on the basis of the calculation of probabilities, eliminating possible arbitrarity. It means that the universe population that makes up the basis of the sample can be subdivided into different units called sampling units. When one says that the sample is randomly determined, it is meant that any of the units or elements that make up the set has the same probabilities of being included in the sample. This procedure has more chances of validity the more homogeneous is the whole.

Tomeo-Perucha and Uña-Juaréz claim that a random sample is that which is obtained in such a way that from all the pertinent points of view the researcher does not have any reason to

believe that it will have to cause some leaning or tendency (Tomeo-Perucha & Uña-Juaréz, 1989). According to Canavos a way of obtaining a good sample when the sampling process provides every object in the population an equal and independent opportunity of being included in the sample (Canavos, 1988). If the population consists of *N* objects and from these is selected a sample of the size *n*, the sampling process must ensure that each sample of size *n* has the same probability of being selected. This procedure leads to what is called random sample or simple random sample. The term "random" is related to the impartiality in the selection of the sample.

The selection of tangible objects of a population consists in a finite number of objects (such as is the case of DVDs or the components of a interactive system: homepage, nodes, links, etc.). In this regard Canavos indicates two ways of obtaining random samples in this kind of population (Canavos, 1988): First, after carrying out an adequate mixture of the objects of the population, one is extracted and the measurable characteristic is observed. This observation will be X_1. The object is returned to the population and this is mixed again, then the second object is extracted, X_2 is chosen for the second observation.

The process is continued in this way until *n* objects have been extracted to get a sample. This technique has the name of sampling with replacement. Second, after carrying out an adequate mixture of the objects of the population *n*, one is extracted and after others without replacement. the measurable characteristic is observed. This technique has the name of sampling without replacement and is the one used in our heuristic techniques and methods for usability and communicability evaluation.

The random sampling without replacement is used when the size of the population is relatively small (not over 100 objects). This is what makes up a hypergeometrical distribution or discreet of probability (Canavos, 1988).

If the sample is made with replacement, it is very likely that the same object is chosen more than once, if the study population is small. On the other hand, if the number of objects in the population is very big, it is irrelevant whether the sampling is made with replacement or without it. The more the size of the population grows, the random replacement sampling is in every intent and purpose the same as the random sampling with a replacement. When certain characteristics of the set or universe are known, one proceeds to group according to stratus, categories or classes the sampling units which are homogeneous among themselves. For instance, the use or content of the DVDs allows to classify them in biographical, geographical, historical, etc. strata a random choice will later be made (simple random). The result of such procedure is known as stratified sampling.

The interested reader can refer to the bibliography in Murray Spiegel and Larry Stephens for get hundreds of examples, solved problems, and practice exercises in statistics (Spiegel & Stephens, 2007).

EXAMPLES ONLINE

Next follows a series of real examples where statistics is manipulated to have a negative influence on the daily life of the users of the global village as defined by McLuhan. Besides, we present a set of instances about star enunciator and collaborators.

Statistics, Surnames and Professional Future

In the Gens Labo website it can be seen that an activity aimed at commercial ends such as printing on a shirt the map of Italy allegedly containing the genealogical information of surnames. However, the current website can entail negative consequences to millions of users because of the bad use of the information contained in the database which a priori is presented as based on census statistics of the Italian population interrelated with the

Annex 1

Figure 1. Physical map

Figure 2. Provincial map

Figure 3. Bordering map

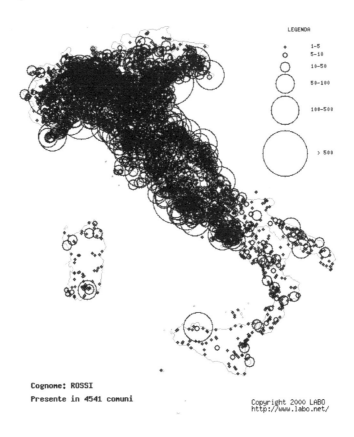

LEGENDA

•	1-5
○	5-10
○	10-50
○	50-100
○	100-500
○	> 500

Cognome: ROSSI
Presente in 4541 comuni

Copyright 2000 LABO
http://www.labo.net/

genealogical trees of the surnames. Everything starts by introducing a surname in the hyperbase and ends with the visualization of the result on a map of Italy.

The system allows one to visualize different kinds of maps: bordering, provincial and physical. In the first and the last some circles of different sizes appear to represent the concentration of the surnames in the scale modality. In the provincial map they resort to the use of colors and range of values. However, if we place the cursor over the provinces appears the title of the autonomous region but not that of the provincial one (see Figure2). That is, the obtainment of the data does not reflect the reality. The territorial division represented by provinces does not serve any longer since the information shown to the user is only regional.

Apparently the circles with the population density which accompany the maps (right area

of Figure3) would ease the progressive reading of those areas where people with the same family name are located. The dots line which splits the table #7 into two indicates that in the upper part are those people who have higher chances of success because of "purity in the family names" issues (that is, who allegedly are few and distributed in regions of the North of Italy) from those in the lower part, regardless of the experience and/or high study levels obtained. The reader who is interested can research in the management posts of the enterprises, industries, regional public institutions, etc. the surnames that appear (a small concentration the surnames between 1 and 350 cities and/or towns –approximately– is a sign of big success in some regions of the North of Italy). Besides, we can observe a second set, that is to say, between 351 and 950 cities and/or towns with big middle level of success. Exceptionally, in this range of

Figure 4. "Purity in the family surnames" –very small circle in regions of the North of Italy

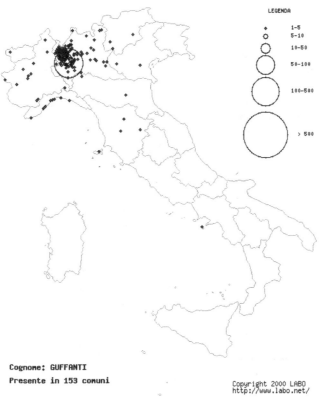

Cognome: GUFFANTI
Presente in 153 comuni

Copyright 2000 LABO
http://www.labo.net/

values, we can find some surnames with a high probably of success.

The surnames of a common use such as Rossi, Bianchi, Conti, Serra or Carusso do not have a high likelihood of success in some environments, through the current system of visualization of surnames, based on the phone directory and not the real census. For instance, we can find Spanish and Portuguese surnames, too. In the alleged hyperbase of Italian surnames we come across some Spanish surnames, without their corresponding accents in the vocals, such as González, García, Rodríguez, etc.

The mistake becomes more apparent as soon as the Spanish surnames are visualized in the USA map. The surname González is widely spread among the peoples of Latin America and not among the Italian community.

In the listing all these surnames focus on the northern regions, excepting the four finals which are distributed among the whole territory. The surnames at the end of the list will not have the same working conditions, that is, labor parity in many institutions, both entrepreneurial and educative, whether they are public or private. This situation does discriminate in educational or employement opportunities or decisions for qualified persons on the basis on the phone directory. A study in the northern regions about the greater labor stability and income per capita of those surnames that occupy the first twelve places of the table (regardless of studies and experience), would show with certainty this statement and with a scarce margin of error.

Star Enunciator and University

The profile of the star enunciators denote a mania towards statistic and gaining visibility on-line. Generally, the star enunciator has web pages and

Figure 5. The González surname is of Spanish origin, and it means «son of Gonzalo"

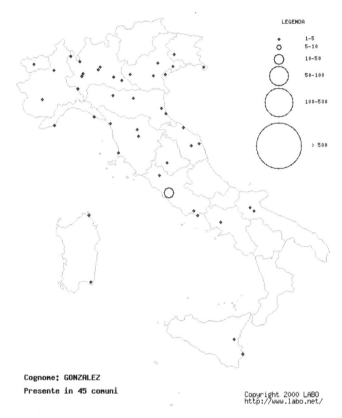

Figure 6. We can see how the surname González is widely spread along all the USA

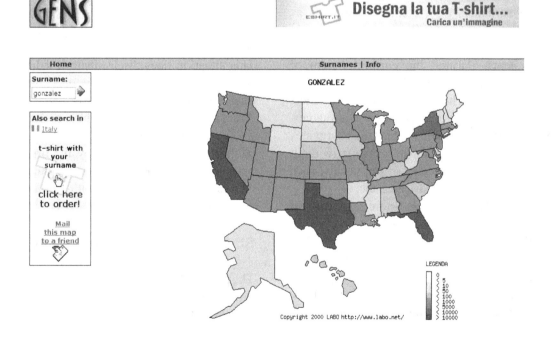

official pages with the site of the university, blog, etc. (the contents are similars) and some social networks: LinkedIn, Facebook, Twitter, Naymz, etc. Their names must appear in the first slots in the main search engines such as Google, Yahoo, MSN, Ask, etc. In the same website of a professor or star enunciator we find the persuasion at the service of the promotion of authoritarianism and the destruction of credibility through the inadequate use of statistics. In the figures 7 and 8, it switches to an alleged daily control from the accesses of students.

The passing of time allows us to see how these new counters engines (Figure9) become something like a personal obsession for some star enunciators or pupils of star enunciators. Besides, thanks to the ease of editing on-line information, sometimes the star enunciator boasts of being a specialist by ridiculing his colleagues (figures 10 and 11). However, through the deeds of his collaborators it is feasible to detect his scarce knowledge of the subjects in which he is allegedly an expert, for instance, usability engineering. Once his on-line smear tactics are detected, he will quickly change the content of the websites that he/she manages but he/she does not respect international usability principles and standards. For instance, different textual content between Italian and English –see figures 12 and 13. Additionally, a way to detect his destructive presence is the constant changes or updates he/she makes in his contents (these examples are dated: August 2009).

Generally, the collaborators of these star enunciators demand help on the issue of the in-

Table 7. Statistics and "purity in the family surnames" in Lombardy, Italy.

Surname	Total cities and/or towns
Dalmagioni	2
Deldossi	7
Selvinelli	10
Cassader	13
Betella	20
Ghilardini	36
Delprato	47
Roggeri	52
Salvaneschi	108
Ghitti	109
Piazzalunga	117
Luoni	125
Guffanti	153
Lancini	172
Mangili	188
Maffeis	263
Cortinovis	267
Tomasoni	342
Castoldi	343
Pesenti	487
Cerutti	688
Gandini	700
Manzoni	828
Beretta	941
Caruso	1776
Serra	1825
Conti	2494
Bianchi	2932
Rossi	4541

Figure 7. Control of the access in a banal exercises area: Word, Write, Excel, etc. – triadic relation between star enunciator/teacher, users/students and Google

UNIVERSITÀ DEGLI STUDI DI BERGAMO

HOME

Univ. di Bergamo > Facoltà di Lettere e Filosofia > Informatica generale

Informatica generale 2004-2005: esercizi di formattazione

ATTENZIONE!!!
Le statistiche del sito indicano che molti visitatori arrivano a questa pagina tramite motore di ricerca; io però ogni anno apro un nuovo sottosito per questo corso e nel nuovo sottosito si possono trovare più materiali che qui, anche se nel ranking dei motori spesso questa pagina compare prima.

VAI AL SITO NUOVO!!!

Figure 8. A referential link to a new page with W3Counter

Fra poco verrete ridiretti alla pagina iniziale del corso di Word ed Excel più recente.
Se però il vostro browser non consente la ridirezione automatica, seguite questo link alla pagina iniziale del corso

W3Counter

Figure 9. Old contents in university website and new counter systems –W3Counter

Figure 10. The contents of the university subjects in audio support show the presence of a star enunciator

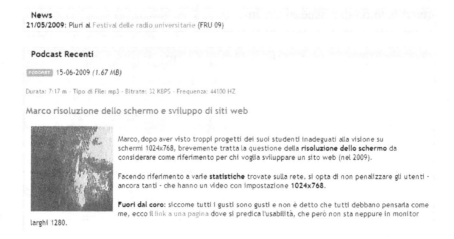

Figure 11. The star enunciator does not respect the freedom of choice of interface resolution in this interface (http://www.agilemodeling.com/essays/agileUsability.htm), forgetting that his knowledge in interfaces are null

Figure 12. The star enunciator does not respect usability standards when the content has two languages, that is to say, we can see a short and long textual information of the same frame –long content in Italian

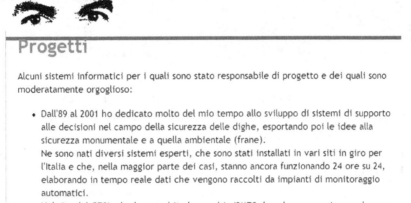

Figure 13. The English version has different order, content and there is a mistake in the title (progetti –is an Italian word)

Figure 14. Credibility arguable in Faz Magazine –www.cadius.org (August 2008)

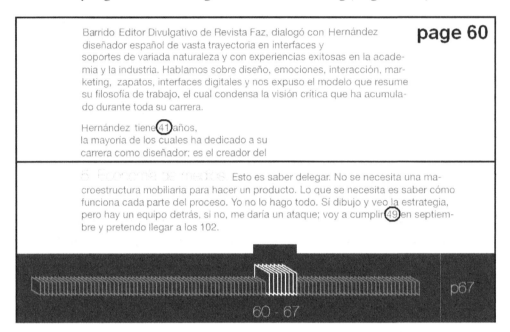

terfaces but leave out the sources or bibliografy references of the received knowledge (i.e., remarks for a final project from Alessandro Venturi about podcasting: http://comesifaunpodcast.wordpress.com/2006/05/10/primo-incontro-podcaster-italiani).

Magazines and Newspapers

The theoretically scientific magazines can be a huge source of credibility destruction, especially in the case that they represent virtual communities allegedly aimed at the issues related to the on-line interactive systems.

A diacronical analysis of the websites of the star enunciator also helps. For instance, in figure 14 we have a digital publication –www.revistafaz.org– in which a lie is said concerning the age of the interview. In page 60 he says. "I am 41 years old" and in the last page #67 "I will turn 49 in September". Oddly enough, in that publication they use an asterisk (the quickest symbol from keyboard to depict a star in informatics) as a separator of the sentences stressed in the text. That is, this is

a multiple stardom example: enunciator, content and presentation. Whenever we come across this triad, the value of the credibility of the means, the interviewer and the interviewee is arguable, not to say equal to zero.

A way of assessing a news item in the current digital newspapers is through the evaluation star rating, its readership, the total of votes and sendings of the news. Besides, a differentiation is qualitatively established among the most seen, the most valued and the total of sendings of the news through an e-mail, that is to say, "E-mail this article to a friend". However, in the statistics graphic of the reading and the sending of the news the timescale of the values in the Y coordinate is not represented (Figure15).

In the following example (Figure16) it can be seen how statistics are used with publicity purposes, but destroying credibility. The destruction is due to the fact that this value of accesses to the homepage of a newspaper obeys to a change of style in the contents (June/July 2009), choosing a line known as tabloid or yellow press such as can be the circulation of multimedia informa-

Figure 15. An excellent idea for the users/readers but they need a complete scale of the values in 'y'coordinate

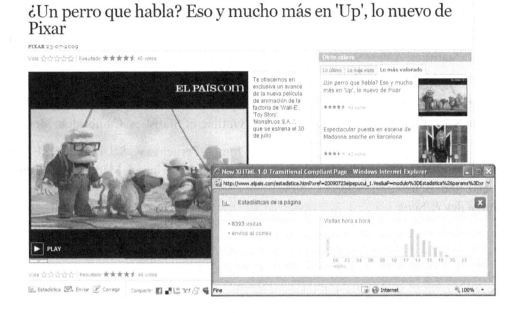

Figure 16. The title of the article should reflect the recent change of orientation of the newspaper editorial

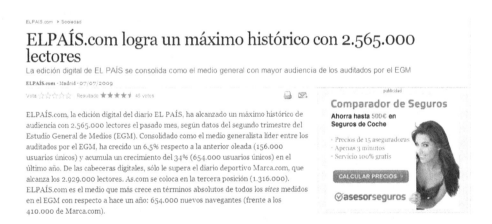

tion (photographies and sound recordings) with worldwide exclusivity.

In the current section it has been seen using two examples how the mixture of scientific academic information and the commercial ends are negative for the credibility of on-line information.

REFERENCES

Berenson, M., Levine, D., & Rindskopf, D. (1998). Applied Statistics. New Jersey: Pretince-Hall.

Bulmer, M. (1979). Principles of Statistics. New York: Dover Publications.

Canavos, G. (1988). Applied Probablity and Statistical Methods. Cambridge: McGraw Hill.

Chatfield, C. (1983). Statistics for Technology. London: Chapman & Hall/CRC.

Hand, D. (2008). Statistics: A Very Short Introduction. Oxford: Oxford University Press.

Johnson, R., & Bhattacharyya, G. (1992). Statistics: Principles and Methods. New York: John Wiley.

Lea, R., & Brooke (2004). Essentials of Statistics for the Social and Behavioral Sciences. New Jersey: John Wiley & Sons.

Moore, D. (1995).The Basic Practice of Statistics. New York: Freeman.

Murat, F. (1971). Estadística. Córdoba: UNC.

Ross, S. (2009). Introduction To Probability and Statistics for Engineers and Scientists. London: Academic Press.

Spiegel, M., & Stephens, L. (2007). Schaum's Outline of Statistics. Cambridge: McGraw Hill.

Tomeo-Perucha, V., & Uña-Juaréz, I. (1989). Estadística descriptiva. Madrid: Alfa Centauro.

Annex 2:
eGovernance Survey on Municipalities Web Sites

Rocío Andrea Rodríguez
National University of La Matanza, Argentina

Daniel Alberto Giulianelli
National University of La Matanza, Argentina

Pablo Martín Vera
National University of La Matanza, Argentina

Artemisa Trigueros
National University of La Matanza, Argentina

Isabel Beatriz Marko
National University of La Matanza, Argentina

INTRODUCTION

This annex shows the 152 aspects considered all along the research with their punctuations. The aspects are organized by categories for their better comprehension.

Each one of the aspects can contribute to one or more design and contents concepts and to the five eGovernance mainstays.

An example is shown in order to understand the aspect's description:

1. **Aspect's description**
2. **Origin:** This item shows the source of aspect. This parameter's value can be: ONTI, W3C, RT (Research Team), PUB (International Publications).
3. **Design and Content:** This item shows the score assigned to the aspect regarding its contribution to each one of the 7 design and content concept. The valid values for the score are integers from 0 to 5. Which are written after each abbreviation: FR (Friendliness), NA (Navigability), US (Usability), AC (Accessibility), IN (Information), VE (Veracity) and FU (Functionality).
4. **Mainstay:** This item shows the score assigned to the aspect regarding its contribution to the fulfillment of each one of the 5 eGovernance mainstays: SER (e-Services), DEM (e-Democracy), ACC (Active Communication), PAC (Passive Communication), TRA (e-Transparency).

Each one of the 152 aspects got a score at least in one of design and contents concepts. Additionally there are 80 aspects from the 152, which got a score in at least one of the 5 eGovernence mainstays. It is important to highlight that an aspect can get score in more than one concept and/or mainstay.

1.1 Category: Technical Aspect

1. When a login form is cancelled it mustn't return "Security error"
   * ORIGIN: RT
   * DESIGN AND CONTENT: FR: 5 - NA: 5 - US: 4 - AC: 0 - IN: 0 - VE: 0 - FU: 0
   * MAINSTAYS: SER: 2 - DEM: 0 - ACC: 0 - PAC: 2 - TRA: 0

2. The web site can be seen in standard resolution (1024x768)
   * ORIGIN: RT
   * DESIGN AND CONTENT: FR: 4 - NA: 5 - US: - AC: 3 - IN: 3- VE: 0 - FU: 0
   * MAINSTAYS: None

3. The web site doesn't have code errors.
   * ORIGIN: W3C
   * DESIGN AND CONTENT: FR: 0 - NA: 0 - US: 0 - AC: 5 - IN: 0 - VE: 0 - FU: 0
   * MAINSTAYS: None

4. The Domain is in clear concordance with local government name.
   * ORIGIN: ONTI
   * DESIGN AND CONTENT: FR: 3 - NA: 0 - US: 5 - AC: 0 - IN: 0 - VE: 0 - FU: 0
   * MAINSTAYS: SER: 1 - DEM: 0- ACC: 1 - PAC: 0 - TRA: 0

5. Web pages do NOT reload automatically
   * ORIGIN: W3C
   * DESIGN AND CONTENT: FR: 4 - NA: 0 - US: 0 - AC: 4 - IN: 0 - VE: 0 - FU: 0
   * MAINSTAYS: None

6. The web pages can be used even when they don't include applets or script support.
   * ORIGIN: W3C
   * DESIGN AND CONTENT: FR: 0 - NA: 0 - US: 0 - AC: 5 - IN: 0 - VE: 0 - FU: 0
   * MAINSTAYS: None

7. The web site does not include images' license errors.
   * ORIGIN: RT
   * DESIGN AND CONTENT: FR: 5 - NA: 5 - US: 0 - AC: 5 - IN: 0 - VE: 0 - FU: 0
   * MAINSTAYS: None

8. The web site does not include not available (broken) images.
   * ORIGIN: RT
   * DESIGN AND CONTENT: FR: 5 - NA: 0 - US: 3 - AC: 0 - IN: 0 - VE: 0 - FU: 0
   * MAINSTAYS: None

9. The web site does not include links to other site's banners.
   * ORIGIN: RT
   * DESIGN AND CONTENT: FR: 3 - NA: 5 - US: 4 - AC: 0 - IN: 0 - VE: 0 - FU: 0
   * MAINSTAYS: None

10. The web site does not include mobile contents that move through the page.
    * ORIGIN: W3C
    * DESIGN AND CONTENT: FR: 3 - NA: 0 - US: 3 - AC: 4 - IN: 0 - VE: 0 - FU: 0
    * MAINSTAYS: None

11. The web site does not include scripts or applets' event controllers depending on the input device.
    * ORIGIN: W3C
    * DESIGN AND CONTENT: FR: 0 - NA: 0 - US: 0 - AC: 4 - IN: 0 - VE: 0 - FU: 0
    * MAINSTAYS: None

12. The web site does not include broken links.
    - ORIGIN: ONTI
    - DESIGN AND CONTENT: FR: 0 - NA: 4 - US: 4 - AC: 4 - IN: 0 - VE: 0 - FU: 0
    - MAINSTAYS: None

13. The web site does not include frames
    - ORIGIN: PUB [2]
    - DESIGN AND CONTENT: FR: 0 - NA: 0 - US: 0 - AC: 5 - IN: 0 - VE: 0 - FU: 0
    - MAINSTAYS: None

14. The web site does not include mark ups to redirection pages automatically.
    - ORIGIN: W3C
    - DESIGN AND CONTENT: FR: 2 - NA: 0 - US: 0 - AC: 4 - IN: 0 - VE: 0 - FU: 0
    - MAINSTAYS: None

15. The web site does not include tables to content organization.
    - ORIGIN: W3C
    - DESIGN AND CONTENT: FR: 0 - NA: 0 - US: 0 - AC: 4 - IN: 0 - VE: 0 - FU: 0
    - MAINSTAYS: None

16. The web site does not include pop ups windows.
    - ORIGIN: W3C
    - DESIGN AND CONTENT: FR: 0 - NA: 0 - US: 0 - AC: 4 - IN: 0 - VE: 0 - FU: 0
    - MAINSTAYS: None

17. If the web site uses ASCII Art, it can be skipped.
    - ORIGIN: W3C
    - DESIGN AND CONTENT: FR: 0 - NA: 0 - US: 0 - AC: 2 - IN: 0 - VE: 0 - FU: 0
    - MAINSTAYS: None

18. The web site includes redundant text links for images maps.
    - ORIGIN: W3C
    - DESIGN AND CONTENT: FR: 0 - NA: 0 - US: 0 - AC: 4 - IN: 0 - VE: 0 - FU: 0
    - MAINSTAYS: None

19. The web site gives security to on line transactions
    - ORIGIN: Research Team
    - DESIGN AND CONTENT: FR: 0 - NA: 0 - US: 0 - AC: 0 - IN: 0 - VE: 5 - FU: 2
    - MAINSTAYS: None

20. The web site offers image maps on the client's side instead of the server's side excepting when the regions cannot be defined by a geometric shape.
    - ORIGIN: W3C
    - DESIGN AND CONTENT: FR: 0 - NA: 0 - US: 0 - AC: 5 - IN: 0 - VE: 0 - FU: 0
    - MAINSTAYS: None

21. The web site uses style sheets.
    - ORIGIN: W3C
    - DESIGN AND CONTENT: FR: 0 - NA: 0 - US: 0 - AC: 4 - IN: 0 - VE: 0 - FU: 0
    - MAINSTAYS: None

22. The web site uses relative units in mark ups and other visual elements.
    - ORIGIN: W3C
    - DESIGN AND CONTENT: FR: 0 - NA: 0 - US: 0 - AC: 4 - IN: 0 - VE: 0 - FU: 0
    - MAINSTAYS: None

1.2 Category: Banner

23. In the banner, the name and municipality's logo is NOT built by Flash or Silverlight
    - ORIGIN: RT
    - DESIGN AND CONTENT: FR: 2 - NA: 0 - US: 0 - AC: 0 - IN: 0 - VE: 0 - FU: 0
    - MAINSTAYS: None

24. The banner refers to municipality name and location
    - ORIGIN: ONTI
    - DESIGN AND CONTENT: FR: 5 - NA: 0 - US: 5 - AC: 0 - IN: 0 - VE: 0 - FU: 0
    - MAINSTAYS: SER: 2 - DEM: 2 - ACC: 0 - PAC: 0 - TRA: 0

25. The banner shows the local government logo
    - ORIGIN: ONTI
    - DESIGN AND CONTENT: FR: 4 - NA: 0 - US: 0 - AC: 0 - IN: 0 - VE: 0 - FU: 0
    - MAINSTAYS: SER: 2 - DEM: 2 - ACC: 0 - PAC: 0 - TRA: 0

26. In the banner, the organization name does not move
    - ORIGIN: RT
    - DESIGN AND CONTENT: FR: 3 - NA: 0 - US: 0 - AC: 0 - IN: 0 - VE: 0 - FU: 0
    - MAINSTAYS: None

1.3 Category: Browsers

27. The browsers´ results, when searching for the municipality web site, include the municipality name and they mention "official web site".
    - ORIGIN: RT
    - DESIGN AND CONTENT: FR: 4 - NA: 0 - US: 4 - AC: 0 - IN: 0 - VE: 5 - FU: 0
    - MAINSTAYS: SER: 2 - DEM: 0 - ACC: 2 - PAC: 0 - TRA: 0

28. It is enrolled in the main web browsers (ALTA VISTA, GOOGLE, LIVE, YA-HOO).
    - ORIGIN: ONTI
    - DESIGN AND CONTENT: FR: 0 - NA: 0 - US: 0 - AC: 4 - IN: 0 - VE: 0 - FU: 0
    - MAINSTAYS: SER: 3 - DEM: 0 - ACC: 3 - PAC: 0 - TRA: 0

29. The web site includes metadata to add semantic information to web pages and sites.
    - ORIGIN: W3C
    - DESIGN AND CONTENT: FR: 0 - NA: 0 - US: 0 - AC: 4 - IN: 0 - VE: 0 - FU: 0
    - MAINSTAYS: SER: 2 - DEM: 0 - ACC: 2 - PAC: 0 - TRA: 0

1.4 Category: General Characteristics

30. The web site offers keyboard shortcuts.
    - ORIGIN: W3C
    - DESIGN AND CONTENT: FR: 3 - NA: 3 - US: 4 - AC: 3 - IN: 0 - VE: 0 - FU: 0
    - MAINSTAYS: None

31. The web site does not include transition music or sounds.
    - ORIGIN: RT
    - DESIGN AND CONTENT: FR: 4 - NA: 0 - US: 0 - AC: 5 - IN: 0 - VE: 0 - FU: 0
    - MAINSTAYS: None

32. The presentation page could be skipped before the site is loaded.
    - ORIGIN: RT
    - DESIGN AND CONTENT: FR: 5 - NA: 0 - US: 0 - AC: 5 - IN: 0 - VE: 0 - FU: 0
    - MAINSTAYS: None

33. The web site shows the path from the home page to any other page inside the site. (breadcrumbs)
    - ORIGIN: ONTI
    - DESIGN AND CONTENT: FR: 5 - NA: 5 - US: 5 - AC: 0 - IN: 0 - VE: 0 - FU: 0
    - MAINSTAYS: None

34. The web site allows using the mouse's right button.
    - ORIGIN: RT
    - DESIGN AND CONTENT: FR: 0 - NA: 3 - US: 3 - AC: 3 - IN: 0 - VE: 0 - FU: 0
    - MAINSTAYS: None

35. The web site allows returning to home page from any page inside the web site.
    - ORIGIN: ONTI
    - DESIGN AND CONTENT: FR: 5 - NA: 5 - US: 5 - AC: 0 - IN: 0 - VE: 0 - FU: 0
    - MAINSTAYS: None

36. The web site allows using the navigator's RETURN button.
    - ORIGIN: ONTI
    - DESIGN AND CONTENT: FR: 5 - NA: 5 - US: 5 - AC: 0 - IN: 0 - VE: 0 - FU: 0
    - MAINSTAYS: None

37. The web site has its logo in the address bar.
    - ORIGIN: RT
    - DESIGN AND CONTENT: FR: 1 - NA: 0 - US: 2 - AC: 0 - IN: 0 - VE: 0 - FU: 0
    - MAINSTAYS: None

38. All the web site functionalities are available into the site.
    - ORIGIN: PUB [2]
    - DESIGN AND CONTENT: FR: 3 - NA: 4 - US: 0 - AC: 3 - IN: 0 - VE: 0 - FU: 0
    - MAINSTAYS: None

1.5 Category: Main Menu's Categories

39. The main menu includes interaction areas option.
    - ORIGIN: ONTI
    - DESIGN AND CONTENT: FR: 1 - NA: 1 - US: 1 - AC: 0 - IN: 0 - VE: 0 - FU: 0
    - MAINSTAYS: SER: 0 - DEM: 5 - ACC: 0 - PAC: 5 - TRA: 0

40. The main menu includes contact option.
    - ORIGIN: ONTI
    - DESIGN AND CONTENT: FR: 5 - NA: 5 - US: 5 - AC: 0 - IN: 0 - VE: 0 - FU: 0
    - MAINSTAYS: SER: 0 - DEM: 5 - ACC: 0 - PAC: 5 - TRA: 0

41. The main menu includes government option.
    - ORIGIN: ONTI
    - DESIGN AND CONTENT: FR: 3 - NA: 3 - US: 3 - AC: 0 - IN: 0 - VE: 0 - FU: 0
    - MAINSTAYS: SER: 0 - DEM: 5 - ACC: 5 - PAC: 0 - TRA: 0

42. The main menu includes services option.
    - ORIGIN: ONTI
    - DESIGN AND CONTENT: FR: 5 - NA: 5 - US: 5 - AC: 0 - IN: 0 - VE: 0 - FU: 0
    - MAINSTAYS: SER: 5 - DEM: 0 - ACC: 5 - PAC: 0 - TRA: 0

1.6 Category: Colors/ Design

43. It provides good background and text contrast to improve reading.
    - ORIGIN: W3C
    - DESIGN AND CONTENT: FR: 4 - NA: 0 - US: 0 - AC: 4 - IN: 0 - VE: 0 - FU: 0
    - MAINSTAYS: SER: 2 - DEM: 0 - ACC: 2 - PAC: 0 - TRA: 2

44. The content area of the page does not have vertical scroll bar, to move through the text.
    - ORIGIN: RT
    - DESIGN AND CONTENT: FR: 5 - NA: 5 - US: 0 - AC: 0 - IN: 0 - VE: 0 - FU: 0
    - MAINSTAYS: None

45. The content area of the page does not have horizontal scroll bar to move through the text.
    - ORIGIN: RT
    - DESIGN AND CONTENT: FR: 5 - NA: 0 - US: 0 - AC: 0 - IN: 0 - VE: 0 - FU: 0
    - MAINSTAYS: None

46. The secondary pages' design coincides with main page's design.
    - ORIGIN: W3C
    - DESIGN AND CONTENT: FR: 5 - NA: 5 - US: 5 - AC: 5 - IN: 0 - VE: 0 - FU: 0
    - MAINSTAYS: None

47. The web shows explanations not only by colors
    - ORIGIN: W3C
    - DESIGN AND CONTENT: FR: 0 - NA: 0 - US: 0 - AC: 5 - IN: 0 - VE: 0 - FU: 0
    - MAINSTAYS: SER: 2 - DEM: 0 - ACC: 2 - PAC: 0 - TRA: 2

48. The only way to access an option into the web site must not be by a banner built with Flash or Silverlight
    - ORIGIN: RT
    - DESIGN AND CONTENT: FR: 3 - NA: 5 - US: 0 - AC: 5 - IN: 0 - VE: 0 - FU: 0
    - MAINSTAYS: None

49. The inner page of the web site must open in the same window used by the main page.
    - ORIGIN: RT
    - DESIGN AND CONTENT: FR: 3 - NA: 5 - US: 3 - AC: 0 - IN: 0 - VE: 0 - FU: 0
    - MAINSTAYS: None

50. The web site uses the same typefont in all its pages.
    - ORIGIN: ONTI
    - DESIGN AND CONTENT: FR: 4 - NA: 0 - US: 0 - AC: 3 - IN: 0 - VE: 0 - FU: 0
    - MAINSTAYS: None

51. The web site does not use green over red or brown contrast (most frequently daltonism type)
    - ORIGIN: PUB [11]
    - DESIGN AND CONTENT: FR: 0 - NA: 0 - US: 0 - AC: 5 - IN: 0 - VE: 0 - FU: 0
    - MAINSTAYS: SER: 1 - DEM: 0 - ACC: 1 - PAC: 0 - TRA: 1

52. The web site must not offer empty pages without the sign "UNDER CONSTRUC-TION"
    - ORIGIN: Research Team
    - DESIGN AND CONTENT: FR: 4 - NA: 3 - US: 2 - AC: 0 - IN: 0 - VE: 0 - FU: 0
    - MAINSTAYS: None

53. The web site must not use blinking text or colors.
    - ORIGIN: W3C
    - DESIGN AND CONTENT: FR: 2 - NA: 0 - US: 0 - AC: 5 - IN: 0 - VE: 0 - FU: 0
    - MAINSTAYS: None

54. The main page must not be too long.
    - ORIGIN: RT
    - DESIGN AND CONTENT: FR: 3 - NA: 4 - US: 2 - AC: 0 - IN: 0 - VE: 0 - FU: 0
    - MAINSTAYS: None

55. All the pages are centered.
    - ORIGIN: RT
    - DESIGN AND CONTENT: FR: 1 - NA: 0 - US: 0 - AC: 0 - IN: 0 - VE: 0 - FU: 0
    - MAINSTAYS: None

1.7 Category: Multimedia Contents

56. The web site offers content's readers for deaf users.
    - ORIGIN: RT
    - DESIGN AND CONTENT: FR: 2 - NA: 0 - US: 0 - AC: 5 - IN: 0 - VE: 0 - FU: 0
    - MAINSTAYS: SER: 3 - DEM: 0 - ACC: 3 - PAC: 0 - TRA: 2

57. The text that reproduce the dynamic content is updated when the content changes.
    - ORIGIN: W3C
    - DESIGN AND CONTENT: FR: 3 - NA: 0 - US: 0 - AC: 5 - IN: 0 - VE: 0 - FU: 0
    - MAINSTAYS: None

58. The web site offers text according the information showed in the multimedia (videos, recordings)
    - ORIGIN: W3C
    - DESIGN AND CONTENT: FR: 0 - NA: 0 - US: 0 - AC: 4 - IN: 0 - VE: 0 - FU: 0
    - MAINSTAYS: SER: 3 - DEM: 0 - ACC: 3 - PAC: 0 - TRA: 1

1.8 Category: Legal Stuff

59. The web site shows the last updating date
    - ORIGIN: ONTI
    - DESIGN AND CONTENT: FR: 0 - NA: 0 - US: 0 - AC: 0 - IN: 0 - VE: 3 - FU: 0
    - MAINSTAYS: SER: 1 - DEM: 0 - ACC: 1 - PAC: 0 - TRA: 0

60. The web site does not include private advertisements.
    - ORIGIN: PUB [2]
    - DESIGN AND CONTENT: FR: 0 - NA: 0 - US: 0 - AC: 0 - IN: 0 - VE: 5 - FU: 0
    - MAINSTAYS: SER: 0 - DEM: 0 - ACC: 3 - PAC: 3 - TRA: 0

61. The web site does not does not disclaim its own information.
    - ORIGIN: ONTI
    - DESIGN AND CONTENT: FR: 0 - NA: 0 - US: 0 - AC: 0 - IN: 0 - VE: 5 - FU: 0
    - MAINSTAYS: SER: 0 - DEM: 5 - ACC: 5 - PAC: 0 - TRA: 3

1.9 Category: Downloads

62. The purpose of the file to be downloaded is mentioned.
    - ORIGIN: ONTI
    - DESIGN AND CONTENT: FR: 5 - NA: 0 - US: 5 - AC: 0 - IN: 0 - VE: 0 - FU: 0
    - MAINSTAYS: None

63. The web site offers alternative file formats.
    - ORIGIN: ONTI
    - DESIGN AND CONTENT: FR: 0 - NA: 0 - US: 0 - AC: 3 - IN: 0 - VE: 0 - FU: 0
    - MAINSTAYS: None

64. The weight of the file to be downloaded is shown.
    - ORIGIN: ONTI
    - DESIGN AND CONTENT: FR: 0 - NA: 0 - US: 5 - AC: 5 - IN: 0 - VE: 0 - FU: 0
    - MAINSTAYS: None

1.10 Category: Published Documents

65. The web site shows the news´ author
    - ORIGIN: ONTI
    - DESIGN AND CONTENT: FR: 0 - NA: 0 - US: 0 - AC: 0 - IN: 1 - VE: 3 - FU: 0
    - MAINSTAYS: SER: 0 - DEM: 3 - ACC: 3 - PAC: 0 - TRA: 3

66. The web site provides news' author contact.
    - ORIGIN: ONTI
    - DESIGN AND CONTENT: FR: 0 - NA: 0 - US: 0 - AC: 0 - IN: 0 - VE: 0 - FU: 3
    - MAINSTAYS: SER: 0 - DEM: 3 - ACC: 0 - PAC: 3 - TRA: 3

67. The web site shows news date.
    - ORIGIN: ONTI
    - DESIGN AND CONTENT: FR: 0 - NA: 0 - US: 2 - AC: 0 - IN: 2 - VE: 4 - FU: 0
    - MAINSTAYS: SER: 3 - DEM: 0 - ACC: 3 - PAC: 0 - TRA: 0

68. The web site doesn't disclaim its own publications.
    - ORIGIN: ONTI
    - DESIGN AND CONTENT: FR: 0 - NA: 0 - US: 0 - AC: 0 - IN: 0 - VE: 4 - FU: 0
    - MAINSTAYS: SER: 0 - DEM: 5 - ACC: 5 - PAC: 0 - TRA: 5

1.11 Category: Forms

69. The forms clearly differentiate the mandatory form's fields.
    - ORIGIN: PUB [11]
    - DESIGN AND CONTENT: FR: 5 - NA: 0 - US: 5 - AC: 0 - IN: 0 - VE: 0 - FU: 0
    - MAINSTAYS: SER: 3 - DEM: 0 - ACC: 3 - PAC: 0 - TRA: 0

70. It offers forms to e-mail web site contents.
    - ORIGIN: ONTI
    - DESIGN AND CONTENT: FR: 0 - NA: 0 - US: 0 - AC: 0 - IN: 0 - VE: 0 - FU: 2
    - MAINSTAYS: SER: 0 - DEM: 3 - ACC: 0 - PAC: 3 - TRA: 0

71. The printable forms are in A4 .pdf format.
    - ORIGIN: ONTI
    - DESIGN AND CONTENT: FR: 0 - NA: 0 - US: 0 - AC: 4 - IN: 0 - VE: 0 - FU: 4
    - MAINSTAYS: SER: 5 - DEM: 0 - ACC: 5 - PAC: 0 - TRA: 0

72. The form's data are validated in the client with clear messages.
    - ORIGIN: RT
    - DESIGN AND CONTENT: FR: 5 - NA: 0 - US: 3 - AC: 3 - IN: 0 - VE: 0 - FU: 0
    - MAINSTAYS: SER: 3 - DEM: 0 - ACC: 0 - PAC: 3 - TRA: 0

73. The forms allow the tabulator use and follow a logic order.
    - ORIGIN: W3C
    - DESIGN AND CONTENT: FR: 5 - NA: 5 - US: 4 - AC: 3 - IN: 0 - VE: 0 - FU: 0
    - MAINSTAYS: SER: 3 - DEM: 0 - ACC: 3 - PAC: 0 - TRA: 0

74. It offers forms to fulfill on line transactions.
    - ORIGIN: ONTI
    - DESIGN AND CONTENT: FR: 0 - NA: 0 - US: 0 - AC: 0 - IN: 0 - VE: 0 - FU: 4
    - MAINSTAYS: SER: 5 - DEM: 0 - ACC: 0 - PAC: 5 - TRA: 0

75. The form's input data are validated to check them.
    - ORIGIN: RT
    - DESIGN AND CONTENT: FR: 0 - NA: 0 - US: 0 - AC: 0 - IN: 0 - VE: 3 - FU: 0
    - MAINSTAYS: SER: 3 - DEM: 0 - ACC: 0 - PAC: 3 - TRA: 0

76. It provides close questions in the forms as frequently as possible.
    - ORIGIN: PUB [11]
    - DESIGN AND CONTENT: FR: 4 - NA: 0 - US: 4 - AC: 0 - IN: 0 - VE: 0 - FU: 0
    - MAINSTAYS: SER: 3 - DEM: 0 - ACC: 3 - PAC: 0 - TRA: 0

77. The forms include elements directly related with the expected options number.
    - ORIGIN: PUB [11]
    - DESIGN AND CONTENT: FR: 4 - NA: 0 - US: 4 - AC: 0 - IN: 0 - VE: 0 - FU: 0
    - MAINSTAYS: SER: 3 - DEM: 0 - ACC: 3 - PAC: 0 - TRA: 0

1.12 Category: Administrative Transactions

78. It allows transaction's condition consulting.
    - ORIGIN: ONTI
    - DESIGN AND CONTENT: FR: 0 - NA: 0 - US: 0 - AC: 0 - IN: 0 - VE: 0 - FU: 5
    - MAINSTAYS: SER: 5 - DEM: 0 - ACC: 0 - PAC: 5 - TRA: 0

79. It offers transaction's information.
    - ORIGIN: ONTI
    - DESIGN AND CONTENT: FR: 0 - NA: 0 - US: 0 - AC: 0 - IN: 5 - VE: 0 - FU: 0
    - MAINSTAYS: SER: 5 - DEM: 0 - ACC: 5 - PAC: 0 - TRA: 0

80. It provides ways to request appointments.
    - ORIGIN: RT
    - DESIGN AND CONTENT: FR: 0 - NA: 0 - US: 0 - AC: 0 - IN: 0 - VE: 0 - FU: 5
    - MAINSTAYS: SER: 5 - DEM: 0 - ACC: 5 - PAC: 0 - TRA: 0

81. It informs about jobs policy and vacancies.
    - ORIGIN: ONTI
    - DESIGN AND CONTENT: FR: 0 - NA: 0 - US: 0 - AC: 0 - IN: 3 - VE: 2 - FU: 3
    - MAINSTAYS: SER: 0 - DEM: 5 - ACC: 5 - PAC: 0 - TRA: 5

1.13 Category: Icons

82. It has an icon to enlarge type fonts
    - 2ORIGIN: ONTI
    - DESIGN AND CONTENT: FR: 3 - NA: 0 - US: 0 - AC: 3 - IN: 0 - VE: 0 - FU: 0
    - MAINSTAYS: SER: 3 - DEM: 0 - ACC: 3 - PAC: 0 - TRA: 2

83. It has an icon to send mail
    - ORIGIN: ONTI
    - DESIGN AND CONTENT: FR: 3 - NA: 0 - US: 0 - AC: 0 - IN: 0 - VE: 0 - FU: 0
    - MAINSTAYS: SER: 3 - DEM: 3 - ACC: 3 - PAC: 3 - TRA: 0

84. It has an icon to print
    - ORIGIN: ONTI
    - DESIGN AND CONTENT: FR: 3 - NA: 0 - US: 0 - AC: 0 - IN: 0 - VE: 0 - FU: 0
    - MAINSTAYS: SER: 3 - DEM: 0 - ACC: 3 - PAC: 0 - TRA: 0

85. It has an icon to see more information
    - ORIGIN: ONTI
    - DESIGN AND CONTENT: FR: 3 - NA: 0 - US: 0 - AC: 0 - IN: 0 - VE: 0 - FU: 0
    - MAINSTAYS: SER: 3 - DEM: 0 - ACC: 3 - PAC: 0 - TRA: 0

1.14 Category: Images and Size

86. When the user moves the mouse over an image or an icon a context text appears
    - ORIGIN: W3C
    - DESIGN AND CONTENT: FR: 4 - NA: 0 - US: 4 - AC: 5 - IN: 0 - VE: 0 - FU: 0
    - MAINSTAYS: None

87. The web site has light images in gif or jpg format.
    - ORIGIN: ONTI
    - DESIGN AND CONTENT: FR: 0 - NA: 3 - US: 0 - AC: 5 - IN: 0 - VE: 0 - FU: 0
    - MAINSTAYS: None

88. The page's weigh is up to 250 KB
    - ORIGIN: ONTI
    - DESIGN AND CONTENT: FR: 0 - NA: 3 - US: 0 - AC: 5 - IN: 0 - VE: 0 - FU: 0
    - MAINSTAYS: None

89. The web site has image's resolution up to 72 dpi
    - ORIGIN: ONTI
    - DESIGN AND CONTENT: FR: 0 - NA: 0 - US: 0 - AC: 4 - IN: 0 - VE: 0 - FU: 0
    - MAINSTAYS: None

1.15 Category: Site's Information

90. It has an icon to enlarge typefonts
    - ORIGIN: ONTI
    - DESIGN AND CONTENT: FR: 0 - NA: 0 - US: 0 - AC: 0 - IN: 2 - VE: 0 - FU: 0
    - MAINSTAYS: SER: 0 - DEM: 3 - ACC: 3 - PAC: 0 - TRA: 3

91. It has an icon to Send Mail.
    - ORIGIN: ONTI
    - DESIGN AND CONTENT: FR: 0 - NA: 0 - US: 0 - AC: 0 - IN: 3 - VE: 0 - FU: 0
    - MAINSTAYS: SER: 0 - DEM: 5 - ACC: 5 - PAC: 0 - TRA: 5

92. It has an icon to print.
    - ORIGIN: ONTI
    - DESIGN AND CONTENT: FR: 0 - NA: 0 - US: 0 - AC: 0 - IN: 5 - VE: 0 - FU: 0
    - MAINSTAYS: SER: 5 - DEM: 0 - ACC: 5 - PAC: 0 - TRA: 0

93. It has an icon to see more information.
    - ORIGIN: ONTI
    - DESIGN AND CONTENT: FR: 0 - NA: 0 - US: 0 - AC: 0 - IN: 3 - VE: 2 - FU: 0
    - MAINSTAYS: SER: 1 - DEM: 0 - ACC: 0 - PAC: 0 - TRA: 0

94. It provides electronic address of government areas.
    - ORIGIN: ONTI
    - DESIGN AND CONTENT: FR: 0 - NA: 0 - US: 0 - AC: 0 - IN: 4 - VE: 2 - FU: 0
    - MAINSTAYS: SER: 0 - DEM: 5 - ACC: 0 - PAC: 5 - TRA: 3

95. It provides information on annual budget.
    - ORIGIN: ONTI
    - DESIGN AND CONTENT: FR: 0 - NA: 0 - US: 0 - AC: 0 - IN: 2 - VE: 0 - FU: 0
    - MAINSTAYS: SER: 0 - DEM: 5 - ACC: 5 - PAC: 0 - TRA: 5

96. It informs municipality's hours of opening.
    - ORIGIN: ONTI
    - DESIGN AND CONTENT: FR: 0 - NA: 0 - US: 0 - AC: 0 - IN: 5 - VE: 0 - FU: 0
    - MAINSTAYS: SER: 5 - DEM: 0 - ACC: 5 - PAC: 0 - TRA: 0

97. It informs on transportation to arrive to the town hall.
    - ORIGIN: PUB [6]
    - DESIGN AND CONTENT: FR: 0 - NA: 0 - US: 0 - AC: 0 - IN: 4 - VE: 0 - FU: 0
    - MAINSTAYS: SER: 3 - DEM: 0 - ACC: 3 - PAC: 0 - TRA: 0

98. It provides information on government areas.
    - ORIGIN: ONTI
    - DESIGN AND CONTENT: FR: 0 - NA: 0 - US: 0 - AC: 0 - IN: 3 - VE: 2 - FU: 0
    - MAINSTAYS: SER: 0 - DEM: 3 - ACC: 3 - PAC: 0 - TRA: 5

99. It provides map with the town hall location.
    - ORIGIN: ONTI
    - DESIGN AND CONTENT: FR: 0 - NA: 0 - US: 0 - AC: 0 - IN: 3 - VE: 0 - FU: 0
    - MAINSTAYS: SER: 2 - DEM: 0 - ACC: 2 - PAC: 0 - TRA: 0

100. It provides information on local government aims and objectives.
    - ORIGIN: ONTI
    - DESIGN AND CONTENT: FR: 0 - NA: 0 - US: 0 - AC: 0 - IN: 2 - VE: 0 - FU: 0
    - MAINSTAYS: SER: 0 - DEM: 2 - ACC: 2 - PAC: 0 - TRA: 2

101. It provides updated news.
    - ORIGIN: ONTI
    - DESIGN AND CONTENT: FR: 0 - NA: 0 - US: 0 - AC: 0 - IN: 4 - VE: 4 - FU: 0
    - MAINSTAYS: SER: 3 - DEM: 0 - ACC: 3 - PAC: 0 - TRA: 5

102. It informs on Projects and Programs.
    - ORIGIN: ONTI
    - DESIGN AND CONTENT: FR: 0 - NA: 0 - US: 0 - AC: 0 - IN: 3 - VE: 0 - FU: 0
    - MAINSTAYS: SER: 0 - DEM: 5 - ACC: 5 - PAC: 0 - TRA: 5

103. It shows the local government's regulations.
     - ORIGIN: ONTI
     - DESIGN AND CONTENT: FR: 0 - NA: 0 - US: 0 - AC: 0 - IN: 2 - VE: 0 - FU: 0
     - MAINSTAYS: SER: 0 - DEM: 5 - ACC: 5 - PAC: 0 - TRA: 5

104. It includes authorities' curriculum vitae.
     - ORIGIN: ONTI
     - DESIGN AND CONTENT: FR: 0 - NA: 0 - US: 0 - AC: 0 - IN: 3 - VE: 3 - FU: 0
     - MAINSTAYS: SER: 0 - DEM: 3 - ACC: 3 - PAC: 0 - TRA: 5

105. It informs the town hall telephone numbers.
     - ORIGIN: ONTI
     - DESIGN AND CONTENT: FR: 0 - NA: 0 - US: 0 - AC: 0 - IN: 5 - VE: 0 - FU: 0
     - MAINSTAYS: SER: 5 - DEM: 0 - ACC: 5 - PAC: 0 - TRA: 0

1.16 Category: Links

106. When placing the mouse pointer over a link, it changes its color.
     - ORIGIN: RT
     - DESIGN AND CONTENT: FR: 5 - NA: 3 - US: 0 - AC: 0 - IN: 0 - VE: 0 - FU: 0
     - MAINSTAYS: None

107. The visited link's color is different from not visited links.
     - ORIGIN: RT
     - DESIGN AND CONTENT: FR: 3 - NA: 4 - US: 3 - AC: 0 - IN: 0 - VE: 0 - FU: 0
     - MAINSTAYS: None

108. The link's text isolated from its context, identifies the link.
     - ORIGIN: ONTI
     - DESIGN AND CONTENT: FR: 3 - NA: 2 - US: 0 - AC: 4 - IN: 0 - VE: 0 - FU: 0
     - MAINSTAYS: None

109. Between two adjacent links, printable characters separated by spaces are always included.
     - ORIGIN: W3C
     - DESIGN AND CONTENT: FR: 0 - NA: 0 - US: 0 - AC: 3 - IN: 0 - VE: 0 - FU: 0
     - MAINSTAYS: None

110. All the links are underlined.
     - ORIGIN: Research Team
     - DESIGN AND CONTENT: FR: 3 - NA: 4 - US: 3 - AC: 0 - IN: 0 - VE: 0 - FU: 0
     - MAINSTAYS: None

111. Links to other web sites open in other window.
     - ORIGIN: ONTI
     - DESIGN AND CONTENT: FR: 4 - NA: 4 - US: 3 - AC: 0 - IN: 0 - VE: 0 - FU: 0
     - MAINSTAYS: None

112. The web site must not include downloads from others web sites.
     - ORIGIN: ONTI
     - DESIGN AND CONTENT: FR: 0 - NA: 3 - US: 0 - AC: 4 - IN: 0 - VE: 5 - FU: 0
     - MAINSTAYS: None

113. The Little hand appears over the link when pointing it with the mouse.
     - ORIGIN: RT
     - DESIGN AND CONTENT: FR: 5 - NA: 4 - US: 4 - AC: 0 - IN: 0 - VE: 0 - FU: 0
     - MAINSTAYS: None

114. If the web site includes link's lists, they must be organized by categories.
     - ORIGIN: RT
     - DESIGN AND CONTENT: FR: 3 - NA: 0 - US: 0 - AC: 3 - IN: 0 - VE: 0 - FU: 0
     - MAINSTAYS: None

115. The web site links the site with sites from national and international organizations.
     - ORIGIN: ONTI
     - DESIGN AND CONTENT: FR: 0 - NA: 3 - US: 0 - AC: 0 - IN: 0 - VE: 0 - FU: 3
     - MAINSTAYS: SER: 3 - DEM: 0 - ACC: 3 - PAC: 0 - TRA: 0

1.17 Category: Lists

116. Nested lists are labeled by level.
     - ORIGIN: ONTI
     - DESIGN AND CONTENT: FR: 3 - NA: 0 - US: 3 - AC: 3 - IN: 0 - VE: 0 - FU: 0
     - MAINSTAYS: None

117. The web site uses numeric or alphabetic labels for the lists.
     - ORIGIN: ONTI
     - DESIGN AND CONTENT: FR: 3 - NA: 0 - US: 3 - AC: 3 - IN: 0 - VE: 0 - FU: 0
     - MAINSTAYS: None

1.18 Category: Main Menu

118. The main menu does not include more than 12 options in the same category.
     - ORIGIN: RT
     - DESIGN AND CONTENT: FR: 4 - NA: 4 - US: 4 - AC: 0 - IN: 0 - VE: 0 - FU: 0
     - MAINSTAYS: None

119. The main menu remains in all the page of the web site.
     - ORIGIN: ONTI
     - DESIGN AND CONTENT: FR: 5 - NA: 5 - US: 5 - AC: 0 - IN: 0 - VE: 0 - FU: 0
     - MAINSTAYS: None

120. If the main menu is built in Flash or Silverlight, all its options appear at the end of the page
     - ORIGIN: ONTI
     - DESIGN AND CONTENT: FR: 0 - NA: 0 - US: 0 - AC: 5 - IN: 0 - VE: 0 - FU: 0
     - MAINSTAYS: None

1.19 Category: Menus in General

121. The menus must not include images without their text.
     - ORIGIN: ONTI
     - DESIGN AND CONTENT: FR: 5 - NA: 0 - US: 3 - AC: 0 - IN: 0 - VE: 0 - FU: 0
     - MAINSTAYS: None

122. When placing over a menu's option, the rest of the options must not move.
     - ORIGIN: Research Team
     - DESIGN AND CONTENT: FR: 5 - NA: 5 - US: 4- AC: 0 - IN: 0 - VE: 0 - FU: 0
     - MAINSTAYS: None

123. When placing over a menu's option, it highlights.
     - ORIGIN: RT
     - DESIGN AND CONTENT: FR: 3 - NA: 3 - US: 3 - AC: 0 - IN: 0 - VE: 0 - FU: 0
     - MAINSTAYS: None

124. The menu's options are representatives.
     - ORIGIN: RT
     - DESIGN AND CONTENT: FR: 5 - NA: 5 - US: 4 - AC: 0 - IN: 0 - VE: 0 - FU: 0
     - MAINSTAYS: None

125. The browser title bar shows actual page-municipality name.
     - ORIGIN: RT
     - DESIGN AND CONTENT: FR: 3 - NA: 3 - US: 3 - AC: 0 - IN: 0 - VE: 0 - FU: 0
     - MAINSTAYS: SER: 1 - DEM: 0 - ACC: 1 - PAC: 0 - TRA: 0

1.20 Category: Navigators

126. The web site is optimized for a specific navigator (Explorer version..., Mozilla Firefox version...)
     - ORIGIN: ONTI
     - DESIGN AND CONTENT: FR: 0 - NA: 0 - US: 0 - AC: 5 - IN: 0 - VE: 0 - FU: 0
     - MAINSTAYS: None

1.21 Category: Resources

127. The search box includes a button to begin searching.
     - ORIGIN: RT
     - DESIGN AND CONTENT: FR: 5 - NA: 5 - US: 3 - AC: 0 - IN: 0 - VE: 0 - FU: 0
     - MAINSTAYS: SER: 2 - DEM: 0 - ACC: 2 - PAC: 0 - TRA: 0

128. It provides Help Area
     - ORIGIN: ONTI
     - DESIGN AND CONTENT: FR: 4 - NA: 0 - US: 0 - AC: 4 - IN: 0 - VE: 0 - FU: 0
     - MAINSTAYS: SER: 0 - DEM: 3 - ACC: 0 - PAC: 3 - TRA: 0

129. The web site includes search.
     - ORIGIN: W3C
     - DESIGN AND CONTENT: FR: 5 - NA: 5 - US: 5 - AC: 5 - IN: 0 - VE: 0 - FU: 3
     - MAINSTAYS: SER: 5 - DEM: 0 - ACC: 0 - PAC: 5 - TRA: 0

130. It provides site's use polls
     - ORIGIN: RT
     - DESIGN AND CONTENT: FR: 3 - NA: 0 - US: 3 - AC: 0 - IN: 0 - VE: 0 - FU: 2
     - MAINSTAYS: SER: 0 - DEM: 3 - ACC: 0 - PAC: 3 - TRA: 3

131. It provides local government's actions and decisions polls.
     - ORIGIN: RT
     - DESIGN AND CONTENT: FR: 3 - NA: 0 - US: 3 - AC: 0 - IN: 0 - VE: 0 - FU: 3
     - MAINSTAYS: SER: 0 - DEM: 5 - ACC: 0 - PAC: 5 - TRA: 5

132. It provides Contact Us Form or E-mail Form.
     - ORIGIN: ONTI
     - DESIGN AND CONTENT: FR: 0 - NA: 0 - US: 0 - AC: 0 - IN: 5 - VE: 2 - FU: 5
     - MAINSTAYS: SER: 0 - DEM: 5 - ACC: 0 - PAC: 5 - TRA: 0

133. The web site includes site map.
     - ORIGIN: W3C
     - DESIGN AND CONTENT: FR: 5 - NA: 5 - US: 0 - AC: 4 - IN: 0 - VE: 0 - FU: 3
     - MAINSTAYS: SER: 3 - DEM: 0 - ACC: 3 - PAC: 0 - TRA: 0

134. It provides e-Newsletter
     - ORIGIN: ONTI
     - DESIGN AND CONTENT: FR: 0 - NA: 0 - US: 0 - AC: 0 - IN: 0 - VE: 0 - FU: 4
     - MAINSTAYS: SER: 0 - DEM: 3 - ACC: 3 - PAC: 0 - TRA: 3

135. It includes Suggestions and Complaints section.
     - ORIGIN: ONTI
     - DESIGN AND CONTENT: FR: 0 - NA: 0 - US: 0 - AC: 0 - IN: 0 - VE: 0 - FU: 3
     - MAINSTAYS: SER: 0 - DEM: 5 - ACC: 0 - PAC: 5 - TRA: 5

136. The web site offers advanced search
     - ORIGIN: W3C
     - DESIGN AND CONTENT: FR: 0 - NA: 0 - US: 0 - AC: 3 - IN: 0 - VE: 0 - FU: 3
     - MAINSTAYS: SER: 2 - DEM: 0 - ACC: 0 - PAC: 2 - TRA: 0

137. It includes Chat Room
     - ORIGIN: ONTI
     - DESIGN AND CONTENT: FR: 0 - NA: 0 - US: 0 - AC: 0 - IN: 0 - VE: 0 - FU: 1
     - MAINSTAYS: SER: 0 - DEM: 5 - ACC: 0 - PAC: 5 - TRA: 0

138. It includes Forums
     - ORIGIN: ONTI
     - DESIGN AND CONTENT: FR: 0 - NA: 0 - US: 0 - AC: 0 - IN: 0 - VE: 0 - FU: 2
     - MAINSTAYS: SER: 0 - DEM: 5 - ACC: 0 - PAC: 5 - TRA: 0

139. The web site offers FAQ and their answers' section.
     - ORIGIN: PUB [10]
     - DESIGN AND CONTENT: FR: 3 - NA: 0 - US: 0 - AC: 0 - IN: 2 - VE: 0 - FU: 0
     - MAINSTAYS: SER: 0 - DEM: 4 - ACC: 4 - PAC: 0 - TRA: 3

140. The web site allows printable version of some of its pages.
     - ORIGIN: PUB [7]
     - DESIGN AND CONTENT: FR: 4 - NA: 0 - US: 0 - AC: 0 - IN: 0 - VE: 0 - FU: 2
     - MAINSTAYS: SER: 4 - DEM: 0 - ACC: 0 - PAC: 4 - TRA: 0

1.22 Category: Technology

141. The web site includes semantic search
     - ORIGIN: RT
     - DESIGN AND CONTENT: FR: 3 - NA: 3 - US: 1 - AC: 0 - IN: 0 - VE: 0 - FU: 4
     - MAINSTAYS: SER: 2 - DEM: 0 - ACC: 2 - PAC: 0 - TRA: 0

142. The web site includes RSS
     - ORIGIN: RT
     - DESIGN AND CONTENT: FR: 0 - NA: 0 - US: 0 - AC: 0 - IN: 0 - VE: 0 - FU: 2
     - MAINSTAYS: None

143. Mobile Site
     - ORIGIN: W3C
     - DESIGN AND CONTENT: FR: 0 - NA: 0 - US: 0 - AC: 3 - IN: 0 - VE: 0 - FU: 0
     - MAINSTAYS: SER: 3 - DEM: 0 - ACC: 3 - PAC: 0 - TRA: 3

1.23 Category: Text

144. The web site includes headers in rows and columns of the tables
     - ORIGIN: W3C
     - DESIGN AND CONTENT: FR: 0 - NA: 0 - US: 0 - AC: 5 - IN: 0 - VE: 0 - FU: 0
     - MAINSTAYS: None

145. It explains the meaning of each abbreviation used in a document the first time it appears
     - ORIGIN: W3C
     - DESIGN AND CONTENT: FR: 3 - NA: 0 - US: 0 - AC: 3 - IN: 0 - VE: 0 - FU: 0
     - MAINSTAYS: SER: 1 - DEM: 0 - ACC: 1 - PAC: 0 - TRA: 2

146. It shows information organized by categories
     - ORIGIN: W3C
     - DESIGN AND CONTENT: FR: 4 - NA: 0 - US: 4 - AC: 4 - IN: 0 - VE: 0 - FU: 0
     - MAINSTAYS: SER: 3 - DEM: 0 - ACC: 3 - PAC: 0 - TRA: 0

147. The special characters can be seen correctly
     - ORIGIN: Research Team
     - DESIGN AND CONTENT: FR: 5 - NA: 0 - US: 3 - AC: 4 - IN: 0 - VE: 0 - FU: 0
     - MAINSTAYS: None

148. It highlights important words
     - ORIGIN: ONTI
     - DESIGN AND CONTENT: FR: 4 - NA: 0 - US: 0 - AC: 4 - IN: 0 - VE: 0 - FU: 0
     - MAINSTAYS: SER: 1 - DEM: 0 - ACC: 1 - PAC: 0 - TRA: 0

149. Technical words are avoided or explained
     - ORIGIN: ONTI
     - DESIGN AND CONTENT: FR: 5 - NA: 0 - US: 0 - AC: 5 - IN: 0 - VE: 0 - FU: 0
     - MAINSTAYS: SER: 1 - DEM: 0 - ACC: 1 - PAC: 0 - TRA: 3

150. Text is organized in paragraphs.
   - ORIGIN: W3C
   - DESIGN AND CONTENT: FR: 0 - NA: 0 - US: 4 - AC: 4 - IN: 0 - VE: 0 - FU: 0
   - MAINSTAYS: SER: 1 - DEM: 0 - ACC: 1 - PAC: 0 - TRA: 0

151. The web site uses SanSerif type fonts
   - ORIGIN: PUB [11]
   - DESIGN AND CONTENT: FR: 3 - NA: 0 - US: 0 - AC: 3 - IN: 0 - VE: 0 - FU: 0
   - MAINSTAYS: None

152. The web site uses dots to join text subsets.
   - ORIGIN: ONTI
   - DESIGN AND CONTENT: FR: 3 - NA: 0 - US: 0 - AC: 0 - IN: 0 - VE: 0 - FU: 0
   - MAINSTAYS: None

Additional Reading

Agrawal, R., & Srikant, R. (1994). Fast algorithms for mining association rules in large databases. In VLDB '94. *In Proceedings of the 20th International Conference on Very Large Data Bases.* San Francisco: Morgan Kaufmann, p. 487-499.

Aguilera, M., & Mendiz, A. (2003). Video Games and Education: Education in the Face of a 'Parallel School'. *Computers in Entertainment.* Vol. 1 (1), p. 1-14.

Aldrich, C. (2005). *Learning by doing: a comprehensive guide to simulations, computer games, and pedagogy in e-learning and other educational experiences.* San Francisco: Wiley.

Anderson, C. (2007). *The long tail: How endless choice is creating unlimited demand.* New York: Random House.

Ankolekar, A., Krotzsch, M., Tran, T., & Vrandecic, D. (2008). The two cultures: Mashing up web 2.0 and the semantic web. *Web Semantics: Science, Services and Agents on the World Wide Web,* Vol. 6 (1), p. 70-75.

Ann, L. (1980). Gardner. Search: An Overview. *AI Magazine,* Vol. 2 (1), p. 23.

Aridor, Y. (1998). Agent Design Patterns: Elements of Agent Application Design. *In Proceedings of Autonomous Agents '98.* New York: ACM Press, p. 108-115.

Armstrong, A., & Casement, C. (2000). *The child and the machine: how computers put our children's education at risk.* Beltville: Robins Lane Press.

Avison, D., & Fitzgerald, G. (2003). Where Now for Development Methodologies? *Communications of the ACM.* Vol. 46 (1), pp. 78-82.

Badiqué, E. (2002). New Imaging Frontiers: 3D and Mixed Reality. In *Proceedings the 1st International Symposium on 3D Data Processing Visualization and Transmission (3DPVT'02),* Padova, Italy, p.296.

Baldi, P. F., Lopes, C. V., Linstead, E. J., & Bajracharya, S. K. (2008). A theory of aspects as latent topics. *ACM SIGPLAN Notices,* Vol. 43 (10), p. 543-562.

Bao, H., & Liu, H, & Yu, J, & Xu, H. (2005). An Ontology-Based Semantic Integration for Digital Museums. In *Proceedings WAIM 2005,* LNCS, Vol. 3739/2005. Berlin: Springer-Verlag, p. 626-631.

Barthes, R. (2009). La Aventura Semiológica. Barcelona: Paidós.

Battelle, J. (2005). *The search: How Google and its rivals rewrote the rules of business and transformed our culture.* New York: Portfolio.

Becher, T. (2001). *Tribus y territorios académicos.* Barcelona: Gedisa.

Beck, K. (2007). *Implementation Patterns.* Massachussets: Addison-Wesley.

Beck, T. (2007). *Web 2.0: User-Generated Content in Online Communities.* Hamburg: Diplomica Verlag.

Bevan, N., Petrie, H., & Claridge, N. (2007). Tenuta: Strategies for Providing Guidance on Usability and Accessibility. In *Proceedings of 4th International Conference on Universal Access in Human-Computer Interaction, Lecture Notes in Computer Science*. Vol. 4556. New Jersey: Lawrence Erlbaum. DOI 10.1007/978-3-540-73283-9_3, p. 20-27.

Bhatnagar, S. (2004). *E-Government: From Vision to Implementation –A Practical Guide With Case Studies*. New Delhi: Sage Publications.

Binkley, D., Ceccato, M., Harman, M., Ricca, F., & Tonella, P. (2005). Automated refactoring of object oriented code into aspects. In *Proceedings of the 21st IEEE International Conference on Software Maintenance (ICSM)*. Washington: IEEE Computer Society, p. 27-36.

Bopp, M. (2006). Didactic Analysis of Digital Games and Game-Based Learning. In Pivec, M. (Ed.), *Affective and Emotional Aspects of Human-Computer Interaction*. Amsterdam: IOS Press, p. 8-37.

British Kinematograph Sound & Television Society (1998). *Diccionario de las tecnologías de la imagen*. Barcelona: Gedisa.

Brooks, D. W., & Nolan, D. E., & Gallagher, S. M. (2001). Informal Education: Museums, Organizations. In *Innovations in Science Education and Technology, Vol. 9: Web-Teaching*. Berlin: Springer-Verlg, p. 209-221.

Brougère, G. (1995). *Jeu et éducation*. Paris: L'Harmattan.

Broy, M. (2006). The 'Grand Challenge' in Informatics: Engineering Software-Intensive Systems. IEEE Computer. Vol. 28 (10), pp. 72-80.

Bruder, I., & Jaworek, G. (2008). Blind and Visually Impaired People: Human-Computer Interaction and Access to Graphics. Introduction to the Special Thematic Session. In *Computers Helping People with Special Needs. Lecture Notes in Computer Science*. Vol. 5105. DOI 10.1007/978-3-540-70540-6_113, p. 767-769.

Brugali, D., & Sycara, K. (2000) Towards Agent-oriented Application Frameworks. *ACM Computing Surveys*, Vol. 32 (1), p. 2.

Buckland, M. (2002). *AI techniques for game programming*. Ohio: Premier Press.

Buckley, J. (2003). E-service Quality and the Public Sector. *Managing Service Quality*. Vol. 13 (6). DOI: 10.1108/09604520310506513, p. 453-462.

Bunge, M. (2006). *A la caza de la realidad*. Barcelona: Gedisa.

Bustamante, E. (2003). *Hacia un nuevo sistema mundial de comunicación*. Barcelona: Gedisa.

Canclini, N. (2007). *Lectores, espectadores e internautas*. Barcelona: Gedisa.

Ceccato, M., Marin, M., Mens, K., Moonen, L., Tonella, P., & Tourwé, T. (2006). *Applying and combining three different aspect mining techniques. Software Quality Control*, Vol. 14 (3), p. 209-231.

Charalabidis, Y., Askounis, D., Gionis, G., Lampathaki, F., & Metaxiotis, K. (2006). Organising Municipal e-Government Systems: A Multi-facet Taxonomy of e-Services for Citizens and Businesses. Berlin: Springer-Verlag. DOI: 10.1007/11823100, p. 195-206.

Chen, H., Brand, L., Gregg, V., Traunmaller, R., Dawes, S., Hovy, E., Macintosh, A., & Larson, C. (2007). *Digital E-Government: E-Government Implementation Information*. New York: Springer.

Cipolla-Ficarra, F. (2002). Heuristic Evaluation of the Internet Cultural Heritage: Spanish and Italian Portals. *In CD-ROM Proceedings Culturtec*. UCM: Madrid. ISBN: 84-7491-710-7.

Cipolla-Ficarra, F. (2005). *Editoria ipermediale: Le nuove frontiere della comunicazione interattiva.* Bergamo: Blue Herons.

Cipolla-Ficarra, F. (2005). Heuristic Evaluation of Animated Help in Hypermedia. *In CD-ROM Proceedings HCI International '05.* HCII '05: Las Vegas, 2005. ISBN: 0-8058-2967-9.

Cipolla-Ficarra, F. (2005). *Interazione uomo-computer nel XXI secolo: Analisi e valutazione euristica della qualità per la comunicazione e l'usabilità.* Bergamo: Blue Herons.

Cipolla-Ficarra, F. (2005). Multimedia and Languages for Children: Semiosis for Universal Access". *In CD-ROM Proceedings HCI International '05.* HCII: Las Vegas, 2005. ISBN: 0-8058-2967-9.

Cipolla-Ficarra, F. (2006). *Podcasting e new media: Miti e realtà nella comunicazione multimediale e l'educazione a distanza.* Bergamo: Blue Herons.

Cipolla-Ficarra, F. (2008). Eyes: A Virtual Assistant for Analysis of the Transparency and Accessibility in University Portal. *In DVD-ROM Proceedings Applied Human Factors and Ergonomics.* AEI: Las Vegas. ISBN: 978-1-60643-712-4.

Cipolla-Ficarra, F. (2008). Guided Tour for International User Interfaces: Multimedia Design in Ecological and Rural Regions". *In DVD-ROM Proceedings Applied Human Factors and Ergonomics.* AEI: Las Vegas. ISBN: 978-1-60643-712-4.

Cipolla-Ficarra, F. (2008). Guided Tour for International User Interfaces: Multimedia Design in Ecological and Rural Regions. *In DVD-ROM Proceedings Applied Human Factors and Ergonomics.* AEI: Las Vegas. ISBN: 978-1-60643-712-4.

Cipolla-Ficarra, F. (2008). HECHE: Heuristic Evaluation of Colours in HomepagE". *In DVD-ROM Proceedings Applied Human Factors and*

Ergonomics. AEI: Las Vegas. ISBN: 978-1-60643-712-4.

Clark, R. C., Richard E., & Mayer, R. E. (2007). *E-learning and the science of instruction: proven guidelines for consumers and designers of multimedia learning.* San Francisco: Wiley.

Cogburn, D. (2003). HCI in the So-Called Developing World: What's in it for Everyone. *Interactions.* Vol. 10 (2), pp. 80-87.

Colorado-Castellary, A. (1997). *Hipermedia visual: El reto hipermedia en el arte y la educación.* Madrid: Universidad Complutense.

Constantine, L., & Lockwood, L. (1999). *Software for use: a practical guide to the models and methods of usage-centered design.* Massachusetts: Addison-Wesley Professional.

Conti, G., & Sobiesk, E. (2009). Malicious Interfaces and Personalization's Uninviting Future. *IEEE Security & Privacy.* Vol. 7 (3), pp. 64-67.

Cooper, A., Reimann, R., & Cronin, D. (2007). *About face 3: the essentials of interaction design.* San Francisco: Wiley.

Cornelissen, B., Zaidman, A., Van Deursen, A., Moonen, L., & Koschke, R. (2009). A systematic survey of program comprehension through dynamic analysis. *IEEE Transactions on Software Engineering.* DOI: http://doi.ieeecomputersociety.org/10.1109/TSE.2009.28

Coutrix, C., & Nigay, L. (2006). Balancing physical and digital properties in mixed objects. In *Proceedings of the working conference on advanced visual interfaces. Interaction environments and semantics based applications.* New York: ACM Press, p. 305-308.

Coutrix, C., & Nigay, L. (2006). Mixed Reality: A model of Mixed Interaction. In *Proceedings of the working conference on advanced visual interfaces. Advanced interaction design.* New York: ACM Press, p. 43-50.

Coyne, R. (1994). Heidegger and Virtual Reality: The Implication of Heidegger's Thinking for Computer Representations. *Leonardo, Vol. 27*, No. 1, p 65-73.

Craig, L. (2005). Applying UML and Patterns. Glenview: Prentice Hall.

Curtin, G., Sommer, M., & Vis-Sommer, V. (2003). The World of E-Government. Routledge: The Haworth Press.

Cuttrell, E., & Dumais, S. (2006). Exploring Personal Information. *Communications of ACM*. Vol. 49 (4), 50-51.

Darley, A. (2003). *Cultura visual digital*. Barcelona: Paidós.

Daston, L. (2007). Things That Talk. New York: Zone Books.

Daston, Lorraine. (2000). *Biographies of Scientific Objects*. Chicago: The University of Chicago Press.

Davidson, D. (2001). *De la verdad y de la interpretación*. Barcelona: Gedisa.

De Freitas, S & Neumann, T. (2009). The use of 'exploratory learning' for supporting immersive learning in virtual environments. *Computers and Education*, 52 (2), p. 343-352.

De Freitas, S. & Maharg, P (forthcoming, 2010). *Transforming professional learning*. In de Freitas, S. Maharg, P. (Eds.). Learning Through Play. Massachusetts: MIT Press.

Deledalle, G. (1996). *Leer a Peirce hoy*. Barcelona: Gedisa.

Dominique, W. (2006). *Salvemos la comunicación*. Barcelona: Gedisa.

Dragos, M.; Voelter, M. & Noble, J. (2006). *Pattern Languages of Program Design*. Vol. 5. Massachusetts: Addison-Wesley.

Dubberly, H. (2009). Models of Models. *Interactions*. Vol. 16 (3), pp. 54-60.

Dunleavy, P., Margetts, H., Bastow, S., & Tinkler, J. (2006). *Digital Era Governance: IT Corporations, the State, and e-Government*. New York: Oxford University Press.

Dunn, F. (2002). *3D Math primer for graphics and game development*. Sudbure: Wordware.

Elster, J. (1997). *El cambio tecnológico*. Barcelona: Gedisa.

Evett, L., & Brown, D. (2005). Text formats and web design for visually impaired and dyslexic readers—Clear Text for All. *Interacting with Computers* Vol. 17 (4), DOI: 10.1016/j.intcom.2005.04.001, p. 453-472.

Fels, S., & Mase, K. (1999). Interactive Video Cubism. In New Paradigms in Information Visualization and Manipulation, Proceedings of the 1999 workshop on new paradigms on information visualization and manipulation in conjunction with the eigth ACM international conference on information and knowledge management, p. 78-82.

Fensel, D., Lausen, H., de Bruijn, J., Stollberg, M., Roman, D., & Polleres, A. (2006). *Enabling Semantic Web Services: The Web Service Modeling Ontology*. Berlin: Springer-Verlag.

Ferretti, S., Mirri, S., Roccetti, M., & Salomoni, P. (2007). Notes for a Collaboration: On the Design of a Wiki-type Educational Video Lecture Annotation System. In *Proceedings of the International Conference on Semantic Computing*. Washington: IEEE Computer Society, p. 651-656.

Findlen, P. (1994). *Possessing Nature*. Berkeley, Los Angeles: University of California Press.

Flake, G., Lawrence, S., Giles, C., & Coetzee, F. (2002). *IEEE Computer*. Vol. 35 (3), p. 66-71.

Fleming, J. (1998). *Web Navigation: Designing the User Experience*. Sebastopol: O'Reilly.

Floyd, M. (2002). *EJB Design Patterns: Advanced Patterns, Processes and Idioms*. New Jersey: John Wiley & Sons.

Foley, J. D., van Dam, A., Feiner, S. K. & Hughes, J. F. (1993). *Introduction to computer graphics.* Massachusetts: Addison-Wesley Professional.

Foley, M. (2003). *UML distilled: a brief guide to the standard object modeling language.* Massachusetts: Addison-Wesley Professional.

Fowler, M. (1997). *Analysis Patterns: Reusable Object Models.* Massachusetts: Addison-Wesley.

Fowler, M. (2002). *Patterns of Enterprise Application Architecture.* Massachusetts: Addison-Wesley.

Fowler, M., Beck, K., Brant, J., Opdyke, W., & Roberts, D. (1999). *Refactoring: Improving the Design of Existing Code.* Massachusetts: Addison-Wesley.

Franson, D. (2002). *2D artwork and 3D modeling for game artists.* Ohaio: Premier Press.

Freeman, D. (2003). *Creating emotion in games: the craft and art of emotioneering.* Berkeley: New Riders Publishing.

Freeman, E.; Freeman, E. Sierra, K. & Bates, B. (2004). Head First Design Patterns. Sebastopol: O'Reilly Media, .

Garoian, C. (2001). Performing the Museum. In Studies in Art Education, Vol. 42 (3), p. 234-248.

Garret, J. (2002). The Elements of User Experience: User-Centered Design for the Web (Voices That Matter). Indianapolis: Peachpit Press.

Gee, J. P. (2007). *What video games have to teach us about learning and literacy.* New York: Palgrave Macmillan.

Gehtland, J., Galbraith, B., & Almaer, D. (2006). *Pragmatic Ajax: A Web 2.0* Primer. Pragmatic Bookshelf.

George F. (2005). *Luger's textbook, Artificial Intelligence: Structures and Strategies for Complex Problem Solving.* 5th Edition. Massachusetts: Addison-Wesley.

Girardi, R., Oliveira, I., & Bezerra, G. (2003). Towards a System of Patterns for the Design of Agent-based Systems. In *Proceedings of The Second Nordic Conference on Agent-Based systems. (VikingPLoP 2003).* Bergen, Norway.

Gladstone, K., Rundle, C., & Alexander, T. (2002). Accessibility and Usability of eCommerce Systems. In *Proceedings of the 8th International Conference on Computers Helping People with Special Needs*, Lecture Notes In Computer Science, Vol. 2398, p. 11–18.

Glitho, R. (2005). *Challenges of Expanding Internet E-Government Communication.* New York: Springer.

Gortais, B. (2003). Abstraction and Art. In *Philosophical Transactions: Biological Sciences*, Vol. 358, (1435), The Abstraction Paths: From Experience to Concept, p. 1241-1249.

Habgood, J., Overmars, M., & Wilson, P. (2006). *The game maker's apprentice: game development for beginners.* New York: Springer.

Hackett, S., Parmanto, B., & Zeng, X. (2004). Accessibility of Internet websites through time, In *Proceedings of ACM SIGACCESS conference on Computers and accessibility*, p. 32-39.

Hailpern, J., Guarino-Reid, L., Boardman, R., & Annam, S. (2009). Web 2.0: blind to an accessible new world. In *Proceedings of the 18th international conference on World Wide Web.* Madrid, p. 821-830.

Hämäläinen, M., Whinston, A., & Vishik, S. Electronic Markets for Learning: Education Brokerages on the Internet. *Communications of the ACM.* Vol. 39 (6), p. 51-58.

Han, J. & Kamber, M. (2006). *Data Mining: Concepts and Techniques.* San Francisco: Morgan Kaufmann.

Hannemann, J. & Kiczales, G. (2002). Design pattern implementation in java and aspectj. In *Proceedings of the 17th ACM SIGPLAN conference on Object-oriented programming, systems, languages, and applications (OOPSLA '02)*. New York: ACM Press, p. 161-173.

Heeks, R. (2005). *Implementing and Managing eGovernment: An International Text*. London: Sage Publications.

Hendler, J. (2009). Web 3.0 Emerging. *IEEE Computer*, Vol. 42 (11), p. 111-113.

Hendler, J. and Golbeck, J. (2008). Metcalfe's Law, Web 2.0, and the Semantic Web. *Web Semant*, Vol. 6 (1), p. 14-20.

Höhler, S. (2002). Dichte Beschreibungen – Die Profilierung ozeanischer Tiefe im Lotverfahren von 1850 bis 1930. In Gugerli, D., & Orland, B. (Ed.), *Ganz normale Bilder – Historische Beiträge zur visuellen Herstellung von Selbstverständlichkeit*. Zürich: Chronos Verlag, p. 19-46.

Holdener, T. (2008). *Ajax: the definitive guide*. Sebastopol: O'Reilly Media.

Holman, J., Lazar, J., Feng, J. H. & D'Arcy, J. (2007). Developing usable CAPTCHAs for blind users. In *Proceedings of the SIGACCESS conference on Computers and Accessibility*. New York: ACM Press, p. 245-246.

Holmes, D. (2001). *eGov: E-Business Strategies for Government*. Boston: Nicholas Brealey Publishing.

Holzinger, A. (2005). Usability engineering methods for Software Developers. In *Communication of the ACM*, Vol. 48 (1), p.71-74.

Homburg, V. (2008). *Understanding E-Government: Information Systems in Public Administration*. Oxon: Routledge-Taylor & Francis.

Huizinga, J. (1938). *Homo ludens*. Hamburg: Rowohlt Taschenbuch Verlag.

Introna, L., & Nissenbaum, H. (2000). Defining the Web: The Politics of Search Engines. *IEEE Computer*. Vol. 33 (1), p. 54-62.

Ivory, M. Y., & Hearst, M. A. (2004). The state of the art in automating usability evaluation of user interfaces. *Computing Surveys, Vol. 2001 (4)*, p. 470-516.

Jeffries, R., Miller, J. R., Wharton, C., & Uyeda K. M. (1991). User Interfaces Evaluation in the Real World: A Comparison of Four Techniques. In *Proceedings of the SIGCHI conference on Human factors in computing systems (CHI'91)*. ACM Press: New York, p. 119-124.

Jenkins, H. (2008). *Convergence culture*. Barcelona, Paidós.

Johnson, J. (2000). Textual Bloopers. *Interactions*. Vol. 12 (5), p. 28-48.

Joly, M. (2003). *La interpretación de la imagen*. Barcelona: Paidós.

Kappel, G., Prýýll, B., Reich, S., & Retschitzegger, W. (2006). *Web Engineering*. New Jersey: Wiley.

Kawanaka, S., Borodin, Y., Bigham, J. P., Lunn, D., Takagi, H., & Asakawa, C. (2008). Accessibility commons: a metadata infrastructure for web accessibility. In *Proceedings of the 10th international ACM SIGACCESS conference on Computers and accessibility*. New York: ACM Press, p. 153-160.

Kazoun, C. & Lott, J. (2008). *Programming Flex 3: The Comprehensive Guide to Creating Rich Internet Applications with Adobe Flex*. Sebastopol: O'Reilly Media.

Kellens, A., Mens, K., & Tonella, P. (2007). A survey of automated code-level aspect mining techniques. In *Lecture Notes in Computer Science*. Vol. 4640/2007. Berlin: Springer-Verlag, p. 143-162.

Kelly, B., Sloan, D., Brown, S., Seale, J., Petrie, H., Lauke, P., & Ball, S. (2007). Accessibility 2.0: people, policies and processes. In *Proceedings of the 2007 international cross-disciplinary conference on Web accessibility (W4A)*. New York: ACM Press, p. 138-147.

Kiczales, G., Lamping, J., Mendhekar, A., Maeda, C., Lopes, C. V., Loingtier, J. M., & Irwin, J. (1997). Aspect-oriented programming. In *ECOOP*, p. 220-242.

Kienitz, G. W. (2007). *Web 2.0, Moses*. Berlin: Springer-Verlag.

King, M., Thatcher, J.W., Bronstadt, P. M., & Easton, R. (2005). Managing usability for people with disabilities in a large Web presence. *IBM Systems Journal* Vol. 44, p. 519-536.

Klein, J. H. (1985). The Abstraction of Reality for Games and Simulations. *The Journal of the Operational Research Society, Vol. 36, No. 8*, pp. 671-678.

Koenig, S.A. (2004). Comparison of Fast Search Methods for Real-Time Situated Agents. In *Proceedings of the International Joint Conference on Autonomous Agents and Multiagent Systems* (AAMAS), p. 864-871.

Kowalski, R. (1979). *Logic for Problem Solving*. Amsterdam: Elsevier North Holland.

Kratky, A. (2009). Mixed Realities - Virtual Object Lessons. In *Proceedings 13th International Conference, HCI International 2009*. Lecture Notes in Computer Science, Vol. 5612. Berlin: Springer-Verlag, p. 440-445.

Laddad, R. (2003). AspectJ *in Action: Practical Aspect-Oriented Programming*. Greenwich: Manning Publications.

Landow, G. (2009). *Hipertexto 3.0*. Barcelona: Paidós.

Lee, R.S.T., & Liu, J.N.K. (2004). iJADE Webminer: An intelligent agent framework for Internet shopping. In *IEEE Transactions on Knowledge and Data Engineering*. Vol. 16 (4), p. 461-473.

Leporini, B., & Paternò, F. (2004). Increasing Usability when Interacting through Screen Readers. *Springer International Journal Universal Access in the Information Society (UAIS)*. "Special Issue on Guidelines, Standards, Methods and Processes for Software Accessibility". Vol. 3 (1), p. 57-70.

Lepouras, G., & Vassilakis, C. (2005). Virtual museums for all: employing game technology for edutainment. *Virtual Reality 8*. p. 96-106.

Levesque, H. Pirri, F., & Reiter, R. (1998). Foundations for the situation calculus. *Electronic Transactions on Artificial Intelligence*. Vol. 2 (3/4), p. 159-178.

Lewis, J. (2006). Sample Sizes for Usability Tests: Mostly Math, Not Magic. *Interactions*. Vol. 13 (6), p. 29-33.

Liarokapis, F., & Newman, R. (2007). Design Experiences of Multimodal Mixed Reality Interfaces. In *Proceedings SIGDOC 07*. New York: ACM Press, p. 34 - 41.

Lih, A. (2009). *The Wikipedia revolution: How a bunch of nobodies created the world's greatest encyclopedia*. New York: Hyperion.

Luesebrink, M. C. (1998). The Moment in Hypertext: A Brief Lexicon of Time. In *Proceedings the 9th Conference on Hypertext and Hypermedia*. New York: ACM Press, p. 106-112.

Lundgren, S., & Hultberg, T. (2009). Time, Temporality, and Interaction. *Interactions*. Vol. 16 (4), p. 34-37.

MacIntyre, B., & Bolter, J. D. (2003). Single-narrative, multiple point-of-view dramatic experiences in augmented reality. *Virtual Reality* (7), p. 10-16.

Maeda, J. (2006). *Las leyes de la simplicidad*. Barcelona: Gedisa.

Maharg, P. (2008). *SIMPLE learning and professional practice*. In Mayer, I., Mastik, H. (eds) Organising and Learning Through Gaming and Simulation. Amsterdam: Eburon Academic Publishers.

Maharg, P., & Nicol, E., (forthcoming 2009). *Cyberdam and SIMPLE: A comparison*. In Warmelink, H., (Ed.) Learning in a Virtual World.

Maldonado, T. (1999). *Lo real y lo virtual*. Barcelona: Gedisa.

Mancini, C., & Buckingham Shum, S. (2004). Towards 'Cinematic' Hypertext. In *Proceedings the 15th Conference on Hypertext and Hypermedia*. New York: ACM Press, p. 215-224.

Mankoff, J., Fait, H., & Tran, T. (2005). Is your Web page accessible? A comparative study of methods for assessing Web page accessibility for the blind. In *Proceedings of CHI2005*. ACM Press: New York, p. 899-908.

Marin, M., Van Deursen, A., & Moonen, L. (2007). Identifying crosscutting concerns using fan-in analysis. *ACM Trans. Software Engineering Methodoly*, Vol. 17 (1), p. 1-37.

Marin, M., Van Deursen, A., Moonen, L., & Van der Rijst, R. (2009). An integrated crosscutting concern migration strategy and its automated application to JHotDraw. *Automated Software Engineering*, Vol. 26 (2), p. 323-356.

Martin, R.; Dirk, R. & Buschmann, F. (1997). *Pattern Languages of Program Design*. Massachusetts: Addison-Wesley.

Mattelart, A. & Mattelart, M. (1997). *Historia de las teorías de la comunicación*. Barcelona: Paidós.

Mattelart, A. (2006). *Diversidad cultural y mundialización*. Barcelona: Paidós.

McCarthy, J.. & Hayes, P. (1969). Some philosophical problems from the standpoint of artificial intelligence. In *Proceedings Machine Intelligence*,

Vol. 4, p. 463–502. Edinburgh: University Press, Edinburgh.

McCrickard, S., & Chewar, C. (2003). Attuning Notification Design to User Goals and Attention Costs. *Communications of the ACM*. Vol. 46 (3), pp. 67-72.

McCue, P. (2005). *The crucial role of animated children's educational games*. Paper presented at the ACM SIGGRAPH'05, Los Angeles. New York: ACM Press.

McEneaney, J. E. (1999). Visualizing and Assessing Navigation in Hypertext. In *Proceedings the 10th Conference on Hypertext and Hypermedia*. New York: ACM Press, p. 61-70.

McLuhan, E. & Zingrone, F. (1998). *McLuhan escritos esenciales*. Barcelona: Paidós.

McLuhan, M. (2009). *Comprender los medios de comunicación*. Barcelona: Paidós.

Mens, T., & Tourwe, T. (2004). A survey of software refactoring. *IEEE Transactions on Software Engineering*, Vol. 30 (2), p. 126-139.

Merritt, R. K. (2001). From Memory Arts to the New Code Paradigm: The Artist as Engineer of Virtual Information Space and Virtual Experience. *Leonardo*, Vol. 34 (5), p. 403-408.

Mika, P. (2007). Social Networks and the Semantic Web (Semantic Web and Beyond). Berlin: Springer-Verlag.

Milgram, P., & Kishino, F. (1994). A Taxonomy of Mixed Reality Visual Displays. *IEICE Transactions on Information Systems*. Vol E77-D (12), p. 1321-1329.

Millington, I. (2006). *Artificial intelligence for games*. San Francisco: Morgan Kaufmann.

Minsk, M. (2007). *The emotion machine: commonsense thinking, artificial intelligence, and the future of the human mind*. New York: Simon & Schuster.

Miyashita, H., Sato, D., Takagi, H., & Asakawa, C. (2007). Aibrowser for multimedia: introducing multimedia content accessibility for visually impaired users. In *Proceedings of the 9th international ACM SIGACCESS conference on Computers and accessibility.* New York, ACM Press, p. 91-98.

Monteiro, M. P., & Jo A. M. (2005). Towards a catalog of aspect-oriented refactorings. In *AOSD '05: Proceedings of the 4th international conference on Aspect-oriented software development.* New York: ACM Press, p. 111-122.

Moore, J., & Bailin, S. (1991). Domain Analysis: Framework for reuse. In IEEE Computer Society Press, p. 179-202.

Mora-Fernández, J. (2008). Multicultural videos: an interactive online museum based on an international artistic video database. In *Proceeding of the 1st ACM international workshop on Communicability design and evaluation in cultural and ecological multimedia system.* New York: ACM Press, p. 23-30.

Moreno-Sánchez, I. (2002). *Musas y nuevas tecnologías: El relato hipermedia*, Barcelona: Paidós.

Mueller, P., Mueller, J. (2003). Accessibility for Everybody: Understanding the Section 508 Accessibility Requirements. Berlin: Springer.

Murphy, E., Kuber, R., McAllister, G., Strain, P., & Yu., W. (2008). An empirical investigation into the difficulties experienced by visually impaired Internet users. *Universal Access in the Information Society.* Vol. 7 (2), Berlin: Springer-Verlag, DOI 10.1007/s10209-007-0098-4, p.79-91.

Murugesan, S. (2007). Understanding Web 2.0. *IT Professional.* Vol. 9 (4), p. 34-41.

Myers, B. (1998). A Brief History of Human-Computer Interaction Technology. *Interactions.* Vol. 5 (2), pp. 44-54.

Nau, D., & Wilkenfeld, J. (2008). Computational Cultural Dynnamics. IEEE *Intelligent Systems.* Vol. 23 (4), pp. 18-19.

Negroponte, N. (1996). *Being digital.* Vintag, New York.

Nichols, B. (1991). *Representing Reality.* Bloomington: Indiana University Press.

Nielsen, J., & Loranger, H. (2006). *Prioritizing Usability (Voices That Matter).* Berkeley: New Riders Press.

Nov, O. (2007). What motivates Wikipedians? *Commununications of the ACM,* Vol. 50 (11), p. 60-64.

Novak, J. (2007). *Game development essentials: an introduction.* Delmar Cengage Learning, Stamford.

Oliver, L., & Sanders, L. (2004). *E-Government Reconsidered: Renewal of Governance for the Knowledge Age.* Saskatchewan Institute of Public Policy –SIPP. Saskatoon: Canadian Plains Research Center, Saskatoon.

Papazoglou, M. (2007). *Web Services: Principles and Technology.* Glenview: Prentice Hall.

Papert, S. (1994). *The children's machine: rethinking school in the age of the computer.* New York: Basic Books.

Pasquali, A. (2007). *Comprender la comunicación.* Barcelona: Gedisa.

Pastoureau, M. (2009). *Diccionario de los colores.* Barcelona: Paidós.

Paulson, L. D. (2005). Building rich web applications with ajax. *IEEE Computer,* Vol. 38(10), p. 14-17.

Petrie, H., & Kheir, O. (2007). The relationship between accessibility and usability of websites. In *Proceedings of the SIGCHI conference on Human factors in computing systems (SIGCHI'07).* New York: ACM Press, p. 397 – 406.

Petrie, H., Badani, A., & Bhalla, A. (2005). Sex, lies and web accessibility: the use of accessibility logos and statements on e-commerce and financial websites. In *Proceedings of Accessible Design in the Digital World Conference 2005*, Dundee.

Pirri, F., & Reiter, R. (1999). Some contributions to the metatheory of the Situation Calculus. *Journal of the ACM*, Vol. 46 (3), p. 325–361. DOI:10.1145/316542.316545

Pitt I., & Edwards A. (2003). Design of speech-based devices. Springer Professional Computing – Practitioner Series. Springer, New York.

Plummer, J. (2004). *A flexible and expandable architecture for computer games*. Tempe: Arizona State University.

Polya, G. (2004). *How to solve it: a new aspect of mathematical method*. Princeton University Press.

Powlik, J. J., & Karshmer, A. I. (2002). When accessibility meets usability. *Universal Access in the Information Society*. Vol. 1 (3), Berlin: Springer-Verlag. DOI: 10.1007/s10209-002-0020-z., p. 217-222.

Reiter, R. (1991). The frame problem in the situation calculus: a simple solution (sometimes) and a completeness result for goal regression. In *Vladimir Lifshitz, editor, Artificial intelligence and mathematical theory of computation: papers in honour of John McCarthy*. New York: Academic Press, p. 359-380.

Reiter, R. (1997). The situation calculus ontology. In *Electronic News journal on reasoning about actions and change*. Linkoping University electronic press. www.ep.liu.se/ej/enrac/1997/

Resnick, M., Martin, F., Berg, R., Borovoy, R., Colella, V., Kramer, K., & Silverman, B. (1998). Digital Manipulatives: New Toys to Think With. In *Proceedings the SIGCHI 98*. New York, ACM Press, p. 281-287.

Richard, G. (1996). *Patterns of Software: Tales From The Software Community*. Oxford University Press. p. 235. http://www.dreamsongs.com/NewFiles/PatternsOfSoftware.pdf.

Rodríguez, A., Giulianelli, D., Vera, P., Marko, I., Trigueros, & A., Larrosa, M. (2008). Analyzing e-governance mainstays on municipalities websites. In *Proceeding of the 1st ACM International Workshop on Communicability Design and Evaluation in Cultural and Ecological Multimedia Systems, CommunicabilityMS '08*. New York: ACM Press, p. 31-38.

Rodriguez, E.P.G., Domingo, M.G., Ribera, J.P., Hill, M.A. & Jardi, L.S. (2006). Usability for All: Towards Improving the E-Learning Experience for Visually Impaired Users. In *Proceedings of ICCHP 2006*, LNCS Vol 4061, p. 1313-1317.

Rosenbloom, A. (2002). How the Virtual Inspires the Real. *Communications of the ACM*. Vol. 45 (7), pp. 28-30.

Rosenfeld, R., Olsen, D., & Rudnicky, A. (2001). Universal Speech Interfaces. *Interactions*. Vol. 8 (6) pp. 34-44.

Russell, S. J., & Norvig, P. (1995). *Artificial intelligence: a modern approach*. Glenview: Prentice Hall.

Sacher, H., & Loudon, G. Uncovering the New Wireless Interaction Paradigm. *Interactions*. Vol. 9 (1), pp. 17-23.

Saddler, H. (2001). Understanding Design Representations. *Interactions*. Vol. 8 (4), pp. 17-24.

Saffer, D. (2009). Designing Gestural Interfaces. Sebastopol, O'Reilly Media.

Salas, N., & Peyton, D. (2009). Reading: Assessment, Comprehension and Teaching. New York: Nova Science.

Schank, R. C. (1997). *Virtual learning: a revolutionary approach to building a highly skilled workforce*. New York: McGraw-Hill.

Schrepp, M. (2006). On the efficiency of keyboard navigation in Web sites. *Universal Access in the Information Society*. Vol. 5 (2), Berlin: Springer-Verlag. DOI: 10.1007/s10209-006-0036-x, p. 180-188.

Scoble, R., & Israel, S. (2006). *Naked conversations: How blogs are changing the way businesses talk with customers.* Hoboken: John Wiley.

Segaran, T. (2007). *Programming Collective Intelligence: Building Smart Web 2.0 Applications.* Sebastopol: O'Reilly Media.

Shalloway, A., & Trott, J. (2001). Design Patterns Explained: A New Perspective on Object-Oriented Design. Massachusetts: Addison-Wesley.

Shapiro, S. (1987). Processing, bottom-up and top-down. In *S. C. Shapiro, editor, Encyclopedia of Artificial Intelligence*, p. 779 - 785. New York: John Wiley & Sons, Inc.

Sharp, H., Rogers, Y., & Preece, J. (2007). *Interaction design: beyond human-computer interaction.* San Francisco: Wiley.

Shipman, F. M., & Marshall, C. C. (1999). Spatial hypertext: an alternative to navigational and semantic links. *ACM Computing Surveys (CSUR)*, Vol. 31, p. 1-5.

Silva, J., Rahman, R., & El Saddik, A. (2008). Web 3.0: A vision for bridging the gap between real and virtual. In *Proceeding of the 1st ACM international workshop on Communicability design and evaluation in cultural and ecological multimedia system.* New York: ACM Press, p. 9-14.

Slaughter, S., & Ang, S. Employment Outsourcing in Information Systems. *Communications of the ACM.* Vol. 39 (4) pp. 47-54.

Snavely, N., & Garg, R., & Seitz, S. M., & Szeliski, R. (2008). Finding Paths through the world's photos. In *International Conference on Computer Graphics and Interactive Techniques, ACM SIGGRAPH 2008.* New York: ACM Press.

Snavely, N., & Seitz, S. M., & Szeliski, R. (2006). Photo Tourism: exploring photo collections in 3D. In *International Conference on Computer Graphics and Interactive Techniques, ACM SIGGRAPH 2006 Papers.* New York: ACM Press, p. 835-846.

Soh, J., & Tan, B. (2008). Mobile Gaming. *Communications of the ACM.* Vol. 51 (3), p. 35-39.

Somerville, I., Stevens, P., & Pooley, R. (2002). *Software engineering.* Massachusetts: Addison Wesley.

Stephanidis C. (2009). *Universal Access Handbook.* Oxon: Taylor & Francis.

Stroulia, E., & Systä, T. (2002). Dynamic analysis for reverse engineering and program understanding. *SIGAPP: Applied Computing Review*, Vol. 10 (1), p. 8-17.

Swamy, N. & Swamy, N. (2006). *Basic game design & creation for fun & learning.* Independence: Delmar Thomson Learning.

Takagi, H., Asakawa, C., Fukuda, K., & Maeda, J. (2004). Accessibility designer: visualizing usability for the blind. In *Proceedings of the ACM SIGACCESS conference on Computers and accessibility (ASSETS '04)*, http://dx.doi.org/10.1145/1028630.1028662.

Tapscott, D. & Williams, D. (2007). Wikinomics. Barcelona: Paidós.

Tapscott, D. (2008). *Grown up digital: how the net generation is changing your world.* New York: McGraw-Hill.

Tarr, P., Ossher, H., Harrison, W., & Jr (1999). N degrees of separation: multi-dimensional separation of concerns. In *ICSE '99: Proceedings of the 21st international conference on Software engineering.* New York: ACM Press, p. 107-119.

Theofanos, M. F., & Redish, J. (2003). Bridging the Gap: Between Accessibility and Usability. *Interactions.* Vol. 10 (6), p. 36-51.

Thiessen, P., & Chen, C. (2007). Ajax Live Regions: ReefChat Using the Fire Vox Screen Reader as a Case Example. In *Proceedings of W4A 2007*, (Banff, Canada, May 2007). New York: ACM Press, p. 136-137.

Tidwell, J. (2005). *Designing interfaces: patterns for effective interaction design*. Sebastopol: O'Reilly Media.

Tonella, P., & Ceccato, M. (2005). Refactoring the aspectizable interfaces: An empirical assessment. *IEEE Transactions on Software Engineering*, Vol. 31 (10), p. 819-832.

Van Dijk, T. (2001). *El discurso como interacción social*. Barcelona: Gedisa.

Verón, E. (1998). *La semiosis social*. Barcelona: Gedisa.

Vickery, G., & Wunsch-Vincent, S. (2007). *Participative Web And User-Created Content: Web 2.0 Wikis and Social Networking*. Paris: Organization for Economic.

Vlissides, J. M. (1998). *Pattern Hatching: Design Patterns Applied*. Massachusetts: Addison-Wesley.

Wagner, I., & Lainer, R. (2003). Designing A Visual 3-D Interface: A Reflection on Methods. *Interactions*. Vol. 10 (6), pp. 12-19.

Wagner, I., Kompast, M., & Lainer, R. (2002). Visualization Strategies for the Design of Interactive Navigable 3-D Worlds. *Interactions*. Vol. 9 (5), pp. 25-34.

West, D. (2007). *Digital Government: Technology and Public Sector Performance*, Princeton: Pricenton University Press.

Wiegers, K. E. (2003). *Software requirements*. Second edition. Redmon: Microsoft Press.

Wilson, R., Landoni, M., & Gibb, F. (2002). A user-centered approach to e-book design. *The Electronic Library*, Vol. 20 (4), p. 322-330.

Xiaoyi, C., Weigiang, K., & Kokichi, F. (2007). Formal Support for e-Government System Design with Transparency Consideration. ICEGOV '07. In *Proceedings of the 1st international conference on Theory and Practice of Electronic Governance*. New York: ACM Press, p. 20-29.

Yee, R. (2007). *Pro Web 2.0 Mashups: Remixing Data and Web Services*.Berkeley: Apress.

Yu, W., Kuber, R., Murphy, E., Strain, P., & McAllister, G. (2006). A novel multimodal interface for improving visually impaired people's web accessibility. *Virtual Reality Journal. Springer London*. Vol. 9, (2/3), p. 133-148.

Yu, W., McAllister, G., Strain, P., Kuber, R., & Murphy, E. (2005). Improving Web Accessibility Using Content-Aware Plug-ins. In *Proceedings of 2005 Conference on Human Factors in Computing Systems (CHI '05 - extended abstracts)*. New York: ACM Pres, p. 1893-1896.

Zweig, J. (1997). Ars Combinatoria: Mystical systems, procedural art, and the computer. In *Art Journal*, Vol. 56 (3), *Digital Reflections: The Dialogue of art and technology*, p. 20-29.

Compilation of References

Adobe. (n.d.). *Accessibility standards compliance.* Retrieved April 30, 2009, from http://www.adobe.com/accessibility/products/compliance/

Adomavicius, G., & Tuzhilin, A. (2005). Toward the Next Generation of Recommender Systems: A Survey of the State-of-the-Art and Possible Extensions. *IEEE Transactions on Knowledge and Data Engineering, 17*(6), 734–749. doi:10.1109/TKDE.2005.99

Agapiou, A., Maharg, P., & Nicol, E. (2009). *Learning contract management and administration via a simulated game environment.* Presented at Viz 09, 13th International Conference on Information Visualisation July 2009, Barcelona.

Agrawal, R., & Srikant, R. (1998). Fast Algorithms for Mining Association Rules. In *Readings in Database Systems,* (3rd Ed.), (pp. pages 580-592). San Francisco, CA: Morgan Kaufmann Series In Data Management Systems.

Amory, A., & Seagram, R. (2003). Educational game models: conceptualization and evaluation. *South African Journal of Higher Education, 17*(2), 206–217.

Ander-egg, E. (1986). *Techniques of Social Investigation.* Buenos Aires, Argentina: Hvmanitas.

Anderson, C. (2006). *The Long Tail: How endless choice is creating unlimited demand.* London: Random House Business Books.

Anderson, P. (2007). What is Web 2.0? Ideas, technologies and implications for education. *JISC.*

Angermeier, M. (2005). *The huge cloud lens bubble map Web2.0.* Retrieved May 8, 2009 from http://kosmar.de/archives/2005/11/11/the-huge-cloud-lens-bubble-map-Web20/

Aranguren, J. (1986). *La comunicación humana.* Madrid: Tecnos.

Arcoverde, R., Lustosa, P., Sousa, A., Soares, S., & Borba, P. (2007). AJaTS – AspectJ Transformation System: Tool Support for Aspect-Oriented Development and Refactoring. In *SBES – TOOLS 2007 Brasil.*

Aridor, Y., & Lange, D. (1998). Agent Design Patterns: Elements of Agent Applications Design. In *Proc. Second Int. Conf. Autonomous Agents,* (pp. 108-115).

Baase, S. (2007). *A Gift of Fire: Social, Legal, and Ethical Issues for Computing and the Internet* (pp. 351). Upper Saddle River: Prentice Hall.

Balakrishnan, R., Fizmaurice, G., & Kurtenbach, G. (2001). User-Interfaces for Volumetric Displays. *IEEE Software, 34*(3), 37–45.

Baldi, P. F., Lopes, C. V., Linstead, E. J., & Bajracharya, S. K. (2008). A theory of aspects as latent topics. *SIGPLAN Not., 43*(10), 543–562. doi:10.1145/1449955.1449807

Ball, T. (1999). The concept of dynamic analysis. In *ESEC/FSE-7: Proceedings of the 7th European software engineering conference held jointly with the 7th ACM SIGSOFT international symposium on Foundations of software engineering,* (pp. 216-234). London: Springer-Verlag.

Bangert-Drowns, R., Kulik, J., & Kulik, D. (1985). Effectiveness of computer-based education in secondary schools. *Journal of Computer Based Instruction, 12*(3), 59–68.

Barthes, R. (1981). *Camera Lucida.* New York: Hill and Wang.

Barton, K., & Maharg, P. (2006). Situated learning and the management of learning: a case study. *The Law Teacher, 34*(2), 141–163.

Basili, V., & Musa, J. (1991). The Future Engineering of Software: A Management Perspective. *IEEE Computer, 24*(9), 90–96.

Beagrie, N. (2005). Plenty of room at the bottom? Personal digital libraries and collections. *D-Lib magazine, 11*(6). Retrieved from http://www.dlib.org/dlib/june05/beagrie/06beagrie.html

Bekebrede, G. (2007). *Playing with multi-actor systems: Evaluation results of the Railway District online simulation-game in Sieberdam/ROCS.* Paper presented at the 38th Annual Conference of the International Simulation and Gaming Association (ISAGA), Nijmegen, The Netherlands.

Bellifemine, F., Caire, G., & Greenwood, D. (2006). *Developing Multi-Agent Systems with JADE,* (Ed.). New York: Wiley & sons.

Ben-Ari, M. (1998). *Constructivism in computer science education.* Paper presented at the SIGSCE - Technical Symposium on Computer Science Education, Atlanta, GA.

Benbunan-Fich, R., & Koufaris, M. (2008). Motivations and Contribution Behaviour in Social Bookmarking Systems: An Empirical Investigation. *Electronic Markets, 18*(2), 150–160. doi:10.1080/10196780802044933

Benett, T. (1995). *The Birth of the Museum.* London: Routledge.

Benjamin, W. (2002). *Medienaesthetische Schriften.* Frankfurt am Main, Germany: Suhrkamp.

Benkler, Y. (2006). *The Wealth of Networks: how social production transforms markets and freedom.* New Haven, CT: Yale University Press.

Bennis, W., & Biederman, P. W. (1998). None of Us Is As Smart As All of Us. *IEEE Computer, 31*(3), 116–117.

Berk, K. (2008). *Greystripe consumer insights report.* San Francisco: Greystripe Inc.

Berners Lee, T. (2006). *developerWorks Interviews,* 22nd August, 2006. Laningham (ed.).

Berners-Lee, T. (1996). WWW: Past, Present and Future. *IEEE Computer, 29*(10), 69–77.

Berners-Lee, T., Hall, W., & Shadbolt, N. (2006). The Semantic Web Revisited. *IEEE Intelligent Systems, 21*(3), 96–101. doi:10.1109/MIS.2006.62

Berners-Lee, T., Hendler, J. & Lassila, O. (May 17, 2001). The Semantic Web. *Scientific American Magazine.* Retrieved on 2008-03-26.

Bethke, E. (2003). *Game development and production.* Plano, TX: Wordware Publishing Inc.

Bevis, E. O., & Watson, J. (1990). *Towards a Caring Curriculum: A New Pedagogy for Nursing.* New York: National League for Nursing.

Bigus, J. P., & Bigus, J. (2001) *Constructing Intelligent Agents Using Java.* New York: Wiley.

Billinghurst, M., Grasset, R., & Looser, J. Designing Augmented Reality Interfaces. *Computer Graphics, 39*(1), 17–21. doi:10.1145/1057792.1057803

Binkley, D., Ceccato, M., Harman, M., Ricca, F., & Tonella, P. (2005). Automated refactoring of object oriented code into aspects. In *21st IEEE International Conference on Software Maintenance (ICSM).*

Birwhistell, R. (1974). *Diccionario de las ciencias sociales.* Madrid: Aguilar.

Bogost, I., & Poremba, C. (2006). (Forthcoming). Can Games get Real? A Closer Look at 'Documentary'. *Digital Games.*

Booch, G., Rumbaugh, J., & Jacobson, I. (2005). *The unified modeling language user guide.* Reading, MA: Addison Wesley.

Book, B. (2004). *Moving beyond the game: social virtual worlds.* Retrieved from http://www.virtualworldsreview.com

Bos, J. E., Bles, W., & Groen, E. L. (2008). A theory on visually induced motion sickness. *Health and Safety Aspects of Visual Displays, 29*(2), 47–57.

Botto, F. (1992). *Multimedia, CD-ROM and Compact Disc.* Wilmslow, UK: Sigma Press.

Bowker, G. C. (2005). *Memory Practices of the Sciences.* Cambridge, MA: MIT Press.

Bowman, S., & Willis, C. (2003). We Media: How Audiences are Shaping the Future of News and Information. *The Media Center at the American Press Institute.*

Boyd, D. M., & Ellison, N. B. (2007). Social network sites: Definition, history, and scholarship. *Journal of Computer-Mediated Communication, 13*(1).

Boyd-Barrett, O., & Rantanen, T. (1998). *The Globalization of News.* London: Sage.

Brajnovic, L. (1979). *El ámbito científico de la información.* Navarra, Spain: EUNSA.

Breu, S., & Krinke, J. (2004). Aspect Mining Using Event Traces. In *Proceedings of the 19th IEEE international Conference on Automated Software Engineering: Automated Software Engineering.* Washington, DC: IEEE Computer Society.

Brewer, J. (2005). *How People with Disabilities Use the Web.* World Wide Web Consortium (W3C), from http://www.w3.org/WAI/EO/Drafts/PWD-Use-Web/

Brin, S. & Page, L. (1998). The Anatomy of a Large-Scale Hypertextual Web Search Engine. *Computer Networks and ISDN Systems, 30*(1-7), 107--117.

Brown, G. (2008). *Social Media, Web 2.0 User-Generated Content and Virtual Communities –100 Most Asked Mass Collaboration Questions.* Brisbane, Australia: Emereo.

Brown, J. S., & Duguid, P. (2000). *The Social Life of Information.* Boston: Harvard Business School Press, Boston.

Brown, R. (1976). *Children and Television.* Beverly Hills, CA: Sage.

Broy, M. (2006). The 'Grand Challenge' in Informatics: Engineering Software-Intensive Systems. *IEEE Computer, 39*(10), 72–80.

Brudvik, J. T., Bigham, J. P., Cavander, A. C., & Ladner, R. E. (2008). Hunting for headings: sighted labeling vs. automatic classification of headings. In *Proceedings of the 10th international ACM SIGACCESS conference on Computers and accessibility,* (pp. 201-208). New York: ACM Press.

Brunet, P. (2002). Virtual Reality. *Infovis.* Retrieved April 2002, from http://www.infovis.net/printMag.php?num=82&lang=2

Bruntink, M., van Deursen, A., van Engelen, R., & Tourwe, T. (2005). On the use of clone detection for identifying crosscutting concern code. *IEEE Transactions on Software Engineering, 31*(10), 804–818. doi:10.1109/TSE.2005.114

Buffa, M., Gandon, F., Ereteo, G., Sander, P., & Faron, C. (2008). SweetWiki: A Semantic Wiki. *Web Semantics, 6*(1), 84–97.

Buie, E. (1999). HCI Standards: A Mixed Blessing. *Interaction, 6*(2), 36–42. doi:10.1145/296165.296177

Bunge, M. (1981). *The science: your method and your philosophy.* Buenos Aires, Argentina: Siglo XXI.

Buzzi, M. C., Buzzi, M., Leporini, B., & Senette, C. (2008). Making Wikipedia Editing Easier for the Blind. In *Proceedings of ACM NordiCHI2008,* (pp. 423-426). New York: ACM Press.

Byrne, T. (2009). *The case against Flex-based application UIs.* CMS Watch. Retrieved on May 15, 2009 from http://www.cmswatch.com/Trends/1492-The-case-against-Flex-based-application-Uis

Cameron, K. (2009). The Road to Greener IT Pastures. *IEEE Computer, 42*(5), 87–89.

Card, S. K., Moran, T. P., & Newell, A. (1983). *The Psychology of Human-computer Interaction* (pp. 29-97). London: Lawrence Erlbaum Associates.

Carey, D. (1996). Is Software Quality Intrinsic, Subjective, or Relational? *Software Engineering Notes, 21*, 74–75. doi:10.1145/381790.565678

Carver, C. A., Howard, R. A., & Lane, W. D. (1999). Enhancing student learning through hypermedia courseware and incorporation of student learning styles. *IEEE Transactions on Education, 42*(1), 33–38. doi:10.1109/13.746332

Casas, S., & Marcos, C. A. (2008). Exploración de Reglas de Inferencia para Automatizar la Refactorización Aspectual. *II Latin American Workshop on Aspect-Oriented Software Development (LA-WASP 2008)*, Campinas, Brasil.

Castro, S., & Mlikota, K. (2002). *Overview On E-Governance. ICTs as Tools for Improving Local Governance*. UNESCO (United Nations Educational, Scientific and Cultural Organization). Retrieved from http://portal.unesco.org/ci/en/files/6532/10391876090Overview_on_e-governance_working_paper.doc/Overview%2Bon%2Be-governance%2Bworking%2Bpaper.doc

Ceccato, M., Marin, M., Mens, K., Moonen, L., Tonella, P., & Tourwé, T. (2006). Applying and combining three different aspect mining techniques. *Software Quality Control, 14*(3), 209–231.

Cerf, V. (2007). An Information Avalanche. *IEEE Computer, 40*(1).

Chalmers, P. A. (2000). User interface improvements in computer-assisted instruction, the challenge. *Computers in Human Behavior, 16*, 507–517. doi:10.1016/S0747-5632(00)00022-4

Champoux, J. E. (1999). Film as a teaching resource. *Journal of Management Inquiry, 8*(2), 240–251. doi:10.1177/105649269982016

Chavan, A. (2009). The Washing Machine That Ate My Sari-Mistakes in Cross Cultural Desing. *Communications of the ACM, 16*(1), 26–31.

Chen, C. L., & Raman, T. V. (2008). AxsJAX: A Talking Translation Bot Using Google IMAxsJAX. Bringing web-2.0 applications to life. In *Proceedings of the 2008 international cross-disciplinary conference on Web accessibility (W4A)*, (pp. 54-56). New York: ACM Press.

Cheok, A. D., Yang, X., Ying, Z. Z., Billinghurst, M., & Kato, H. (2002*)*. Touch Space: Mixed Reality Game Space Based on Ubiquitous, Tangible, and Social Computing. *Personal and Ubiquitous Computing 6*. London: Springer Verlag.

Chiang, A. (2007). Motivate AI class with interactive computer game. In *Proc. of IEEE Int. Workshop on Digital Game and Intelligent Toy Enhanced Learning, 1*(1).

Chisolm, W., Vanderheiden, G., & Jacobs, I. (2001). Web Content Accessibility Guidelines. *Interaction, 13*(4), 34–53.

Cipolla-Ficarra, F. (1994). Sistemas Multimediales Interactivos: Aproximación a la Perspectiva Comunicacional. *Novática, 112-113*, 4–6.

Cipolla-Ficarra, F. (1996). A User Evaluation of Hypermedia Iconography. In *Proceedings Computergraphics* (pp. 182-191). Paris: GRASP.

Cipolla-Ficarra, F. (1997a). Evaluation of Multimedia Components. In *Proceedings IEEE* [Washington, DC: IEEE Computer Society.]. *Multimedia Systems, 97*, 557–564.

Cipolla-Ficarra, F. (1997b). Method and Techniques for the Evaluation of Multimedia Applications. In *Proceedings HCI International '97*, (pp. 635-638). San Francisco: Elsevier.

Cipolla-Ficarra, F. (1998). Method for evaluation of hypermedia usability. In *Proc. 7th IFAC/IFIP/IFORS/IEA Symposium on Analysis, Design and Evaluation of Man Machine Systems and Human Interface*, (pp. 173-178). Kyoto, Japan: Elsevier.

Cipolla-Ficarra, F. (1999). MEHEM: A Methodology for Heuristic Evaluation in Multimedia. In *Proceedings Sixth International Conference on Distributed Multimedia Systems - DMS'99 (KSI), IFIP* (pp. 89-96). Aizu, Japan: Elsevier.

Cipolla-Ficarra, F. (2001). Panchronics: An Attribute of the Quality for Hypermedia Systems. In *Proceedings In-*

ternational Conference on Information Systems Analysis and Synthesis, (pp. 289-294). Orlando, GA: ISAS.

Cipolla-Ficarra, F. (2002). Homepage and Communications: Quality Metrics. In *Proceedings Eight International Conference on Distributed Multimedia Systems,* (pp. 202-209). San Francisco: DMS.

Cipolla-Ficarra, F. (2003). Table of Heuristic Evaluation for Communication of the Multimedia Systems. In *Proceedings HCI International '03,* (pp. 940-944). Crete: LEA.

Cipolla-Ficarra, F. (2005). An Evaluation of Meaning and Content Quality in Hypermedia. In *CD-ROM Proceedings.* Las Vegas: HCI International.

Cipolla-Ficarra, F. (2007). A Study of Acteme on Users Unexpert of Videogames. [). Berlin: Springer-Verlag.]. *Lecture Notes in Computer Science, 4553,* 215–224. doi:10.1007/978-3-540-73111-5_25

Cipolla-Ficarra, F. (2008). *Communicability Design and Evaluation in Cultural and Ecological Multimedia Systems.* In Communicability MS 08' October 31 2008, Vancouver BC, Canada, (pp. 1-8). New York: ACM Press.

Cipolla-Ficarra, F. (2008a). Dyadic for Quality in Hypermedia Systems. In *DVD Proceedings Applied Human Factors and Ergonomics.* Las Vegas: AEI.

Cipolla-Ficarra, F. (2008b). HECHE: Heuristic Evaluation of Colours in HomepagE. In *DVD Proceedings Applied Human Factors and Ergonomics.* Las Vegas: AEI.

Cipolla-Ficarra, F. (2009). Persuasion On-Line and Communicability: The Destruction of Credibility in the Virtual Community and Cognitive Models. *Psychology of Persuasion.* New York: NovaPublishers.

Cipolla-Ficarra, F. (2009). Virtual Classroom and Communicability: Empathy and Interaction for All. *New Directions in Intelligent Interactive Multimedia Systems and Services,* (LNCS, pp. 117-127). Berlin: Springer-Verlag.

Cipolla-Ficarra, F., & Cipolla-Ficarra, M. (2008). Interactive Systems, Design and Heuristic Evaluation: The

Importance of the Diachronic Vision. In *Proceedings International Symposium on Intelligent Interactive Multimedia Systems and Services, KES IIMSS,* (pp. 625-634). Berlin: Springer-Verlag.

Cipolla-Ficarra, F., & Cipolla-Ficarra, M. (2008). Multimedia, User-Centered Design and Tourism: Simplicity, Originality and Universality. *New Directions in Intelligent Interactive Multimedia* (pp. 461-470). Berlin: Springer-Verlag.

Cipolla-Ficarra, F., & Cipolla-Ficarra, M. (2009). Attention and Motivation in Hypermedia Systems. In *Proceedings HCI International 2009,* (LNCS, pp. 78-87). Berlin: Springer-Verlag.

Cipolla-Ficarra, F., Vivas, E., & Romo, J. (2009). Credibility On-line: Quality Metrics for Evaluation. Online Communities. [). Berlin: Springer-Verlag.]. *Lecture Notes in Computer Science, 5621,* 172–181. doi:10.1007/978-3-642-02774-1_19

Colapietro, V. (1993). *Glossary of Semiotics.* New York: Paragon House.

Collis, J. Ndumu, D. & van Buskirk, C. (2000) The Zeus. *Agent Building Toolkit – ZEUS Methodology Documentation.* Retrieved from http://labs.bt.com/projects/agents/zeus

Cornelissen, B., Zaidman, A., van Deursen, A., Moonen, L., & Koschke, R. (2009). A systematic survey of program comprehension through dynamic analysis. *IEEE Transactions on Software Engineering, 20*(6), 476–493.

Craven, J., & Brophy, P. (2003). *Non-visual access to the digital library: the use of digital library interfaces by blind and visually impaired people.* Technical report. Manchester, UK: Centre for Research in Library and Information Management (CERLIM). Retrieved from http://www.cerlim.ac.uk/pubs/index.php

Csikszentmihályi, M. (1990). *Flow: the psychology of optimal experience* (1 ed.). New York: Harper Perennial.

Csikszentmihalyi, M. (1996). *Creativity-flow and the psychology of discovery and invention.* New York: Harper perennial.

Cutumisu, M. (2006). Generating Ambient Behaviors in Computer RolePlaying Games. *IEEE Intelligent Systems*, *21*(5), 19–27. doi:10.1109/MIS.2006.92

Cyberdam. (n.d.). Retrieved from http://www.cyberdam.nl

Cych, L. (2006). Social Networks. In *Emerging Technologies for Education, BECTA* (ed.). Coventry, UK: Becta ICT Research.

Dahlbom, B., & Mathiassen, L. (1997). The Future of Our Profession. *Communications of the ACM*, *40*(6), 80–89. doi:10.1145/255656.255706

Dance, F. (1973). *Teoría de la comunicación humana*. Buenos Aires: Troquel.

Daston, L., & Gallison, P. (2007). *Objectivity*. New York: Zone Books.

Davies, J., Goel, A. K., & Nersessian, N. J. (2005). *A cognitive model of visual analogical problem-solving transfer*. Paper presented at the Nineteenth Annual International Joint Conference on Artificial Intelligence, Denver, CO.

De Souza, C. (2004). The *semiotic engineering on human-computer interaction*. Cambridge, UK: The MIT Press.

De Souza, C., Barbosa, S., & Silva, S. (2001). Semiotic Engineering Principles for Evaluating End-User Programming Environments. *Interacting with Computers*, *13*, 467–495. doi:10.1016/S0953-5438(00)00051-5

Debray, R. (1995). *Vie et mort de l'image*. Paris: Gallimard.

Department of the Premier and Cabinet - Office of e-Government. (2006). *Guidelines for State Government Websites Version 2.1*, Australia. Retrieved from http://www.egov.dpc.wa.gov.au/documents/WebGuidelines-Version2.1_final.doc

Desurvire, H., Caplan, M., & Toth, J. A. (2004). *Using heuristics to evaluate the playability of games*. Paper presented at the Conference for human-computer interaction, Vienna, Austria.

Dharaskar, R., Bajpayee, V., Chube, N., & Thakre, V. (2005). E-learning software for mathematical concepts and algorithms of computer graphics. *Information Technology Journal*, *5*(1), 172–176.

Dias, B., & Brewer, E. (2009). How Computer Science Serves the Developing World. *Communications of the ACM*, *52*(6), 74–80. doi:10.1145/1516046.1516064

Dileep, K., Yeonseung, R., & Hyksoo, J. (2008). Quality of Service (QoS) of Voice over MAC Protocol 802.11 using NS-2. In *Proc. MSCommunicability '08* (pp. 39-44). New York: ACM Press.

Dillard, J., & Pfau, M. (2002). *Persuasion Handbook*. Thousand Oaks: Sage.

Doctorow, C., Dornfest, F., Johnson, J., & Powers, S. (2002). *Essential Blogging*. Sebastol, CA: O'Reilly.

Dondlinger, M. J. (2007). Educational video game design: a review of the literature. *Journal of Applied Educational Technology*, *4*(1), 21–31.

Downes, S. (2004). Educational Blogging. *EDUCAUSE Review*, *39*(5), 14–26.

Dubberly, H., Pangaro, P., & Haque, U. (2009). What is Interaction? Are There Different Types? *Interaction*, *16*(1), 69–75. doi:10.1145/1456202.1456220

Ebersbach, A., Glaser, M., & Heigl, R. (2006). *Wiki: Web Collaboration*. Berlin: Springer-Verlag.

Eberts, R. (1992). *User Interface Design*. London: Pretince-Hall.

Eco, U. (2001). *Apocalitici e integrati*. Milano: Bompiani.

Edmundson, A. (2008). *Globalized E-learning –Cross Cultural Dimension*. Saarbrücken, Germany: VDM Verlarg.

Egenfeldt-Nielsen, S. (2005). *Beyond edutainment: exploring the educational potential of computer games*. University of Copenhagen.

Ehman, L. H., & Glenn, A. D. (1987). *Computer-based Education in the Social Sciences,* (pp. 284 825). Bloom-

ington, IN: Social Studies Development Center and ERIC Clearing house for Social Studies/Social Science Education, ED.

Ellison, N., Lampe, C., & Steinfield, C. (2009). Social Network Sites and Society: Current Trends and Future Possibilities. *Interaction, 16*(1), 6–9. doi:10.1145/1456202.1456204

Engelhardt, M., Hildebrand, A., Lange, D., & Schmidt, T. C. (2006). Reasoning about eLearning Multimedia Objects. In J. Van Ossenbruggen, G. Stamou, R. Troncy & V. Tzouvaras (Ed.) *Proceeding of First International Workshop on Semantic Web Annotations for Multimedia (SWAMM).*

Ernst, M. D. (2003). Static and dynamic analysis: Synergy and duality. In *WODA 2003: ICSE Workshop on Dynamic Analysis* (pp. 24-27), Portland, OR.

European Union. (2008). *Communication from the Commission to the European Parliament, the Council, the European economic and social Committee and the Committee of the regions.-"Towards an accessible information society."* Retrieved from http://eur-lex.europa.eu/LexUriServ/LexUriServ.do?uri=CELEX:52008DC0804:EN:NOT

Facer, K. (2003). *Computer Games and Learning* (Report). Bristol, UK: FutureLab.

Farooq, U., Kannampallil, T. G., Song, Y., Ganoe, C. H., Carroll, J. M., & Giles, L. (2007). Evaluating tagging behavior in social bookmarking systems: metrics and design heuristics. In *'GROUP '07: Proceedings of the 2007 international ACM conference on Supporting group work,'* (pp. 351—360). New York: ACM.

Fayad, M. E., & Johnson, R. E. (1999). Domain-Specific application Frameworks. *Frameworks experience by Industry.* New York: John Wiley & Sons, Inc.

Felder, R. M., & Breng, R. (2004). *The ABC's of engineering education: Abet, Bloom's taxonomy, cooperative learning, and so on.* Paper presented at the American Society for Engineering Education Annual Conference & Exposition.

Fenton, N. (1994). Software Measurement: A Necessary Scientific Basis. *IEEE Transactions on Software Engineering, 20*(3), 199–206. doi:10.1109/32.268921

Fenton, N. (1997). *Software Metrics: A Rigorous Approach.* Cambridge, UK: Chapman & Hall.

Fernandes, T. (1995). *Global Interface Design: A Guide to Designing International User Interfaces.* San Diego: Academic Press Professional.

Ferres, L., Verkhogliad, P., & Boucher, L. (2007). L. Natural language interaction with graphical representations of statistical data. In *Proceeding of ACM International cross-disciplinary conference on Web accessibility (W4A),* (pp.132-133). New York: ACM Press.

Fisch, S. M. (2005). *Making educational computer games 'educational'.* Paper presented at the 4th International Conference for Interaction Design and Children, Boulder, CO.

Fischer, G. (2006). Distributed intelligence: extending the power of the unaided, individual human mind. In *AVI '06: Proceedings of the working conference on Advanced visual interfaces,* (pp.7-14). New York: ACM Press.

Fleming, J. (1998). *WEB navigation: designing the user experience.* Sebastapol, CA: O'Reilly.

Foraker Design. (2005). *Usability first. Accessibility: Types of Accessibility Aids.* Retrieved April 30, 2009, from http://www.usabilityfirst.com/accessibility/types.txl

Fowler, M. (1999). *Refactoring: Improving the Design of Existing Code.* Reading, MA: Addison Wesley.

Frasca, G. (2003). Simulation versus Narrative – Introduction to Ludology. In Wolf, M. J. P., & Perron, B. (Eds.), *The Video Game Theory Reader.* New York, London: Routledge.

Furlong, E. J. (1961). *Imagination.* London: George Allen & Unwin.

Furnas, G. (1987). The Vocabulary Problem in Human–System Communication. *Communications of the ACM, 30*(11), 964–971. doi:10.1145/32206.32212

Galvão, J. R. (2000). *Modeling reality with simulation games for a cooperative learning.* Paper presented at the Winter Simulation Conference.

Gamma, E., Helm, R., Johnson, R., & Vlissides, J. (1995). *Design patterns - Elements of reusable object-oriented software.* Reading, MA: Addison Wesley.

Gamma, R., & Vlissides, J. (1995). *Design Patterns: Elements of Reusable Object-Oriented Software,* (Ed.). Boston: Addison-Wesley Professional Computing Series.

Garrett, J. J. (2005). Ajax: a new approach to Web applications. *AdaptivePath.com.* Retrieved on May 15, 2009.

Gee, J. P. (2004). *Situated Language and Learning: A Critique of Traditional Schooling.* London: Routledge.

Gendarmi, D., & Lanubile, F. (2006). *Community-Driven Ontology Evolution Based on Folksonomies, On the Move to Meaningful Internet Systems 2006: OTM 2006 Workshops,* (pp. 181—188).

Gerbier, L. (2001). Découpage fantastique et continuité graphique dans la bande dessinée. *Image and Narrative, 2.* Retrieved Sept. 12, 2008 from http://www.imageandnarrative.be/

Ghezzi, C., Mandrioli, D., & Jazayeri, M. (2003). *Fundamentals of Software Engineering.* Upper Saddle River, NJ: Prentice Hall.

Gillmor, D. Noren, A., (eds.). (2004). *We the Media: Grassroots Journalism by the People, for the People.* Sebastopol, CA: O'Reilly Media, Inc.

Ginzburg, C. (1989). *Clues, Myths, and the Historic Method.* Baltimore: Johns Hopkins University Press.

Glaser, M. (2006, September 27). *Your Guide to Citizen Journalism.* Public Broadcasting Service. Retrieved on May 9, 2009.

Gobet, F., Lane, P. C. R., Croker, S., Cheng, P. C.-H., Jones, G., Oliver, I., & Pine, J. (2001). Chunking mechanisms in human learning. *Trends in Cognitive Sciences, 5*(6), 236–243. doi:10.1016/S1364-6613(00)01662-4

Goble, C., Harper, S., & Stevens, R. (2000). The travails of visually impaired web travellers. In *Proceedings of the Eleventh ACM on Hypertext and Hypermedia* (pp. 1–10). New York: ACM Press.

Golder, S., & Huberman, B. A. (2006). The Structure of Collaborative Tagging Systems. *Journal of Information Science, 32*(2), 198–208. doi:10.1177/0165551506062337

Google. (2007). *Google Web Toolkit Mission Statement.* Retrieved on May 15, 2009 from http://code.google.com/Webtoolkit/makinggwtbetter.html#introduction

Gould, H., Hughes, M., Maharg, P., & Nicol, E. (2008). The narrative event diagram: a tool for designing professional simulations. In D. Gibson, (Ed.), *Digital Simulations for Improving Education: Learning Through Artificial Teaching Environments,* (pp. 111-114).

Gray, J. (1996). Evolution of Data Management. *IEEE Computer, 29*(10), 47–58.

Grimes, J., & Potel, M. (1991). What is Multimedia? *IEEE Computer Graphics, 11*(1), 49–52. doi:10.1109/38.67700

Han, J., & Kamber, M. (2006). *Data Mining, Second Edition: Concepts and Techniques.* San Francisco: The Morgan Kaufmann Series in Data Management Systems.

Hanenberg, S., Oberschulte, C., & Unland, R. (2003). Refactoring of aspect-oriented software. In *4th International Conf. on Object-Oriented and Internet-based Technologies, Concepts, and Applications for a Networked World,* (pp. 19-35), Erfurt, Germany.

Hannemann, J. (2006). Aspect-Oriented Refactoring: Classification and Challenges. In *Workshop on Linking Aspect Technology and Evolution (LATE'06), 5th International Conference on Aspect-Oriented Software Development (AOSD'06),* Bonn, Germany.

Hannemann, J., & Kiczales, G. (2002). Design Pattern Implementation in Java and AspectJ. In *Proceedings of the 17th ACM conference on Object-oriented programming, systems, languages, and applications,* (pp. 161-173). New York: ACM Press.

Hannemann, J., Murphy, G. C., & Kiczales, G. (2005). Role-based refactoring of crosscutting concerns. In

Proceedings of the 4th international conference on Aspect-oriented software development, (pp. 135–146). Chicago: ACM Press.

Hardaway, D., Hogan, M., & Mathieu, R. (2005). Outsourcing the University Computer Lab. *IEEE Computer, 38*(9), 100–102.

Hastings, R. (2009). *Web 1.0.* Retrieved July 19, 2009 from http://en.wikipedia.org/wiki/Web_1.0

Hébert, S., Béland, R., Dionne-Fournelle, O., Crête, M., & Lupien, S. J. (2005). Physiological stress response to video-game playing: the contribution of built-in music. *Life Sciences, 76,* 2371–2380. doi:10.1016/j.lfs.2004.11.011

Hegland, M. (2003). *Algorithms for association rules,* (LNAI, pp. 226-234). New York: Springer-Verlag.

Hemmeninger, D. (2007). The ACM and IEEE-CS Guidelines for Undegraduate CS Education. *Communications of the ACM, 50*(5), 46–53. doi:10.1145/1230819.1230838

Hildmann, H., Hainey, T., & Livingstone, D. (2007). *Psychology and logic: design considerations for a customisable educational resource management game.* Paper presented at the Fifth Annual International Conference in Computer Game Design and Technology, Liverpool, UK.

Hingston, P., Combes, B. & Masek, M. (2006). Teaching an undergraduate AI course with games and simulation. *LNCS 3942,* (vol. 1, pp. 494-506).

Hirose, M. (2006). Virtual Reality Technology and Museum Exhibit. *The International Journal of Virtual Reality, 5*(2), 31–36.

Holzhauer, R. W. (2004). *Sieberdam – Designing a Virtual Town for Academic Legal Education.* Retrieved from: http://oldwww.frg.eur.nl/lia/icto/projecten/rechtenonline/sieberdam.pdf

Horn, R. (1989). *Mapping Hypertext.* Waltham: Lexington Press.

Horst, B. (2000). Leibniz' Theater der Natur und Kunst. In Bredekamp, Brüning, Weber, *Theater der Natur und Kunst,* (pp. 12-19). Berlin: Henschel Verlag.

Howard, C. (2006). *Learning, study and review methods: a fun way to learn and study complex theoretical content.* Paper presented at the Annual ASCILITE Conference: Who's learning? Whose technology? Sidney, Australia.

Hughes, A. L., Palen, L., Sutton, J., Liu, S. B., & Vieweg, S. (2008), Site-seeing in disaster: An examination of on-line social convergence. In *Proceedings of the 2008 ISCRAM Conference,* Washington, 2008.

INDEC - Statistics and Census National Institute. (2001). *Censo Poblacional.* Argentine. Retrieved from http://www.indec.mecon.ar/

International Society for Augmentative and Alternative Communication. (n.d.). Retrieved from http://www.isaac-online.org/en/home.shtml

International Standard Organization [ISO]. (1998). *ISO 9241-11: Ergonomic Requirements for Office Work with Visual Display Terminals (VDTs), Part 11: Guidance on Usability,* (1st Ed.), 1998-03-15. Geneva, Switzerland: International Organization for Standardization.

Ivory, M. Y., Yu, S., & Gronemyer, K. (2004). Search result exploration: a preliminary study of blind and sighted users' decision making and performance. In *Extended abstracts of CHI 2004* (pp. 453-1456). New York: ACM Press.

Iwamoto, M., & Zhao, J. (2003). Refactoring aspect-oriented programs. In *Proc. of 4th AOSD Modeling With UML Workshop, UML'2003,* San Francisco.

Jacobson, I. (1995). *The use-case construct in object-oriented software engineering,* (pp. 309-336).

Johnson, L. A., & Schleiyer, T. K. L. (2003). Developing high-quality educational software. *Journal of Dental Education, 67*(11), 1209–1220.

Johnson, R., & Foote, B. (1988). Designing Reusable Classes. *Journal of Object-Oriented Programming, 1*(2), 22–35.

Jonassen, D. H. (2003). *Handbook of Research on Educational Communications and Technology.* Mahwah, NJ: Lawrence Erlbaum, Inc. *KODOS.* (n.d.). Retrieved from http://cps.tbm.tudelft.nl/node/95

Jones, M. L. (2006). *The Good Life in the Scientific Revolution*. Chicago: University of Chicago Press.

Kellens, A., Mens, K., & Tonella, P. (2007). A Survey of Automated Code-Level Aspect Mining Techniques. In *Transactions on Aspect-Oriented Software Development IV*, (LNCS Vol. 4640 pp. 143-162). Berlin: Springer Verlag.

Kessler Piveta, E., Hecht, M., Soares Pimenta, M., & Price, R. T. (2006)... *Detecting Bad Smells in AspectJ. JUCS*, *12*(7), 811–827.

Kiczales, G., Hilsdale, E., Hugunin, J., Kersten, M., Palm, J., & Griswold, W. G. (2001). An overview of aspectj. In J.L. Knudsen, & J.L. Knudsen, (Eds.), *ECOOP*, (LNCS Vol. 2072, pp. 327-353). Berlin: Springer.

Kim, I.C. (2006). 3D interactive computer games as a pedagogical tool. *LNCS 4270*, (Vol. 1, pp. 536-544)

Kit, E. (1995). *Software Testing in the Real World –Improving the Process*. New York: Addision Wesley.

Kleinberg, J. (2008). The Convergence of Social and Technological Networks. *Communications of the ACM*, *51*(11), 66–72. doi:10.1145/1400214.1400232

Kleinberg, J. (2008). The Convergence of Social and Technological Networks. *Communications of the ACM*, *51*(11), 66–72. doi:10.1145/1400214.1400232

Klemperer, P. (2006). *Network Effects and Switching Costs: Two Short Essays for the New Palgrave*. Working Paper series, Social Science Research Network. Retrieved on May 21, 2009 from http://papers.ssrn.com/sol3/papers.cfm?abstract_id=907502

Koivunen, M., & May, M. (2002). *Exploring Usability Enhancements in W3C Process* [PowerPoint slides]. Retrieved from http://www.w3.org/2002/Talks/0104-usabilityprocess/slide3-0.html

Koschke, R., & Quante, J. (2005). On dynamic feature location. In *ASE '05: Proceedings of the 20th IEEE/ACM international Conference on Automated software engineering*, (pp. 86-95). New York: ACM Press.

Köstering, S. (2003). *Natur zum Anschauen*. Köln, Germany: Böhlau Verlag.

Kotsiantis, S., & Kanellopoulos, D. (2006). Association rules mining: A recent overview. In *International Transactions on Computer Science and Engineering*, (pp. 71-82).

Kraemer, K., Dedrick, J., & Sharma, P. (2009). One Laptop Per Child: Vision vs. Reality. *Communications of the ACM*, *52*(6), 66–73. doi:10.1145/1516046.1516063

Lasica, J. D. (2003, August 7). What is Participatory Journalism? *Online Journalism Review*. Retrieved on May 9, 2009.

Lassila, O., & Hendler, J. (2007). Embracing Web 3.0. *Internet Computing*, *11*(3), 90–93. doi:10.1109/MIC.2007.52

Lazar, J., Allen, A., Kleinman, J., & Malarkey, C. (2007). What frustrates screen reader users on the web: A study of 100 blind users. *International Journal of Human-Computer Interaction*, *22*(3), 247–269.

Lee, E. A.-L., & Wong, K. W. (2008). A Review of Using Virtual Reality for Learning. In Pan, Z. et al. (Eds.), *Transactions on Edutainment I*, (LNCS Vol. 5080). Berlin: Springer Verlag.

Lee, M., & Hsu, W. (2005). Improving data quality: eliminating dupes & I-D-ing those spurious links. *IEEE Potential*, *24*(2), 35–38. doi:10.1109/MP.2005.1462465

Leporini, B., Andronico, P., Buzzi, M., & Castillo, C. (2008). Evaluating a modified Google user interface via screen reader. *Universal Access in the Information Society*, *7*(3), 155–175. doi:10.1007/s10209-007-0111-y

Leporini, B., Paternò, F., & Spano, L. D. (2009). *Is flash really accessible when interacting through screen readers?* Accepted by AAATE conference, 30 August - 2 September, 2009, Florence, Italy.

Leuthold, S., Bargas-Avila, J. A., & Opwis, K. (2008). Beyond web content accessibility guidelines: Design of enhanced text user interfaces for blind internet users. *International Journal of Human-Computer Studies*, *66*(4), 257–270. doi:10.1016/j.ijhcs.2007.10.006

Life, S. (n.d.). Retrieved from http://secondlife.com/

Light, A. (2004). Audience Design: Interacting with Networked Media. *Interaction, 11*(2), 60–62. doi:10.1145/971258.971279

Lindgaard, G. (1989). Testing the Usability of Interactive Computer Systems, In G. Lindgaard & J. Millar (Ed.), *Testing the Usability of Interactive Computer Systems, Proceedings of Workshop at HCI Australia'89,* (pp. 1-13). Ergonomics Society of Australia, Computer-Human Interaction Special Interest Group.

Liu, S. B., Palen, L., Sutton, J., Hughes, A. L., & Vieweg, S. (2008), In search of the bigger picture: The emergent role of on-line photo sharing in times of disaster. In *ISCRAM '08: Proceedings of the 5th International ISCRAM conference,* (pp.140–149).

Macdonald, N. (2004). Can HCI Shape the Future of Mass Communications? *Interaction, 11*(2), 42–47. doi:10.1145/971258.971272

Maes, P. (1995). Intelligent Software. *Scientific American, 273*(3), 84–86.

Maharg, P. (2006a). Authenticity in learning: transactional learning in virtual communities. *Innovating E-learning 2006: Transforming Learning Experiences.* Retrieved from http://www.jisc.ac.uk/elp_conference06.html

Maharg, P. (2006b). On the edge: ICT and the transformation of professional legal learning. *Web Journal of Current Legal Issues, 3.* Retrieved from http://wejcli.ncl.ac.k/2006/issue3/maharg3.html

Maharg, P., & Owen, M. (2007). Simulations, learning and the metaverse: changing cultures in legal education. *Journal of Information, Law, Technology, 1.* Retrieved from http://www2.warwick.ac.uk/fac/soc/law/elj/jilt/2007_1

Malizia, A., Bellucci, A., Levialdi, S. G., Diaz, P., & Aedo, I. (2009). A visual Storyboard System to support back-channel communication for emergencies. Submitted to *Journal of Visual Languages and Computing (JVLC).*

Mallone, T. W. (1980). *What makes things fun to learn? Heuristics for designing instructional computer games.* Paper presented at the Symposium on Small Systems, Palo Alto, CA.

Mandl, H., Gruber, H., & Renkl, A. (1994). Knowledge application in complex systems. In S. Vosniadou, E.D. Corte & H. Mandl, (Eds.), *Teachnology-based Learning Environments* (pp. 47-50). Berlin: Springer-Verlag.

Marcos Mora, M., & Rovira Fontanals, C. (2005). *Usability Evaluación de la Usabilidad en Sistemas de Información Web Municipales: Metodología de análisis y desarrollo.* Barcelona, Spain: Pompeu Fabra University. Retrieved from http://www.semanticaweb.net/archives/2005_evaluacion-municipales-isko.pdf

Marcus, A. (1993). Human Comunications Issues in Advanced UIs. *Communications of the ACM, 36*(4), 101–109. doi:10.1145/255950.153670

Marcus, A., Gould. (2000). Crosscurrents –Cultural Dimensions and Global Web User-Interface Design. *Interaction, 12*(4), 32–46. doi:10.1145/345190.345238

Marin, M. (2004). Refatoring Jhotdraw's Undo Concerns to AspectJ. In *Proceedings For Workshop Aspect Reverse Engineering (WARE2004).*

Marin, M., Moonen, L., & van Deursen, A. (2005). An approach to aspect refactoring based on crosscutting concern types. In *Proceedings of the 2005 workshop on Modeling and analysis of concerns in software,* (pp. 1-5). St. Louis, MO: ACM Press.

Marin, M., Van Deursen, A., & Moonen, L. (2007). Identifying crosscutting concerns using fan-in analysis. *ACM Transactions on Software Engineering and Methodology, 17*(1), 1–37. doi:10.1145/1314493.1314496

Marin, M., van Deursen, A., Moonen, L., & van der Rijst, R. (2009). An integrated Crosscutting Concern Migratin Strategy and ts Semi-Automated Application to JHotDraw. *Automatic Software Engieneering, 16,* 323–356. doi:10.1007/s10515-009-0051-2

Marvin, C. (1988). *When Old Technologies Were New.* New York: Oxford University Press.

Mathes, A. (2004). *Folksonomies --- Cooperative Classification and Communication Through Shared Metadata.* Technical report, Computer Mediated Communication (LIS590CMC), Urbana-Champaign, Illinois.

Mayer, R. E., & Anderson, R. B. (1992). The instructive animation: helping students build connections between words and pictures in multimedia learning. *Journal of Educational Psychology, 84*(4), 444–452. doi:10.1037/0022-0663.84.4.444

McFarland, D., & Wolpaw, J. (2008). Brain-Computer Interface Operation of Robotic and Prothetic Devices. *IEEE Computer, 10*(4), 52–56.

McLuhan, M., & Power, B. (1992). *The Global Village: Transformations in World Life and Media in the 21st Century.* Oxford, UK: Oxford University Press.

McQuail, D. (2002). *Reader in Mass Communication Theory.* London: Sage.

McQuail, D. (2005). *Mass Communication Theory.* London: Sage.

Meleis, H. (1996). Toward the Information Network. *IEEE Computer, 29*(10), 59–67.

Mens, K., Kellens, A., & Krinke, J. (2008). Pitfalls in aspect mining. In *WCRE '08: Proceedings of the 2008 15th Working Conference on Reverse Engineering,* (pp. 113–122). Washington, DC: IEEE Computer Society.

Mitchell, W., & McCullough, M. (1995). *Digital Design Media.* New York: ITP.

Monteiro, M. P. (2004). *Catalogue of refactorings for AspectJ.* Universidade do Minho.

Monteiro, M. P., & Fernandes, J. M. (2005). Towards a catalog of aspect-oriented refactorings. In *Proceedings of the 4th international conference on Aspect-oriented software development,* (pp. 111–122). Chicago: ACM Press.

Mozilla Developer Center. (n.d.). *AJAX.* Retrieved April 30, 2009, from http://developer.mozilla.org/en/docs/AJAX

Mulholland, J. (1994). *Handbook of Persuasive Tactics: A Handbook of Strategies for Influencing Others Through Communication.* London: Routledge.

Muller, N. (1996). Multimedia over the Network. *Byte, 31*(3), 73–83.

Murugesan, S. (2007). Understanding Web 2.0. *IT Professional, 9*(4), 34–41. doi:10.1109/MITP.2007.78

Myers, B. A., Ko, A. J., & Burnett, M. M. (2006). Invited research overview: end-user programming. In *CHI '06 Extended Abstracts on Human Factors in Computing Systems,* Montréal, Québec, Canada, April 22 - 27, 2006, CHI '06, (pp. 75-80). New York: ACM.

Nielsen, J. (1990). *Hypertext and Hypermedia.* San Diego: Academic Press.

Nielsen, J. (1992). The Usability Engineering Life Cycle. *IEEE Computer, 25*(3), 12–22.

Nielsen, J. (1993). *Usability engineering.* San Diego: Morgan Kaufmann.

Nielsen, J. (1996). Usability Metrics: Tracking Interface Improvements. *IEEE Software, 13*(6), 12–13.

Nielsen, J. (2001) *Coordinating User Interfaces for Consistency.* San Francisco: Morgan Kaufmann Publishers.

Nielsen, J. (2001). *Designing Web Usability: The Practice of Simplicity.* San Francisco: New Riders Publishing.

Nielsen, J., & del Galdo, E. (1996). *International User Interfaces.* New York: John Wiley & Sons.

Nielsen, J., & Loranger, H. (2006). *Prioritizing Web Usability.* San Francisco: New Riders Publishing.

Nielsen, J., & Mack, R. (1994). *Usability Inspection Methods.* New York: Wiley.

Norman, D. (2004). *Emotional Design: Why We Love (or Hate) Everyday Things.* New York: Basic Books.

Nöth, W. (1995). *Handbook of Semiotics.* Indianapolis: Indiana University Press.

O'Reilly, T. (2005, September 30th). *What is Web 2.0: Design Patterns and Business Models for the next generation of software.* Sebastol, CA: O'Reilly Media Inc. Retrieved 08/05/09 from http://www.oreillynet.com/pub/a/oreilly/tim/news/2005/09/30/what-is-Web-20.html

O'Reilly, T. (2006, December). *Web 2.0 compact definition: Trying again.* Retrieved from http://radar.oreilly.com/archives/2006/12/Web-20-compact.html

O'Reilly, T. (2007). What is Web 2.0: Design Patterns and Business Models for the Next Generation of Software, Communications & Strategies. *International journal of digital economics, 65,* 17-37.

One Laptop Per Child. (2009). Mission Statement. *One Laptop Per Child.* Retrieved February 28, 2009, from http://laptop.org/en/vision/mission/index2.shtml

ONTI - National Bureau for Information Technologies. (2005). E-Governance Plan Decree 378/2005; Argentine. http://www.sgp.gov.ar/contenidos/onti/productos/pnge/docs/pnge_decreto_378_2005.pdf

Oren, E., Breslin, J., & Decker, S. (2006). How Semantics Make Better Wikis. In *Proceedings of WWW2006,* May 23-26, 2006, Edinburgh, Scotland. New York: ACM Press.

Owen, M. (2004). *An anatomy of Games, a discussion paper.* Bristol, UK: Futurelab.

Pantic, M., Zwitserloot, R., & Grootjans, R. J. (2005). Teaching introductory artificial intelligence using a simple agent framework. *IEEE Transactions on Education, 48*(3), 382–390. doi:10.1109/TE.2004.842906

Parkes, A., Poupyrev, I., & Ishii, H. (2008). Designing Kinetic Interactions for Organic User Interfaces. *Communications of the ACM, 51*(6), 58–65. doi:10.1145/1349026.1349039

Paternò, F. (1999). *Model-Based Design and Evaluation of Interactive Application.* London: Springer-Verlag.

Pernice, K., & Nielsen, J. (2001). *Beyond ALT Text: Making the Web Easy to Use for Users with Disabilities.* Fremont, CA: Nielsen Norman Group. Retrieved from http://www.nngroup.com/reports/accessibility/beyond_ALT_text.pdf

Petrie, H., Fraser, H., & Neil, K. (2004). Tension, what tension? website accessibility and visual design. In *Proceeding of International World Wide Web Conference* (pp. 13-18). New York: ACM Press.

Pfleeger, S. (2008). Software Metrics: Progress after 25 Years. *IEEE Software, 25*(6), 32–34. doi:10.1109/MS.2008.160

Piaget, J. (1993). *The Children Machine.* New York: Basic Books.

Pontifical Catholic University of Chile. (2006). *Estudio Sitios Web Municipales: e-Government en Chile.* Retrieved from http://www.cetiuc.cl/wp-content/uploads/2007/01/presentacion-estudio-municipalidades.pdf

Porter, J. (2006). *The del.icio.us lesson.* Retrieved May 11, 2009 from http://bokardo.com/archives/the-delicious-lesson/

Pree, W. (1996) *Patterns.* Sigs books and multimedia, New Cork.

Preece, J. (1998). Empathic Communities: Reaching Out Across the Web. *Interaction, 5,* 32–43. doi:10.1145/274430.274435

Pressman, R. (2005). *Software Engineering –A Practitioner's Approach.* New York: McGraw-Hill.

Reardon, K. (1981). *Persuasion. Theory and Context.* London: Sage.

Reeves, B., & Nass, C. (1998). *The Media Equation –How People Treat Computers, Television, and New Media Like Real People and Places.* Cambridge, UK: Cambridge University Press.

Rieber, L. P., & Parmley, M. W. (1995). To teach or not to teach? Comparing the use of computer based simulations in deductive versus inductive approaches to learning with adults in science. *Journal of Educational Computing Research, 14*(4), 359–374.

Roa, J., Gutierrez, M., & Stegmayer, G. (2008). FAIA: Framework para la enseñanza de agentes en IA. *IE Comunicaciones: Revista Iberoamericana de Informática Educativa, 1*(7), 1–10.

Robinson, G., & Cargill, C. (1996). History and Impact of Computer Standards. *IEEE Computer, 29*(10), 79–85.

Rollings, A., & Morris, D. (2000). *Game architecture and design.* The Coriolis Group.

Russell, S., & Norvig, P. (2003). *Artficial Intelligence: A Modern Approach,* (2nd Ed.). New York: Prentice-Hall.

Russo, P., & Boor, S. (1993). How Fluent is Your Interface? Designing for International Users. In *Proceedings IN-TERCHI '93,* (pp. 342-347). Amsterdam: ACM Press.

Ruthven, I. (2008). Contextual factors affecting the utility of surrogates within exploratory search. *Information Processing & Management, 40*(2), 437–462. doi:10.1016/j.ipm.2007.08.002

Rystedt, H., & Lindwall, O. (2004). The interactive construction of learning foci in simulation-based learning environments: a case study of an anaesthesia course. *PsychNology, 2*(92), 168–188.

Salah, M., & Mancoridis, S. (2004). A hierarchy of dynamic software views: from object-interactions to feature-interactions. In *Software Maintenance, 2004, Proceedings 20th IEEE International Conference,* (pp. 72-81).

Sanders, L. (2008). An Evolving Map of Deing Practice and Design Research. *Interaction, 15*(6), 13–17. doi:10.1145/1409040.1409043

Sartre, J.-P. (2006). *The Imaginary.* Abingdon, UK: Routledge.

Satava, R. M. (2001). Surgical education and surgical Simulation. *World Journal of Surgery, 25*(11), 1484–1489. doi:10.1007/s00268-001-0134-0

Saussure, F. (1990). *Course in General Linguistics.* New York: McGraw-Hill.

Scapin, D., & Vanderdonckt, J. Farenc, C.H., Bastide, R., Bastien, CH., Leulier, C., Mariage, C. & Palanque, P.H. (2000). Transferring Knowledge of User Interfaces Guidelines to the Web. In *Proceeding of International Workshop on Tools for Working with Guidelines TF-WWG'2000* (pp. 293-303). London: Springer-Verlag.

Schachter, J. (2006), TR35 2006 Young Innovator: Joshua Schachter, 32 (Del.icio.us [Yahoo])". *Technology Review.* Retrieved on May 21, 2009.

Schaffer, D. W. (2004). Pedagogical praxis: the professions as models for post-industrial education. *Teachers College Record, 106*(7), 1401–1421. doi:10.1111/j.1467-9620.2004.00383.x

Schoen, D., & Bennett, J. (1996) Reflective Conversation with Materials. In T.A. Winograd (Ed.) *Bringing Design to Software* (pp. 171-184). New York: ACM Press.

Scott, K. (2009). Is Usability Obsolete? *Interaction, 16*(3), 6–11. doi:10.1145/1516016.1516018

Sears, A. (2007). *The Human-Computer Interaction Handbook: Fundamentals, Envolving Technologies and Emerging Applications.* New York: LEA.

Shadbolt, N. (2006). Private conversation at *Memories for Life: the future of our pasts* event. British Library, London, Dec. 12th 2006.

Shaffer, D. W. (2006). *How computer games help children learn.* New York: Palgrave.

Shaw, R. (2005). *Web 2.0? It doesn't exist.* Retrieved from http://blogs.zdnet.com/ip-telephony/?p=805

Shepherd, D., Gibson, E., & Pollock, L.L. (2004). Design and evaluation of an automated aspect mining tool. In *Arabnia, H. R., Reza, Software Engineering Research and Practice,* (pp. 601-607).

Shepherd, D., Pollock, L. L., & Tourwé, T. (2005). Using language clues to discover crosscutting concerns . *ACM SIGSOFT Software Engineering Notes, 30*(4), 1–6. doi:10.1145/1082983.1083129

Shih, E. (2008). IT Diffusion in Developing Countries. *Communications of the ACM, 51*(2), 43–48. doi:10.1145/1314215.1340913

Shneiderman, B. (2005). *Designing the User Interface.* Reading, MA: Addision Wesley.

SimPLE: Simulation Professional Learning Environment. (n.d.). Final project report. Retrieved from http://www.jisc.ac.uk/media/documents/programmes/elearninginnovation/simple_final_report.pdf

Sloan, D., Heath, A., Hamilton, F., Kelly, B., Petrie, H., & Phipp, L. (2006). Contextual web accessibility - maximizing the benefit of accessibility guidelines. In *Proceedings of the 2006 international cross-disciplinary workshop on Web accessibility* (pp. 121-131). Berlin: ACM Press.

Snyder, J., Carpenter, D., & Slauson, G. J. (2006). *Myspace. com: a social networking site and social contract theory.* Dallas, TX: ISECON 23.

Squire, K. (2003). Video games in Education. *International Journal of Intelligent Simulations and gaming, 2*(1).

Squire, K. (2005). *Game-based learning: an emerging paradigm for instruction.* Academic ADL Co-Lab Initiative. Retrieved from http://www.academiccolab.org/initiatives/papershtml

Stafford, B. M. (1999). *Artful Science.* Cambridge, MA: MIT Press.

State Services Commission. (2007). *NZ Government Web Standards and Recommendations; Version 1.0; New Zealand.* Retrieved from http://www.e.govt.nz/standards/web-guidelines/web-standards-v1.0/web-standards-v1.0.rtf

Steinkuehler, C., & Williams, D. (2006). Where everybody knows your (screen)name: online games as 'third places'. *Journal of Computer Mediated Communication, 11*(4). Retrieved from http://jcmc.indiana.edu/vol11/issue4/steinkuehler.html.

Stroulia, E., & Systä, T. (2002). Dynamic analysis for reverse engineering and program understanding. *SIGAPP Appl. Comput. Rev., 10*(1), 8–17. doi:10.1145/568235.568237

Stvilia, B., Twidale, M. B., Gasser, L., & Smith, L. C. (2005). *Information quality discussions in Wikipedia.* Technical Report, Florida State University. Retrieved May 11, 2009 from http://mailer.fsu.edu/~bstvilia/

Suh, B., Chi, E. H., Kittur, A., & Pendleton, B. A. (2008). Lifting the veil: improving accountability and social transparency in Wikipedia with wikidashboard. In *Proceeding of the Twenty-Sixth Annual SIGCHI Conference on Human Factors in Computing Systems,* Florence, Italy, April 05 - 10, 2008, CHI '08. New York: ACM, New York.

Surowiecki, J. (2004). *The wisdom of crowds: Why the many are smarter than the few and how collective wisdom shapes business, economies, societies, and nations.* New York: Doubleday Books.

Sutton, J., Palen, L., & Shklovsky, I. (2008). Back-channels on the front lines: Emergent uses of social media in the 2007 southern california wildfires. In *Proceedings of the 2008 ISCRAM Conference,* Washington.

Tan, J., & Biswas, G. (2007). *Simulation-based game learning environments: building and sustaining a fish tank.* Paper presented at the IEEE International Workshop on Digital Game and Intelligent Toy Enhanced Learning, Taiwan.

Thatcher, J. (2006). Assistive Technology: Screen Readers and Browsers. In *Web Accessibility,* (pp. 103-124). San Francisco: Apress. Wikipedia. (n.d.). *Wictionary project.* Retrieved from http://en.wikipedia.org/wiki/Wiktionary

Tompa, F. (1989). A Data Model for Flexible Hypertext Database System. *ACM Transactions on Information Systems, 1,* 85–100. doi:10.1145/64789.64993

Tonella, P., & Ceccato, M. (2004). Aspect mining through the formal concept analysis of execution traces. In *WCRE '04: Proceedings of the 11th Working Conference on Reverse Engineering (WCRE'04),* (pp. 112-121). Washington, DC: IEEE Computer Society.

Tonella, P., & Ceccato, M. (2004). Migrating interface implementation to aspects. *Software Maintenance, IEEE International Conference,* (pp. 220-229).

Tonella, P., & Ceccato, M. (2005). Refactoring the Aspectizable Interfaces: An Empirical Assessment. *IEEE Transactions on Software Engineering, 31*(10), 819–832. doi:10.1109/TSE.2005.115

Tourwé, T., & Mens, K. (2004). Mining aspectual views using formal concept analysis. In *Proc. Of the Fourth IEEE International Workshop on Source Code Analysis and Manipulation (SCAM 2004)* (pp. 97-106).

Tourwé, T., Kellens, A., Vanderperren, W., & Vannieuwenhuyse, F. (2004). Inductively Generated Pointcuts to Support Refactoring to Aspects. In *Proceeding Software Engineering Properties of language for Aspect Technology (SPLAT) Workshop at AOSD'04.*

Tscheligi, M., & Reitberger, W. (2007). Persuasion as an Ingredient of Societal Interfaces. *Interaction, 14*(5), 41–43. doi:10.1145/1288515.1288538

Turkle, S. (1995). *Life on the Screen: Identity in the Age of the Internet.* New York: Simon and Schuster.

Ullman, C., & Dykes, L. (2007). *Beginning AJAX (Programmer to Programmer).* Hoboken, NJ: Wrox.

UNESCO - United Nations Educational, Scientific and Cultural Organization. (n.d.). *E-Governance: Engaging E-Governance Capabilities.* Retrieved from http://portal.unesco.org/ci/en/files/14896/11412266495e-governance.pdf/e-governance.pdf

Valenza, C., Adkins, J. (2009). Understanding Visual Thiking: The History and Future of Graphic Facilitation. *Interactions, 16* 4), 38-43.

Van der Hijden, P. (2007). *Enabling Teachers in Higher Education to Develop their Own Simulations: The Virtual City of Cyberdam.* Berlin: Online Educa.

Van der Vlist, E., Ayers, D., Bruchez, E., Fawcett, J., & Vernet, A. (2006). *Professional Web 2.0 Programming (Wrox Professional Guides).* Wrox.

Van der Wal, T. (2005). *Explaining and showing broad and narrow folksonomies.* Retrieved on May 11, 2009 from http://www.vanderwal.net/random/category.php?cat=153

van Deursen, A., Marin, M., & Moonen, L. (2005). *A Systematic Aspect-Oriented Refactoring and Testing Strategy and its Application to JHotDraw.* Amsterdam: CWI.

Vickery, G., & Wunsch-Vincent, S. (2007). *Participative Web And User-Created Content: Web 2.0 Wikis and Social Networking.* Organization for Economic.

Virzi, R. (1997). Usability Inspection Methods. In *Handbook of Human-Computer Interaction,* (p. 705-716). Amsterdam: Elsevier.

W3C - World Wide Web Consortium. (2008). *Web Accessibility Brief guide.* Retrieved from http://www.w3c.es/divulgacion/guiasbreves/Accesibilidad

W3C. (2004). *Web Services Glossary.* W3C Working Group Note 11 February 2004. Retrieved on May 21, 2009 from http://www.w3.org/TR/ws-gloss/

Weaver, A., & Morrison, B. (2008). Social Networking. *IEEE Computer, 41*(2), 97–100.

Web Managers, & the Requirements and Best Practices Checklist for Government. (2005). Retrieved from http://www.usa.gov/webcontent/reqs_bestpractices/checklist/long.pdf

Wiesing, L. (2005). *Artifizielle Präsenz.* Frankfurt am Main, Germany: Suhrkamp.

Wilson, C. (2007). The Problem with Usability Problems: Context is Critical. *Interaction, 14*(5), 46–47. doi:10.1145/1288515.1288542

Wimmer, R., & Dominick, J. (2006). *Mass Media Research: An Introduction.* Belmont, CA: Thompson-Wadsworth.

Windschitl, M., & Andre, T. (1998). Using computer simulations to enhance conceptual change: the roles of constructivist instruction and student epistemological beliefs. *Journal of Research in Science Teaching, 35*(2), 145–160. doi:10.1002/(SICI)1098-2736(199802)35:2<145::AID-TEA5>3.0.CO;2-S

Wong, J., & Hong, J. (2008). What do we "mashup" when we make mashups? In *Proceedings of the 4th international Workshop on End-User Software Engineering,* Leipzig, Germany, May 12 - 12, 2008, WEUSE '08, (pp. 35-39). New York: ACM.

Wong, J., & Hong, J. I. (2007). Making mashups with marmite: towards end-user programming for the Web. In *Proceedings of the SIGCHI Conference on Human Factors in Computing Systems,* San Jose, CA, April 28 - May 03, 2007, CHI '07, (pp. 1435-1444). New York: ACM.

Wooldridge, M. (2002). *Introduction to Multiagent Systems.* New York: John Wiley & Sons.

World Health Organization. (2001). *International Classification of Functioning, Disability and Health.* Retrieved from http://www.who.int/classifications/icf/en/

World Wide Web Consortium. (W3C). (2005). *Social Factors in Developing a Web Accessibility Business Case for Your Organization*. Retrieved from http://www.w3.org/WAI/bcase/soc

World Wide Web Consortium. (W3C). (2008a). *Techniques for WCAG 2.0*. W3C Working Group Note. Retrieved December 11, 2008, from http://www.w3.org/TR/WCAG-TECHS/

World Wide Web Consortium. (W3C). (2008b). *WAI-ARIA Overview*. Retrieved from http://www.w3.org/WAI/intro/aria.php

World Wide Web Consortium. (W3C). (2008c). *Web Content Accessibility Guidelines 2.0. Recommendation*. Retrieved from December 11, 2008, from http://www.w3.org/TR/WCAG20/

World Wide Web Consortium. (W3C). (2009). *WAI-ARIA Best Practices*. W3C Working Draft. Retrieved 24 February 2009, from http://www.w3.org/TR/wai-aria-practices/.

Yesilada, Y., Harper, S., Goble, G., & Stevens, R. (2004). Screen Readers Cannot See (Ontology Based Semantic Annotation for Visually Impaired Web Travellers). In *ICWE 2004 Proceedings* (LNCS, pp. 445-458). Berlin: Springer.

Zang, N., & Rosson, M. B. (2008). What's in a mashup? and why? studying the perceptions of Web-active end users. In *Visual Languages and Human-Centric Computing, 2008. VL/HCC 2008. IEEE Symposium on*, (pp. 31-38).

Zhang, C., & Jacobsen, H. A. (2007). Efficiently mining crosscutting concerns through random walks. In *AOSD '07: Proceedings of the 6th international conference on Aspect-Oriented Software Development*, (pp. 226-238). New York: ACM Press.

Zviran, M., Te'eni, D., & Gross, Y. (2006). Does Color in Email make a Difference? *Communications of the ACM*, *49*(4), 94–99. doi:10.1145/1121949.1121954

About the Contributors

Francisco V. Cipolla-Ficarra is a professor, researcher and writer. PhD. Area: Multimedia (1999). B.A. in Social Communication (1988). B.A. in Computer Programming and Systems Analysis (1983). Manager and coordinator of the first Human-Computer Interaction Lab. in Barcelona, Spain (1997 – 1999). Professor in American and European universities, technical and professional colleges (1981 – present), subjects: computer science, computer graphics and animation, human-computer interaction, design and multimedia. Scientific journalist and writer (1989 – present). CEO: Blue Herons Editions. Coordinator of AInCI (*International Association of Interactive Communication –www.ainci.com*) and ALAIPO (*Latin Association International of Human-Computer Interaction –www.alaipo.com*). Main research interests: HCI, communicability, quality, auditory and evaluation of interactive systems, computer graphics and animation, social communication, semiotics, e-learning, video games, ecological and cultural heritage. ACM and IEEE member.

* * *

Esteban S. Abait is a PhD student at the Universidad Nacional del Centro de la Provincia de Buenos Aires (UNCPBA). He is doing his research activities at the ISISTAN Research Institute. His main research interest includes aspect-oriented software development, particularly the evolution of legacy object-oriented systems to aspect-oriented ones. He received his B.S. degree from the UNCPBA State University in 2009, the same year when he was awarded with a postgraduate research fellowship grant from CIC (Comisión de Investigaciones Científicas) .

Ignacio Aedo Cuevas holds a degree in Computer Science and Ph.D. in Computer Science from Universidad Politécnica de Madrid. He's currently full professor at the Universidad Carlos III de Madrid and his interests mainly focus on topics such as hypermedia, interactive systems, web systems, learning technologies, development methodologies and information systems for emergency situations. Since 2001, he is technical advisor of the Ministry of Internal Affairs for the application of ICT in the civil protection domain. He co-organized the "HCI for emergencies" workshop for CHI 2008 conference and a special session with the same name in the ISCRAM 2008 conference. He was also General Co-Chair of IEEE ICALT 2008.

Andrea Bellucci is currently a researcher of the DEI group at Universidad Carlos III de Madrid, Spain. He holds a degree in Computer Science from University Sapienza of Rome, Italy (thesis title: Spatio-temporal analysis of georeferenced images). He attended in 2005 the IBM EMEA Top Students

Recognition Event at Stuttgart, Germany. From 2006 to 2007 he worked for the CATTID (Television and Long Distance Educational Techniques Application Centre) of University Sapienza of Rome, conducting advanced research activities on RFID technology. His main research activities focused on Human Computer-Interaction and Interaction Paradigms, Computer Supported Cooperative Work, Web Systems and Social Networks.

Maria Claudia Buzzi earned her Master's Degree in Computer Science from the University of Pisa in 1995. She works at the "Istituto di Informatica e Telematica" of the Italian National Research Council in Pisa, in the research group 'Innovative Web Technologies'. She has more than thirteen years' experience in Web application design, network infrastructure, and e-Government services, with special focus on certification and Quality of Services. Technical skills include coordination of several technological and research projects. In the last few years she has dedicated extensive study to accessibility and usability aspects for disabled users, related to user interface design.

Marina Buzzi earned her Master's Degree in Computer Science from the University of Pisa in 1991. At present she works in the 'Ubiquitous Internet' research group of the "Istituto di Informatica e Telematica" of the Italian National Research Council in Pisa. She has extensive experience in design of network services and Web applications. Technical skills include coordination of several technological and research projects. Since 2003 she has been studying user interface design, with special focus on usability and accessibility for the blind. Current research is on accessibility of Web systems (search engines, wikis, eLearning systems) and performance of complex systems (RFID systems). She has been a professional member of ACM and has participated in the activities of the Accessibility and Computing group (SIGACCESS) since 2004.

Sandra Casas is a professor of Universidad Nacional de la Patagonia Austral (UNPA) since 1995. She has obtained the Master degree in Software Engineering in 1999 from Universidad de Deusto (Spain). She received her PhD in computer science from the University of Vigo (Spain). Since 2005 she is working in Aspect-Oriented Programming research area.

Miguel Cipolla-Ficarra is a professor and researcher. PhD. Area: Power Electronic Engineering (1996). B.A. Electronic Engineering – Telecommunications (1990). B.A. Electric Engineering (1999). Professor in European universities, technical and professional colleges (1987 – present). Software project manager: design, development and implementation of algorithms. Product manager, application engineer and technical sales engineer in international projects. CEO: Alfacis S.L. –Industrial automation: electronic, electrical and mechanical systems. Director of laboratory in F&F Multimedia Communic@ tions Corp. Technical manager in AInCI (*International Association of Interactive Communication –www. ainci.com*) and ALAIPO (*Latin Association International of Human-Computer Interaction –www.alaipo. com*). Main research interests: interfaces, usability engineering, interactive systems, telecommunication, computer sciences, networks, industrial design, programmation, automation, motors on microprocessor, ecological energy, e-commerce and computer aided education.

Paloma Díaz Pérez is full professor at Universidad Carlos III de Madrid (Escuela Politécnica Superior) and head of the DEI research group. She holds a Degree in Computer Science and Ph.D. in Computer Science from Universidad Politécnica de Madrid. Her research interests mainly focus on web

and hypermedia/web engineering methods combining usability principles and practices as well as their practical application to different kinds of interactive systems including e-learning and e-gov. Since 2001, she is technical advisor of the Ministry of Internal Affairs for the application of ICT in the domain of civil protection. She's senior member of ACM and IEEE.

Maria Valeria Ficarra is a lawyer. B.A. Union lawyer (2003). Master in International Legal Practice (2008). Public Relations: AInCI (*International Association of Interactive Communication*) and ALAIPO (*Latin Association International of Human-Computer Interaction*) Barcelona, Spain. Main research interests: labour and international law, legal and business strategies, problem-solving techniques, leadership, psychology, sociology, communication, cultural understanding and cooperation.

Daniel Alberto Giulianelli: Bachelor in Computer Science (National Technological University – UTN). Master in Computer Science (La Matanza National University – UNLaM, Buenos Aires, Argentina). Actually PhD student in Computer Science in La Plata National University (UNLP), Buenos Aires, Argentina. Areas of interest: Software Engineering, Information and Communication Technologies. Chair on High Council of UNLaM, representing Professors. Coordinator of Computer Science Engineering. (UNLaM). UNLaM's representative in the Electronic Governance in Argentine Electronic Governance Net. Chair on Engineer Faculty Advisor Commission UNLaM. Post grade and grade Professor in National Universities. Researcher designated by Categorization National Commission depending of Science and Technology Secretary. Research Projects director and co-director. Post grade thesis director. Science and Technology's Projects Evaluator. Chair of National and International Scientific Committees. Author and co-author of national and international publications. Organizer, presenter and expositor of national and international congresses. Professional Activity: Director of Engineering Technology Applied to Technological Security S.A.

Ma. De los Milagros Gutiérrez is a PhD student at Universidad Tecnológica Nacional. She is an Information Systems Engineering graduate from the Universidad Tecnológica Nacional. She is teaching Artificial intelligence in the Systems Department at the Facultad Regional Santa Fe, Universidad Tecnológica Nacional. She is undertaking research into the use of simulation technologies within Business Processes and Engineering Design Environment. She obtained her Systems Information specialization degree in 2004. She is promoter member of the Research Center for Information Systems (CIDISI). Her current research interests are distributed simulation and intelligent agents.

Born in Korea, **Juri Hwang** lives and works in Los Angeles as an independent filmmaker and sound designer. Her work focuses on film and other media projects dealing with cultural issues and explores the relationship between fiction film and documentary. Juri Hwang was involved into the creation of numerous media projects and worked as an independent artist in the research initiative. The Labyrinth Project at the University of Southern California. Her work has been shown and exhibited internationally.

André Koscianski received his B.S. in Computer Science in 1994, from the Paraná's State University of Maringá, Brazil. In 2000 he obtained his M. S. in Industrial Informatics from CEFET – Paraná, Federal Center of Technology Education, participating in the development of a Flexible Manufacturing System simulator. In 2001 he went to France, where he obtained his Dr. degree in Mechanical Engineer from INSA de Rouen, for his dissertation "Mechanics Modelling for Real-Time", once again working in

the development of simulation software. Currently he teaches in a Computer Technology undergraduate course and a professional master degree in Science and Technology Education, at UTFPR, Federal University Of Technology of Paraná, at Ponta Grossa, Brazil. His research interests include computer simulation and games, with particular attention to the development of educational software.

Born in Berlin, **Andreas Kratky** lives and works in Berlin and Los Angeles. He studied visual communication, philosophy and fine arts in the Humboldt University and the University of the Arts in Berlin. Andreas Kratky is a media artist and visiting assistant professor in the Interactive Media Division of the School for Cinematic Arts of the University of Southern California. He has worked on several award winning projects like "That's Kyogen", "Bleeding Through – Layers of Los Angeles 1920-1986", "Soft Cinema" and the interactive costume projection in the opera "The Jew of Malta". His work has been shown internationally in Europe, the USA and Japan. Previously Kratky used to work in the ZKM | Center for Art and Media where he was the head of the Multimedia Studio.

Barbara Leporini obtained her PhD in Computer Science at the University of Pisa in 2003 with a dissertation on Web accessibility and usability. Since the beginning of her PhD project, Barbara has carried out her research at the National Research Council in Pisa in the "Human Interfaces in Information Systems" laboratory of the Institute for Information Science and Technology (ISTI), where she is now a researcher. In theory and practice, she investigates techniques and methods for making websites, publishing, museum content, search engines, e-learning systems and identification systems for electronic signatures accessible and usable for special-needs users. She has also provided technical support for accessibility and usability at various levels, particularly in boards and groups working on different problems concerning the visually-impaired.

Alessio Malizia is currently with the DEI group holding a Lecturer position at the University Carlos III, at Madrid, Spain. He holds a degree in Computer Science and Ph.D. in Computer Science from University Sapienza of Rome, Italy (Thesis title: a Cooperative-Relational Approach to Digital Library Environments). From 1999 to 2002 he worked for the Rome IBM Tivoli Laboratory, and Silicon Graphics. From 2003 to 2004, he was Visiting Researcher at the XEROX PARC (Palo Alto Research Center, Palo Alto, CA, USA) in the ISTL (Information Science and Technology) Lab working on visualization and small display devices. He authored the book "Mobile 3D Graphics" published by Springer (September 2006). Until February 2007, he was a Research Fellow at the Computer Science Department of the University Sapienza of Rome, Italy. In the past his research activities focused on theory and algorithms for pattern recognition, machine learning and visualization. Today he is working on Human Computer Interaction, Visual Languages and Social Networks.

Claudia A. Marcos has been a Professor in the School of Computer Science at Universidad Nacional del Centro de la Provincia de Buenos Aires (UNCPBA) since 1991. From 2000 to 2005 she was co director of the ISISTAN Research Institute. Her main research area is in aspect-oriented software development, UML and agile development. She teaches several undergraduate and postgraduate courses at the UNICEN and has also national and international publications in the area. She leads several university research projects in Argentina as well as abroad. Currently, she is advising postgraduate and undergraduate students. Dr Marcos received her B.S. degree in 1993 from the UNCPBA State University in 1993. She obtained her PhD degree in Computer Science in 2001.

Isabel Beatriz Marko: Electronic Engineer Buenos Aires National University (UBA, Ciudad Autónoma de Buenos Aires, Argentina). Master in Universitary Teaching Technological National University (UTN, Buenos Aires, Argentina). Professor in Computer Science Engineering and Electronics Engineering (UNLaM, Buenos Aires, Argentina). Head of Advanced Computer Science (UNLaM). User interface for industrial control developer. Tailored software developer in PLC's controlled systems into the industrial process control environment. Grade thesis director: Control and Graphics of networks in telephony (UNLaM). Associated teacher of the Computing Department and member of the advisory commission on universitary ambit of the J. F. Kennedy University (Ciudad Autónoma de Buenos Aires, Argentina). Researcher in UNLaM in the following projects: Electronic Government, Intelligent Environments applied to Sports, Pedagogic and Technical Methodology Development that allow the students to develop their capabilities of reasoning logic.

Emma Nicol MSc BSc Hons (Glasgow) has been based at the University of Strathclyde in Glasgow, Scotland since 2002. She has been involved in the evaluation of a number of educational technology projects, notably the EU-funded WEBKIT project on tangible user interfaces for children (2004) and the JISC funded SIMPLE (SIMulated Professional Learning Environment) project (2008). Her main research interest is the searching behaviour of school age children. She has published in the fields of Education, Information Retrieval and Human-Computer Interaction. Emma is currently a PhD candidate in the Department of Computer and Information Sciences.

Milton Pividori is an Information Systems Engineering student at Universidad Tecnológica Nacional. Currently He has a scholarship in the research and development Center in Information System (CIDISI) at Universidad Tecnológica Nacional where develops his works. He is the primer promoter of the software free laboratory at Universidad Tecnológica Nacional. His current research interests are Intelligent agents and free software development.

Jorge Roa is a PhD student at Universidad Tecnológica Nacional. He received his degree in Information System Engineering in 2008 from Universidad Tecnológica Nacional (UTN). He has been working at the Research and Development Center in Information System (CIDISI) since 2005. In 2008 he received a 4 years fully-funded PhD fellowship position at UTN-CIDISI. His current research interests include artificial intelligence and B2B collaborations.

Rocío Andrea Rodríguez: Computer Science Engineer from La Matanza National University (UNLaM), Buenos Aires, Argentina. Actually PhD student in Computer Science in La Plata National University (UNLP), Buenos Aires, Argentina. Professor in the following careers: Computer Science Engineering, Electronic Engineering and Industrial Engineering (UNLaM). Industrial Engineering National Technological University (UTN), Haedo, Buenos Aires, Argentina. Researcher in UNLaM in the teams of Electronic Governance, Networking and Information Technologies. Actually she has got a research scholarship from the Science, Technology and Production Research Department. National and international researcher's paper reviewer. Author and co-author of national and international publications. Frequently assistant to national and international Computer Science and Technology Congresses. She has submitted more than thirty papers in countries like: Argentina, Canada, Chile, Colombia, Ecuador, Egypt, Spain, United States of America and Peru.

Osiris Sofia is a professor of Universidad Nacional de la Patagonia Austral (UNPA) since 1992. He has obtained the Master degree in Nets and Communications System in 2000 and the Speciality in Software Engineering in 2000 from Universidad Politécnica de Madrid (Spain). His main research area is in parallelism and distributed systems. He teaches several undergraduate courses at the UARG and has also national and international publications in the area. He leads several university research and institutional projects.

Georgina Stegmayer is currently professor at Universidad Tecnológica Nacioanl (Argentina) and assistant researcher in the Research Center for Information Systems (CIDISI - CONICET). She obtained her PhD degree in neural networks for mobile communications devices modeling at Politecnico di Torino in 2006. Her current research interests include computational intelligence models applied to data mining, pattern recognition and bioinformatics.

Artemisa Trigueros: Computer Science Graduate, Buenos Aires National University (UBA, Ciudad Autónoma de Buenos Aires, Argentina). Teacher Degree (Provincia de Buenos Aires, Argentina). Completed all courses in the Master in Computer Sciece program in La Matanza National University (UNLaM, Buenos Aires, Argentina). Actually writing the Master Thesis Theme: m-Governance and m-Learning applications to University learning subject. Professor in Information and Communication's Technologyies, and Programming in the careers of Computer Science Engineering, Electronics Engineering and Industrial Engineering (UNLaM). Head of Computer Science Department. professor, coordinator and maintenance of Computer Science Laboratory San Carlos Borromeo High School. English Teacher. Researcher in UNLaM in the Electronic Government research team. Author and co-author of national and international publications. Assistant to national and international educational Computing Congresses.

Pablo Martín Vera: Computer Science Engineer from La Matanza National University (UNLaM) Buenos Aires, Argentina. Actually PhD student in Computer Science in La Plata National University (UNLP) Buenos Aires, Argentina. Thesis Theme: Semantic SOA for robust business applications. Professor in UNLaM. Member of several research teams in UNLAM: Electronic Governmance, High Speed Networking and Parallel Applications Modeling. Paper reviewer of congresses from Argentina, Chile and United States of America. Author and co-author of national and international publications. Frequently assistant and expositor to national and international Computer Science and Technology Congresses. Professional activity: Project Leader in Computer Science Technology S.A. (TISA), an ISO 9001 certified software factory company which develops business applications using new technologies in mobile and web environments. Experience in Quality System orchestration for ISO 9001 certification.

Santiago A. Vidal is a PhD student at the Universidad Nacional del Centro de la Provincia de Buenos Aires (UNCPBA). He is doing his research activities at the ISISTAN Research Institute. His main research area is in aspect-oriented development, particulary the automation of aspect refactorings for evolving object-oriented systems into aspect-oriented systems. He received his B.S. degree from the UNCPBA State University in 2008. He also has a postgraduate fellowship granted by CONICET (National Council for Scientific and Technological Research of Argentina) since 2009.

Index

A

Accessibility 64, 65, 70, 72, 73, 74, 75, 77, 87, 89, 90
algorithms 91, 98
anthropologists 209, 212, 217
Application Programming Interface (API) 44
Apriori algorithm 183
architectural complexity 164
architecture of participation 39, 40, 41, 42, 58
Archive 202, 203
ARIA landmarks 80
Artificial Intelligence 121, 124, 139, 164
Aspect-Oriented Programming (AOP) 177
Aspect-Oriented Software Development (AOSD) 176
AspectRT 178, 185, 186
Assistive Technology 89
audiovisual systems 206
auditory stimuli 165
Augmentative and Alternative Communication (AAC) 68
authentic element 175
Authenticity 14, 17, 18
authentic manner 165

B

bidirectional interactive communication 92, 120
Blackberrys 14
blackboard 162
business-oriented factors 204, 207

C

Calvin-Benson Cycle 166, 168
Cascading Style Sheets (CSS) 37
causal rules 127, 135
CERN 36
Code Library 175
cognitive environment 164
cognitive models 209, 212, 217, 221
cognitive systems 65, 66, 67
Collaborative tagging 47
collaborative tagging systems 45, 48, 58
collective human intelligence 57
collective intelligence 37, 39, 40, 43, 46, 57
combinatorial approach 198
communicability 204, 206, 207, 209, 210, 211, 212, 213, 215, 216, 217, 218, 219, 220, 222, 223, 224, 227
communication-aimed social sciences 117
Communication and information theory 210
Communication social 210
communico 94
community-shared material 47
complex organic compound 166
composition style 198
computer animation 210
computer-based collections 203
computer developers 162
computer games 162
computer-generated images 28
computer graphics 210
computer hardware 23
computer program 109
computer science 206, 208, 210, 211, 212, 222, 223, 224